INTERPRETING
SAMSON AGONISTES

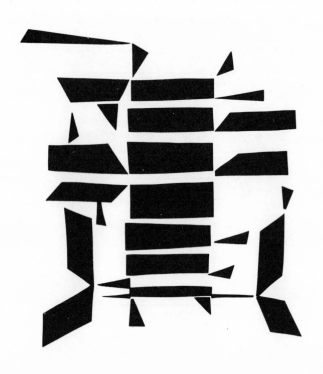

INTERPRETING

$\mathcal{S}AMSON\ \mathcal{A}GONISTES$

JOSEPH WITTREICH

Princeton University Press

Library of Congress Cataloging in Publication Data will be found
on the last printed page of this book

ISBN 0-691-06671-X

Publication of this book has been aided by a grant from the
General Research Fund of the University of Maryland and a grant
from the Paul Mellon Fund of Princeton University Press

This book has been composed in Linotron Caslon

Clothbound editions of Princeton University Press books are
printed on acid-free paper, and binding materials are chosen for
strength and durability

Printed in the United States of America by Princeton
University Press, Princeton, New Jersey

*Frontispiece: "A ship in full rig—Dalila," lithograph by Robert
Medley from his illustrated edition of Samson Agonistes (1979)*

CONTENTS

. . . the Eye altering alters all . . .
—WILLAM BLAKE

One begins by reading or seeing a play like other plays, subject to the conditions and limitations of its own age and to our corresponding limitations in receiving it. One ends with the sense of an exploding force in the mind that keeps destroying all the barriers of cultural prejudice that limit the response to it. In other words, we begin with a notion of what the play might reasonably be assumed to mean, and end with realizing that what the play actually does mean is so far beyond this as to be in a different world of understanding altogether.
—NORTHROP FRYE

PREFACE

. . . *Do generations press*
On generations, without progress made?
—WILLIAM WORDSWORTH

Beyond the desert of criticism, we wish to be
called again.
—PAUL RICOEUR

Jonathan Culler maintains that "One thing we do not need is
more interpretations of literary works."[1] Instead, according
to Culler, we should assay what we are doing, emphasize
matters theoretical, and engage in intertextual discourse. There
is an inexorable logic to this argument, which, crediting the
Yale School of Criticism with exposing interpretation as mis-
interpretation, proceeds to discredit further the already dis-
credited. Some may wish to follow Culler in his restless movement beyond interpretation—in his devaluing of interpretation
by way of valorizing theoretical discourse and dispute. However, I am inclined to follow those who espouse a hand-in-
glove relationship between theory and interpretation and correspondingly believe that the only inducement for scuttling
interpretation (and then only as a temporary measure) occurs
when it becomes blocked by unexamined and erroneous premises. Such an inducement for abandoning interpretation is

[1] *The Pursuit of Signs: Semiotics, Literature, and Deconstruction* (Ithaca: Cornell
Univ. Press, 1981), p. 6.

there, as it happens, in Milton criticism and nowhere more abundantly evident than in readings of *Samson Agonistes*, which, all too frail in their methodologies, are also too commonly founded upon suspect suppositions and dubious declarations, upon the sometimes uncritical paraphernalia and platitudes of the interpretive community.

Miltonists have approached *Samson Agonistes* in much the same way that Peter Martyr pursued the Samson story in the Book of Judges, and with many of the same results. The easy correlations and oversimplifications of the typologist have displaced narrative, as well as dramatic, ambiguities. Typological reading has thus militated against narrative and dramatic probity, with Milton's critics seeming to say with Peter Martyr that we should not search the Samson story too curiously, especially the matter of his marriages, for whatever has been surmised is surely right. Samson's marriages must be divinely instigated, "otherwise it had not bene lawfull . . . to mary one of a contrary religion"; to think of Samson as other than a magistrate, or public man, would be to credit him with the sort of heinous acts to which "God hym selfe [never would have] appoynted" a private man.[2] The fact is that Milton's poem, no less than its sourcebook, opposes automatism in perception; it teases us out of, instead of coercing us into, tired formulas, redundant patterns, and calcified religiosity; it operates against the tendency of taking things for granted, making us see the Samson story anew. Milton cannot be expected to conform so easily to a tradition that in his own day is on trial.

Yet, as with the Judges narrative in the hands of Peter

[2] For these commonplaces of Peter Martyr (P. Vermigli), see *Most Fruitfull and Learned Comentaries* (London: John Day, 1564), ff. 212ᵛ-213, 235ᵛ, 236ᵛ. Martyr's views have persisted through the centuries; thus John M'Clintock and James Strong write, "We must not attribute too scrupulous views to the times of the Judges" (*Cyclopaedia of Biblical, Theological, and Ecclesiastical Literature* [12 vols.; 1880; rpt. Grand Rapids: Baker Book House, 1970], IX, 313).

Martyr so with *Samson Agonistes* in the hands of most of Milton's critics: the Samson story, glossed by commonplaces, is made to engender still other commonplaces, all of which Milton's poem is thought to confirm rather than challenge. For example, Northrop Frye hypothesizes that, were it not for *Samson Agonistes*, "we could say with some confidence that Milton could never have chosen Samson for a hero." For Frye, this statement remains "essentially true" even after we have encountered the "transmuted" hero of Milton's tragedy. Frye's essay, nevertheless, dismantles its own hypothesis by flattening the "savage and primitive" story of the biblical Samson into the nearly as "savage and primitive context" of the Judges narrative, and by offering Milton's Samson to us, in contrast, as "a human analogy" and "dramatic prototype of Christ." For Frye, the catastrophe at the pillars is the true similitude of the apocalyptic drama in which Christ comes in judgment, and the entire Samson story is "a natural sequel" and "Old Testament counterpart" to *Paradise Regained*.[3] *Samson Agonistes* is a recapitulation of Milton's own progress as a wayfaring Christian and of his emerging political program for England.

Frye's hypothesis is nonetheless beset with contradictions: "Samson in the Bible . . . lounges about the Philistine countryside killing and destroying and burning crops and sleeping with their women, but with no hint of any organization behind him," yet "in Milton all Samson's exploits are carefully integrated into a consistent crusade for God's people against God's enemies" and in such a way as to show Samson to be a "born leader under all the rags and filth and chains."[4] It is difficult to deduce from Frye's statement why, given this rehabilitated and regenerate Samson, Milton would be reluctant

---

[3] *Spiritus Mundi: Essays on Literature, Myth, and Society* (1976; rpt. Bloomington: Indiana Univ. Press, 1983), pp. 218, 205, 209, 217.

[4] *Ibid.*, p. 221.

to place him in a pantheon of heroes, although Frye's conception of Milton's Samson may in fact be just another manifestation of the critical tendency to discredit Samson's limitations and shortcomings—"his all too human character."[5] Frye's premise, that Milton's Samson stands in marked contrast to Samson in the Book of Judges, would hardly be worth mentioning if it were not the cornerstone on which criticism of *Samson Agonistes*, now for nearly a century, has rested and if it did not yield the conclusion on which so much criticism of Milton's tragedy has foundered: that the figure scripture excoriates for his sins is by Milton forgiven or excused from them, at least in *Samson Agonistes*.

It is time to test an alternative set of hypotheses: (1) that the scriptural story of Samson is set within a far more civilized and humane narrative than is currently allowed; (2) that, whether within the context afforded by the Judges narrative or the one provided by *Paradise Regained*, the Samson story functions as a warning prophecy, an oracular threat, that would avert the disaster it announces and contravene the situation it seems to court; (3) that rehabilitation of the Samson story is not the driving conception behind Milton's poem but is rather a phenomenon especially of one phase of seventeenth-century Protestant hermeneutics, providing a context with which Milton's tragedy interacts; (4) that into the Samson story Milton, like the Judges narrator, knits a snare for the reader; (5) that Milton's *Samson Agonistes* is more a companion piece to the myth of a lost paradise than to the myth of paradise regained; (6) that like *Paradise Regained*, however, it proceeds by frustrating rather than fostering then current typologies; and (7) that, in this way, Milton's Samson appears in the image and likeness—as the similitude—of the biblical Samson and hence not as the counterpart but as the countertype of Christ, and

[5] Donald F. Bouchard, *Milton: A Structural Reading* (Montreal: McGill-Queen's Univ. Press, 1974), p. 141.

of the poet's own true self, and as a foil to the political program Milton urges upon his people in the aftermath of a failed revolution. In *Samson Agonistes* a great work of biblical history and an important philosophy of history, lest either become outdated, are reborn as art.

The story of Samson, long and complicated in its history, has, over the ages, passed through distinguishable phases: the original tale and the Judges retelling; later versions and variations, a proliferation of them during the Renaissance; and finally Milton's interpretation or reinterpretation, which is a radical ambiguation of an already equivocal tale. The Judges narrative is one nodal point in a long history, apparently releasing the Samson story from mere apologetics and thereby transmuting legend into explanatory history. *Samson Agonistes* is yet another such nodal point, marking still another shift in which, as Paul Ricoeur might say, explanatory modulates into interpretive history; that is, a history perceived as peculiar to a time and place is now reconceived as a universal history.[6] The Judges narrative and Milton's poem relate to one another as would a dialogue between a story and its interpretation. The Samson story had been fettered by time. *Samson Agonistes* examines the stuff of which those fetters are made by subjecting received interpretation of its story to interrogation.

What Frye has perceived, and what is customarily credited to Milton, is his ranging of a new ideology against the outmoded and primitive one of the Judges narrative; yet these discrepant ideologies can be found within the confines of either the biblical or Miltonic text. We witness here not so much an ideology changing its import and form as it moves through time as an ideological conflict that persists in time and that, less obtrusive in the biblical story, is magnified by Milton's poem. Perhaps we will never know why the Samson story

---

[6] "Narrative Time," *Critical Inquiry*, 7 (1980), 187.

originally came into being, or what meanings that story (in its hypothesized folk-tale stage) was meant to convey. With others, though, we can conjecture that the story enshrined an ethic, a code of behavior that had become, or that should have become, outworn. Milton seems not to have worried over the issue of the story's origin, although he clearly brooded over the implications of that story once it had become appropriated and then integrated within the Judges narrative. His concern, in this instance, is not with the origins of a story but with its functions. We may assume that for him this was both *a good story* and one deeply troubling in its implications no less than in its narrative setting, and that, given its immense popularity yet diversity of function and meaning in the seventeenth century, it was also a story with a natural appeal for this poet. Milton was attracted to the Samson story probably for the reasons enunciated by Sir Thomas Browne in his *Religio Medici*:

> . . . there are in Scripture Stories that do exceed the Fables of Poets, and to a captious Reader sound like *Garagantua* or *Bevis*: Search all the Legends of times past, and the fabulous conceits of these present, and 'twill be hard to find one that deserves to carry that Buckler unto *Sampson*; yet is all this of an easie possibility, if we conceive a divine concourse, or an influence but from the little Finger of the Almighty. It is impossible that either in the discourse of man, or in the infallible Voice of God, to the weakness of our apprehensions, there should not appear irregularities, contradictions, and antinomies. . . .[7]

It is as if Milton were saying through *Samson Agonistes*: the versions of the Samson legend current in his century are not

[7] *The Works of Sir Thomas Browne*, ed. Charles Sayle (3 vols.; Edinburgh: John Grant, 1927), I, 34.

the whole story, or even the only story; the real story, confused rather than clarified in its long evolution through time, has for too long remained unsung. In its diverse forms and different meanings, the Samson story sensitized Milton's age—and presumably Milton himself—to the multiple functions such a story was serving and to still others it might serve. That story, whatever its earlier history, had no single function or meaning as Milton inherited it but was being used, as Barbara Herrnstein Smith tells us narratives are typically used, here to reflect and there to supplement the existing reality, here to uphold and there to topple reigning ideologies, now to burden us with our mortality and now to provide us with intimations of our immortality.[8]

Allusions to the Samson story are ubiquitous in the seventeenth century, in both low-brow and high-brow culture, among Royalist apologists and Puritan pamphleteers. Now Charles I invokes the Samson legend—and now John Milton. There were various reasons for telling Samson's story, and perhaps still others for listening to it. Milton, of course, had his own reasons for retelling this oft-told tale and for wanting us to listen to it again, but this time in a new register. Those reasons are the subject of this book and unfold from the separate contextualizations afforded by individual chapters: on Samson in the Book of Judges, on the Renaissance Samsons and different Renaissance representations of his story, and finally on Milton's Samsons and his contextualizations of that story, principally the one provided by *Paradise Regained*. *Samson Agonistes* relies on contexts, which is to say that this text is resonant with continuities, and sometimes disjunctive continuities, with other texts.

The interpretation of *Samson Agonistes* that the following chapters invite does not accord with the received reading of

---

[8] "Narrative Visions, Narrative Theories," *Critical Inquiry*, 7 (1980), 235.

Milton's poem. Indeed, a comparison of some recent criticism of the poem (like that provided by John Carey and Irene Samuel) with more conventional interpretations may turn out rather like William Riley Parker's comparison of recent with early criticism, which led him "to wonder . . . if the critics were writing about the same work."[9] But, more, the comparison may serve to remind us that if certain interpretive choices, and hence critical readings, have in some measure failed Milton's poetry, we nonetheless learn from that poetry about the efficacy of second choices, even in the affairs of literary criticism. Contextualizations for the Samson story inherited by the Renaissance, and those manufactured by the age, afford new interpretative options even as they remind us, in the words of Stephen Booth, of those "conditioned reflexes by which we take contextual probabilities for certainties"[10] when in fact the text of Milton's poem, coupled with the time of its publication, renders certain probabilities improbable. Or to put this another way, the problem of contextualization is one of locating the relevant contexts for criticism; it is finally a problem of value and is likely to result in turning present critical skirmishes over, let us say, typological interpretation into a warfare of ideology before a truce can be called.

More than any other of Milton's works, *Samson Agonistes* is a reflection on both the politics of writing and the politics of reading, on Milton's politics no less than on those of his interpreters. The work of criticism must not be altogether unlike Milton's work, which would untangle the ideologies that had become almost hopelessly knotted in the Samson story and, untangling, restructure them. Futhermore, critics must

[9] *Milton: A Biography* (2 vols.; Oxford: Clarendon Press, 1968), II, 937. See also Carey, *Milton* (London: Evans Brothers, 1969), pp. 138-46, and Samuel, "*Samson Agonistes* as Tragedy," in *Calm of Mind: Tercentenary Essays on "Paradise Regained" and "Samson Agonistes,"* ed. Joseph Wittreich (Cleveland: Press of Case Western Reserve Univ., 1971), pp. 235-57.

[10] *"King Lear," "Macbeth," Indefinition, and Tragedy* (New Haven: Yale Univ. Press, 1983), p. 61.

learn, especially with *Samson Agonistes*, to elide the politics of poetry with the politics of its interpretation by way of reconstituting both. This critical enterprise will be accomplished only in the recognition that, at least in Milton's day, a criticism of politics inevitably turned into a criticism of theology and vice versa, and in the awareness that, though "Milton's politics underlie much of what must be seen as the politics of Milton criticism,"[11] there has been and remains much confusion over which politics belong to whom. In the instance of *Samson* criticism, for example, the interpreter has presumed that he knows what Milton's politics are and then proceeds to assert a concord or discord between Milton's politics and his own. More often than not, Milton's politics are misunderstood, and disagreement is mistaken for agreement.

It has been a commonplace of criticism that a poem is self-contained, self-sufficient, and that in the interpretive act all else must be subordinated to it: the poem exists in its own right and constitutes the only necessary datum for literary criticism. Especially in the aftermath of New Criticism, some poems aspire to this condition, comply with this "idealism." But not Milton's, and most emphatically not Milton's *Samson Agonistes*. His is another order of art, the meaning of which completes itself outside the poem—in history—although some would say within the experience of the audience that receives the poem. They are more nearly right than is sometimes supposed, especially if the contexts of literature are valued as the mental constructs informing the minds of a poem's audience and hence enabling that audience to decipher the meaning of what it reads. What is predictably within the mind conditions, perhaps even determines, interpretive activity. What *Samson Agonistes* would mean as a document of the Protestant Ref-

[11] I am quoting from Jackie DiSalvo's *War of Titans: Blake's Critique of Milton and the Politics of Religion* (Pittsburgh: Univ. of Pittsburgh Press, 1983), p. 7; equally relevant here is the entire fourth chapter of Maureen Quilligan's *Milton's Spenser: The Politics of Reading* (Ithaca: Cornell Univ. Press, 1983).

ormation is different from what it means, or can mean, as a
flowering of the Puritan Revolution; what it means within the
context of Milton's early prose writings is qualitatively different from the meaning it derives from its placement with
Paradise Regained; what it meant to the seventeenth century is
probably not what it means to certain airy-headed readers of
our own time, impoverished as they are by the lack of much
historical sense. Almost effortlessly now, we can determine
what the poem has meant to this or that age; but what perplexes
us still, and confounds criticism, is the question of what the
historically determinate meanings of *Samson Agonistes* are: what
are the poem's relevant contexts? why are they to be regarded?
how are they to be valued? why—and how—does any of this
matter? These questions are the preoccupation of this book and
provide it with an agenda.

Criticism of *Samson Agonistes* needs to examine its own
premises and assay its own conclusions and, in doing so, is
likely to discover a haunting analogy between its exegetes and
Ricoeur's theologians of faith. In each instance, there is a
general community (here of readers) and a community of
interpreters, together with an ecclesiastical, or a critical, magisterium. The contamination of criticism moves downward in
this implied hierarchy, losing its inquiring spirit, its diversity
and richness, as it places itself increasingly under "the tutelage
of the fixed assertions of the magisterium."[12] As Ricoeur might
say, Milton's critics have made us confront a monolithic conception of the Samson story instead of, as we should, a story
that is pluralistic, polysemic, and analogical rather than typological, in most of its seventeenth-century forms. Not Milton's poems but his critics have encouraged the reductive tendencies that are ubiquitous in interpretations of *Samson Agonistes*.

The greatest threat to literary interpretation continues to be

[12] *Essays on Biblical Interpretation*, ed. Lewis S. Mudge (London: SPCK, 1981),
p. 74.

the unreflecting transference of ill-suited theory to texts whose own ideological commitments that theory may contravene. There is the example of some very distinguished feminist critics appropriating, without ever questioning, the theories of Stanley Fish, Harold Bloom, and Lawrence Stone which often, and necessarily, are at cross-purposes with their own objective of liberating a text from the orthodoxies, the very politics, with which Fish, Bloom, and Stone in different ways damage their texts. The eye of criticism is not altered by feminists who persist in seeing through, not with, the eyes of Fish, Bloom, and Stone; who have become unwitting mediators of a distinctly patriarchal version of texts; who therefore minimize the contradictions within a text and thereby stabilize instead of unsettling existing critical discourse. A feminist criticism should, but does not always, remove the crooks from a straight line. Interpretation of *Samson Agonistes* is endangered in much the same way: by those who impose theories upon a text with which they do not mesh and whose ideological commitments they muddle. Such critics are prone to fashioning out of the text their own beliefs and then to fashioning their beliefs into those of Milton or even his period's beliefs; they tend to cover over the very fissures in a text that their theories expose, in the process compromising not the theory but themselves as its practitioners. Too often such critics manufacture fictions out of history and then represent them as history instead of as its mutilations.

It is tempting to say that what *Samson Agonistes* begs for most of all is a New Historicism. That is in the most neutral way what I am saying, but I am saying it without any wish to align my own critical enterprise with those who would perpetrate new forms of elitism in what, at its best, has been an egalitarian academy. The sometimes monolithic perspectives of a past criticism, in the case of *Samson Agonistes* anyway, often embody the commonplaces of history that, enmeshed within this tragedy, hence relevant to it and to its critics, are also under challenge within the poem. A past criticism is *past* only because it is partial (in all senses of the word) and should be *passed by* only in an act of absorption that acknowledges its bearing upon, and even its operations within, the larger dynamic of the poem. Stephen Greenblatt is one of the new historicists who understands this principle and whose own critical efforts, apposite to the largest objectives of my book, encourage the placement of *Samson Agonistes* among the many writings of the sixteenth and seventeenth centuries that are "fields of force, places of dissension and shifting interests, occasions for the jostling of orthodox and subversive impulses."[13]

Indeed, the chapters that follow ask of *Samson Agonistes* and its critics the same sorts of questions that Greenblatt asks of Shakespeare's *Richard II*—of Queen Elizabeth's, of contemporary response to the play and of now current yet altogether different responses to it: why *Samson* Agonistes? why *this* story at *this* particular moment in English history? what are the personal ramifications of this poem when we remember that in the years immediately before its publication Milton had been identified by his detractors with the legendary Samson and that, earlier still, Samson himself had been proclaimed the patron saint of the revolutionary cause? Yet it is also important to remember that some texts are immune to Greenblatt's deconstructive skepticism. *Samson Agonistes* does more than bring contending world-views, conflicting ideologies into its reader's gaze: it is a poetry of choice, of mediation, and

[13] "Introduction," in *The Forms of Power and the Power of Forms in the Renaissance*, ed. Stephen Greenblatt (Norman: Univ. of Oklahoma Press, 1982), p. 6; see also pp. 4-5. This volume is a special issue of *Genre*. Or as Greenblatt writes elsewhere: "great art is an extraordinarily sensitive register of the complex struggles and harmonies of culture" (*Renaissance Self-Fashioning: From More to Shakespeare* [Chicago: Univ. of Chicago Press, 1980], p. 5).

hence a poem in which "the volcanic heat of thought," ethical and political, always smolders under the religious drama.[14]

Any poem about Samson written or published during the years of the Civil War, or in its aftermath, would predictably involve some reflection on a revolution that had found its identity in, and drawn much of its spirit from, the Samson story. A poem about Samson *written by John Milton* would, just as predictably, involve reflections upon a revolution which Milton had championed and self-reflection by virtue of the fact that Milton himself had been given an identity with Samson and certainly preserves a measure of that identity in his poem. It is conceivable that Milton wrote his poem simply accepting that identity with Samson and, through him, urging another, this time successful, revolution; it is equally conceivable that, divorcing himself from Samson, Milton composed this poem as a retrospective repudiation of the cause he once championed. It is probable however—for this is the direction in which the evidence drifts and in which the pressures of the poem point—that Milton accepts the historical and personal identifications, much as he did in *Paradise Lost* through analogous identifications involving Satan. In his epic, according to Jackie DiSalvo:

> We are . . . faced with the contradiction that, in identifying Satan with the English Revolution, Milton would seem to be either renouncing that struggle or supporting Satan's attack on God. Rather, I would suggest that Milton knew exactly what he was doing in making Satan a revolutionary. The only plausible explanation for his denigration is that, through him, Milton wishes to criticize not only the old order but also those aspects of the revolution which he believed

[14] George Clark, *The Seventeenth Century*, 2nd ed. (1947; New York: Oxford Univ. Press, 1961), p. 337.

responsible for its failure and from which he wished
to separate himself.[15]

As with Satan even more grandly so with Samson: Milton
now glimpses through his elected figure both history and himself in history; he embraces the revolutionary but not the
revolution. The Whitmanesque proverb—*there is the knit of
identity but always distinction*——summarizes the situation of a
poem where Milton's critique of the Revolution, now more
centered and comprehensive, is also more keenly conscious of
the extent to which the Revolution was defeated not only by
enemies without but, even more, by contradictions within—
and *still within* the history Milton would inaugurate.

Milton's critics, the very best of them, come in for hard
questioning in this book; and because it assumes a polemical
posture, this book necessarily dwells on what is mistaken in
their readings rather than on what is eminently acceptable—
and right. In this context, I should mention first of all Barbara
K. Lewalski, Mary Ann Radzinowicz, and Stanley Fish.[16]
Their readings of *Samson Agonistes* are not mine, and yet they
are three of the critics whose interpretive efforts have made
Milton's tragedy a poem that really matters. If careful examination causes me to challenge certain of their premises in
the chapters that follow, it also corroborates Lewalski's contention that the Book of Revelation provides the authority and

---

[15] *War of Titans*, p. 252. Given DiSalvo's argument, it is noteworthy that at least
in some quarters it was thought that Milton had deliberately attributed the same
characteristics to the apostate angels in *Paradise Lost* as belonged to his rebellious
brethren (see *Memoirs of Thomas Hollis*, comp. Francis Blackburne [2 vols.; London:
Printed by J. Nichols, 1780], I, 226).

[16] See Lewalski, "*Samson Agonistes* and the 'Tragedy' of the Apocalypse," *Publications of the Modern Language Association*, 85 (1970), 1050-62; Radzinowicz, *Toward
"Samson Agonistes": The Growth of Milton's Mind* (Princeton: Princeton Univ. Press,
1978), and Fish, "Question and Answer in *Samson Agonistes*," in "*Comus*" and
"*Samson Agonistes*": A Casebook, ed. Julian Lovelock (London: Macmillan, 1975),
pp. 209-45.

sanction for Milton's conception of history as a Christian tragedy, no less than Radzinowicz's claim that, once the Revolution
was lost, "Milton undertook the intellectual and moral analysis
of failure" with *Samson* providing the record of "all that is
permanently salvageable in the experience; a vision embracing
both the individual and the community . . . ; a vision of how
one might face the facts of human defeat with some kind of
intelligible hope and how that hope might be transmitted by
the poet to the future."[17] We differ on the particularities of
that vision, the complexity of which is discerned by Fish in
his argument that *Samson* contains no pattern of regeneration,
only disconnected patterns of seeming regeneration that frustrate all expectations of a neat, evolving, progressive spiritual
history for Samson. Interpreters of *Samson Agonistes* will go
nowhere unless they continue to stand on the shoulders of these
three commentators—and until they recognize that, in keeping
with Old Testament narrative art, Milton creates in Samson
a character "constantly emerging from and slipping back into
a penumbra of ambiguity."[18]

Within this same context, but separately, I wish also to
mention Christopher Hill. He is singly responsible for making us question what it means to align Milton with "the Chris-

[17] I quote from Radzinowicz's inaugural statement on *Samson*, "*Samson Agonistes*
and Milton the Politician in Defeat," in "*Comus*" *and* "*Samson Agonistes*," ed. Lovelock, p. 207.

[18] See Robert Alter, *The Art of Biblical Narrative* (New York: Basic Books, 1981),
p. 129; and cf. Herbert Schneidau, *Sacred Discontent: The Bible and Western Literature*
(Baton Rouge: Louisiana State Univ. Press, 1976), who observes that, in the scriptural
narratives, "the 'ring of truth' is heard not in spite of but *in* the ambiguity and
inconsistency" (p. 279; my italics). When post-structuralists (like R. A. Shoaf)
speculate that Milton adds the feature of Samson's weak-mindedness to a tradition
where this feature is otherwise not to be found and then maintain that Samson is "an
Old Testament hero . . . of unambiguous fame" (p. 188, but see also p. 187), they
reveal the extent to which theorists, in departing from the historicity of traditions
and texts, are not always up to the potentiality of their theory; see *Milton, Poet of
Duality: A Study of Semiosis in the Poetry and Prose* (New Haven: Yale Univ. Press,
1985), pp. 181, 188, and also p. 187.

tian tradition" and thus for eroding what for a long time has been a precept of Milton's interpreters: "To understand the significance of the [Samson] story for Milton one must . . . recall the reading of the story by, say, St Augustine and St Thomas Aquinas."[19] Hill may not have gotten the significance of that story exactly right, but he is certainly correct in urging upon us the Samson literature of Milton's own time (instead of that of earlier times); he is correct, too, in pressing for historical readings sensitive to political implications. Hill is in the vanguard of a criticism which would promote the view, recently set forth by Nicholas Jose, that *Samson Agonistes* is "a political drama" forged from a story "traditionally available for political interpretation" and offering a political judgment on the state and on the current moment of history.[20]

In the seventeenth century, the Samson legend may not be surrounded by a field of unified opinion, but it does provide a zone for diversified political discussion. And perhaps in ways undreamt of by Hill, the Samson legend affords a perspective on Milton's own experience of defeat, which, as Hill rightly remarks, never eventuated in Milton's shifting God's kingdom away from its earthly foundations: "The happier Paradise within was still to be regained on earth."[21] Among those commentators taking their interpretive leads from Hill, there may

[19] I quote from Herbert J. C. Grierson, *Milton and Wordsworth, Poets and Prophets: A Study of Their Reactions to Political Events* (London: Chatto and Windus, 1950), pp. 137-38; and see Hill's argument against such propositions in *Milton and the English Revolution* (New York: Viking, 1977), esp. pp. 428-48. Frank Kermode comments incisively: "Milton . . . had said enough in his time about moldy exegetes to discourage us from thinking they could explain his tragedy. In making sense of the bully-boy of Judges he imposes his own interpretations and uses those of the exegetes merely as instances of erroneous opinion"; see "Milton in Old Age," *Southern Review*, 11 (1975), 523.

[20] See *Ideas of the Restoration in English Literature 1660-71* (Cambridge, Mass.: Harvard Univ. Press, 1984), p. 143.

[21] *The Experience of Defeat: Milton and Some Contemporaries* (New York: Viking, 1984), p. 318; see also p. 315.

be disagreement over the extent to which Milton breaks loose, or even wished to break loose, from polemics in *Samson Agonistes* and over the extent to which Samson's bringing down of the temple signals the moment of exultation when that paradise is regained by Samson himself. But such disagreements exist within the shared understanding that *Samson* is no poem floating free from history but is instead a poem which, wishing to undo the Restoration and committed to upside-downing it, "raises historical anxiety to tragic power"—in the words of Jose, "giving full moving utterance to an important element in contemporary experience," while achieving its greatness as an utterance through the sheer force and quality of its political and historical intelligence.[22] What that intelligence insists upon is that history is open and is what we ourselves make of it.

My own efforts, particularly in the first chapter of this book, are directed toward separating, for the moment, the dance from the dancer. With regard to Fish and Hill, Lewalski and especially Radzinowicz, I have no doubt whatever that each critic has presented Milton's poem in an illuminating way. Yet each of these critics has also succumbed to an ideology (not in every instance the same ideology) from which I would release Milton's poem. Ideology, especially when its workings are unrecognized, unacknowledged, distorts and disfigures interpretation; yet even its limitations do not prevent these very different critics from achieving luminous moments of interpretation. They may not afford the ultimate illumination for *Samson Agonistes*, but each does provide an enabling viewpoint which inches us closer to that ultimate illumination. Still, what these and many other critics are wont to forget is that poetry—and especially Milton's poetry—is actively complicated by "persistent refusals *merely* to mirror the orthodoxies

---

[22] *Ideas of the Restoration in English Literature 1660-71*, p. 165; see also p. 159.

of the time; and by . . . refusals to interfere with our freedom
to 'see and know', and interpret for ourselves, the truth about
human experience, as they [the poets] have recreated it before
us, in its infinite and disturbing variety." But also, as Harriett
Hawkins goes on to say, critics, especially of the last few
decades, have exacerbated the problematics of poetry by denying its authors *their* freedom, which is also their privilege,
"to criticize established assumptions; or, rather, a series of
orthodox interpretations have been imposed on works which
seem, very conspicuously, to rebel against easy orthodoxies."[23]
The imposition of orthodoxies on Milton's poetry constitutes
a large part of the history of its criticism; and it was one such
recent imposition—that by Georgia Christopher[24]—which
caused me to cease in my contemplations of the present book
and to commence its composition. Once the book was under-
way, I found myself drawn more than ever to the illustrations
for *Samson Agonistes* by Robert Medley. Two of them—"The
Ruin of the City" and "A Ship in Full Rig"—appear,
respectively, on the dustjacket and as frontispiece to this book.
They appear with the kind permission of the artist and afford
a visual counterpart to Milton's own endeavor, which involves
abstracting the mutilated forms of the Samson legend from
tradition and then subjecting them to scrutiny.

In one sense, this book has been a long time in the making.
I first encountered *Samson Agonistes* as an undergraduate during
the late 1950s. So far as I knew, the reading of the poem I
set before my teacher was unprecedented in the critical community and to that teacher no more than a mild annoyance—
an aberration of critical judgment, he seemed to think. During
the 1960s I found (and I think this not a false surmise) but

[23] *Poetic Freedom and Poetic Truth: Chaucer, Shakespeare, Marlowe, Milton* (Oxford: Clarendon Press, 1976), pp. xi (my italics), xii.
[24] *Milton and the Science of the Saints* (Princeton: Princeton Univ. Press, 1982).

one sympathetic ear. At the 1964 Democratic Convention in Atlantic City, Adlai Stevenson addressed a group of diplomats more interested in foreign policy than in the electoral process he was there to explain. Once his remarks to the diplomatic corps were completed, he was queried not on how Americans elect a president but on whether, as a former presidential candidate, he believed that physical strength alone was enough to recommend a nation for leadership. With lightning speed, Stevenson retorted by quoting these lines from *Samson Agonistes*: "what is strength without a double share / Of wisdom" (53-54).

A then would-be Professor of English was impressed by this citation of his favorite poet, and from a poem he had not yet fathomed, yet impressed even more by this instance—and there was another that day, Robert Kennedy's citation from *Romeo and Juliet*: "when he dies, we'll 'take him and cut him out in little stars . . .' "—by these instances of poetry invading the world of politics and being bent, by virtue of such concerns, into its rhetoric. The would-be professor became a professor in 1966 and in the years following has watched the emergence of a new, or alternative, *Samson Agonistes*, the architects of which are John Carey, Donald Bouchard, Helen Damico, and, chief among them, Irene Samuel.[25] *Their* Samson is *my* Samson, and I am convinced (and what critic dares

---

[25] For the statement by Carey, see n. 9 above, by Bouchard n. 5, and by Samuel n. 9; for Damico's essay, see "Duality and Dramatic Vision: A Structural Analysis of *Samson Agonistes*," *Milton Studies*, 12 (1979), 91-116. Although he does not finally reject the orthodox reading of *Samson*, Ralph Waterbury Condee locates the troubling features of such a reading: a facile identification of Milton with Samson, its swerve from the mode of Greek tragedy, its antithetical relationship to the value system inherent in Milton's epics and representation of a heroism that is "violent, vengeful, and bloody." See *Structure in Milton's Poetry: From the Foundation to the Pinnacles* (University Park: Pennsylvania State Univ. Press, 1974), p. 144; see also pp. 125-26, 139-40, 143-45.

come forward without this conviction?) that *ours* is *Milton's* Samson. I am likewise convinced that the enterprise of literary criticism should be Milton's literary enterprise: the recovery of the true form of the Samson story, disfigured by time and denied by historical realities. The enterprise of literary criticism should produce, in its most important outcome, the emancipation of consciousness.

This book is written as a parent not of settlement but of further critical inquiry. My debts are not legion; they are owed in part to students who remained patient with my reading of *Samson Agonistes* in the face of my impatience with the readings of others and in part to those who vested faith in a project to which I was sometimes faithless: the John Simon Guggenheim Memorial Foundation, my provost Shirley Strum Kenny at the University of Maryland, the Graduate School of the University of Maryland, and the Henry E. Huntington Library and Art Gallery. My friends Leopold Damrosch, Ernest Gilman, Richard Ide, Barbara Lewalski, Annabel Patterson, and Gary Schmidgall, as well as Stuart Curran, have read the manuscript in some version. Richard/ Aleks Campbell may have read nothing of the book, but he did help to create the happy environment in which it was written. Other friends at the Newberry Library, Pennsylvania State University at State College, the University of Illinois at Chicago Circle, the University of Michigan at Dearborn, and the University of Kentucky heard parts of this book and promptly proceeded to help me revise what clearly needed revising. I also owe a considerable debt to the libraries of the University of Maryland, the University of Pennsylvania, Princeton University, as well as to the British Library, the Bodleian Library, the Folger Shakespeare Library, and the Henry E. Huntington Library.

Jean Hagstrum of Northwestern University and Thomas

Roche of Princeton University must be singled out for the enthusiastic encouragement each gave me early on. The Press readers—Galbraith Crump, Mary Ann Radzinowicz and John Steadman—helped to improve this book immeasurably: Crump and Steadman through calm reassurance, and Radzinowicz through a charitable sternness. My research assistants, Christine Gray especially and Michael Selmon, and my splendid editor, Jerry Sherwood, bestowed unlimited care and uncommon intelligence on the manuscript as it was being readied for the printer. Finally, generous assistance was provided me by those editors who agreed to publish parts of this book while it was still in progress: " 'Strange Text!': PARADISE REGAIN'D . . . To Which Is Added *Samson Agonistes*," in *Poems in Their Place*, ed. Neil Fraistat (Chapel Hill: University of North Carolina Press, 1986), " 'In Copious Legend, or Sweet Lyric Song': Typology and the Perils of the Religious Lyric," in *"Bright Shootes of Everlastingnesse": The Seventeenth-Century Religious Lyric*, ed. Claude J. Summers and Ted-Larry Pebworth (Columbia: Univ. of Missouri Press, 1986).

My largest debt for this book, however, is owed to my parents and to Aunt Angeline Karlinger. In collusion with my parents, I suspect, and as a last-ditch effort to get me out of academe into politics, Aunt Angeline took me to the Democratic Convention of 1964 and negotiated my way to the top of the Convention Center where Stevenson was speaking. They may have failed in their immediate objective, but I doubt they would think that I have now failed them: without them this book simply would not be. And it is only fitting that a book of mine, so long coming to term, be dedicated to my parents: they have been together now for fifty years, are still loving and still much loved. I had thought once of including on the dedicatory page the following passage: "The voice of parents is the voice of gods, for to their children they are heaven's

lieutenants." But in the present context these lines are embarrassingly inapt: this book is written by a son who did *not* listen
to his parents and who, alas, cannot lay claim to having heard,
ever, the voice of God.

J. W.

Provincetown, Massachusetts
23 July 1984

CITATIONS

All citations of Milton's writings are given parenthetically
within the text and, unless otherwise indicated, are (for the
poetry) to *The Works of John Milton*, ed. Frank Allen Patterson
(18 vols.; New York: Columbia Univ. Press, 1931-38) and
(for the prose) to *Complete Prose Works of John Milton*, ed.
Don M. Wolfe et al. (8 vols.; New Haven: Yale Univ. Press,
and London: Oxford Univ. Press, 1953-83). For Milton's
last poems, I have used the standard abbreviations: *PL (Paradise Lost)*, *PR (Paradise Regained)*, *SA (Samson Agonistes)*.
Quotations from the Bible, unless I document them differently, accord with the King James version. Throughout, I
refer to the female character in the Book of Judges as *Delilah*
and to the same character in Milton's dramatic poem as *Dalila*.

INTERPRETING
SAMSON AGONISTES

CHAPTER I

SAMSON AGONISTES AND THE
STATE OF MILTON CRITICISM

> . . . *the best way of resisting the dominant*
> *ideology . . . is not surprisingly, to bring its*
> *existence out into the open and to discuss it.*
> —Christopher Butler

No sooner had Raymond Waddington told us what we could all agree upon—that *Samson Agonistes* is a drama of regeneration—than Irene Samuel declared she could not agree, and in such a way as to remind us of the Johnsonian proposition: "this is the tragedy which ignorance has admired, and bigotry applauded."[1] It has been suggested that we will never know exactly what Johnson meant inasmuch as published commen-

---

[1] See Samuel, *"Samson Agonistes* as Tragedy," in *Calm of Mind: Tercentenary Essays on "Paradise Regained" and "Samson Agonistes,"* ed. Joseph Wittreich (Cleveland: Press of Case Western Reserve Univ., 1971), p. 235, and in the same volume see Waddington, "Melancholy Against Melancholy: *Samson Agonistes* as Renaissance Tragedy," p. 259. For Johnson's critique, see *The Poetical Works of John Milton,* ed. Henry John Todd (7 vols.; London: Printed for J. Johnson, 1801), IV, 347. The regenerist theory espoused by Waddington marks the progress of Samson's mind, tracing a "steady psychological progression from despair through heroic conflict upward to exultation and the final assumption into beatitude"; see Una Ellis-Fermor, *The Frontiers of Drama,* 2nd ed. (London: Methuen, 1946), p. 32, and also G. A. Wilkes, "The Interpretation of *Samson Agonistes,*" *Huntington Library Quarterly,* 26 (1963), who similarly describes the poem as a drama of Samson's developing awareness (pp. 367, 378-79). Cf. Mason Tung, *"Samson Impatiens*: A Reinterpretation of Milton's *Samson Agonistes,*" *Texas Studies in Language and Literature,* 9 (1968), who, while he continues to posit a regenerate Samson at the end of Milton's poem, protests that this is not a drama of regeneration but of "sudden conversion" (p. 477; see also p. 492).

tary on Milton's tragedy hardly existed at the time. Some commentary did exist, however, both visual and verbal, with illustrative criticism (a good index to any text's status in the culture) foregrounding the catastrophe at the pillars and arraying around that subject Samson meditating and Samson encountering Dalila. Verbal criticism was more various still, with *Samson Agonistes* being regarded as a tragedy that, even if unadapted to general taste, was Milton's most nearly faultless, most finished work. Recognized as "a perfect model and standard of tragic poetry" and then ranked third among Milton's poems—above *Lycidas* but below *Paradise Lost* and *Comus*—*Samson* continued to be praised, as it had been anonymously praised in 1692, for its exquisite descriptions (especially of Samson's death) and delicate narrations, for the turn of the whole, for its being so intricately of a piece with Milton's entire canon, and for its "terrible *Satyr* on *Woman*."[2] Dr. Johnson may never have worried over the poem's alleged misogyny; but he was clearly unsettled by a poem whose unorthodox aesthetic features bespoke what was for Johnson Milton's more objectionable unorthodoxies in matters of religion and politics.

Moreover, such criticism as existed by mid-century received codification in Thomas Newton's variorum commentary where

---

[2] See Bishop Atterbury's Letter to Pope (15 June 1722), in *The Works of John Milton*, ed. Thomas Birch (2 vols.; London: Printed for A. Millar, 1753), I, lxix; and Joseph Warton quoted in *Poems upon Several Occasions*, ed. Thomas Warton (London: Printed for James Dodsley, 1785), p. 34. But see also *Milton: The Critical Heritage*, ed. John T. Shawcross (London: Routledge and Kegan Paul, 1970), p. 98, and *Milton 1732-1801: The Critical Heritage*, ed. Shawcross (London: Routledge and Kegan Paul, 1972), pp. 148, 226, 268. Alongside the opinion that *Samson Agonistes* "passed through the Classical and Romantic movements of the Eighteenth Century with little more than the perfunctory attention of scholarly criticism" (John Walter Good, *Studies in the Milton Tradition* [Urbana: Univ. of Illinois Press, 1915], p. 210) should be placed the observation that *Samson*, translated into Greek, was also adapted for music and for the stage in the eighteenth century and that Handel's musical adaptation was published at least nine times before 1800.

Milton is regularly beheld "in the person of Samson" and where, repeatedly, Milton's dramatic poem is regarded in its political aspect as a reproach to his countrymen, and in its religious aspect as "a concealed attack on the church of England" whose "opulent Clergy . . . he tacitly compares with the lords and priests of the idol Dagon."[3] Many of the notes printed by Newton cross-reference passages in *Samson Agonistes* to the classics and the Bible, to Spenser, and especially to *Paradise Lost*. Yet the most provocative of these notes represent *Samson* as a deeply autobiographical poem steeped in political awareness and concern. Samson's "That fault I take not on me" speech (241 ff, but see 679-709) is said to address, as plainly as Milton dared, "the Restoration of Charles II, which he accounted the restoration of slavery," with the annotator Jortin wondering "how the Licensers of those days let it pass."[4] Reflecting upon lines 628 ff, the annotator Newton suggests that Milton probably intended them as "a secret satir upon the English nation, which according to his republican politics had . . . chosen *bondage with ease* rather than *strenuous liberty*."[5] Manoa's application for Samson's deliverance is thereupon paralleled with Marvell's petition for Milton's deliverance; Dalila is represented as a composite portrait of Milton's first two wives; and Milton, while brooding over "the trials and sufferings of his party after the Restoration," is thought also to focus upon his own situation, and probably that of Sir Henry Vane, and then to describe through the sufferings of Samson his own grief and misery, his own melancholy.[6]

It is misleading to argue that in the eighteenth century

---

[3] See *"Paradise Regain'd"* . . . *"Samson Agonistes,"* 2nd ed., ed. Thomas Newton (2 vols.; London: Printed for W. Strahan, 1785), I, 269, and *The Poetical Works of John Milton*, ed. Todd, IV, 466-67 (cf. *SA* 1418 ff).

[4] *"Paradise Regain'd"* . . . *"Samson Agonistes,"* ed. Newton, I, 277.

[5] *Ibid.*, I, 229.

[6] *Ibid.*, I, 303, 277, 286, 249.

Samson Agonistes received only perfunctory attention and exerted little influence, for by the end of that century the premises for a criticism of the poem were firmly established: this is a poem in which Milton creates a new type of heroic character, the likes of which are not to be found even in Homer; it is a poem in which, through the character of Samson, Milton paints himself and one that, because it records so poignantly Milton's experience of defeat, must have been composed early in the 1660s. Eighteenth-century criticism simply paves the way for the dicta of the next century: that Milton is "a second Samson" or the "Samson among Poets," that "Samson *is* Milton in hard Hebrew form," and that *Samson Agonistes* is the poet's "last effort . . . to rescue the English nation from disgrace and servitude." In the words of Sir Egerton Brydges, this is a poem in which we see Milton "revenging himself on his age," crushing "the Philistines, as Samson in death buried his enemies"; this is a poem, in the eloquent formulation of Richard Garnett, that is at once national and prophetic:

> "Samson Agonistes" deserves to be esteemed a national poem, pregnant with a deeper allusiveness than has always been recognized. . . . Particular references to the circumstances of his life are not wanting. . . . But, as in the Hebrew prophets, Israel sometimes denotes a person, sometimes a nation, Samson seems no less the representative of the English people in the age of Charles the Second. . . . The English nation is . . . the enslaved and erring Samson—a Samson, however, yet to burst his bonds and bring down ruin upon the Philistines. "Samson Agonistes" is thus a prophetic drama, the English counterpart of the world-drama of "Prometheus Bound."[7]

[7] See, respectively, Max Ring, *John Milton and His Times: A Historical Novel in Three Parts*, trans. John Jefferson, 2nd ed. (London: John Heywood, 1889), p. 467; *Poetical Works of John Milton* (London: Suttaby, Evance, and Fox, 1821), p. xiv;

Though criticism of *Samson Agonistes* had become more finely nuanced in the nineteenth century, its basic concerns are nonetheless epitomized by an estimate of Milton's tragedy reprinted in the *Memoirs of Thomas Hollis* and offer clues, certainly, to the kind of interpretation that caused Dr. Johnson to recoil from the poem:

> Let us consider . . . [Milton's] tragedy in this allegorical view. Samson imprisoned and blind, and the captive state of Israel, lively represents our blind poet, with the republican party after the Restoration, afflicted and persecuted. But these revelling idolators will soon pull an old house on their heads; and GOD will send his people a deliverer. How would it have rejoiced the heart of the blind seer, had he lived to

---

The Complete Poetical Works of John Milton, ed. George Gilfillan (2 vols.; Edinburgh: James Nichol; London: James Nisbet, 1853), II, xxx (my italics); and Walter Savage Landor's remark in *The Romantics on Milton: Formal Essays and Critical Asides*, ed. Joseph Wittreich (Cleveland: Press of Case Western Reserve Univ., 1970), p. 332. For Brydges' comment, see *Letters from the Continent* (Kent: Printed by Lee Privy, 1821), pp. 106, 108; and for Garnett's, see *Life of John Milton* (New York: Walter Scott Publishing Co., n.d.), pp. 184-85. It is of some interest that, once the stitching of Milton to Samson comes apart in the nineteenth century, it is proposed that *Samson Agonistes* must have been written before Milton lost his sight; see Joseph Ivimey, *John Milton: His Life and Times* (New York: D. Appleton, 1833), p. 236. William Hayley's dating of the poem in 1662 is thus moved back by Ivimey to the late 40s or early 50s in anticipation of a dispute that continues to vex many of Milton's most distinguished critics. In our own time, Nicholas Jose brings into conjunction the private and the public, the cultural and the cosmic aspects of Milton's tragedy: "*Samson Agonistes* is impressive for its struggle to bring into conjunction . . . disparate orders of experience: politics and history, the purposes and ways of providence, and the psychology of the solitary man" (*Ideas of the Restoration in English Literature 1660-71* [Cambridge, Mass.: Harvard Univ. Press, 1984], p. 164). In his brilliant chapter on "The Politics of Milton's Early Poetry," David Norbrook observes that in the political tracts of the 1640s "Milton viewed the development of English history in terms that mirrored his own self-development"; see *Poetry and Politics in the English Renaissance* (London and Boston: Routledge and Kegan Paul, 1984), p. 236. I would note only an adjustment of this strategy in *Samson Agonistes*; here Milton mirrors in Samson the course of English history and thereby distinguishes his own development from that of most of his countrymen.

have seen with his mind's eye the accomplishment
of his prophetic predictions![8]

Judging from the off-hand remark by Walter Savage Landor,
this is the sort of interpretation that, engulfing *Samson Agonistes*
in the eighteenth century, continued well into the next century.
The revolutionary call is there in the play; but Landor remains
"reluctant to see disturbed [by it] the order and course of
things, by alterations at present unnecessary." Milton's tragedy
may be urging that "when an evil can no longer be borne
manfully and honestly and decorously, then down with it, and
put something better in its place"; yet Landor counsels
"guard[ing] strenuously against such evil," for "the vigilant
will seldom be constrained to vengeance."[9]

For Johnson, presumably, this is just the sort of play,
though devoid of Landor's prudent counseling, that the surly
and acrimonious Milton could be expected to write; it is just
the kind of play that Christopher Hill credits him with having
written. "About *Samson Agonistes*," Hill writes:

> . . . "neo-Christians" are as mealy-mouthed as they
> are about Milton's defence of polygamy. They em-
> phasize that the poem is about the regeneration of
> Samson. They do not emphasize that it is also about
> revenge, about political deceit and murder, and that
> the two themes are inseparable. . . . Milton's mes-
> sage seems clear: however difficult the political cir-
> cumstances, be ready to smite the Philistines when
> God gives the word.[10]

[8] See "An Answer to Some Criticism on Milton's Paradise Lost" (*London Chronicle*, April 28, 1764), in *Memoirs of Thomas Hollis*, comp. Francis Blackburne (2 vols.; London: Printed by J. Nichols, 1780), II, 624.

[9] *The Romantics on Milton*, ed. Wittreich, p. 330.

[10] *Milton and the English Revolution* (New York: Viking, 1977), p. 442. Although Hill's celebration of "Samson's vengeance" persists in *The Experience of Defeat: Milton and Some Contemporaries* (New York: Viking, 1984), his attitude toward those who

Johnson and Hill discern in *Samson Agonistes* the same sentiments; it is just that what appalls Dr. Johnson Professor Hill
applauds. In this connection, it should be noticed that the critic
cited in the *Memoirs of Thomas Hollis* represents a reading of
Samson apparently current in the eighteenth century but one
from which he himself would divest the poem: "these mystical
and allegorical reveries [representing Milton as a spiteful
Samson] have more amusement in them, than solid truth, and
savour but little of cool criticism."[11] What is evident from
this brief foray into the record of criticism is that *Samson
Agonistes*, like its titular hero, is the captive of history—of a
history from which one hopes a new criticism can release the
poem. There is no doubt, if we credit at all the critical observations of Johnson and Hill, that *Samson Agonistes* is a
polemical poem; but criticism has yet to investigate the polemics of Milton's polemic, and its authors would be well-
advised to begin such a task in the understanding that Hill's
Samson is *the* Samson of most of Milton's editors and commentators from Thomas Newton to David Masson.

In the past decade, it has become increasingly apparent that
Miltonists cannot agree on the most fundamental issues concerning Milton's "tragedy": on whether, for instance, *Samson
Agonistes* is a tragedy or a divine comedy. And, of late, there
is the curious spectacle of conventional interpreters confirming
their orthodoxies by sidling up to Professor Hill and using
his rhetoric to dispose of Irene Samuel's argument which is
that:

---

think otherwise is considerably tempered: "It is a credit to their hearts, but not to
their knowledge of the world in which Milton lived" (pp. 314, 317). Even Hill's
expansive knowledge of Milton and his times requires expansion.

[11] *Memoirs of Thomas Hollis*, comp. Blackburne, II, 624. The critic here cited is
identified by Sir Egerton Brydges as John Upton; see *The Poetical Works of John
Milton* (London: William Tegg, 1862), p. 494.

Milton's critical and religious thought, his view of tragedy, his habit as a poet, the nature of tragedy generally and of tragedies like *Samson* in particular—none of these supports such a reading of the play [as is provided either by the regenerist critics or by Dr. Johnson].

According to Samuel, Milton's "poetry shows a sensibility hardly narrower than Shakespeare's and a moral vision rather finer"; and what seems always to wedge itself between Milton and his readers is a false assumption:

> . . . that he is less poet than polemicist, doctrinaire rather than doctrinal, rigidified by his Christian convictions into inhumanity rather than illumined to a clearer reading of the human condition. It is understandable that Dr. Johnson preferred to read Milton as narrowly partisan and bigoted. It is less understandable that Milton's professed admirers so consistently diminish his whole human awareness.

Samuel's *Samson Agonistes* is no martyr play, nor is it about Milton's protagonist's being restored to divine favor. Rather, this poem is emphatically a tragedy about a man defeated who, despite his virtues, "has a *hamartia* so deep in his ethos that he snares himself in folds of dire necessity more subtly woven even than those in which Clytemnestra netted Agamemnon."[12]

No two critics summarize better than Samuel and her respondent, Wendy Furman, the interpretive issues governing the criticism of Milton's poem, nor better illustrate the ideological underpinnings of that criticism. Their controversy is methodological and, in the broadest sense, political. Furman's formulations derive from a methodology whose chief propo-

---

[12] "*Samson Agonistes* as Tragedy," in *Calm of Mind*, ed. Wittreich, pp. 235, 254, 256.

nent, at least in terms of *Samson Agonistes*, is Michael Krouse. If Krouse's premises go unexamined, so too do his conclusions:

> That part of hermeneutic literature which pertains to Samson was affected surprisingly little by the great break in the Christian tradition which began at the opening of the sixteenth century when Luther posted his theses in Wittenberg. The Reformation . . . left few traces in interpretation of the Old Testament. This fact is best demonstrated by reference to Renaissance commentaries which are omnium gatherums, drawing together and interweaving great quantities of earlier exegesis to expound a single biblical text.[13]

To restrict attention to, or even settle it upon, such gatherings of previous, mostly Medieval, exegesis is to insure continuity between its and the Renaissance Samson. On the other hand, to redirect attention to sermons (often prophesyings in the sense that they articulate freshly emerging interpretations of biblical texts) and to political tracts (often dependent upon, and developments of, the new discoveries of such prophesyings) is to enlarge the historical perspective by engaging the contrary evidence. Such an effort contributes complexity and nuance to what survives as an inadequate and flattened historical record. To look beyond the theologians to the poets is to

---

[13] *Milton's Samson and the Christian Tradition* (Princeton: Princeton Univ. Press for the Univ. of Cincinnati, 1949), p. 63. The altering eye *does* alter all. Writing nearly eighty years before Krouse, M'Clintock and Strong contend that "The older writers on Samson contribute nothing to the interpretation of the history" and thus turn to the period from 1674 to 1751, when Renaissance exegesis is being codified, to provide them with the best that has been thought and said about the Samson story. The authorities here cited are Hilliger (1674), Weissenborn (1705), Lehmann (1711), Oeder (1718), Vriement (1738), Maichel (1739), Hauke (1740), and Gasser (1751), under whose sway (owing largely to the influence of seventeenth-century exegesis on the Samson story), this "wilful and rough hero" is judged "unworthy of comparison with Christ" (*Cyclopaedia of Biblical, Theological, and Ecclesiastical Literature* [12 vols., 1880; rpt. Grand Rapids: Baker Book House, 1970], IX, 316).

augment that record still further, and further yet by glancing beyond *Samson Agonistes* to a later commentary, especially when it can be shown that Milton's text helped to spawn a later Samson hermeneutic, the outlines of which accord with Samuel's, but not with Furman's, profile of Samson.

This controversy also has a conspicuously political aspect, making such matters as the politics of reading and of interpretation special concerns here. Michael Walzer, for example, poses questions concerning Puritanism that Furman and Samuel present in reference to *Samson Agonistes*. Conceding that Puritanism is "an ideology of the transition" within which the chain of being is "transformed into a chain of command" and within which "the emphasis of political thought [is shifted] from the prince to the saint," thus providing continuing religious sanction for political action,[14] Walzer addresses the same issue to which Furman and Samuel respond so differently. Where does Milton stand in relation to this ideology, he asks, on the near or far side of it? Is he an adherent to the Puritan ideology or a critic of it? And is *Samson Agonistes* written to engender, or to repudiate, a state of mind that would confront the existing order in an attitude of war, urging sympathizers to strike when the iron is hot and to impose justice rather than wait upon its eventual implementation? These are questions that do not easily answer themselves. But they may at least begin to answer themselves in the realization that political discourse often solidifies into formulaic language and subjects its mythic content to hackneyed interpretation; it mesmerizes its audience into accepting this, not that, perspective on an inherited story. A vital part of seventeenth-century political rhetoric, the Samson story is reincarnated by Milton as tragedy, with *Samson Agonistes* affording a good example of

[14] *The Revolution of the Saints: A Study in the Origin of Radical Politics* (Cambridge, Mass.: Harvard Univ. Press, 1965), pp. 2, 166, 300.

how a nearly obsolete political language, and a story engrafted with its commonplaces, is given a new lease on life.

In *"Samson Agonistes* as Christian Tragedy: A Corrective View," Furman responds tartly to Samuel, "if it is 'the tragedy ignorance has admired and bigotry applauded', so be it," even as she contends that Samuel "is speaking of a system of values clearly at odds with the Bible." Then Furman accuses Samuel of pursuing interpretive options "possible since the advent of higher criticism in the nineteenth century . . . but . . . hardly . . . open to the seventeenth-century Christian" who would never have encountered "Samson's accomplishments [being] belittled or criticized," not even in the Book of Judges and whose Samson, in any event, would be the apotheosized Samson of St. Paul's Epistle to the Hebrews.[15]

For Furman, presumably, the Samson of the Higher Criticism, a Samson without precedent in the seventeenth century, is conceptualized in the nineteenth century, probably by the likes of George Bush, who writes, "No part of the Scripture has afforded more occasion for the doubts of sceptics, or the scoffs of infidels, than the history of Samson. His character is indeed dark, and almost inexplicable. By none of the judges of Israel did God work so many miracles, and yet by none were so many faults committed." As others had been, Bush is troubled by Samson's marriage to the Woman of Timnath which, despite the fact that it is entered upon without the consent of his parents, has seemed "highly deserving of commendation"; by the foxes episode where there is on Samson's part a mingling of "ridicule with revenge"; and by the temple catastrophe where Samson is "the instrument of a signal act of vengeance."[16] Bush's conceptualization persists into the

[15] *"Samson Agonistes* as Christian Tragedy: A Corrective View," *Philological Quarterly*, 60 (1981), 169, 170, 171, 172.

[16] *Notes, Critical, and Practical, on the Book of Judges* (New York: Saxton and Miles, 1844), pp. 184, 198, 215.

twentieth century with William Kelly, for example, lamenting that we do not find in this unworthy instrument "the generous disinterestedness of grace"; we have here "the strangest and most humbling of histories" boldly marking "how little moral strength keeps pace with physical power."[17] And in our own time there is the further, and still more striking, example provided by Steven Brams, who finds in the Samson story an outstanding instance of sexual desire overriding political judgment. Samson is "ecumenical" in his carnal desires and "surreptitiously manipulat[es] events"; he avenged his captors in "an unprecedented biblical reprisal that sealed both his doom and the Philistines' "; and this "harassment" story, however difficult for Samson, sends out confusing signals about God's purpose in history and control over historical events.[18]

The lineaments of such a portrait, it is true, have a strong resemblance to the one drawn by Samuel; yet if we can trust Bush's acknowledgments to lead us to the derivation of this portrait, its source is not Germany and the Higher Criticism but the Renaissance hermeneutics of Martin Bucer (1554), Peter Martyr (1561), Victorinus Strigel (1575, 1586), David Chytraeus (1589), Nicolas Serrarh (1604), Jacob Bonfreri (1631, 1659), and John Osiander (1682). The English commentator regularly invoked by Bush to authorize such a portrait is Bishop Hall of the seventeenth century. Despite such a list of authorities and the sanction they would seem to provide for Samuel's Samson, in Furman's opinion the Samson of *Samson Agonistes* is the Samson of another Renaissance hermeneutic, his brutality here muted by a poet who merely alludes to Samson's more questionable exploits and who, like Samson, is in a historical quagmire "where vengeance is the only kind of justice there is."[19] Adherents to the belief that

[17] *Lectures on the Book of Judges* (London: C. A. Hammond, 1945), pp. 42, 54, 67.

[18] See *Biblical Games: A Strategic Analysis of Stories in the Old Testament* (Cambridge, Mass.: MIT Press, 1980), pp. 154, 156, 159, 160.

[19] "*Samson Agonistes* as Christian Tragedy," p. 173. It must be acknowledged,

Milton's Samson is a deliberately aggrandized, regenerate hero need to be reminded that such a conception, by the time of *Samson*'s publication, is a dead orthodoxy. We need to question whether this is the kind of poem Milton has really written, whether the Milton of *Samson Agonistes* hardens into orthodoxy or is rather its interrogator, whether Milton's Samson is a mountain heightened to sublimity or rather a volcano erupting.

The Samson of modern-day biblical hermeneutics could easily be disregarded were it not for the fact that so often (witness the instance provided by Daniel Smith) *Samson Agonistes* is invoked as a crucial precedent and principal sanction for this supposedly modern-day Samson. Serving also as a dissuasive to ignoring modern commentary is the additional fact that, whatever the relationship between this Samson and Milton's, this Samson bears a striking resemblance to both the Reformation Samson of Luther and the Samson of post-Civil-War-years commentators. Milton's *Samson* is cited by Smith to evidence that of all his calamities Samson most resented his loss of sight and to illustrate not only his consummate foolishness in his dealings with Delilah but also how Israelite history might have been different if only it had joined with Samson in his conflicts. Yet in summary, Smith must say of Samson what Luther had said, and what many of Milton's contemporaries were saying, that, however strong and at times noble his passions, Samson often exhibits feebleness of mind:

> He was raised up for important purposes, . . . but not always with the best motives, and a great part of which he thwarted by his bad conduct. It is possible that he repented and found pardon. . . . If so, the Scriptures remain silent on the subject. But while

certainly, that the authorities enlisted by Bush in support of his representation of a degenerate Samson (especially Bucer and Martyr) could have been invoked by Furman in support of her representation of a regenerate Samson. The point is that in the sixteenth century Samson's character is typically shrouded in ambiguity so that now this, now that aspect of his character predominates.

charity may hope this was the case, let it be remembered that the sacred history is far from holding him
up as a model for imitation. His vices were those
that the Word of God denounces in the most alarming language, and he is rather held up as a beacon
light for our warning, showing us the fearful consequences of transgressing the laws of purity.[20]

For good reason apparently, Milton casts the Samson story as
a tragedy, exemplifying through its protagonist what not to do.

An argument like that advanced by Furman rests rather
uneasily on the assumption that Milton is loyal to the donées
of Scripture and especially those of its Renaissance commentators—donées which Samuel is said to ignore, her interpretation to eschew, and which Furman herself seems unable to
articulate with accuracy. Very different mind-sets inform the
criticism of Furman and Samuel. Furman's attention is fixed
on the Samson of critical tradition, which she alleges to be the
Samson of traditional biblical hermeneutics; Samuel's concern
is with Milton's Samson, and she pays little mind to whether
this Samson is coincident with the Samson of either biblical
tradition or traditional commentary on Milton's poem. Furman thus vests her confidence in contextual possibilities that
Samuel thinks Milton's own writings render improbable. Furman would use historicity to negate the claims of a seemingly
unhistorical inquiry and would use the commonplaces of the
critical community to interpret *Samson Agonistes* as a poetry
redundant in its commonplaces. From such a viewpoint, Milton seems to be less a poet than Hieronymous Ziegleus, who
declares in the prologue to *Samson, Tragoedia Nova* (1547):
"base it were / Merely to parrot what was said before."[21]

[20] *The Life of Samson* (New York: T. Mason and G. Lane, 1840), pp. 93-94, but
see also pp. 67, 75-76, 80-82; and cf. W. A. Scott, *The Giant Judge: or the Story
of Samson, the Hebrew Hercules*, 2nd ed. (San Francisco: Whitton, Towne, and
Company, 1858), p. 253.

[21] See Watson Kirkconnell, *That Invincible Samson: The Theme of "Samson Agonistes"
in World Literature* (Toronto: Univ. of Toronto Press, 1964), p. 4.

Samuel, on the other hand, recognizes that art is formative of reality and not just a reflection of it. Her strategy is to correlate—to the extent that correlation is possible—various critical responses with a stable text, and in such a way as to pursue a line of inquiry that raises historical questions anew: what kind of ethical system does the Samson legend harbor and has it fostered? what is Milton's attitude toward Samson, both in his play (which, though it is a play, *must* be read as a poem) and in his other writings? And Samuel raises these questions in such a way as to root out commonplaces which have come to figure uncritically in writing about Milton's tragedy. Furman reads white where Samuel reads black, urges identity where Samuel would force distinction, skirts the issues that Samuel searches, and generally would silence the debate that Samuel has instigated. Both critics comprehend the need for contextualizing *Samson Agonistes* but meet that need differently: Furman by binding the poem to the orthodoxies of Christian tradition and to what has been called "the ahistorical idealism of mainstream literary criticism"[22] of *Samson Agonistes*, and Samuel by correlating the same poem with the heterodoxies of Milton's other writings even if this tactic involves flying in the face of the platitudes of Christian tradition uttered by the critical community.

Furman declares but does not demonstrate that Samuel's Samson—"a Hebrew fact" certainly[23]—lies beyond the historical scope of Milton's poem; and her regard for the apotheosized Samson of St. Paul's Epistle to the Hebrews does not allow her to acknowledge that, in the seventeenth century, it is especially the commentators on the Hebrews text who throw the nature of Samson's heroism into question, who see Samson as an angry spirit never healed nor harmonized. Great diversity

---

[22] See Andrew Milner, *John Milton and the English Revolution: A Study in the Sociology of Literature* (Totowa: Barnes and Noble, 1981), p. 195.

[23] The phrase is Sir Richard Jebb's and is quoted from "*Samson Agonistes* and the Hellenic Drama," in "*Comus*" and "*Samson Agonistes*": *A Casebook*, ed. Julian Lovelock (London: Macmillan, 1975), p. 180.

of character is represented in this roll-call, according to David
Dickson, writing in 1637: some are strong like David, "some
weaker, as the rest; some base Bastardes . . . [and] some of
them tainted with notorious falles in their life." We are left
to wonder whether Samson belongs to the line of David (Milton did not think so) or is representative of the baser sort.[24]
Dickson does not say, although he can be expected to have in
mind the kinds of misgivings already registered by Samuel
Bird in 1598. Bird is uncertain whether Samson was right in
taking an infidel bride and, more, whether the Lord really
prompted such doings; he allows no more to Samson than this:
"one good thing we may learne of him, that he asked his
parents consent."[25] Even when heroism is granted to Samson,

[24] A Short Explanation of the Epistle of Paul to the Hebrewes (Dublin: Printed by
the Society of Stationers, 1637), annotation to 11:32. For the alternative tradition
that Furman would represent, see Henry Ainsworth, The Communion of Saincts (n.p.:
n.p., 1628): on all the judges—Otheniel, Gideon, Jephthah, and Samson—says
Ainsworth, "the spirit of the Lord came, clothed them, strengthned them, and
prospered upon them; whereby they went boldly unto great battels, overcame their
enemies, and rent the wilde beasts that roared upon them" (pp. 217-18; see also p.
240). No sooner do M'Clintock and Strong invoke the seemingly positive representation of Samson in Hebrews and oppose it to the obviously negative one in Judges
than they begin to speak guardedly:

> The enrolment of his name by an apostolic pen (Heb. XI, 32) in the list
> of the ancient worthies . . . warrants us, undoubtedly, in a favorable
> estimate of his character on the whole, while at the same time the fidelity
> of the inspired narrative has perpetuated the record of infirmities which
> must forever mar the lustre of his noble deeds.

According to M'Clintock and Strong, consideration of Samson's strength and accomplishments "may palliate, it cannot excuse the moral delinquencies into which he was
betrayed, and of which a just Providence exacted so tremendous a penalty in the
circumstances of his degradation and death." Their authorities are Weissenborn
(1705) and Maichel (1739); see Cyclopaedia of Biblical, Theological, and Ecclesiastical
Literature, IX, 312-13. It is very clear that for all these commentators, the "awe"
and "astonishment" expressed by Samson's parents at the annunciation of his birth
sit against Samson's "vindictive cunning" exhibited in his various deeds; "his supernatural bodily prowess . . . [contrasts with] his moral infirmities, and his tragic end"
(IX, 312-13).
[25] The Lectures of Samuel Bird . . . upon the 11. Chapter of the Epistle unto the
Hebrewes (London: John Legate, 1598), p. 95.

it is granted in such a way as to excuse, not deny, that he was
motivated by revenge: "He desired to be revenged, not of
rancour of mind but of zele of justice . . . so al the elect &
glorified Sainctes desire revenge."[26] Samson's supposed heroism comes under challenge not just here, but in commentary
on the Book of Revelation; and insofar as this critical attitude
toward Samson infiltrates readings of the Book of Judges, it
is to be found not in hefty Bibles with their compendious
annotations but in political tracts that derive historical analogies
from the Judges narrative and in sermons on Judges that are
themselves prophesyings.

Furman is culpable of doing no more than what the rest of
us have been doing for far too long: of listening to F. Michael
Krouse rather than to seventeenth-century writers. According
to Krouse, no Renaissance writer questioned "whether, having
fallen, Samson repented his sins"; that is, no one ever questioned Samson's regeneration.[27] But listen also to Daniel Dyke
writing in 1635. Having already observed that the Spirit of
God leads us always to the Word, never to the theater, and
having submitted the view that all impulse to kill derives from
Satan, not from God, Dyke, through a series of slippery
equations, sermonizes Samson into Satan:

> . . . as the Philistins got away the Israelites weapons,
> so doth Satan in getting away faith from us, disarme
> us, and make us naked. . . . And in this faith ap-
> prehending Gods strength lies our strength, as *Sam-
> sons* in his lockes, and therefore the Divell knowing
> this, labours to do to us, which *Dalelah* did to *Sam-
> son*, even to cut off our lockes. And indeed when he
> doth this, he doth to us, which *Samson* did to the
> Philistins, hee pluckes downe the pillers of the
> house, and so overthrowes us.[28]

[26] *The Holie Bible* (2 vols.; Doway: Printed by Laurence Kellam, 1609), I, 552.
[27] *Milton's Samson and the Christian Tradition*, p. 77.
[28] *Michael and the Dragon, or Christ Tempted and Satan Foyled*, in *Two Treatises:*

First the Philistines are Satan, then Delilah becomes Satan, and finally Samson is Satan. Consider further the evidence against Krouse's position provided by commentators like Thomas Goodwin (1643): "We find Samson a godly man (whom yet we would scarce have thought such, but that we find his name in the list of those worthies, Heb. xi., ensnared with a Philistine woman, against the counsel of his parents . . . who clearly laid open his sin to him. And he was in the event reproved for his folly. . . . it came to pass he fell in love with another, as bad as any of the former, Delilah, who was his ruin. But his returning thus to folly cost him dear, for in the end he was taken as a captive to the Philistines, his enemies . . . and himselfe made a fool of, to make his enemies sport. . . . no child of God can take any great encouragement thus to return to folly."[29] For Goodwin, only those who, unlike Samson, repent and return from their folly can take comfort from this negative example. Were Samson really "a holy man, that had his eyes in his head, [he] could not but see his error."[30] Nor apparently has Krouse taken into account John Trapp on the same passage in Hebrews: "Here the Names only of sundry Worthies of old time *per praeteritionem conglobantur*, are artificially wound up together for brevity sake. All these were not alike eminent, and some of them such, as, but that we finde them here enrolled, we should scarce have taken them for honest men."[31] St. Augustine may have wished to settle

---

The One of Repentance, the Other of Christs Temptations (London: Printed by John Beale, 1635), pp. 216, 219, 241-242.

[29] *The Works of Thomas Goodwin*, ed. John C. Miller and Robert Halley (12 vols.; Edinburgh: James Nichol; London: James Nisbet, 1861-66), III, 419-20.

[30] *Ibid.*, III, 419.

[31] *Annotations upon the Old and New Testament* (5 vols.; London: Printed for Robert White, 1662), V, 890. Trapp's comment, and Goodwin's above (n. 29), expose the naiveté of Krouse's proposition that the omission of Samson's name from a commentator's listing of the heroes cited in Hebrews means no more probably than that "he saw no reason to explain their inclusion" (*Milton's Samson and the Christian Tradition*, p. 49). Surely some of the time the omission is calculated to imply a negative

all dispute over the Samson story in the rhetorical question, "Who can draw up a brief against religious deference to God?"; but commentators again become disputatious as they come increasingly to recognize, with Trapp, that always when the Lord "goes out, some judgment comes in" as was the case with Samson who, forsaking God, is forsaken by Him.[32]

When Miltonists insist that Samson the saint predominates in seventeenth-century hermeneutics, no less than in Milton's own interpretation of the Samson legend, they are simply tracking in the footing already provided by Krouse. Without regard for the aforementioned evidence, nor for that provided by certain seventeenth-century renderings of the lives of the saints,[33] Krouse maintains that Rupert of Heribert is "the only commentator who ever called Samson's sainthood into question" and further states that "the principal reason why [fit readers of Milton's poem] found justification for all of Samson's deeds was the fact that they had accepted his sainthood as incontrovertible." Despite evidence to the contrary (the

---

evaluation. In a sermon probably dating from the 1650s or 60s, John Lightfoot offers the following comment on Hebrews 32:

> Gideon, and Samson, and Jephthah: men, indeed, that had done great acts, but that, in the close, came off with some foul blot. . . . Gideon made an ephod. . . . Samson pulled down the house upon his own head, and so became "felo-de-se," or guilty of his own death.

See "A Sermon Preached upon Judges, XI. 39: Prudence in Making Vows," in *The Whole Works*, ed. John Rogers Pitman (13 vols.; Oxford: J. Parker, 1822-25), VII, 151. Lightfoot may pay lip-service to the notion that Samson is "a type of Christ" but does so by way of registering his deeper concern with the fact that "No judge, of all the twelve, had fallen into the enemies' hand, and under their abuse, but only Samson" (*A Chronicle of the Times and the Order of the Texts of the Old Testament*, in *The Whole Works*, ed. Pitman, II, 161-62).

[32] See St. Augustine's *The City of God* (I.xxvi), ed. George E. McCracken (7 vols.; London: William Heinemann; Cambridge, Mass.: Harvard Univ. Press, 1957-72), I, 111, and Trapp's *Gods Love-Tokens, and the Afflicted Mans Lessons* (London: Printed by Richard Badger, 1637), pp. 113-14.

[33] See, e.g., Samuel Clarke's *The Marrow of Ecclesiastical History*, 3rd ed. (London: Printed for W. B., 1675), pp. 15, 21.

hedged celebrations of Samson, often in the compendious Bibles; the mutilation of the Samson legend by the harsh political rhetoric of the age), Krouse concludes that "Milton did not abandon the view of Samson as saint in using him as the hero of tragedy. . . . The Samson whom we meet in Milton's play is a saint."[34] There is, of course, no logical connection between these two statements: to enlist a conception from tradition is not necessarily to espouse it. In fact, through Manoa's urging that Samson's acts be enrolled "In copious Legend, or sweet Lyric Song" (1737), Milton very cunningly points to decidedly different portraits of Samson: the highly ambiguous figure deriving from legend, and the unblemished image characteristic of the seventeenth-century religious lyric.

It is easy to forget that not just of late, but always, there have been commentators representing "two lines of approach: those who see in Samson a religious hero with tragic elements, and others who make an essentially negative evaluation of him, as an example not to be imitated, the opposite of the true hero." In a recent study by Gerhard von Rad, Samson appears as "a negative example"; yet von Rad does no more than continue in "a line begun by Martin Luther."[35] For a while,

[34] *Milton's Samson and the Christian Tradition*, pp. 130, 97, 104. According to Krouse, "allegorical interpretation of the saints of the Old Testament seems to have been most fully developed in connection with Samson." In the Renaissance, moreover, "Samson was still regarded as a saint. Not even the popular secular notion of Samson as a ruined lover affected this ancient conception. . . . Along with this conviction that Samson was a saint went a desire to absolve him from whatever faults he had been charged with" (p. 74; but see also pp. 15-16). In isolated instances, Krouse glimpses the ambiguities in Samson's character, as when he speaks of a "swaggering," yet "consecrated, folk hero" (p. 13); but almost always Krouse's accents are misplaced.

[35] J. Alberto Soggin, *Judges: A Commentary* (London: SCM Press, 1981), pp. 258-59. Observing that "the stories in Judges contain matter of very different historical value, ranging from the high level of the Gideon and Abimelech narratives . . . to the low level of the pericope of Samson," William Foxwell Albright proposes that the Book of Judges "illustrates the common attitude toward the charismatic leader rather than any phase of the hero's life"; see *From the Stone Age to Christianity: Monotheism and the Historical Process* (Baltimore: The Johns Hopkins Press, 1940), pp. 209, 217. That the Book of Judges was being read in this manner, at least some

this essentially negative view may have enjoyed parity with a more positive view of Samson as hero and saint; but in the seventeenth century it would gradually deepen until, in the 1650s and 60s, it became the reigning view of Samson. Von Rad speaks very well not only for himself, but for the last half of Milton's century, when he proclaims Samson to be "the oddest figure amongst the judges" and then posits that most readers "will indeed find it absolutely impossible to understand him as judge over Israel."[36] It just will not do to continue talking in general terms about the Christian tradition in *Samson Agonistes*, to say with William Riley Parker that "In general, the Christian tradition treated Samson as a hero of serious purpose, whose exploits against the Philistines were . . . not the pranks of an adventurous bully. . . . In the tradition Samson was God's agent and champion, strengthened supernaturally to begin Israel's deliverance."[37] *In the tradition*, as it happens, Samson is much more—and much less.

The Furman-Samuel controversy is an extreme instance of the propensity for criticism to privilege not a literary text, nor even its antecedent traditions, but blinkered interpretations of that text current in the critical community; it is an extraordinary instance of critical intelligence collapsing into the grip of convention and thus opposing the thrust of *Samson Agonistes* away from orthodox toward revisionist interpretation of the Samson story. Furman reinforces, whereas Samuel resists, the critical tendency to purvey received ideas and established at-

---

of the time in the seventeenth century, is suggested by John March, *A Sermon . . . on the 30th of January 1676-7* [Judges 19:30] (London: Printed for Richard Randell, 1677) and by Christopher Wyvill, *An Assize-Sermon Preached . . . March the 8th 1685-6* [Judges 17:6] (London: Printed for Walter Kettilby, 1686).

[36] *Old Testament Theology: The Theology of Israel's Historical Traditions*, trans. D.M.G. Stalker (2 vols.; New York: Harper and Brothers, 1962), I, 333.

[37] John Steadman has kindly made available to me Parker's portion of the *Samson* variorum which, once Steadman's portion of the commentary is completed, will be published under the title, *A Variorum Commentary on the Poems of John Milton: "Samson Agonistes"* (New York: Columbia Univ. Press). I quote from ms. pp. 40-41.

THE STATE OF MILTON CRITICISM

titudes as continuous, processive traditions accommodated by a poem that never conveys differences, that is reflective of but unreflecting on those traditions. Despite their disagreements, however, Furman and Samuel share a concern fostered for them by Barbara Lewalski and more recently furthered by Georgia Christopher: whatever its ties with classical tragedy, *Samson Agonistes* is wrought as a Christian poem out of the Protestant tradition of Reformation and Renaissance England. Implicit in that proposition is another: that we must desist from representing Medieval importations as clichés of Renaissance—and certainly of Milton's—thought. Moreover, what becomes apparent as we expand the field of evidence provided by Christopher and Lewalski is that not even allowably Renaissance commonplaces figure, or can figure, in *Samson Agonistes* in ways some critics have led us to believe. What such critics demonstrate is that when art is confined to mere reflection its significance is necessarily restricted to what is already known. We need to have opened what has for too long been foreclosed—the revolutionary character of art. When this happens, as Hans Robert Jauss remarks, we will be led "beyond the stabilized images and prejudices of [our] . . . historical situation toward a new perception of the world or an anticipated reality."[38]

Conventional interpretation of *Samson Agonistes* has surely alerted us to a part of what would be within the horizon of expectation of Milton's contemporary audience—but only to a part and not to the most important part. It has ignored the fact that poetry often is written to expand that horizon of expectation. Samson as a type of Christ and a hero of faith, as an image of regeneration swallowing up generation, survives within the consciousness of the seventeenth century, but in tandem with the realization that Samson's character is a riddle,

[38] *Toward an Aesthetics of Reception*, trans. Timothy Bahti (Minneapolis: Univ. of Minnesota Press, 1982), p. 14.

so contrived that even Delilah remains confounded by it. Abiezer Coppe can thus imagine himself as a Samson confounding base things by base things into "eternall Majesty, unspeakable glory, my life, my self" even as Vondel (in a play from which Milton was once thought to have stolen his poem) can posit that the Philistines are "Wrathful with reason." Vondel then has his Chorus propose that Samson "complains / And talks, but all untimely, of revenge," the Chorus having already urged: "Let revenge / Be now abated. There will follow you / The honour of forgiveness to a foe."[39] We must learn to ask with Jauss: what would be the audience's expectations? how various might its expectations be? does a work like *Samson Agonistes* satisfy or suppress, foster or frustrate them? does it offer a congenial or alienating perspective to its audience? Such questions, in turn, may open to us a *Samson Agonistes* that is not "an enfeeblement of imaginative power but . . . an intensification of it."[40]

Let us now turn attention to Georgia Christopher who would do for Milton what Roland Frye has already done for Shakespeare—who would revert to Martin Luther and John Calvin for epitomes of religious attitudes, for the theological commonplaces of the poet's culture, for the base line of a hermeneutic that Milton's poetry is everywhere thought to affirm.[41] Yet in reverting to Luther and Calvin, Christopher

[39] See Coppe's "A Fiery Flying Roll" (1649), in *A Collection of Ranter Writings from the Seventeenth Century*, ed. Nigel Smith (London: Junction Books, 1983), p. 108; and Vondel's *Samson, a Holy Revenge* (1660), in Kirkconnell, *That Invincible Samson*, pp. 79, 95, 119. Goodwin provides a superb example of how a regenerate and degenerate Samson can be hosted by the same consciousness; see *The Works of Thomas Goodwin*, ed. Miller and Halley, III, 319-20, and cf. VIII, 508-09.

[40] T.J.B. Spencer, *"Samson Agonistes* in London," in *Twentieth Century Interpretations of "Samson Agonistes,"* ed. Galbraith M. Crump (Englewood Cliffs: Prentice-Hall, 1968), p. 97.

[41] See Christopher, *Milton and the Science of the Saints* (Princeton: Princeton Univ.

often omits the crucial detail, or the complicating piece of
evidence, as when, through an epigraph derived from Luther,
she places the figure of Samson among those biblical heroes
who sunk low but mounted high:

> Samson, David, and many other celebrated men who
> were full of the Holy Spirit fell into huge sins. . . .
> Such errors and sins of the saints are set forth in
> order that those who are troubled and desperate may
> find comfort. . . . No man has ever fallen so griev-
> ously that he could not have stood up again.[42]

The Samson story, Christopher argues, is (1) a Christian
affirmation against life's darkness, (2) a typological affirmation
of Christ's ultimate victory, and (3) the legend of a Hebrew
hero who in the seventeenth century became an honorary Puritan saint. And more, in *Samson Agonistes*, according to Christopher, "the latter line of interpretation dominates and subsumes the first two interpretive routes."[43]

The entire discussion of Milton's tragedy turns round the
argument that "Luther and Calvin were convinced that the
Holy Spirit moved in the lives of the patriarchs," hence in
Samson's life, and the argument that in this, Milton's last
poem, the climax is reached in "God's 'leading' the hero to
perform a specific and unexpected action of deliverance."[44]

Press, 1982); and cf. Frye, *Shakespeare and Christian Doctrine* (Princeton: Princeton
Univ. Press, 1963). The principal challenge to Christopher's argument comes from
Christopher Hill: "Seventeenth-century religious radicals looked back to Wyclif and
Hus rather than to Luther and Calvin, the persecuted, not the successful" (*The
Experience of Defeat*, p. 303).

[42] *Luther's Works*, ed. Jaroslav Pelikan et al. (55 vols.; St. Louis: Concordia Press;
Philadelphia: Fortress Press, 1955-76), XXVI, 109. See also Rudolf Hermann, *Die
Gestalt Simsons bei Luther* (Berlin: A. Töpelmann, 1952).

[43] *Milton and the Science of the Saints*, p. 226. But see Krouse's argument that "In
Luther's view Samson was a negative exemplum, an object lesson teaching us by his
killing and his lechery not to do likewise" (*Milton's Samson and the Christian Tradition*,
p. 70).

[44] *Milton and the Science of the Saints*, pp. 231, 232.

Christopher's discussion turns around this argument but not around what Luther and Calvin actually say; and they do not say the same thing certainly, nor even within their own writings speak as univocally as Christopher would lead us to believe. The diversity of their observation, especially of Luther's—indeed much that would complicate and, as it happens, compromise Christopher's argument—is ignored. We learn only that Christopher is impatient, that we should be impatient, with those who see Milton, in his tragedy, fracturing rather than securing received typological associations, with those who dwell on Samson's barbarism in breaking God's laws and hence in killing so many Philistines. Such readings, Christopher contends, are "at odds with the prevailing Protestant hermeneutic"; for Luther and Calvin "held that the patriarchs were illuminated by God's Spirit and saw through their dark oracles to the promise of immortality. . . . The puritan reader," she continues, "would easily discount the emphasis upon revenge and mass slaughter as belonging to the ethics of a bygone age and focus instead upon the unchanging spiritual issue: faith in God's words."[45] No Puritan authority is cited, however. Had the field of evidence been enlarged to include the diverse Puritan literature, it would have become quickly evident that not all Puritans said the same thing about Samson. Moreover, the Puritan literature that does confront Samson in the 1640s and 50s is a literature of shifting accents and concerns, where an initial muddling of differences between Samson and Christ modulates into an accentuation of their differences.

No doubt there were those in the seventeenth century, such as Samuel Mather, who blurred distinctions in order to portray Samson as "a bright and glorious Representation of the Messiah," as "a little Sun . . . [who] gave . . . some dawnings of the Day, some beginnings of Light and Liberty in that deep night of Darkness and Bondage."[46] The Samuel Mathers

---

[45] *Ibid.*, pp. 247, 248.

[46] *The Figures or Types of the Old Testament* (Dublin: n.p., 1683), p. 132. What

of Milton's age may encourage the view that Samson, purged
of his sin, exhibits in his lifetime a pattern of experience
mysteriously arranged by God and even, as Christopher would
have it, a pattern extrapolated from Christ's passion and resurrection as "a pastoral simplification" of that experience.[47]
The "critical" question, however, is whether *Samson Agonistes*
is, in this sense, of its age or dwells apart from it or, more
exactly perhaps, whether Milton's poem better accords with
an alternative tradition of the age and one that, nominally the
subject of Christopher's book, is never really represented by
it. Even Mather must cluster types in order to produce an
ample portrait of Christ, and so invokes not just Samson but
David and Solomon, "all which three put together, gives a
bright and glorious representation of Jesus Christ: *Sampson* in
his Death and Sufferings, *David* in his Victories and Con-
quests, *Solomon* in the peace, and quiet establishment of his
Kingdom."[48] Samson simply cannot figure forth the conquering Christ or the kingdom to come, since for many a bondage
lurked under this apparent shape of good.

As early as Calvin certainly, alongside the acknowledgment
that Samson "was a type of Christ, and represented Him," is
the admission—indeed a steadily deepening awareness—that
Samson, even at the end, is governed by "passionate wrath
and vengeance."[49] Samson may be cited to illustrate that "*God*

is characteristic of the sixteenth century loses its typicality in the seventeenth. For
characteristically sixteenth-century formulations standing behind this one by Mather,
see *The Sermons of Edwin Sandys* (1585), ed. John Ayre (Cambridge: Cambridge
University Press, 1841), pp. 370-71, and Edward Vaughan, *An Introduction into the
Bookes of the Prophets and Apostles* (London: Printed for William Holme, 1598),
unpaginated "An Introduction to Booke of Judges." Of course, this older typology
survives in the seventeenth century, not only in Mather's writings but in Benjamin
Keach's discussion of "Sampson *Type of Christ*" in *Troposchematologia: Tropes and
Figures; or, a Treatise of the Metaphors, Allegories, and Express Similitudes, &c.
Contained in the Bible* (London: Printed for John Hancock, 1682), p. 418.

[47] *Milton and the Science of the Saints*, p. 231.
[48] *The Figures or Types of the Old Testament*, p. 116.
[49] See *Commentaries: On the Last Four Books of Moses*, trans. Charles William

hearkens even to defective prayers . . . perverted prayer"; but
what Calvin emphasizes is that those prayers "burst forth from
a heart not at all peaceful or composed" and that "even though
there was some righteous zeal mixed in, still a burning and
hence vicious longing for vengeance was in control."[50] This
is the Calvin of the *Institutes*; and such views also persist in
his *Commentaries*, where they gather around not the Book of
Judges but the Epistle to the Hebrews. Of St. Paul's listing
of Old Testament heroes (11:32), Calvin observes that "there
was not one of them whose faith did not halt. . . . [I]n all
the saints, something reprehensible is ever to be found." In
Samson, he continues, we encounter a figure who has "incon-
siderately betrayed the safety of the whole people." Samson
may be a hero of faith, but of a faith that is "halting and
imperfect."[51]

Pronouncements of this sort begin to etch a portrait not of
an apotheosized but of a tragic hero who, though not a glorious
image of deity, is nonetheless a profoundly moving depiction
of mistaken and suffering humanity. They also make it inevitable that subsequent Protestant commentators setting forth
Christ's types, especially Samson, will emphasize with William Guild *"The Disparitie"*:

> *Samson* lost his former strength when hee was be-
> trayed . . . but so lost not Christ Iesus his powerfull
> strength . . . Also, *Samsons* Wife was taken from
> him, and given to another: but the Spouse of Christ
> his Church, can no creature take from him. . . .
> The ouerthrowe of his [Samson's] enemies, was his
> ouerthrow likewise, and as they dyed, so he dyed;

Bingham (51 vols.; Edinburgh: Calvin Translation Society, 1844-53), I, 487, and
Institutes of the Christian Religion, ed. John T. McNeill, trans. Ford Lewis Battle (2
vols.; Philadelphia: Westminster Press, 1960), II, 870.

[50] *Institutes*, trans. Battle, II, 870.

[51] *Commentaries: On the Epistle of Paul the Apostle to the Hebrews*, trans. Bingham,
L, 302-03.

but so it was not with Christ, for they onely did
bruise his heele: but hee did breake their head: they
assaulted him onely violently: but he wounded them
mortally, and ouercame.[52]

The point is repeated insistently throughout the century: Jesus
excels his types, "was stronger then Sampson"; for as Barten
Holyday explains, Jesus "deliuered Sampson from the cap-
tiuitie of the cordes: which he did not breake by his owne
strength."[53] As a "strong man" Samson is but a "shadow" of
the true strong man in whose power it is, according to Thomas
Goodwin, "to overcome all our enemies, and to lift hell gates
off their hinges, and to carry them up the mountains."[54] What
was for some a sign of identity between Samson and Christ
was for others a mark of difference: there was a long-standing
tradition that Antichrist would arise out of the tribe of Dan
and an accompanying belief that the gates of the city were a
protection against the onslaught of Antichrist and their removal, an opening of its doors to him.[55]

Luther is less guarded than Calvin in his praise of Samson

[52] *Moses Vnuailed: or, Those Figures which Served unto the Patterne and Shaddow of
Heavenly Things* (London: Printed for J. Budge, 1620), pp. 159-60. Though Keach
sets forth "Express Similitudes," his habit is to present, along with the "Parallel,"
the "Disparitie" as in *Tropologica: A Key to Open Scripture Metaphors* (London: Printed
for Enoch Prosser, 1682).

[53] *Three Sermons . . . Preached at Oxford* (London: Printed for N. Butter, 1626),
p. 3.

[54] *The Works of Thomas Goodwin*, ed. Miller and Halley, III, 419.

[55] See Marjorie Reeves, "The Development of Apocalyptic Thought: Medieval
Attitudes," in *The Apocalypse in English Renaissance Thought and Literature*, ed.
C. A. Patrides and Joseph Wittreich (Manchester: Manchester Univ. Press; Ithaca:
Cornell Univ. Press, 1984), p. 47. Cf. Krouse, *Milton's Samson and the Christian
Tradition*, pp. 52-54. This tradition may have greater relevance here than Krouse
allows. Edward Vaughan instructed the Renaissance that in Revelation 7, when the
tribes are enumerated, "*Dan* . . . is left out, wherby it is thought that Antichrist
should come of him: he caused the first Idolatrie" (*Method, or Briefe Instruction; Verie
Profitable and Speedy, for the Reading and Understanding of the Old and New Testament*
[London: Printed by T. Orwin, 1590], p. 56).

and hence more the exponent of the received typology, even on occasion advancing Samson to the head of Christ's types:

> Samson . . . bit the cavalry and the infantry of the Philistines. For Samson never had an army, as the other leaders or Judges of Israel had. But all alone, without help and arms, he did very great things at the urging of the Spirit. He tore asunder the ropes and bonds with which he was tied up, as though they were threads of yarn. He overthrew exceedingly strong forces of infantry and cavalry, and on one occasion he even slew 1,000 men with the jawbone of an ass. Many quaked and fled when they saw him. In the end, he killed more when he died than others killed when they were alive.
>
> Accordingly, Samson was a remarkable warrior and savior above all others. He did everything at the prompting and impulse of the Spirit, even in death itself. Therefore he is depicted by Moses in a remarkable manner. . . . 'He will be a serpent,' he says, not against his own people but against his foes and enemies. And he says the same thing twice: 'He will be a viper by the path' which immediately avenges the injury with its poisonous sting and bite when it is trodden on. Thus Samson . . . trusted in God and rushed against the foe with the same fury. And nowhere in . . . Holy Scripture is there a similar example of a warrior so brave and invincible.[56]

Still, Luther is compelled at times to moderate, even curtail, his praise. Samson may have performed incredible feats; but Abraham's victory, because he did not spurn "ordinary means" or act on "some rash impulse," is "far more glorious." Nor

[56] *Luther's Works*, ed. Pelikan, VIII, 281.

is Samson set before us as an example for imitation: "We must distinguish between a miracle and examples. The latter we should imitate, but the former [which Samson exemplifies in abundance] we cannot imitate without presumption. Indeed, it would be useless and dangerous to imitate it."[57] Saints like Samson, Luther argues, have not been "viewed aright," for we should be emulating their faith, not imitating their deeds.[58] And elsewhere, admitting that he himself has been charged with "mak[ing] bloodshed such a precious work," Luther allows that if the Christian soldiers "are not doing right in shedding blood . . . , then . . . Samson must have done wrong when . . . [he] punished evildoers and shed blood"; and we, in turn, "ought to let the sword alone."[59] Often wondering about, even brooding over, the example of Samson, Luther concedes rather plaintively that "There must have been a strong forgiveness of sins in his case."[60]

Even if Luther believes that Samson's acts of harassment were divinely sanctioned, he declines to use the sword himself, saying that miracles of the sword are "rare and hazardous":

> For we read thus of Samson . . . that he said, "As they did to me, so have I done to them," even though Proverbs . . . says to the contrary, "Do not say, I will do to him as he has done to me," and . . . adds, "Do not say, I will repay him his evil."[61]

If we are going to remember, as Christopher does, that Samson is the Puritan saint (a stature won by him through his related role as the patron saint of the Puritan revolutionary cause),

[57] *Ibid.*, II, 375-76. Even Augustine understands, as Krouse reports, "that the saints are not necessarily to be imitated in *all* their acts" (*Milton's Samson and the Christian Tradition*, p. 37).
[58] *Luther's Works*, ed. Pelikan, XXII, 273.
[59] *Ibid.*, XLVI, 83.
[60] *Ibid.*, LIV, 79.
[61] *Ibid.*, XLV, 104.

then we are obliged to represent Luther's effort as depoliticizing and deradicalizing the Samson legend. A myth that
would become politically profitable in the hands of the Puritans
was for Luther problematical in the extreme:

> Münzer, a stupid man, read the histories . . . of
> Joshua, Samson, and David; and from the pulpit he
> impressed their examples on the peasants. "You are
> the people of God," he shouted. "Therefore you
> should follow the examples of the saints, of Samson
> and Joshua; and by killing the princes you should
> change the political state of affairs." But the conclu-
> sion is false, for heroic men who have special im-
> pulses are excepted from the rule. We, too, who are
> under the rule, neither can nor should imitate them.

Münzer's Samson, from Luther's point of view, should be
handed down through the generations "not as an example but
in order that we may abstain from the example and from
imitating it."[62] Samson, in his deeds, simply provides no example from which to adduce a pattern. This is a crucial aspect
of Luther's portrait, one eschewed by Christopher presumably
because it confutes the very terms by which many Puritans,
during the 1640s, restored Samson to heroism and established
him as their patron saint. Luther's condemnation is the Puritans' (perhaps even the early Milton's) commendation.
Christopher reveals the risk in disregarding hermeneutical
texts crucial to the full historical record, even as she resists
what should be a guiding principle of Milton studies: strong
evidence of indebtedness is typically accompanied by sharp
disagreement between debtor and those to whom the debts are
owed. Efforts to lay Milton's poetry in the lap of orthodoxy
inevitably result in that poetry's being shorn of its strength.

There is a sense in which Milton is a traditionalist; and in

[62] *Ibid.*, V, 311, 326; cf. III, 30-31.

his epics especially, traditions are fully represented in both their multifaceted detail and their discrepant aspect, and in such a way as to suggest that Milton is not so much their marshal as their manipulator. The appearance of tradition, of a society's orthodoxies, in a poem may (but does not necessarily) subvert revolutionary aims. What is important, always, is not the appearance of orthodoxies but the attitude a poet assumes toward them. Milton's is a poetry of choice, even of second choices, where one interpretation is *not* as good as any other. Often the strongest interpretive leads are coded into silences, or submerged rather than foregrounded in the text. Repeatedly, the tradition is less important than the poet's swerve from it, though the swerve is sometimes rendered inconspicuous by so ample, so exhaustive a representation of the tradition itself. The swerve teaches us how to read silences and what to make of omissions from, or submersions within, the text; it insinuates how additions to a text may constitute acts of interpretation. The swerve also signals the kind of poetry Milton writes—not one of commonplaces but one that interrogates commonplaces; not a poetry that is Augustinian, Boethian, and Aquinian (as Stanley Fish implies[63]) but one that is fired in the furnace of its own age. Additionally, the swerve indicates the importance of reading poetry with attention to implication and through intelligent inference. These latter features, sometimes missing from Christopher's criticism, are abundantly evident in Lewalski's. But even here certain inferences, intriguing and often ingenious, remain insubstantial; and still the commonplaces of Renaissance exegesis pertaining to the Samson story are too easily, and uncritically, assimilated to Milton's poem.

To Krouse's unimpeached chapters on the Patristic, Scholastic, and Renaissance Samsons, Lewalski is said, by Thomas

[63] "Question and Answer in *Samson Agonistes*," in *"Comus" and "Samson Agonistes,"* ed. Lovelock, p. 220.

Kranidas, to have added the unimpeachable component of a typology that displaces the usual correlation of Samson and Christ with an equation of Samson and the Church—or the Christian elect.[64] This is Lewalski's argument:

> The tragic theory which can be extrapolated from the Protestant commentary designating the Book of Revelation as tragedy identifies the Church as tragic protagonist enduring painful agony and suffering thoughout the entire scope of the "play" in this theater, by reason of the radical imperfection of its members. Yet it also engages in struggle and conflict, winning the spiritual triumphs of patience and faith, and it endures and struggles in hope of the apocalyptic victory which, at the end of time, the Elect will share with Christ. The Saints' story, as recorded in the Book of Revelation, is a tragedy of suffering and struggle, yet at its conclusion the providence of God visits the tragic catastrophe not upon the suffering faithful but upon their enemies and persecutors. It seems clear that this theory of tragedy has some relevance to the action in *Samson Agonistes*. Samson throughout the play is the greatly suffering and struggling hero, engaged, as are all the Elect, in the conquest of himself, in the process of spiritual growth, and in spiritual combat with his enemies. And at the tragic catastrophe he is the instrument of God's power (as the Elect will be at the end of time) wrecking the judgment of God upon his and God's

---

[64] See Krouse's *Milton's Samson and the Christian Tradition*, and Lewalski's "*Samson Agonistes* and the 'Tragedy' of the Apocalypse," *Publications of the Modern Language Association*, 85 (1970), 1050-62. For the aforementioned assessment of Lewalski's essay, see Kranidas, "*Samson Agonistes*," in *A Milton Encyclopedia*, ed. William B. Hunter, Jr., et al. (9 vols.; Lewisburg: Bucknell Univ. Press; London: Associated Univ. Presses, 1978-80), VII, 148.

enemies. However—and this point significantly separates the tragedy of Samson from the triumphant
victory and glorification of the Saints in the last
chapters of the Apocalypse—in the play the hero is
himself involved in and subjected to the final
catastrophe.[65]

This is an argument that, rightly, finds the tragic analogy for
Samson Agonistes in the Book of Revelation but that, wrongly,
deprives exegetical history of complexity and nuance by failing
to observe the actual status assigned to Samson by Revelation's
commentators, especially during the seventeenth century. It
also denies us, in the process, a full array of Renaissance
portrayals of Samson, or even an ample sense of the deep

[65] "*Samson Agonistes* and the 'Tragedy' of the Apocalypse," p. 1054. Among the
most enlightening pages in Krouse's study, *Milton's Samson and the Christian Tradition*,
are those charting the progressive adjustments in Samson portraiture that yielded for
the Renaissance a tragic hero (see esp. pp. 12, 57-62, 83-85, 88). Given Lewalski's
attention, altogether appropriate, to David Pareus's conception of apocalyptic tragedy,
it is of equal importance that we mesh that conception with Pareus's representation
of Samson as a type of Christ who, nonetheless, sins grievously and who, in his
failings, requires no less charity of us than Judas did of Jesus—whose sins, once we
begin to canvas them, are to be deplored, if not censured; see *Operum Theologicorum*
(2 vols.; Frankfurt: John Rose, 1647), I, 490-92, and also Pareus's theological
miscellanies in Zacharias Ursinus's *The Summe of Christian Religion . . . To This
Work . . . Annexed the Theologicall Miscellanies of David Pareus*, trans. A. R. (London:
Printed by James Young, 1645), esp. pp. 727-32, 843. Pareus's reflections on the
civil magistrates in the latter of these works include David, Ezekiel, Joseph, David
and (among the judges) Moses, Joshua, and Gideon, although they do not encompass
Samson but do include this telling observation: "The summe of all this is . . . That
it is the duty of a Christian Prince and Magistrate, to rule their subjects according
to the Morall Law of God . . . from which rule they are not to depart a haires
breadth" (p. 732). It is clear from Pareus's remarks in *Opera Theologicorum* that
Samson does depart from God's laws and hence is never regarded by his people as
acting according to God's ordinances. The only copy of *Theologicall Miscellanies* I
could locate is in the McAlfin Collection of the Burke Library at the Union Theological Seminary. A much earlier essay by Albert S. Cook stresses that the tragedy
of the Apocalypse is truly prophetical—that it envisions the tragic end of the wicked
themselves; see "Milton's View of the Apocalypse as Tragedy," *Archiv für das Studium
der Neueren Sprachen und Literaturen*, 129 (1912), 74-80.

structure of ambiguity that those portraits seem to share. Insistently, Lewalski speaks of "Protestant exegesis"[66] during the Renaissance where God is present with, not parted from, Samson in the end—where Samson's vengeful qualities are not a failing in his person but attributes (proper ones) of his judgeship. Here it is as if all Protestants spoke of Samson in the same language and with the same accents and, indeed, as if there were one Samson instead of many distinguishable Samsons to be found in this vast and important body of commentary. In the Renaissance, as it happens, even those who say of Samson, "neuer was there any Israelite more miraculously victorious ouer the enemies of God," are obliged to admit that the Apocalypse complicates their argument by eliminating Dan from its enumeration of the twelve tribes. The serpent in the way, the viper in the path of Genesis, it was thought, is the Samson of Judges who, though he may have been commissioned as a deliverer of his people from Antichrist, once the evidence of Revelation is factored in, may in the end be that Antichrist.[67] "Gods people tread so hard upon the Devills head," writes Trapp, "that he cannot but turne againe, bite them by the heeles, with *Dans* adder in the path."[68]

The fact is that by Revelation's commentators Samson is sometimes placed in the line of Michael and Christ, like them triumphing in his death, and sometimes is aligned with the party of Satan. Here he is represented as one of the saints against whom Antichrist wages battle; he plays Christ to "the cursed Philistines" who make a festival of his afflictions. And there he is himself that Antichrist, now doing to the Lord's

[66] "*Samson Agonistes* and the 'Tragedy' of the Apocalypse," esp. pp. 1055-56.

[67] See Francis Rollenson, *Twelve Prophetical Legacies: or Twelve Sermons vpon Iacobs Last Will and Testament* (London: Printed for Arthur Johnson, 1612), p. 141; see also pp. 143-53. Rollenson presumably would number Samson among the twenty-four Elders in Revelation who represent the saints of both the Old and New Testaments (p. 77); and for other of his comments on the Samson story, see pp. 38, 92, 173.

[68] *Gods Love-Tokens*, p. 60.

teachings what earlier he had done to the foxes.[69] Among those who read the Book of Revelation as a book of blood crying out for more blood and who believed that God deliberately delays his victory in order to devote more time to vengeance, Samson is treated as a more positive image than by those for whom such thinking is anathema. For those who aver that men now "Canonize Devils for Saints; if they would adventure to kill Kings,"[70] Samson becomes a very problematical figure indeed. Here Samson is a man of great courage, smiting a thousand men with the jawbone of an ass; but there he is a man rebuked by God for his foolishness, who has visited upon himself blindness, affliction, and death and who, according to

[69] See, e.g., Hezekiah Holland who writes that "our *Michael* overcame (as *Sampson*) by his death," having already explained that "Christ is *Michael* in this place" (*An Exposition, or a Short, but Full, Plaine, and Perfect Epitome of the Most Choice Commentaries upon the Revelation of Saint John* [London: Printed for George Calvert, 1650], p. 91); cf. Sampson Price, *Ephesus Warning Before Her Woe* (London: Printed for J. Barnes, 1616), p. 52. See also Thomas Taylor, *Christs Victorie over the Dragon: or Satans Downfall* (London: Printed for R. Dawlman, 1633), pp. 363, 452-53, 461-62, 745. On Samson as a saint, see the anonymous *A Breife Exposition of the XI. XII. and XIII. Chapters of the Revelation* (London: Printed by M. Simmons, 1651), p. 47, and also the negative representation by William Guild, *The Sealed Book Opened* (London: Printed for Anthony Williamson, 1656), p. 65. And on Samson as a limb of Antichrist, an idea implicit in identifications of Samson with the third angel of the Apocalypse, see William Perkins' formulation: "As Samson slue more by his death, then by his life: so Christ . . . saved more by death then by life" (*Lectures upon the Three First Chapters of the Revelation* [London: Printed for Cuthbert Burbie, 1604], p. 272). Especially in the 1650s and 60s, it appeared as if Samson might have disguised himself and so deceived the world into believing he was a saint; see Christopher Hill, *Antichrist in Seventeenth-Century England* (London: Oxford Univ. Press, 1971), pp. 126-27. Samson is associated with Antichrist by Richard Bernard, *A Key of Knowledge for the Opening of the Secret Mysteries of St Johns Mysticall Revelation* (London: Felix Kyngston, 1617), p. 76, and with the Church by Daniel Featley, "The Stevvards Summons; or the Day of Account" (1639), in *Threnoikos: The House of Movrning* (London: Printed by John Dawson, 1640), p. 8.

[70] Nathaniel Grenfield, *The Great Day, or a Sermon, Setting Forth the Desperate Estate and Conditions of the Wicked at the Day of Judgement* (London: W. Stansby, 1615), p. 18.

Trapp, by "continuance in an evill course," is punished "one Sinne with another." When Samson leaves God, God leaves Samson, with the result that disaster is visited upon him. Then Trapp continues: "*Sampsons* eyes were the first offendours, which betrai'd him to lust, therefore his eyes are the first pul'd out, and he is led a blind captive to *Gaza*, where he first gaz'd on his curtisan *Dalilah*."[71]

With Samson the question is not so much, as it would be with Satan, is he a hero or a fool? Rather, Samson was regularly represented as a figure whose foolishness qualified his heroism, as a Christian soldier in the Erasmian sense, who shows very little resemblance to Christ and is always shouldered over by those who are truly of the Christian elect. Despite the fact that "war is so savage a thing that it befits beasts than men, so outrageous that the very poets feigned it came from the Furies, so pestilent that it corrupts all men's manners, so unjust that it is best executed by the worst men, so wicked that it has no agreement with Christ," there are always those fools, says Erasmus, who represent themselves, or are represented by others, as soldiers for Christ and who, governing by the sword, omitting all else, make war, savagery, and retaliation their business.[72] Samson never really escaped being numbered among such fools, especially by Revelation's commentators. And Milton's Samson acknowledges as much: he calls himself a "Fool" and asks, "Am I not sung and proverbd for a Fool / . . . do they not say, how well / Are come upon him his deserts?" (201, 203-05; cf. 77). He admits to bearing "The mark of fool" (496) and finally declares, in response to the

---

[71] Trapp, *Gods Love-Tokens*, p. 141; see also pp. 113-14, 131, and Taylor, *Christs Victorie over the Dragon*, p. 279.

[72] *The Praise of Folly*, trans. John Wilson (1668; rpt. Ann Arbor: Univ. of Michigan Press, 1963), pp. 119-20. Trapp uses the Samson story to illustrate that God reprimands us for our foolishness: "How far would not *Samson* have run, being once out, if God had not stopt him with the crosse?" (*Gods Love-Tokens*, p. 63).

summoning officer, that he will not go to the temple. No longer a fool, Samson will not now "be . . . fool or jester" to the Philistines (1338). That he does eventually go to the temple reveals Samson, at least for some, as a consummate fool.

For one commentator on Revelation, Samson is a representative and for another he is the opposite of the Christian elect; for one he is God's avenging angel, and for another he is an angel fallen away from the divine vision, poisoning the earth and its waters, opposing the way of the Lord and burning up the Gospel. As a minister of God's wrath, Samson illustrates that, however many and excellent the graces bestowed upon a man, "he is not to execute any function, especially publiquely, before he receive a particular warrant and calling from God."[73] In this way, Samson is invoked as a sanction for carnal warfare; but he is also cited, as he will be cited in the next century by Jonathan Edwards, to illustrate the paradox of strength in weakness: "Samson, out of weakness, received strength to pull down Dagon's temple, *through prayer*. . . . So the people of God, in the latter days, will out of weakness be made strong, and will become the instruments of pulling down the kingdom of Satan, *by prayer*."[74] In this way, with the emphasis falling so emphatically on his *prayer*, Samson becomes a type of the spiritual warriors of Revelation.

During the 1640s, it may have been argued that the sword and the spear were as necessary as the pen and the pulpit to the tearing down of Antichrist, that "the people of God have a commission not onely for a defensive, but an offensive Militia, and posture of warre"; it may even have been asked, "what losse is it [if you die at war] to be translated from

---

[73] See the anonymous *A Plaine Explanation of the Whole Revelation of Saint John* (London: Printed for Nathaniel Newberry, 1622), sig. N4ᵛ.

[74] *Apocalyptic Writings of Jonathan Edwards*, ed. Stephen J. Stein (New Haven: Yale Univ. Press, 1977), p. 355.

earthly prisons, to heavenly enlargements?"[75] But a decade later, the heavy accent falls on the Apocalypse as a book that, opposing "the beastlie nature of men" to "the Lamb-like holie nature," would foster spiritual warfare: "the beastlie partie," says John Durie, "fight's onely to maintein the interest of flesh and blood, which is self-greatness, . . . against the interest of the Spirit; which is self-denial, . . . serving others in the Kingdom of Christ through love."[76] Even typologists like Thomas Taylor have a difficult time squaring their precepts with the Samson story. The Christian soldier, Taylor will argue, earns his crown by repudiating the devices of the common soldier and like any king must fight to protect that crown, but not as an ordinary soldier would fight: both types of soldier must follow their captains even unto death; but the Christian soldier, scorning revenge, must do it much more since he is led into a warfare not physical but mental.[77]

In their association of Samson with the third angel of the Apocalypse, Revelation's commentators issue their sternest rebuke; for this is the angel who, embracing error, becomes the mangler of God's word and who, corrupting the Gospel, comes to emblematize the false prophet.[78] The true prophets, we are

[75] Joseph Boden, *An Alarme Beat up in Sion, to War against Babylon* (London: Printed for Christopher Meredith, 1644), pp. 15, 32. John Lilburne uses Samson to illustrate Boden's point: either Lilburne will be delivered from this "causelesse and illegall imprisonment," or he will "by his death, so doe them [his oppressors] (*Sampson* like) more mischiefe, then he did them all his life" (see *The Resolved Mans Resolution* [London: n.p., 1647], p. 1).

[76] *The Revelation Reveled by Two Apocalyptical Treatises* (London: Printed by William Du-Gard, 1651), pp. 70, 73; see also pp. 48, 52, 66-67.

[77] *Christs Victorie over the Dragon*, p. 89. At the same point in his argument, Taylor urges: "Bee armed like Princes, with the armour of God, and weapons mighty through God against all principalities and enemies."

[78] For the identification of Samson with the third angel of the Apocalypse, see Guild, *The Sealed Book Opened*, p. 65; and for typical explanations of the significance of that angel, see, e.g., Augustine Marlorate, *A Catholike Exposition upon the Revelation of Sainct John* (London: Printed by H. Binneman, 1574), ff. 121, 123ᵛ; Taylor, *Christs Victorie over the Dragon*, pp. 226-27; and David Pareus, *A Commentary*

THE STATE OF MILTON CRITICISM

told, subscribe to the doctrine of God's love and mercy, but the false prophets adhere to the doctrine of his wrath and justice; the true prophets alone understand that God's way is not to "kyll us with swoordes" but to "chastice us with roddes," that they "do not revenge themselves by strength of hand, not with sword, or poyniards . . . ; but the revenge proceedeth out of *their mouthes*."[79] Throughout the seventeenth century, the third angel of the Apocalypse was represented as a militarist, an agent of carnal warfare, who, falling from the heavens, enters into "*the* low estate of Subjection" and betokens "the slaughter of many in wars" and who, falling "*inwardly*," symbolizes those great men of history who abandon "the care of heavenly things, to pursue and cleave to those of the Earth."[80] An infection upon true vision, a corrupter and counterfeiter of Christian doctrine, burying it under human traditions, a falsifier of Gospel teachings, this angel, says Joseph Mede, is "*A Prince of bitternes and sorrows*," whose lot is to bring those qualities upon both himself and others.[81]

Samson is by no means a centerpiece of Revelation commentary, yet when he does figure therein it is often to undo altogether the received typology and to undermine inherited conceptions of Samson's heroism. One link between Samson and Christ is weakened by Thomas Taylor in his description of "*Michael* [i.e., Christ] . . . [as] the true *Sampson*, who with the jawbone of his owne mouth smites them downe, heapes upon heapes."[82] Another link is virtually broken by John

---

upon the Divine Revelation of the Apostle and Evangelist John, trans. Elias Arnold (Amsterdam: C. P., 1644), pp. 161-63.

[79] See William Fulke, *Praelections upon the Sacred and Holy Revelation of S. John*, trans. George Gifford (London: Thomas Purfoote, 1573), p. 25, and Joseph Mede, *The Key of the Revelation*, 2nd ed., trans. Richard More (London: Printed for Phil. Stephens, 1650), pt. ii, p. 10.

[80] See Henry More, *Apocalypsis Apocalypseos; or the Revelation of St. John the Divine Unveiled* (London: Printed for J. Martyn and W. Kettilby, 1680), pp. 76, 78, and the anonymous *A New Systeme of the Apocalypse* (London: n.p., 1688), pp. 170-71.

[81] *The Key of the Revelation*, trans. More, p. 96.

[82] *Christs Victorie over the Dragon*, pp. 461-62.

Trapp when he urges: follow the way of Christ, assume his burden, take up his cross rather than treading upon it, "be sensible of the weight of it, and not runne away with it as *Sampson* did with the gates of *Gaza*."[83] Once the received typology is eroded, Samson can be scrutinized anew as a fallen, tragic figure from whom God hides and to whom light is now darkness. The point is illustrated first by reference to the Philistines, then by reference to Samson himself. When God leaves man, the evil spirit comes upon him as the Philistines came upon Samson; yet again, when God leaves men, judgment is passed upon them as it is upon Samson, the wages of whose sin *"is death,"* both "Temporall, Spirituall."[84]

Among Revelation's commentators, no facts pertaining to Samson—certainly not, as Parker would have it, the "fact" of his election—are "accepted as incontrovertible."[85] Elected by God before his birth, Samson in his lifetime betrays his election, and God flees from him. The question here and elsewhere is whether Samson, once of the elect, can, at the end of his life, be numbered among the redeemed or whether instead he should be sorted with the reprobate. Far from sanctioned by Revelation's commentators, Lewalski's new typology, within the context these commentators afford for reading the Samson story, is rendered suspicious. Indeed, it is only through such fanciful allegorizations of the Samson story that some of Revelation's commentators can present Samson in a favorable light. Patrick Forbes identifies Satan with "that Lion, whom *Sampson* rent," while Nathaniel Grenfield portrays Samson's foxes as sin and explains Samson's slaying of them as a sublime act of judgment.[86]

[83] *Gods Love-Tokens*, p. 42.

[84] *Ibid.*, p. 114.

[85] Again I quote from Parker's portion of the forthcoming *Samson* variorum (see n. 37 above), ms. pp. 41-42.

[86] See Forbes, *An Learned Commentarie upon the Revelation of Saint John* (Middelburg: Printed by Richard Schilders, 1614), p. 23, and Grenfield's *The Great Day*, p. 62. Alternatively, among commentators on the Book of Judges, the lion will be

Richard Bernard may be one of the commentators who placed Samson, along with Joshua and David, among "The Lords most valiant and religious General[s]."[87] However, even if Samson is thus cited, it is usually the careers of Joshua and David that are elaborated upon. And it is also Bernard who fully lays out the terms for a contrast between Christ and Samson, redeemer and destroyer, true and false prophet. The former, a proponent of mental fight, subdues his enemies by the sword which comes out of his mouth; the latter, who has recourse to force and violence, uses the carnal sword. The one has his bride, the other his whore; the one rises into a new life, the other goes down to destruction; the one lives by the waters of the Gospel, the other is drunk with the blood of murder and sacrifice. Such antitheses, when set against the stories of Jesus and Samson, place those figures in dramatic opposition. And Bernard advances still other antitheses, contrasting those who go forth with the everlasting gospel and those who ignore it; those who are killed for preaching God's word and those who put others to death, thereby exalting the sacrifice of death over the gospel of love. The former, Bernard

---

identified with the Old Adam, with a principle within, that needs conquering (Joseph Hall, *Contemplations on the Historical Passages of the Old and New Testaments* [3 vols.; Edinburgh: Willison and Darling, 1770], I, 340-42); and Samson's foxes will be identified with "all fanatics" as in *Luther's Works*, ed. Pelikan et al., XLVII, 175, or with the Anabaptists which whether "there bee two and thirty sects" of them, with their tails afire, would burn down the true church (Joseph Wybarne, *The New Age of Old Names* [London: Printed for William Barret and Henry Fetherstone, 1609], p. 117, and also p. 132). According to Matthew Griffith, "Presbyterians, Independents, Anabaptists, and all other Schismatiques and Sectaries" are emblematized by "*Samsons* Foxes" (*The Fear of God and the King* [London: Printed for Thomas Johnson, 1660], p. 91); cf. Griffith, *A Patheticall Perswasion to Pray for Publick Peace* (London: Printed for Richard Royston, 1642), p. 40. Francis Rollenson says that all the fraudulent and tyrannical people of the world are represented by Samson's foxes; see *Twelve Prophetical Legacies: or Twelve Sermons vpon Iacobs Last Will and Testament* (London: Published for Arthur Johnson, 1612), p. 274.

[87] *The Bible-Battells; or the Sacred Art Military* (London: Printed for Edward Blackmore, 1629), p. 25; see also pp. 32, 79, 165.

concludes, are virgins, whereas the latter are spiritual and corporeal fornicators; the former are Christian in deed, whereas the latter are Christian in name only. Given this context, it is noteworthy that Bernard should later invoke the Samson story, representing Samson as a type of the great Dragon, Antichrist, and Delilah as a type of the Great Whore.[88] This alternative tradition of Revelation commentary needs to be accommodated to Lewalski's argument, or, more likely, that argument needs to be modified in accordance with this tradition of interpretation. Only in Revelation, and certainly not in Judges, is tragedy relieved and mitigated by hope. Judges, that is, represents the times as they are and does not, as Revelation will do, overlay that representation with the image of a better future.

There are obvious typological links between the Book of Revelation and the Book of Judges; yet they pertain, for the most part, outside the Samson story and are forged for purposes of contrast rather than comparison. Where such links do involve the Samson story with the catastrophe at the pillars or with the holocaust at the end of time they serve to contrast the false with the true apocalypse, a failed with a successful deliverance. Through such contrasts, we are enabled to examine Samson's supposed heroism, whether he is a limb of Christ or Antichrist. "The adumbrations of the antitype in the type," as Lewalski remarks, "may seem to mitigate the tragic effect by reference to the Apocalyptic hope"[89] but only, it should be added, if we assume a comparative rather than contrastive relationship between Judges and Revelation and thereby conceal the ironies meant to be revealed. Only if we sort Samson with Christ and not Antichrist, only then can we continue to

[88] *A Key of Knowledge*, pp. 34-38, 76. Importantly, Bernard is here contrasting the Mighty Angel of the Apocalypse with the third and fifth angels (often thought to be the same).

[89] *"Samson Agonistes* and the 'Tragedy' of the Apocalypse," p. 1062.

regard Samson's tragedy as a necessary episode leading toward the divine comedy instead of seeing in the recurrence of this tragedy an episode that prevents the divine comedy from playing itself out because such episodes repeatedly stall history before the stroke of end-time.

Miltonists are among the most learned and innovative critics in the academy; but when they are in the arms of *Samson Agonistes*, their Morpheus it seems, even the best of them nods. They—indeed *we*—have at times aggrandized Samson by contradicting the text of Milton's poem, by arguing that Milton says nothing about the Woman of Timnath or the law of an eye for an eye, despite repeated references to "the *Timnian* bride" (1018; cf. 219-20, 382-83) and Samson's own insistence that he will repay his "underminers in thir coin" (1204). We have not only diminished and sometimes altogether discounted the revenge motive in the poem but have also distorted telling details, detoured crucial facts, such as the dating of Marvell's dedicatory poem to *Paradise Lost* in order to silence the notion of a vengeful Samson. Milton's critics sometimes contradict themselves, telling us here that Samson prays and there that he does not pray, here that there is violence and elsewhere that there is no violence in *Samson Agonistes*. Other times these same critics contradict one another, arguing now that Marvell could not possibly have heard about and read *Samson Agonistes* and now that he must have heard of, and read, that poem.[90] Most alarming of all, however, are those

---

[90] See, e.g., Chauncey Tinker, "*Samson Agonistes*," in *Tragic Themes in Western Literature*, ed. Cleanth Brooks (New Haven: Yale Univ. Press, 1955), pp. 61-62; Anthony Low, *The Blaze of Noon: A Reading of "Samson Agonistes"* (New York: Columbia Univ. Press, 1974), p. 187; Mary Ann Radzinowicz, *Toward "Samson Agonistes": The Growth of Milton's Mind* (Princeton: Princeton Univ. Press, 1978), pp. 269-70, 390, and also by Radzinowicz, "*Samson Agonistes* and Milton the Politician in Defeat," in *"Comus" and "Samson Agonistes,"* ed. Lovelock, p. 201, and

critics who contradict not just isolated details of Milton's text ("Israel is sometimes at variance with God which Samson never is"), but the very spirit that informs Milton's writings, their abiding humanity ("There is no room for pity, not for the people. Milton would not have us believe that Israel merits any sympathy"). Such are "the fruits"—a programmatic inhumanity—that, for some, come from a "rereading" of *Samson Agonistes*[91] and that for others come from rereading the Book of Judges, which, cleansing our minds of present-day religious and ethical conceptions, is said to put us in touch with a religion not averse to holding its enemies in derision, to trampling and despoiling them, or exacting an eye for an eye. Both Milton and the Book of Judges require interpretation (such as they have not always received) that is germane to their essence.

What are we to say of this tradition of confusion and misrepresentation (perhaps extend to critics generally what Coleridge said of one of *Samson*'s critics?): that they "require . . . a telescope . . . , with . . . [their] contracted intellectual vision, to see half a quarter as far" as Milton saw?[92] What are we to conclude: that criticism of *Samson* has assumed a fictive form which preys upon the text? that we have become embarrassingly distanced from that text and the exegetical traditions impinging on its story? that in their capacity as literary and cultural historians, certain Miltonists are engaging in a

"The Distinctive Tragedy of *Samson Agonistes*," in *Composite Orders: The Genres of Milton's Last Poems*, ed. Richard S. Ide and Joseph Wittreich (Pittsburgh: Univ. of Pittsburgh Press, 1983), pp. 254, 256, 275 (a special issue of *Milton Studies*). Christopher Hill, "Milton and Marvell," in *Approaches to Marvell: The York Tercentenary Lectures*, ed. C. A. Patrides (London and Boston: Routledge and Kegan Paul, 1978), p. 22; and Sanford Budick, *Poetry of Civilization: Mythopoeic Displacement in the Verse of Milton, Dryden, Pope, and Johnson* (New Haven: Yale Univ. Press, 1974), pp. 48, 56.

[91] See Zillur Rahman Siddiqui, "On Re-Reading *Samson Agonistes*," in *Essays on John Milton*, ed. Asloob Ahmad Ansari (Aligarh: Aligarh Muslim Univ., 1976), pp. 68, 69.

[92] *The Romantics on Milton*, ed. Wittreich, p. 196.

form of historical writing which, paradoxically, operates out-side the historical dimension of their text? Or more, that the "most dreadful enemy" of which Wordsworth speaks—"our own preestablished codes of decision"[93]—our own (not to be confused with Milton's) ideologies have come between the text of this poem and its criticism? Both interpretation and ide-ology, it appears, are less progressive, more under the control of provisional historical frameworks, than we have thought. What have been posing as critical operations mounted on his-torical information are, in fact, exercises of a critical imagi-nation sometimes without historical moorings at all, and often without textual sanction either. Such readings, having finally very little to do with Milton's poem and practically everything to do with readers who are busy objectifying their own, and recapitulating others', ideological commitments, are misread-ings. And such misreadings, as Edward Tayler has remarked in another context, "do not inspire confidence in our profes-sion."[94] They are a measure of, indeed a case study in, the involvement of literary criticism with ideology, of the capacity of ideology to overrun a text and overrule interpretation.

Such misreadings derive in part from a later historical van-tage point, which has created, in the words of William Ellery Channing, "a consciousness of defect, rather than [an aware-ness of] the triumph of acquisition."[95] But they derive, in the main, from mistaken delegations of authority: to critics who continue to handle Milton's poems tendentiously, indeed to an entire critical community, much of whose historical "sense" is unauthorized to the very point of being invalidated by the

---

[93] *Lyrical Ballads 1798*, 2nd ed., ed. W.J.B. Owen (London: Oxford Univ. Press, 1969), p. [3].

[94] *Milton's Poetry: Its Development in Time* (Pittsburgh: Duquesne Univ. Press, 1979), p. 254.

[95] *Remarks on the Character and Writings of John Milton*, 2nd ed. (London: Printed for Edward Rainford, 1828), p. 35.

THE STATE OF MILTON CRITICISM

documents of history. Nor is faithlessness to the text of the
poem, and to the record of history, the only culprit. Such
misreadings also derive from an oversimplified conception of
tradition and the operations of the individual talent, from a
desire to aggrandize Milton's Samson by differentiating him
from the Samson of the Book of Judges and thereupon asso-
ciating his "heroism" with that of Jesus in the New Testament.
Typological reading, in this instance, subtends misreading; as
Frank Kermode might say, it reinforces, to the detriment of
Samson Agonistes, "the superiority of latent over manifest
sense"[96] by obliterating the literal meaning altogether. The
New Testament, we know, altered the sense of the Old,
through typology's blotting out its narratives and thus sanctioning institutional inattention to them. If the Old Testament
was still licensed for exegesis, the licensing agents were typologists who, as they issued the license, included with it tacit
instructions for restricting interpretation. Perhaps, as Kermode has gone on to instruct us, we are hosts to mistaken
assumptions about scriptural narratives, making them subsid-
iary to the myth they enwrap and to the meaning, often typological, they are thought to encode. Typology, we should
remember, is a way of writing history and a way of abolishing
old history except as a type-source for new history; in terms
of that old history, its function is obfuscating rather than
restorative.

Historical critics seem convinced that, at least in the case
of *Samson*, they have already done their job. I shall argue, on
the contrary, that the job has hardly yet begun, and will begin
only in the recognition that Milton's poem comes at the end
of a long tradition of heavy-handed interpretation and is part

[96] *The Genesis of Secrecy: On the Interpretation of Narrative* (Cambridge, Mass.:
Harvard Univ. Press, 1979), p. 2; see also p. 107. And cf. Kermode's *The Art of
Telling: Essays on Fiction* (Cambridge, Mass.: Harvard Univ. Press, 1983), esp.
pp. 185-200.

of a processive interpretation of the Samson story that has been excessively censored. In this instance, a biblical narrative has generated the new text of *Samson Agonistes*, which, though faithful to the spirit of its source, does not always adhere to the particularities of its story. This scriptural book is a reminder: that Milton's poem contains an embedded narrative; that, like biblical art generally, "whatever is reported . . . can be assumed to be essential to the story"[97] and whatever is relegated to the margins may be more essential still; that Milton's omissions from the biblical narrative are no less cunning than his redactions or repetitions; that a new version of a story, despite obvious departures from, and silences about, an earlier version, can nonetheless remain faithful to its scriptural meaning and can, through those very strategies of apparent subversion, restore meanings obfuscated by time's transhifting. What discrepancies exist between the new and older versions of the Samson story are a further reminder, first, that "Fame [including Samson's own] if not double-fac't is double-mouth'd, / And with contrary blast proclaims most deeds, / On both his wings, one black, th' other white, / Bears greatest names in his wild aerie flight" (971-74). Second, this poem is not, as New Criticism would have it, a sealed universe, but one that begs for contextualization, with both tradition and Milton's other writings, as a preliminary effort of all interpretation. Interpretation of *Samson Agonistes* will advance no further until it becomes responsive to Rosemond Tuve's plea for more study of Milton in his "historical context."[98]

Yet contextualization has generated its own problems, bringing criticism of *Samson Agonistes* to an impasse. Like any

---

[97] Robert Alter, *The Art of Biblical Narrative* (New York: Basic Books, 1981), p. 80.

[98] "New Approaches to Milton," in *Essays by Rosemond Tuve: Spenser, Herbert, Milton*, ed. Thomas P. Roche, Jr. (Princeton: Princeton Univ. Press, 1970), p. 261.

other critical method, contextualization, which may generate meaning, permits it to arise most completely when there is the attendant understanding that a great work never really transcends but does always exceed its contexts. The current anarchy of pluralisms has supplemented without subverting existing historical contextualizations. The array of new contexts for interpreting the poem, only some of them historical, has enlarged as the conceptual frameworks of criticism have changed. Disagreements are likely to arise not over the efficacy of contextualization but over concern whether this or that context is the relevant one, the valid tradition—over concern with promoting one ideology, while protecting the poem from another. Others may claim for their studies what Krouse has claimed for his own, that the center of their concern is the "complex tradition behind *Samson Agonistes*, the ideological context of the poem";[99] but such claims are not now likely to produce critical advances unless they are coupled with the intention of revising historical contexts for the poem and conferring upon it new ideological perspectives.

Criticism requires specifications, but also theorizations, of its contexts. Its enterprise is complicated by the fact that, as Christopher Butler explains, "the text alone under-determines its own context of interpretation (or . . . is not sufficient alone to help us decide on a context for interpretation)." Criticism may advance by hazarding a guess, but only to the extent that it also avoids the false surmise. Assisted by inflections from within the text, it creates a "context of situation" or what Butler calls a "co-text."[100] What here follows, then, is a series of contextualizations, all historical and, I hope, all finding a

[99] *Milton's Samson and the Christian Tradition*, p. 16.
[100] *Interpretation, Deconstruction, and Ideology: An Introduction to Some Current Issues in Literary Theory* (Oxford: Clarendon Press, 1984), pp. 88, 136.

sanction in a text rich in implication, rife with inferences, and informed by and interacting with a variety of valid traditions. *Samson Agonistes* is not a representation of this *or* that tradition but an embodiment of both; in the words of J. B. Broadbent, it is a "ritualizing of conflict, word by word, phrase by phrase, representing sides and states in the struggle."[101] In this way, *Samson* may be seen as a poem about the interpretive conflicts it has spawned, about the ideological rifts they have opened; it does not proselytize or propagandize but instead exposes ideological differences and mediates the space between them. Such is the manner of this "Strange text!" where we witness Milton "brooding in his blindness" yet "seeing all"[102]—a Milton, to appropriate his own words from *Of True Religion*, with "Senses awakt" and "Judgement sharpn'd" (VIII, 437).

---

[101] *"Samson Agonistes," "Sonnets," and "Comus,"* ed. J. B. Broadbent and Robert Hodge (Cambridge: Cambridge Univ. Press, 1977), p. 138.

[102] I quote first from Hilaire Belloc, *Milton* (Philadelphia: J. B. Lippincott, 1935), p. 280, and then from Allen Ginsberg, "Poem Rocket," in *Collected Poems 1947-1980* (New York: Harper and Row, 1984), p. 164.

CHAPTER II

SAMSON AGONISTES AND
THE SAMSON STORY IN JUDGES

*Has any historical narrative ever been written
that was not informed not only by moral
awareness but specifically by the moral authority of
the narrator? It is difficult to think of any
historical work . . . that was not given the force
of a moral judgement on the events it narrated.*
                                    —HAYDEN WHITE

The history of the Old Testament, of the formation of certain
books into a canon, is, in part, the history of what happens
when prophetic literature is invested with priestly understanding. Prophecy is lost in the appropriation, which is to say that
the prophetic word loses its urgency and hence its bearing on
the moment at hand; its relevance to the present is displaced
by binding the text to the past, the future, or both. One set
of questions involves: what did it mean for this particular set
of books to become bound, and binding? under what conditions
did their canonization occur? against what forces? to what end?[1]
But once canonization has occurred and, then, once the Old
Testament, appropriated to the New, is interpreted in terms
of it, another phenomenon occurs, another set of questions
emerges. Why these correlations of Old and New Testament
stories and not others? Why, at a particular moment in history,
is one set of correlations displaced by another? Why are certain

[1] See the fine discussion provided by Gerald L. Bruns, "Canon and Power in the
Hebrew Scriptures," *Critical Inquiry*, 10 (1984), 462-80.

books of the Old Testament propelled into prominence? How—and why—does this or that story achieve popularity, hence privileging over others?

During the Renaissance, for example, and especially in England, the Book of Judges was one book that became dis-bound from the Old Testament and that was thereupon re-bound now with this set of passages, now with that from the New Testament. One consequence of isolating and thereby privileging this book was to restore its prophetic significance by asserting its special bearing on history here and now. This book asserted itself first in the interest of monarchy and later in the interests of the Puritan Revolution; was used by one political party against another and even, at times, was deployed by a party against itself—as a way of addressing its own prob-lems and of admitting to its own failings. The Samson story in Judges moved now with, now against, powerful political agents and forces. It was here an instrument of power and there an instrument against certain forms of power. The po-litical edge, or edges, of the Samson story were hewn sharply by the 1640s after which time Milton wrote *Samson Agonistes*. This poem interacts intriguingly with the Samson story as it is narrated in Judges and with the politicized versions of that story which came to the fore during the seventeenth century. Terry Eagleton provides a handle on such a phenomenon when he writes that literature "does not stand in some reflective, symmetrical, one-to-one relation with its object. The object is deformed, refracted, dissolved—reproduced less in the sense that a mirror *re*produces its object than, perhaps, in the way that a dramatic performance re*produces* the dramatic text."[2] The reproduction, as Eagleton would have it, is not a reflec-tion, then, but an interpretation.

Typology was an important agent in both interpreting and

[2] *Marxism and Literary Criticism* (Berkeley and Los Angeles: Univ. of California Press, 1976), p. 51.

politicizing the Samson story; and though more remains to be said about typology in relation to both processes, at this juncture we need to address the biblical narrative that in our own time, as in Milton's, is frequently overshadowed by typology, even obliterated by it. It has been said that "writing typologically was for Milton a means to embrace Scripture while escaping its bonds."[3] Typology is, in fact, just that for other writers but not for Milton, whose concern, especially with Old Testament stories, is not with relinquishing but with restoring the bonds of scriptural meaning, not with barring history from his poetry but with embodying it therein. If it is possible to typologize history out of a book, it is also possible to typologize history back into that same book, and history in all its aspects—social, political, religious, and even literary.

Early on in its critical history, *Samson Agonistes* was linked to *King Lear* by way of punctuating the autobiographical element in a poem where "Milton, in the person of Samson, describes exactly his own case" and, especially in this poem's reflections on women, reminds us that he was "almost as unfortunate in his daughters as the Lear of Shakespeare."[4] However, there is a more apt and obvious connection between the two tragedies: both are fictionalized histories cast as tragedies; if *Lear* is a representation of the tragedy of Christian humanism, *Samson* is similarly and simultaneously a representation of the tragedy of Renaissance Puritanism and of the English Civil War. Allowing for the caesura that history places between

[3] Gregory Goekjian, "Deference and Silence: Milton's Nativity Ode," *Milton Studies*, 21 (1985).

[4] See *The Poetical Works of John Milton*, ed. Henry John Todd (7 vols.; London: Printed for J. Johnson, 1801), IV, 403, 366. For a discussion of *King Lear* and its sourcebooks, which has significant bearing on *Samson Agonistes* and the Book of Judges, see Joseph Wittreich, *"Image of That Horror"*: *History, Prophecy, and Apocalypse in "King Lear"* (San Marino: Huntington Library, 1984), esp. pp. 14-46; see, too, Joseph H. Summers, "Response to Anthony Low's Address on *Samson Agonistes*," *Milton Quarterly*, 13 (1979), 103.

these two plays, if we can say that English tragedy through
the time of Shakespeare is severing connections with what
sustains the dominant culture and is thus, "at bottom, . . .
nothing less than the negation and dismantling of the Eliza-
bethan World Picture,"[5] we may also surmise that the dismantling process continues in a play like *Samson Agonistes* but
also is extended to the dominant forms of Christianity, to the
very ways people were thinking about the issues—moral, political, and theological—for which the Samson story had become a fulcrum.

Milton's eschewing of the usual Samson typology is part
and parcel of his acceptance of the implications of the Judges
story and of his attendant rejection of certain contemporary
formulations concerning that same story. In wresting from the
Judges narrative what he regards as the original prophetic
understanding of the Samson saga, Milton mocks Samson's
failings and not, as is too often supposed, the book that first
exposed them. What survive into the seventeenth century are
disarrayed readings, the now distorted fragments of an earlier
understanding of the Samson story. Milton clearly expects his
audience to be conscious of a variety of constructions, at various
times but especially in his own time, placed upon that story
and hence to be alert to the numerous ironies he directs against
partial, misshapen, erroneous interpretations. When *Samson
Agonistes* is set against the sourcebook of Judges, we become
immediately sensitized to what Hayden White would call Milton's "creative distortions"; when the same poem is aligned
with Renaissance interpretations of the Judges narrative, it
becomes abundantly evident that Milton's purpose in retelling
the Samson story is to correct the "fraudulent outline" that,

---

[5] Franco Moretti, " 'A Huge Eclipse': Tragic Form and the Deconstruction of
Sovereignty," in *The Forms of Power and the Power of Forms in the Renaissance*, ed.
Stephen Greenblatt (Norman: Univ. of Oklahoma Press, 1982), p. 12 (a special
issue of *Genre*).

historically, had been imposed upon that story.[6] Neither the Bible nor *Samson Agonistes* takes as its ultimate objective the mirroring of attitudes and opinions its readers already hold; they are devoted instead to alienating their readers from the reigning orthodoxies. *Samson Agonistes* is not an encoding but a decoding of the Samson story, the original presentment of which Milton alters but without deforming it; thus his poem relates to the Book of Judges as a literature of fiction relates to a literature of fact. Yet what is remarkable about the relationship is the congruence, finally, between the two texts.

It is a sad fact of much criticism organized around source study that its authors have read about Milton's sources instead of having read them, or have simply read extracts from a source (for example, the Samson story as related in Judges 13-16), a habit of mind that has altogether distorted the significance of that narrative. Criticism of *Samson Agonistes* is still perpetrating interpretations whose credibility is rendered dubious by disfiguring representations of the Judges narrative. In consequence, the confusions of the critic about Milton's sourcebook become our confusions. Thus Chauncey B. Tinker instructs us, through a curious upside-downing of the Judges narrative, that because of the trouble in which Samson involved them, "his wife and her father were burned alive by their countrymen" and *then* Samson, "by way of revenge, catches three hundred foxes, ties them together, attaches torches to their tails, sets them ablaze and turns the wretched animals loose in the fields of the Philistines." What is represented as *effect* by Tinker is *cause* in the Judges narrative where these two events appear in reverse order. Or again, Tinker instructs

<hr/>

[6] *Tropics of Discourse: Essays in Cultural Criticism* (Baltimore: Johns Hopkins Univ. Press, 1978), pp. 47, 57. Kenneth Gross's brilliant discussion of the "poetics of idolatry" taking the form of revisionary narrative is of signal importance here; see *Spenserian Poetics: Idolatry, Iconoclasm, and Magic* (Ithaca: Cornell Univ. Press, 1985), pp. 30, 41-53, 59-61.

us that human slaughter in Judges allows us to feel "nothing but satisfaction" inasmuch as it is a given of this narrative that Jehovah wills "that the enemies of Israel should be wiped out, men, women, servants too, and cattle." Tinker insists upon such a reading of Milton's sourcebook despite the narrator's intrusions and demurrals and, more, despite the fact that Jehovah declines to intervene in such a way precisely because he wishes to test Israel by her enemies. The supposed "givens" of the Judges narrative, hence of Milton's poem, are not givens at all. While the holocaust may be a memorable spectacle, it is not, in either the Bible or Milton's poem, "a thrilling catastrophe."[7] Milton's creative distortions of the Judges narrative are of a completely different order from subsequent critical misreadings of Milton's poem.

Additions and omissions, suppressions and silences, truncations no less than repetitions, are significant in Milton's retelling of the Samson story, but in a way that directs attention back to, instead of diverting it from, that story and in the recognition apparently that, despite discrepancies of awareness between playwright and player, in Christian drama the artist and his audience are guided, as Klaus Peter Jochum observes, "by the invariable biblical framework."[8] They are guided without being confined by the scriptural tale; and, more, they are supremely conscious of the larger context from which such stories derive and to which they must be restored in order to ascertain the fullness of their meaning. There is scanning and rescanning of the same history both within and between individual books of the Bible so that, for example, "even as the two books of the Kings and Chronicles do contain the stories of the same course of time from David unto the captivity . . .

[7] See Tinker, "*Samson Agonistes*," in *Tragic Themes in Western Literature*, ed. Cleanth Brooks (New Haven: Yale Univ. Press, 1955), pp. 59, 64-65, 69.

[8] *Discrepant Awareness: Studies in English Renaissance Drama* (Bern: Peter Lang, 1979), p. 273.

book of the Kings handles most the affairs of the Kings
rael; and that of the Chronicles more eminently holds
forth the story of the kings of Judah."[9] This strategy makes
for multiperspectiveness and finds its counterpart in the Book
of Judges, which contains not one but several in-set narratives;
there is continuity between them, inner form and connection,
as well as an organic relationship between the parts and the
whole. Milton's tragedy follows suit by threading into its
Samson story, and thus involving it with, other episodes recounted in Judges and other of the scriptural histories with
which the Judges narrative was thought to intersect.

The Samson story from Judges serves Milton in the same
way that the Lear story from the chronicles serves Shakespeare:
each source provides the poet-dramatist with the elements of
a history, private and public, forged by him into a story. In
both instances, the poets, so to speak, are processing the un-
processed historical record. As Hayden White observes in
another context, "The events are *made* into a story by the
suppression or subordination of certain of them and the high-
lighting of others, by characterization, motific repetition,
variation of tone and point of view . . . no historical event is
intrinsically tragic; it can only be conceived as such from a
particular point of view or from within the context of a structured set of events."[10] In retelling the Samson story, Milton
could have shifted point of view and changed the scope of his
perceptions; or, as White might say, he could have changed
the "emplotment" of his story so as to achieve a comic vision.
Milton does neither however, and so retains the tragic sense
and structure of the Judges narrative. Yet Milton's story is
more than a simple redaction of this biblical tale. Certain of

9 "An Exposition of the Revelation" (1639), in *The Works of Thomas Goodwin*,
ed. John C. Miller and Robert Halley (12 vols.; Edinburgh: James Nichol; London,
James Nisbet, 1861-66), III, 18.
10 *Tropics of Discourse*, p. 84.

its details are altered—not to diminish but to deepen their significance, not to obscure but to reveal the implications of Milton's original. Moreover, Milton's story is simultaneously a response to the Judges narrative and to the constructions Renaissance interpreters had placed upon that narrative. In the Book of Judges, the Samson story is aligned with a cyclical, deterministic view of history; during the Renaissance, however, it became increasingly a type of eschatological and apocalyptic history. Milton's poem not only reflects these contrary views of history but, more important perhaps, mediates between them.

In altering the Judges story, Milton gives it a new shape, and gives priority not to the content of the story but to the rhythms of history captured within it. His objective is to wring from scriptural history its highest truths; and if attaining that goal necessitates the creation of certain fictions (that Samson and Dalila were married, for instance), Milton plays with those fictions as the child of truth in the belief, apparently, that what are fictions in form may in their substance be truth. Milton reaches for the truth of history, then, by compelling ideas about history in the Judges narrative into their most perfect shape. As Paul Ricoeur has remarked, there is a paradox here, for when the poet enters such a fiction he most speaks truth: "fiction and redescription . . . go hand in hand. Or, to speak like Aristotle in his *Poetics*, the *mythos* is the way to true *mimesis*, which is not slavish imitation, . . . or mirror-image, but a transposition or metamorphosis—. . . a redescription."[11] Rather as Shakespeare does in *King Lear*, by modifying inherited material and deviating from an authoritative source, Milton implies that elements in his poem not found in the Book of Judges may nonetheless be true to history and are, moreover, a way of clarifying the history expounded

[11] *Essays on Biblical Interpretation*, ed. Lewis S. Mudge (London: SPCK, 1981), p. 102.

by Judges. Thus, by virtue of the relationship it strikes with its source, *Samson Agonistes* should be accorded the status of what Frank Kermode calls an interpretative fiction.[12] As such, the poem can be seen, in terms of the conceptual model provided for it by the Book of Judges, as engaged in a variety of fiction-making operations: it *condenses* by including some events and excluding others; it *displaces* by foregrounding this and backgrounding that; it *encodes* some events as causes, others as effects, joining this group of events even while disjoining that group. In this way, as White explains, the historian—in this case the poet—represents "his distortion as a plausible one, and creates another discourse, a 'secondary elaboration' running alongside"[13] another's discourse, in this instance the Judges narrative.

About *Samson Agonistes*, Milton's critics customarily tell us this: that Samson's life is recounted in the Old Testament Book of Judges and that later Samson is himself canonized in the New Testament Epistle of St. Paul to the Hebrews. The Bible, in other words, affords two widely discrepant portraits of Samson, and to each accrues a strikingly different hermeneutic. Milton's Samson, in turn, is thought to derive not from the somewhat negative example of Judges but from the positively heroic portrait derived from Hebrews; that is, from a story which, once decontextualized, is recontextualized in terms of the New Testament. Criticism of *Samson* has thus evolved by darting glances at Christian tradition but without devoting studied attention to the scriptural book on which that tradition is ultimately founded. It is this space in critical discourse that needs filling, but in the full recognition that, though the in-

[12] *The Genesis of Secrecy: On the Interpretation of Narrative* (Cambridge, Mass.: Harvard Univ. Press, 1979), p. 109.
[13] *Tropics of Discourse*, p. 112.

volvement of history and tragedy remains a point of continuity between *Samson Agonistes* and its source story, Milton's poem deviates notably from the account of Samson in Judges and interacts uneasily with the portrait of him etched by Hebrews. There are different kinds of truth, Milton seems to be saying, some of which are ascertainable only through fictional representation.

That there is calculated interplay between the Old- and New-Testament Samsons is made abundantly evident by a poetic text which, depending upon Judges for most of the particularities of the Samson story, still places that story within the perspective of St. Paul's roll-call of Old Testament heroes: "of Gideon . . . and *of* Samson, and *of* Jephthah" (11:32). Samson's words here concerning his divine favor and heroic deeds bring into the mind of the Chorus "The matchless *Gideon* in pursuit / Of *Madian* . . . / And how ingrateful *Ephraim* / Had dealt with *Jephtha*" (280-83). And thereupon Samson, in a clear evocation of St. Paul, instructs the Chorus: "Of such examples adde mee to the roul" (290).

In Judges, Samson and Delilah are not married, none of the Philistines is saved, there is no character named Harapha, no Public Officer to summon Samson to the temple, and no Messenger to report the catastrophe at the pillars. Furthermore, the episode with the foxes and Samson's prayer are accentuated. Milton's departures from his sourcebook have been described unabashedly as a "reconstruction . . . designed . . . to rehabilitate a highly embarrassing biblical narrative";[14] but they may be explained more accurately by St. Jerome's assertion that the history recorded here is to be observed, "but the spiritual understanding rather [is] to be folowed."[15] Mil-

[14] Philip J. Gallagher, "The Role of Raphael in *Samson Agonistes*," *Milton Studies*, 18 (1983), 272.

[15] Quoted from *The Holie Bible* (2 vols.; Doway: Printed by Laurence Kellam, 1609), I, 516.

ton's departures from the Judges narrative are to be understood, then, as fictions deployed against the falsehoods of superstition and tradition that over the ages have tainted the Word, whose "truth," as Michael tells Adam, is "left onely in those written Records pure, / Though not but by the Spirit understood" (*PL* XII.511-14). As David Masson reports, nowhere has Milton "overstrained" his source and, despite deviations from it, has "inserted [nothing] that is out of keeping with the incidents of the Hebrew legend, as they might be reconceived for narration by the coolest poetic artist."[16] Facts do not necessarily speak for themselves but often require that another speak for them, even explain them. Without such explanation, we may not know what the facts actually are, and different representations of them invariably foster variant but not necessarily discrepant interpretations.

Virtually every episode in the biblical story is encompassed by Milton's retelling: the annunciation of Samson's birth, the tearing of the lion, Samson's riddle, his slaying of a thousand Philistines with the jawbone of an ass, the jawbone miracle, Samson's carrying away of the gates of the city, his marrying of and betrayal by the Woman of Timna, his retreat to Etham, his subsequent betrayal of God and betrayal by Dalila, his murder of the thirty men at Askalon and of many thousands more in the play's catastrophe. Still, in his retelling which amounts to yet another version of the Samson story, Milton foregrounds two of these episodes—Samson's marriage to and betrayal by Dalila and his slaughter of many thousands in the play's catastrophe. All other episodes in Samson's life are arrayed around these events, some emphasized over others by insistent repetition (the annunciation of Samson's birth, his supposed inspiration, his role as a deliverer, his first marriage,

---

[16] *The Life of John Milton: Narrated in Connexion with the Political, Ecclesiastical, and Literary History of His Time* (6 vols.; 1880; rpt. Gloucester, Mass.: Peter Smith, 1965), VI, 670.

his repeated slayings of others); and a few of the episodes in the Judges narrative are rendered conspicuous only by Milton's evasion of them. "It is in the significant *silences* of a text, in its gaps and absences," says Terry Eagleton, "that the presence of ideology can be most positively felt. It is these silences which the critic must make 'speak'."[17]

Samson's plea for private revenge ("only this once" in the Book of Judges 16:28) is excised from Milton's account, and so is the reason for Samson's being at Gaza (his spending the night there), though not the episode of his tearing down and carrying away the gates of the city. Too often excisions from, and suppressions of, the Judges narrative are cited only to illustrate "how the wild berserker of . . . Judges has been so tamed by Milton,"[18] when, in fact, Milton has not banished such issues as Samson's private revenge and whoremongering from his tragedy but rather, in this telescoped version of the biblical story, has simply relocated and given a different focus to those issues, turning the former around Samson's first marriage and then revolving questions concerning the propriety of Samson's marriages around his union with Dalila. More startling perhaps than Milton's emending the Judges version in order to represent Samson and Dalila as husband and wife is his suppression of the love motive that highlights their relationship in the Book of Judges: "And it came to pass afterward, that he loved a woman in the valley of Sorek, whose name *was* Delilah" (16:4). Milton may not excise the love motive from his version of the story, but he does submit it to ironic treatment, and he does subordinate it to other motives. The love motive figures in Samson's double-talk: to Dalila he confesses his private feelings, saying he was driven by love into this marriage; but to the Chorus which chastizes Samson

[17] *Marxism and Literary Criticism*, pp. 34-35.

[18] See Northrop Frye, *Spiritus Mundi: Essays on Literature, Myth, and Society* (1976; rpt. Bloomington: Indiana Univ. Press, 1983), p. 218.

for this and his previous marriage, Samson acknowledges only the public obligation to use this marriage to seek an occasion against the Philistines.

Frank Kermode formulates the artistic principle that pertains in *Samson Agonistes*: "Secrets . . . are at odds with sequence, . . . one way we can find the secret is to look out for evidence of suppression, which will sometimes tell us where the suppressed secret is located."[19] In *Samson Agonistes*, two notably suppressed details are Samson's firing of the foxes' tails and the subsequent burning alive of the Woman of Timna and her father. Milton consigns the first of these events to oblivion and pushes the other into the basement of his poem. The effect, especially of the latter strategy, is not so much the aggrandizing of Samson as the organizing of the philosophical and moral concerns of Milton's story around Samson's actions, not those of the Philistines, and the aggrandizing of those concerns over such theatrical spectacle. Or to make the point another way: the two episodes are of a piece, exist in a causal relationship with one another; Samson's burning of their crops prompts the Philistines into retaliation. However, it is not the retaliatory acts of the Philistines, but Samson's, that are at issue here. Through Samson's character and actions, Milton's poem reflects upon the nature of good and evil and upon the moral codes by which men distinguish between them. Milton's silence concerning Samson's foxes submits to the same kind of explanation. The episode had been so heavily allegorized by the Renaissance that it now enhanced rather than detracted from Samson's character. It was a signal instance of Samson acting as God's agent to rid the world of wickedness and the church of heretics. To eliminate the episode is to excise from his own version of the Samson legend an event in which Samson, embodying the forces of good, opposes the powers

---

[19] "Secrets and Narrative Sequence," *Critical Inquiry*, 7 (1980), 87-88.

of evil. Obliterating this episode from his poem, Milton disallows its customary figuring of Christ's tentative, and later total, triumph over Antichrist. Thus he avoids risky moments in the Judges narrative.

But not *just* risky moments. What separates the foxes episode from all other events, often repeatedly represented in *Samson Agonistes*, is the fact that it alone is not shrouded in claims, implicit or explicit, to divine inspiration. There is no spirit rushing on Samson when he ignites the foxes' tails and destroys the Philistines' crops. On the other hand, those episodes emphasized by repetition—Samson's slaying of the thirty men at Askalon, his then slaying a thousand more with the jawbone and many thousands more in hurling down the temple—these episodes are each allied with a claim to divine commission and, in conjunction, alert us to what will be the crucial issue in Milton's retelling of this story: Samson's claims to be acting by divine commission and the legitimacy of those claims. Their legitimacy is made an issue, emphatically so, by Milton's suppression of Samson's prayer which, reading backward from it, commentators had used to sanction all of Samson's previous deeds.

Milton may be selectively silent in *Samson Agonistes*, but always in a purposeful way, as is strikingly evident in the fact that he also suppresses any mention of Samson's judgeship. Milton, it is true, had little regard for the judges, a fact which has led some to conjecture that in excising all notice of Samson's office Milton eliminates an offensive part of Samson's life from his account, thereby exalting his hero over his counterpart in Judges. Nevertheless, this explanation misses the crucial point. Samson's judgeship, mentioned in verses that conclude both the fifteenth and sixteenth chapters in the Judges narrative, was used to excuse Samson from his most heinous crimes according to the argument that they belong to his public life and because performed by a magistrate are sanctioned from above. To excise any mention of Samson's judgeship from his own rendering of the story is, in effect, to silence this argument. Instead of exonerating Samson by incorporating such episodes into his public life, Milton implicates Samson in error by opening the possibility that actions presumed to belong to his public life are actually performed in his private person.

By virtue of his being appointed to office before his birth, Samson is unique among the judges. Yet by placing all Samson's actions under the aspect of his judgeship, the biblical narrative throws the very nature of that judgeship into question. Unlike kings, the judges were empowered not to make laws, but only to uphold those already made by God. The swordbearers of His Word, the judges were, according to John Trapp, "Gods Lieutenants extraordinarily raised up" and charged with executing His judgments, not their own, while preserving *"true Religion in purity and sincerity."*[20] According to John Diodati, a judge "could not bear any sign of a violent, proud, or absolute domination," for he is dependent "onely upon Gods election, command, approbation and guide, aiming onely at the publick good and safety of his People."[21] A judge, as Robert Norwood reminds us, is "to be judged, as well as to judge"—is to be judged whether worthy, even after anointment, "both in regard of . . . Knowledge, and . . . Vertue."[22]

It is too often forgotten that righteousness in the Old Testament is a legal, not a moral, term. As E. W. Heaton remarks, "it is the business of a judge to decide who is 'in the right'. By dispensing justice, he maintains the *norm* of society,"

[20] See Trapp, *Annotations upon the Old and New Testament* (5 vols.; London: Printed by Robert White, 1662), I, 43, 109, and John Downame et al., *Annotations upon All the Books of the Old and New Testaments* (2 vols.; London: Printed by Evan Tyler, 1657), I, "The Argument" to the Book of Judges.

[21] *Pious and Learned Annotations upon the Holy Bible*, 4th ed. (London: Printed by Thomas Roycroft, 1664), "Argument" to the Book of Judges.

[22] *An Additional Discourse* (London: Printed for Richard Moon, 1653), pp. 18-19.

THE SAMSON STORY IN JUDGES

always judging by reference to normal standards of conduct
and through his judgment revealing his society, its norms and
values. Indeed, says Heaton, the decision by a judge, the very
term of his judgment, means "done thing"—refers, that is,
to the customary manner of doing things in a given community.[23] The Samson story may be founded upon the irony
that God expected morality but found murder, riotousness
instead of righteousness; but that story eventually turns on the
irony of Samson and his judgeship, that Samson's own life—
his marriages and cavorting, his plundering and slaughtering—involves repeated departures from the accepted standards
of behavior that were to be his constant point of reference and
that in his own life, and in whatever judgments he rendered,
Samson was expected to uphold.

Milton comments appositely in *The Doctrine and Discipline
of Divorce*: "But for a Judge, but for a Magistrate the Shep-
heard of his people to surrender up his approbation against
law & his own judgment to the obstinacie of his heard, what
more un-Judge-like, more un-Magistrate-like, and in warre
more un-commander-like?" (II, 314-15) Here Milton seems
to be saying with Luther that "in these days the sheep have to
beware of the shepherd more than of the wolves."[24] The Book
of Judges is, then, a summoning to judgment and, especially
in the instance of Samson, yields to the perception of Northrop
Frye: "The final sentence in the Book of Judges, 'He judged
Israel twenty years,' comes as a considerable shock: *that* Samson
has never shown the slightest capacity to judge anything, much
less lead a nation."[25] In regard to such capacities, Milton's
Samson is no more than *that* Samson; and Milton himself is
no less able than the Hebrew writers in "produc[ing] a certain

[23] *The Old Testament Prophets*, rev. ed. (London: Darton, Longman, and Todd,
1977), p. 66.
[24] *Luther's Works*, ed. Jaroslav Pelikan et al. (55 vols.; St. Louis: Concordia Press;
Philadelphia: Fortress Press, 1955-76), XXXIX, 271.
[25] *Spiritus Mundi*, p. 221.

THE SAMSON STORY IN JUDGES

indeterminacy of meaning, especially in regard to motive, moral character, and psychology," for such "complexities of motive and ambiguities of character" are essential aspects of his, and their, vision of man.[26] Moreover, Milton shares with the Old Testament writers a strategy through which, instead of enunciating moral judgments, he elicits moral inferences from carefully planted ambiguities.

Repeatedly Samson disregards God's laws—in marrying infidels without parental consent, in feasting his marriage among drunken idolaters, in touching the corpse of the torn lion, in defiling the bodies of the men slain at Askalon, in the indiscriminate slaughter of the "choicest youth" (264) at Ramathlehi, after which time the spirit of God that once rushed upon Samson departs from him. The only way of redeeming Samson for heroism, Milton well knew, was to argue for God's suspension of his own laws. The Chorus does exactly this while reflecting upon Samson's plight, saying that God is not bound by his own prescripts which were made for us, not him: "[He] hath full right to exempt / Whom so it pleases him by choice / From National obstriction, without taint / Of sin, or legal debt; / For with his own Laws he can best dispence" (310-14). Samson, in turn, appeals to this same argument in justifying to the Chorus his going to the temple even though, as he earlier tells the Public Officer, "Our Law forbids at thir Religious Rites / My presence" (1320-21). Despite that "Law," Samson will argue that commands are not commandments, commandments are "no constraints"; that God "may dispense with me or thee / Present in Temples at Idolatrous Rites / For some important cause, thou needst not doubt" (1372, 1377-79). Arguments of this order compromise the very idea of judgeship and confound the notion that "the contradiction / Of their own deity, Gods cannot be" (898-99).

Such arguments are but a part of the pernicious casuistry

[26] See Robert Alter, *The Art of Biblical Narrative* (New York: Basic Books, 1981), pp. 12, 22.

that accrued to the Samson story by way of allowing him to be acclaimed a hero and are, or should be, disposed of by Milton himself when he argues in *The Doctrine and Discipline of Divorce* that he wants to be "able to shew . . . the waies of the Lord, strait and faithfull as they are, not full of cranks and contradictions, and pit falling dispenses" (II, 230). In *Tetrachordon*, Milton makes clear that there are dispensations, *and there are dispensations*: "A dispensation is for no long time, is particular to som persons rather then generall to a whole people; alwaies hath charity the end, is granted to necessities and infirmities, not to obstinat lust." There is this form of generous dispensation, and there is the other sort that Samson exhibits in Milton's poem: "This permission is another creature . . . and is the very *antarctic pole* against charity, nothing more advers, ensnaring and ruining those that trust in it, or use it" (II, 658-59).

Samson Agonistes is full of "studied reticences," "stubborn contradictions," and "patterned ambiguities"—is marked by "cryptic conciseness," "terse understatement," planned evasions and conspicuous silences.[27] What may be in the background of Judges is here foregrounded; what there is centered is here pushed to the periphery. Thus though *Samson* recapitulates many episodes in Judges, Milton's inflections, though not his revelations, differ from those of the biblical redactor. Milton relates to scriptural history in much the same way as an historian relates to the chronicles, arranging previously chronicled events within "a hierarchy of significance by assigning events different functions as story elements" so as to

[27] That is, *Samson Agonistes* possesses the very features characteristic of Old Testament narrative art as Alter describes them, *ibid.*, pp. 17, 101, 126, 154. Or as Kenneth Burke proposes, the Milton of *Samson Agonistes* has perfected the "roundabout device" through which, by "dramatic subterfuge," he can "include what he would have had to exclude, if reduced to a conceptually analytic statement" (*A Grammar of Motives and a Rhetoric of Motives* [Cleveland and New York: Meridian Books, 1962], p. 529).

disclose, in the words of Hayden White, "the formal coherence of a whole set of events" when they are gathered around a single figure and when they are as the elements of a carefully crafted plot "with a discernible beginning, middle, and end."[28]

The slaying of Samson's bride and father-in-law, an act of retaliation against them for Samson's running the foxes through the fields and destroying the crops, if not alluded to specifically, is presumably within the consciousness of Dalila when she expresses her fear that Samson will deal with her as earlier he dealt with his Timnian bride, within the consciousness of the Chorus when it reminds Samson of that bride and of "Thy Paranymph . . . / Successour in thy bed" (1020-21), and within Samson's own consciousness when, as Milton reports, he is dwelling in the rock of Etham, which in the Judges story is Samson's refuge after having taken revenge upon those Philistines who killed his wife and father-in-law. On the margins of their consciousness, this episode is allowed to sit on the margins of ours as well; and only on the margins, for in scrupulous fairness to Samson Milton blames him for nothing of which he is not directly accountable. As a poet familiar with the art of narrative and now appropriating certain of its principles for a dramatic poem, Milton surely recognized that "Narrative always says less than it knows, but it often makes known more than it says."[29] That principle informs the narrative discourse in *Samson Agonistes*, and so too does the correlative strategy of omitting some important action of which neither the author nor his characters can be ignorant but which there is a pointed purpose to concealing. Such deliberate omissions often contribute to the final revelation.

One critic expresses bewilderment at Milton's omitting the

[28] *Metahistory: The Historical Imagination in Nineteenth-Century Europe* (Baltimore: The Johns Hopkins Univ. Press, 1973), p. 7.

[29] Gérard Genette, *Narrative Discourse: An Essay in Method*, trans. Jane E. Lewin (Ithaca: Cornell Univ. Press, 1980), p. 198; see also p. 196.

scene in which Samson's wife and father-in-law are murdered by their own people, especially in view of the fact that Milton could have here used Samson as a foil for exhibiting Philistian vengeance: Milton could—*should*—have capitalized on an event that instead he chose to ignore. For this critic, apparently, the exclusion of the event is worth noting, but only as an opportunity lost by Milton for further glorifying Samson in a contrast with Philistian vengeance.[30] The omission of the episode, surely purposeful, may in fact signal another intention, that of withholding such a contrast with the implied purpose of making vengeance an attribute that Samson shares with the Philistian foes. And in any event, given the reigning reading of *Samson Agonistes* as a drama of regeneration, the more striking silence concerns what happens to Samson at Etham, where according to tradition Samson undergoes an experience of great moment for his inner life: here repentance is made and grace in him revived.[31] Whatever Milton may excise from the Judges narrative, he refuses to omit the primitive ethic that governs Samson and the Philistines alike—and Samson no less than the Philistines. Instead of casting off the old man and renewing himself at Etham, Samson, "retir'd" there, plots more revenge, "Not flying, but fore-casting in what place / To set upon them, what advantag'd best" (253-55). The Philistines will do to Samson what he had done to them; but Samson, in turn, will do unto them what they have done to him: he repays them "in thir coin" (1204). The violence of his rhetoric—he will tear Dalila limb from limb and bare his fists against Harapha—is the same violence that turned God from Samson's people in the first place, when they showed

[30] Thomas Kranidas, "*Samson Agonistes*," in *A Milton Encyclopedia*, ed. William B. Hunter, Jr., et al. (8 vols.; Lewisburg: Bucknell Univ. Press; London: Associated Univ. Presses, 1978-80), VII, 147.

[31] See W. A. Scott, *The Giant Judge: or the Story of Samson, the Hebrew Hercules*, 2nd ed. (San Francisco: Whitton, Towne, and Company, 1858), pp. 241, 246.

themselves wont to cut off the thumbs and toes of their enemies (Judges 1:6-7).

Samson's violence is of a piece with that violence which repeatedly, relentlessly manifests itself throughout the Book of Judges—in Ehud's slaying of the fat King Eglon: "Ehud came unto him, and . . . put forth his left hand, . . . took the dagger from his right thigh, and thrust it into his belly: And the haft also went in after the blade, . . . so that he could not draw the dagger out of his belly; and the dirt came out" (3:20-22); in Jael's murder of Sisera: "She put her hand to the nail, and her right hand to the workmen's hammer; . . . she smote off his head, when she had pierced and stricken through his temples" (5:26; cf. 4:21); and in the Levite's dismembering of his concubine: "he took a knife, and laid hold on his concubine, and divided her, *together* with her bones, into twelve pieces, and sent her into all the coasts of Israel" (19:29). Samson's violence is of a piece with the various scenes of massacre where thousands upon thousands are slain (1:4; 3:29, 31; 8:11; 9:49; 20:35, 44).

Moreover, by questioning whether Samson was actually at prayer, as he had done in the *First Defense*, Milton casts a dubious eye on the whole matter of Samson's rousing motions coming from God. There Milton wonders aloud whether Samson acts in accordance with divine command, or by self-prompting, or some other inducement. Here the matter is presented covertly, with Samson standing at the pillars "as one who pray'd," according to the Messenger, "*Or* some great matter in his mind revolv'd" (1637-38; my italics). There are those who believe that "or" means "and" in this poem and who, by this logic, would make "life" a "crown" of "shame" (1579).[32] If that logic betrays the critic's own argument, it

---

[32] See Edward Tayler, *Milton's Poetry: Its Development in Time* (Pittsburgh: Duquesne Univ. Press, 1979), pp. 120-21, and, more curiously, given his finely nuanced argument, which is otherwise so attentive to complexities, Stanley Fish, "Question

nevertheless buttresses the argument implicit in Milton's poem: that Samson's own life *is* a crown of shame. Still, the fact is that, though Samson is often at prayer in the Book of Judges, not only at the pillars but before going to Etham and after the slaughter at Ramathlehi, prayer is not a part of the patterned repetitions in *Samson Agonistes*. There is a difference between praying to God and pondering matters of self-concern and interest, Milton seems to be saying; and so only once in the poem is its protagonist shown indubitably at prayer, and then the prayer is for his own death—an "oft-invocated death" that will be "the welcom end" of all his pains, its "benumming Opium," its "only cure" (575-76, 630): "This one prayer yet remains . . . / . . . speedy death, / The close of all my miseries, and the balm" (649-51). That prayer is spoken by one who, in the end, is said to be "over-strong" against himself (1590).

The Messenger's own uncertainties about motivation become a reflection of uncertainty concerning Samson's motives—whether they derive from "providence *or* instinct of nature . . . / *Or* reason . . . disturb'd, and scarse consulted" (1545-46; my italics). Perhaps more remarkable than Milton's equivocation on Samson's prayer is his displacement of Samson's last, pitiful words in the Judges account: "O LORD GOD, remember me, I pray thee, and strengthen me, I pray thee, only this once, O God, that I may be at once avenged of the Philistines" (16:28). This verse from the Judges account is replaced in *Samson Agonistes* by the ominous words addressed to the Philistines: "Hitherto, Lords, what your commands impos'd / I have perform'd . . . / Not without wonder or delight beheld. / *Now of my own accord* such other tryal / I mean to shew you of my strength yet greater; / As with amaze shall strike all who behold" (1640-45; my italics). What was in Judges a prayer is here a thinly veiled threat; what was

and Answer in *Samson Agonistes*," in *"Comus" and "Samson Agonistes": A Casebook*, ed. Julian Lovelock (London: Macmillan, 1975), p. 234.

there a plea for divine infusion and sanction is here a declaration that what is done is done *of my own accord.*

There has been a marked tendency in Milton criticism to discount the significance of Milton's displacing Samson's prayer. From St. Augustine onward, this prayer provided the crucial piece of inferential evidence that Samson's acts were divinely sanctioned. There is the problem of his marrying the Woman of Timnath without parental consent, now obviated by the argument that if Samson acts with God's approval at the temple he must have acted with God's approval earlier on. The complications of the Judges narrative can thus be overcome: a text that says Samson *looks* at the Woman of Timnath, and is "pleased" by her, must mean that Samson *loved* her; a text that remains silent about Samson's telling his parents about his divine commission must mean to speak through that silence and to say that actually Samson did tell his parents and win their reluctant consent for the marriage. A text that seems to build sympathy for the Woman of Timnath's being burned alive must actually mean to deprive her of any sympathy, suggesting instead that there is poetic, even divine, justice in her meeting the fate she hopes to avoid by betraying Samson. Whatever the appearances, this argument goes, Samson never acts as a private person to gratify his desire for revenge; he acts only in his public person to deliver his people.[33]

Without the prayer, there would not even be a hint in the Judges narrative that God, who had earlier departed from Samson, now returns to him. The quick sequence is crucial to this line of commentary: there is Samson's prayer to God followed immediately by Samson's miraculous feat. Not only do the prayer and the temple holocaust stand in a causal relationship, but the prayer is the bit of testimony valorizing

[33] Simon Patrick (1626-1707) provides a startling example of such argumentation in *A Commentary on the Old Testament,* in *A Critical Commentary and Paraphrase of the Old and New Testament,* comp. Simon Patrick et al. (4 vols.; Philadelphia: Carey and Hart; New York: Wiley and Putnam, 1844-45), II, 1-96.

Samson as a public person. The prayer proves to Simon Patrick, for example, that Samson once again is "moved by a heroical spirit from God himself"; the catastrophe simply would not have "proceeded from a spirit of private revenge, God would not have heard his prayer (for he doth not love to justify men's passions): but that is *a proof* that his desire proceeded from God, who intended to punish the Philistines."[34] To hedge the prayer is to hedge the proof; to replace the prayer with a threat is to remove that proof altogether. It is also to problematize Samson's death without declaring outright that his death is a suicide.

If Samson's marriages are not testimony to his divine commission, they may be (as they were for Robert Burton) evidence of his "insatiable lust":

> *Solomon's* wisdom was extinguished in this fire of lust, *Sampson's* strength enervated. . . . Human, divine laws, precepts, exhortations, fear of God and men, fair, foul means, fame, fortunes, shame, disgrace, honour, cannot oppose, stave off, or withstand the fury of it. . . . No cord, nor cable, can so forcibly draw, or hold so fast. . . .

The very best men, Burton continues, "if once they be over-

---

[34] *Ibid.*, II, 76, 95 (my italics). Cf. "Sermon VIII: The Good Mans Epitaph; or, the Happiness of Those That Die Well" (1639), Daniel Featley et al., *Threnoikos: The House of Movrning* (London: Printed by John Dawson, 1640), p. 183: "It is not valour for to flie a danger: it is valour to beare it. If any example can bee alledged to this purpose, that of *Sampsons* may. But Saint *Austin* hee answereth. The Spirit of God secretly commanded him to doe it . . . : for if the Spirit of God had not commanded it, yea, and assisted him in it too, hee had never done that he did, in pulling downe the house upon him selfe and the Philistims" (I am grateful to Alinda Sumers-Ingraham for this citation). See also Richard Capel, *Tentations: Their Nature, Danger, Cure* (2 vols.; London: Printed for John Bartlet, 1650), II, 284: "*Sampson* I know did kill himself, and did well in it, but he had special order for it from God: shew the like order, and then do the like as *Sampson* did: but without the same order, the same act which was not sin but a duty in *Sampson*, is a great sin in any of us."

taken with . . . passion . . . commit many absurdities, many indecorums, unbefitting their gravity and persons. . . . *Sampson, David, Solomon, Hercules, &c.* are justly taxed of indiscretion in this point."[35] Only by death does Samson free himself from this plight and its attendant misery. In that death, he is a reminder that not even the strong men of the world are immune to death, as well as an object lesson "that no man should glorie in anything without, *Neither the strong man in his strength, nor the wise man in his wisdome, or the rich man in his wealth, but if hee glory in any thing, to glory in the Lord.*" Samson did not even give thanksgiving to the Lord when he killed the thousand men with the jawbone of an ass.[36]

In "The Argument" to his poem, Milton delivers his protagonist from the burden of suicide—"what *Samson* had done to the *Philistins*, and by accident to himself"—and thereby delivers Samson's life to us as a tragedy. If Samson is to be the hero of a tragedy, an intermediary man (as Aristotle might call him), he must not be represented as a suicide victim, "This . . . being so grieuous a sinne, we must not thinke that Samson was guiltie of it," says Samuel Bird.[37] To present Samson as "self-kill'd / Not willingly, but tangl'd in the fold" (1664-65), more nearly conforms to the demands of a Christian tragedy where Milton will nonetheless place an increased burden of responsibility on Samson by rendering Dalila as his wife and, later, by releasing the vulgar from the slaughter.

[35] *The Anatomy of Melancholy*, ed. A. R. Shilleto (3 vols.; London: George Bell and Sons, 1893), III, 60-61, 176. For other of Burton's references to Samson, see II, 181; III, 3, 237.

[36] *Ibid.*, II, 301, and Featley et al., "Sermon VII: The Worlds Losse and the Righteous Mans Gaine," *Threnoikos*, p. 159.

[37] *The Lectures of Samuel Bird . . . upon the 11. Chapter of the Epistle unto the Hebrewes* (Cambridge: John Legate, 1598), p. 101. Burke captures the complexity of *Samson Agonistes* in his observation that, through "dramatic subterfuge"—through a deliberate complication of Samson's supposed suicide—Milton suggests, in his edging toward yet still hedging the topic, not "a recipe for suicide . . . but a mere dash, or soupçon, of such an ingredient" (*A Grammar of Motives and a Rhetoric of Motives*, pp. 529, 530).

To do this, Milton must alter the description of "the house" in Judges which "was full of men and women; and all the lords of the Philistines *were* there; and *there were* upon the roof about three thousand men and women" (16:27). In Milton's poem "the house" of Judges becomes "a spacious Theatre . . . / With seats where all the Lords and each degree / Of sort, might sit in order to behold, / The other side was op'n, where the throng / On banks and scaffolds under Skie might stand" (1605-10). And instead of perishing as in the Judges account, they escape. This alteration of his source has led Christopher Hill to propose that Milton "went out of his way to save the people from destruction":

> Milton is unique in putting the common people out-
> side, safe from Samson's vengeance. He also inno-
> vated when he made a priest urge Dalilah to betray
> Samson which leads up to his other departure from
> the Bible in insisting that only the Philistine aris-
> tocracy and clergy perished.[38]

It is true: this is an astonishing revision of Milton's source, but also one submitting to another construction of meaning.

More boldly than the introduction of the Public Officer or Messenger, this revision of the Judges narrative subverts Samson's heroism. Both characters, introduced as dramatic neces-sities, reinforce the poem's humanitarian impulses: The Mes-senger paints an image of the final horror, and the Public Officer provokes Samson into a posture at odds with, and an embarrassment to, his supposed heroism. Unlike Harapha, who now appears too much like Samson, the Public Officer "is not imperious, or even hostile," but on the contrary, as Stanley Fish observes, is "solicitous," caring for, even com-plimentary of, a Samson whose prophetic irony, " 'Perhaps

[38] *The Experience of Defeat: Milton and Some Contemporaries* (New York: Viking, 1984), p. 314.

thou shalt have cause to sorrow indeed' . . . is at the expense of someone we . . . like. This is not the Nazarite's finest moment."[39] And given Manoa's portrait of the Philistines (a few still set on revenge, but most of them not), at least some of them seem undeserving of the destruction soon to be visited upon them and are properly the object of our compassion, if not of Samson's.

Milton does not allow us to accept this mass slaughter unquestioningly. Moreover, that the vulgar should finally escape is of Milton's and God's, surely not of Samson's, devising and implies a contrast between their distributive, as opposed to Samson's retributive, justice. Samson thus becomes progressively ensnared in a web of guilt. The violent catastrophe brings out of concealment an element of Samson's character harbored in the poem's parenthetical references to earlier episodes in his life: to Samson's exploits as a warrior generally (126-31, 341-45, 438-39, 638-40, 1180); and specifically to his slaying of the lion (128), of the thirty men at Askalon (1186-88, 1196-1204), and of a thousand men with the jawbone of an ass (142-45, 262-64, 581-83, 1093-95, 1189-91). But more, that catastrophe, the only significant action here, maintains the focus of Milton's sourcebook on Samson's vengeance. No sooner is the catastrophe reported than Samson's countrymen celebrate him for his act of vengeance valiantly and willfully performed, taking "joy presumptuous" in the image of a Samson walking "over heaps of slaughter'd [foes]" (1530-31). It has been proposed that, "If the poem is 'about' Samson's regeneration, it is incompetent to leave his last action ambiguous."[40] Yet in anticipating just this sort of objection,

---

[39] "Question and Answer in *Samson Agonistes*," in *"Comus" and "Samson Agonistes,"* ed. Lovelock, p. 236. Even apologists like Patrick are obliged to concede that the Philistines are true to their word: they promise to humble and not kill Samson; they do humble without killing him (*A Critical Commentary and Paraphrase of the Old and New Testament*, II, 75).

[40] Hill, *The Experience of Defeat*, p. 316.

that "if the author had meant all this, he would have said so more clearly," Tzvetan Todorov offers the appropriate rejoinder: "if the author could not quite understand what he was writing, the tale itself knew all along."[41] Milton, though, is more alert to the implications of the Samson story than many of his contemporaries. Hence Samson's last act is left ambiguous, deliberately so, with the probable implication that Milton's poem is not *about* Samson's regeneration but, instead, about his second fall. And *Samson Agonistes* is, after all, a poem.

These alterations of Milton's source amount to intensifications of certain of its concerns—with reprobation, cruelty, and vengeance certainly, but also with marriage and deliverance. Through a rigorously exercised principle of selection, Milton establishes foci and asserts emphases for the already organized history related in the Book of Judges. Paradoxically, Milton's departures from his source, which have seemed to have an ennobling effect on Samson's character, to have so tamed this "merry butcher,"[42] also underscore the concerns of that source, and of Milton's poem, with debasement through marriage and deliverance into further servitude. Samson and his people finally tyrannize themselves. Because of their record of backsliding, God eventually refuses to extirpate corrupt nations, choosing instead "to prove Israel by them" (3:1); but the Israelites subvert the divine plan by turning to such nations and then taking their daughters to be their wives and giving their daughters to their sons. In this, we are told, "the Children of Israel did evil in the sight of the LORD" (3:7). Although,

---

[41] *The Poetics of Prose*, trans. Richard Howard (Ithaca: Cornell Univ. Press, 1977), p. 142.

[42] See A. Smythe Palmer, *The Samson Saga and Its Place in Comparative Religion* (London: Sir Isaac Pitman and Sons, 1913), p. 71.

with reference to Samson, we are informed that "the Spirit of the LORD began to move him at times" (13:25) and, later, that "it *was* of the LORD, that he sought an occasion against the Philistines" (14: 4), we are never apprised that the Lord sanctioned Samson's marriage to the Woman of Timnath. We are told only that such marriages are forbidden and that they are a mark of the Israelites' increasing debasement. What is a framing device in the Book of Judges—the matter of marrying infidels (3:5-7; 21:1-7)—is foregrounded in *Samson Agonistes* through Milton's centering of his drama in the story of Samson's liaison with Dalila.

As a correction to William Empson's proposition that Dalila is "a deeply wrong wife" and without regard for his claim that the Samson-Dalila marriage "is essential to the poem, because it yields a particularly shocking moral paradox," Irene Samuel, not altogether playfully, responds that "Dalila is . . . the most bird-brained woman to have ever gotten herself involved in major tragedy."[43] Whatever the merits of that contention, the marriage *is* crucial to Milton's poem because Milton makes of it a moral problem, perhaps "want[ing] to save the lady's dignity, not the hero's,"[44] but most assuredly wanting to introduce a moral quandary to the poem and, through this marriage, to problematize Samson's character. Samson himself becomes a riddle.

[43] See Empson, *Milton's God*, rev. ed. (London: Chatto and Windus, 1965), pp. 211, 218-19, and Samuel, "*Samson Agonistes* as Tragedy," in *Calm of Mind: Tercentenary Essays on "Paradise Regained" and "Samson Agonistes*," ed. Joseph Wittreich (Cleveland: Press of Case Western Reserve Univ., 1971), p. 248.

[44] Empson, *Milton's God*, p. 224. For a noble (and historically grounded) defense of Dalila, see Heather Asals, "In Defense of Dalila: *Samson Agonistes* and the Reformation Theology of the Word," *Journal of English and Germanic Philology*, 74 (1975), 183-94, and Joyce Colony, "An Argument for Milton's Dalila," *Yale Review*, 66 (1977), 562-75. Cf. Mary S. Weinkauf, "Dalila: The Worst of All Possible Wives," *Studies in English Literature*, 13 (1973), 135-47, along with these two essays by Marlyn Millner Kahr: "Delilah," in *Feminism and Art History* (New York: Harper and Row, 1982), pp. 119-25, and "Rembrandt and Delilah," *The Art Bulletin*, 55 (1973), 240-59.

It is of some interest that Milton's contemporaries acknowledge that "the Rabbines make Delilah to have been . . . [Samson's] wife, and further say, that he taught her the Law of *Moses* before he took her; But none of this," they concede, "is likely to be true."[45] And it is of some amusement that commentators subsequent to Milton will allow, in the same breath that they proclaim "I have not travelled out of the sacred record concerning Samson," that Milton represents Samson and Dalila as married in order to give "Mrs. Delilah Samson" her "due"; and, observing that in scripture Delilah is nowhere called Samson's wife, they will nonetheless conclude that "Milton considers her . . . [Samson's] *second* wife, which seems . . . most likely."[46] What in Milton's time seemed highly *un*likely is perceived after his time, and owing to his influence, as *most likely* indeed.

As if to remove his poem from what had become a highly controversial issue in Renaissance biblical commentary, Milton locates the matter of Samson's marriage in his betrothal to Dalila, telling us very pointedly, first, that Samson thought his marriage acceptable to the Lord, not that it was acceptable to the Lord: "I thought it lawful from my former act," Samson confides to the Chorus (231); second, that only by arguing that God dispensed with his laws can we explain what might have prompted Samson, against his vow of strictest purity, to enter upon a marriage with "that fallacious Bride, / Unclean, unchaste" (320-21); and third, that the marriage was never approved by Samson's parents: "I cannot praise thy Marriage choises, Son, / Rather approv'd them not," Manoa confesses (420-21). For some, there is a "lingering ambivalence" to

---

[45] Trapp, *Annotations upon the Old and New Testament*, I, 90. See also Patrick who writes that "St. Chrysostom and others are of opinion, that he was married to her" (*A Critical Commentary and Paraphrase of the Old and New Testament*, II, 73).

[46] See Scott, *The Giant Judge*, pp. xvii, 253, 256. This piece of intellectual history makes an important point to Miltonists: having already engaged the subject of the Bible's influence on Milton, they might now turn their attention to the related topic of Milton's influence on the Bible.

these lines: surely "Milton's God (no less than the Bible's) urges Samson to marry the Timnite as a pretext for harrying Philistines—foreknowing . . . [Samson] will interpret the marriage as precedent-setting and so marry Dalila."[47] For Edward Tayler, however, these are "fiercely farcical" lines intended to remind the reader of what he assuredly knows, that Samson's marriage choices, deriving from divine impulsion, are "praiseworthy 'choices' indeed."[48]

Actually, Manoa's lines, with their evident moral verdict, have just the opposite effect: one of challenging rather than crediting such knowledge and thus of peeling away from the Samson story those platitudes that by the Renaissance had come to overlay it. Indeed, it is just the kind of platitude enunciated by Tayler that, during the seventeenth century, was being stripped from the Samson story, with Samson in his encounter with Delilah being cited as a signal instance of those who mistakenly "flye to their owne wisedome, and their owne strength, and their owne policy, and their owne knowledge."[49] The same sort of platitude is pulled away from the Samson story by Milton's poem where, as Fish well knows, "the relationship between Samson's marriages and God's will [becomes] progressively less clear"[50] and certain and where, even at the end, we are not allowed to forget that the virgins visiting

[47] See Gallagher, "The Role of Raphael in *Samson Agonistes*," p. 279.

[48] *Milton's Poetry*, p. 111. Before the fact, Charles Dunster offers the appropriate rejoinder to such an argument: "Milton may be understood to have imagined Samson, in his marriage with Dalila, acting from inclination, and . . . falsely attributing and ascribing it to divine impulse. This is consistent with what is said, ver. 532." Dunster's note is printed by Sir Egerton Brydges, *The Poetical Works of John Milton* (London: William Tegg, 1862), p. 494.

[49] Lewis Thomas, *Seauen Sermons, or the Exercises of Seauen Sabbaths* (London: Printed for John Wright, 1615), A7ᵛ; and for Thomas Goodwin what we see in Samson is the "unmortifyed lusts" of a man whom "none of the daughters of Israel could please but he must have one of the Philistims" (*The Works of Thomas Goodwin*, ed. John C. Miller and Robert Halley [12 vols.; Edinburgh: James Nichol; London: James Nisbet, 1861-66], II, 369).

[50] "Question and Answer in *Samson Agonistes*," in *"Comus" and "Samson Agonistes,"* ed. Lovelock, p. 217.

Samson's tomb will remember and forever bewail "His lot unfortunate in nuptial choice, / From whence captivity and loss of eyes" (1743-44). In *Samson Agonistes*, Dalila is Samson's wife not because Samson's marriage is praiseworthy but because that marriage is necessary, as Northrop Frye reports, if the poem is going to absorb Milton's thinking on divorce.[51]

Milton's thesis is clear: marriage is a matter of love and divorce, a matter of charity. In *The Doctrine and Discipline of Divorce*, Milton seems to allow for a hate such as Samson eventually displays for the Woman of Timna—"not that Hate that sins, but that which onely is . . . the turning aside from a mistaken object," allows for such hate so long as it leads the aggrieved party "to seek a fit help" to mend rather than, as seems the case with Samson's liaison with Dalila, to multiply his mistakes (II, 253). Milton also allows for the believer to remain within an idolatrous marriage so long as there are "better hopes," and "to forbear departure . . . till nothing have bin neglected to set forward a conversion" (II, 265-66; cf. *Tetrachordon*, II, 683, 686). Without the conversion, there can be no "due company . . . no human society," only "a brutish congresse" (II, 275) ending in "rancor and strife, a thing so opposite both to mariage and to Christianitie, it would perhaps be lesse scandal to divorce a natural disparity, then to link violently together an unchristian dissention, committing two ensnared souls inevitably to kindle one another, not with the fire of love, but with a hatred *inconcileable*" (II, 280; cf. *Colasterion*, II, 731).

Samson's reason for entering upon a second marriage is thus rendered suspect, not only because Dalila violates Milton's standard for fitness that makes second choices acceptable, but because the acceptance of such a marriage requires the argument that for a second time now God has revoked his laws,

---

[51] *Spiritus Mundi*, p. 219.

allowing Samson to make still another compact with sin. Yet
Milton himself never argues in this way. "[T]he Law is the
Israelite," Milton declares in *The Doctrine and Discipline of
Divorce*, "and hath this expresse repeated command *to make
no cov'nant with* sin *the Canaanite*, but to expell him, lest he
prove a snare" (II, 288). And later he says: "To make a
regularity of sin by law, either the law must straiten sin into
no sin, or sin must crook the law into no law" (II, 321).
Milton's thinking here casts suspicion not only on Samson's
second marriage but on his first divorce. Samson may have
returned to the Woman of Timna but only after having deserted her and subsequent to her having been given away to
another: "a person deserted which is something lesse then
divorc't, may lawfully marry again" (II, 338). Not only Samson's motives in these marriages—to seek an occasion against
the Philistines—but many of his actions are called into question
by Milton's insistence that "He who doth evil that good may
come thereby, approves not what he doth, and yet the grand
rule forbids him, and counts *his damnation* just if hee doe it"
(II, 314).

Virtually everyone in Milton's century, of whatever religious or political persuasion, registered uneasiness concerning
Samson's marriage. By fixing attention upon Dalila, Milton
can reflect upon Samson's marrying, without the encumbrance
of having to dispute with commentators from Luther onward
who, however troubled by Samson's alliance with the Woman
of Timnath and his seeming disregard of parental consent in
forging that alliance, can appeal to textual ambiguity in order
to make the case that *in this one instance* God suspended his
marriage laws so as to seek an occasion against the Philistines.
This one time God encourages an infidel marriage, allows the
Nazarite Samson to celebrate that marriage at Timnath rather
than at home, excluding his parents from the entire affair, in
these manipulations, or so the argument goes, God allowing

himself to vent his anger and deliver his revenge. What had always seemed to compromise Samson and to confound his claim of divine instinct, that he celebrated his marriage away from home and among a group of idolaters, instead of being supressed in Milton's account, is there witnessed to by Samson himself: "in your City held my Nuptial Feast" (1194).

It would be obvious to any reader of Judges that this book's stories are framed by discussions of marriage, which themselves emblematize the continual backsliding and continuing debasement of the Israelites. Moreover, to the extent that the foes of Israel are accorded attention in the Judges narrative, it is with the intention not of anatomizing and exposing *their* failures, which are obvious and not at issue, but of revealing the character of the Israelites whose God opposes the extermination of the enemies by whom, repeatedly, he plots to test his people. Here, and presumably in Milton's tragedy, the Philistines are a revelation of the Israelites and Dalila, a revelation of Samson. Encounters thought by Dr. Johnson to have the "effect . . . of raising the character of Samson"[52] instead expose his failings. The marriage with Dalila, in the process, replicates Samson's first marriage instead of providing an image in reverse of it. There is testimony to this replication in the seventeenth century, coming from Richard Capel for example, who conflates Delilah and the Woman of Timnath,

[52] See *The Poetical Works of John Milton*, ed. Todd, IV, 346. Wolfgang Iser sets forth the proper corrective principle: minor characters surround the protagonist, their perceptions are posed against his, in order "to illustrate the negative aspects of the hero, and as these diminish so do the minor characters themselves become superfluous"; or alternatively, as the negative features become increasingly a center of concern, minor characters proliferate and their various perceptions become all the more crucial; see "Narrative Strategies as a Means of Communication," in *Interpretation of Narrative*, ed. Mario J. Valdés and Owen J. Miller (1978; rpt. Toronto: Univ. of Toronto Press, 1981), p. 115. This principle may account for a proliferation of characters in Milton's rendering of the Samson story, and the same principle may also explain the appearance of Harapha, who boldly underscores Samson's more negative features.

speaking of the former as if she were the latter: "*Dalilah* did lie to save her fathers house from burning, but we see that her fathers house was burned."[53] Similarly, Milton's Dalila is a mirror on Samson, so that what the Chorus says of her rebounds as a criticism of Samson as well: "inward gifts / Were left for hast unfinish't, judgment scant, / Capacity not rais'd to apprehend / Or value what is best / In choice . . . / Or was too much of self-love mixt" (1026-31). The principles governing the biblical narrative pertain in *Samson Agonistes* as well, and they find still further elucidation in Milton's thoughts on marriage and divorce.

Samson's plight is probably remembered in *The Doctrine and Discipline of Divorce* as Milton observes, sadly, that "to grind in the mill of an undelighted and servil copulation" may become the "forc't work of a Christian mariage" (II, 258); and conversely, as David Masson perceives, the Samson-Dalila episode "is almost literal excerpt from Milton's Divorce Pamphlets."[54] Milton's words on divorce in these pamphlets offer an intriguing perspective on Samson's marriage in the later tragedy. For one thing, marriage and the ruin of an individual man are equated with ill-government and the ruin of a whole people, Milton here capitalizing on the Samson analogy that informs, and indeed frames, the Judges narrative (II, 229). And for another, second choices, because they are informed by the wisdom of experience and thus are a reparation for a first mistake, should be allowed in marriage (II, 249-50). With respect to mixed marriages, the New Testament allows (hence Milton allows) that "all living creatures were sanctify'd to a pure and Christian use. . . . *The unbeleeving wife is sanc-*

---

[53] *Tentations*, I, 362. In our own time, this sort of conflation is evident in the following observation of Robert Graves and Raphael Patai: "This Palestinian custom [of leaving one's parents and cleaving to one's wife] is proved by the account in *Judges* of Samson's marriage to Delilah" (*Hebrew Myths: The Book of Genesis* [Garden City: Doubleday, 1964], p. 13; see also p. 122).

[54] *The Life of John Milton*, VI, 674.

tify'd by the husband, that is, made pure and lawfull to his use" (II, 261-262). The only proper motive for such marriages is love, the one spouse winning the other's conversion *by love*, which is *"onely . . . the fulfilling of every Commandment"* (II, 258).

No other motive, no other objective, is countenanced; and where another pertains, such as the performing of *other* duties (II, 254), one is likely to find seducement and defilement, "a spirituall contagion," says Milton, and to feel "a certain religious aversation and abhorring," neither of which sorts well with marriage (II, 262). Where there is lust and not love, there is, for Milton, a weakening of Christian fortitude; and the Book of Judges is cited by him to instance fornication and whoredom, nothing being "so opprobrious to . . . parents" as the woman who plays the harlot (II, 263, 336). Milton's reflections on divorce explain why Samson may not have won the consent of his parents, nor of his countrymen, for either of his marriages, especially the second one; they make clear that Samson's motives in marriage—to satisfy his lust, to seek an occasion against the Philistines—not only ensure that his marriages will be a bondage and a snare, but defy the very principles that govern such marriages, as well as Milton's own expectations of them, that the heart will be gradually opened to faith and that a conversion will be effected (II, 266). Milton explains that no marriage can be sustained without love: "where love cannot be, there can be left of wedlock nothing, but the empty husk of an outside matrimony; as undelightful and unpleasing to God, as any other kind of hypocrisie" (II, 256). In marrying infidels, enemies of his own people, Samson links himself with what Milton, in *Tetrachordon*, calls "the meer carcas of a Mariage" (II, 603). No wonder that Milton should say with St. Paul, *"Mis-yoke not together with Infidels"* and thereupon ask with him what, in effect, Manoa asks of his son and what, ironically, Samson asks of Dalila: *"what part*

hath he that beleeveth with an Infidell?" (II, 262; cf. *SA*
882-86).

Milton is steadfast in his conviction that "a right beleever
ought to divorce an idolatrous heretick . . . that idolatrous
mariage is . . . hatefull to God" (II, 264-65). The burden
falls upon those who continue to regard Samson as a saint,
and excuse his marriages as divinely inspired, to square their
propositions with Milton's own principles as they are articulated in *Tetrachordon*: "when a Saint is joyn'd with a reprobate," when there is "no love, no goodnes, no loyalty, but
counterplotting, and secret wishing one anothers dissolution,
this is to me the greatest mystery . . . of ought, unless it bee
the mystery of iniquity" (II, 607). Not only must God suspend
his laws to legitimate such marriages, but Milton must suspend
his own doctrines and disciplines concerning divorce. Samson
enters upon his second marriage not out of love but again to
seek an occasion; the "smooth hypocrisie" (872) of which he
accuses Dalila, that of pretending love, is, in fact, his own
hypocrisy. Unless conversion is won, as Milton insists, there
can only be enmity between the parties; for each of them will
tear away at the other, both owing and observing different
allegiances. The situation Dalila describes is in such marriages
predictable, inevitable; and it is no different from Samson's,
except for the fact that each is subject to and thus serves a
different deity:

> It was not gold, as to my charge thou lay'st,
> That wrought with me: thou know'st the Magistrates
> And Princes of my countrey came in person,
> Sollicited, commanded, threatn'd, urg'd,
> Adjur'd by all the bonds of civil Duty
> And of Religion, press'd how just it was,
> How honourable, how glorious to entrap
> A common enemy, who had destroy'd

> Such numbers of our Nation: and the Priest
> Was not behind, but ever at my ear,
> Preaching how meritorious with the gods
> It would be to ensnare an irreligious
> Dishonourer of *Dagon* . . . (849-61)

Here is the problem of marrying an infidel without first winning a conversion, and here is the irony in Milton's presenting Samson and Dalila as married against a minor tradition that had invented this relationship by way of arguing that Samson learns from his first mistake, this time winning the conversion that with the Woman of Timnath he had not sought. The effect of this tradition is to render Delilah's betrayal all the more offensive; the effect of Milton's silencing this part of the tradition is to render Samson all the more culpable. The only control in such a marriage can come from the "due awe" of the female exacted by the "despotic power" of the male (1054-55). Samson and the Chorus may argue in this way, but Milton *never* does.

So astonishingly misogynous were these and other lines in *Samson Agonistes* that early editors felt obliged to distinguish this "sudden start of resentment" from the "cooling and sober reasoning" of *Paradise Lost*. It is as if Milton were transferring to *Samson Agonistes* the harsh sentiments expressed about Eve, and women generally, in the Fall story from Genesis. According to one spokesman of Milton's age, "*Adams* sin was as no sin in comparison of the sin of *Eve*."[55] Newton quotes Thyer as saying: "however just the observation may be, that Milton, in his *Paradise Lost*, seems to court the favour of the female sex, it is very certain, that he did not carry the same complaisance into . . . [*Samson Agonistes*]," where he "outgoes" even Euripides as a "*woman-hater*." And Newton himself observes that here Milton "indulges his spleen a little, de-

[55] Capel, *Tentations*, II, 89.

preciates the qualifications of the women, and asserts the superiority of the men; and, to give these sentiments the greater weight, puts them into the mouth of the Chorus."[56] In an imaginary conversation with Walter Savage Landor, Robert Southey is even more severe: "The chorus in this tragedy is not always conciliating and assuaging. Never was anything more bitter against the female sex. . . . The invectives of Euripides are never the outpourings of the chorus, and their venom is cold as hemlock; those of Milton are hot and corrosive."[57] The fact is that such sentiments are out of harmony with Milton's thinking anywhere, at any time, and that their being placed in the mouth of the Chorus is of a piece with Milton's larger strategy of having the Chorus utter the commonplaces that he himself will discredit.

There are those who believe that Milton's Chorus is an idealized spectator and that, imbued with "vitalizing energy," it assumes "the role of a moral preceptor"; more typically, the Chorus is regarded as "highly platitudinous," even at times "pietistic," and is said to have a full range of commonplaces at its command and to use them in a "wholly conventional" way, with Milton's point being that "The Chorus embodies . . . a mentality universally found, and one all too common among the Christians of his own day."[58] Yet *Samson Agonistes*

[56] See *The Poetical Works of John Milton*, ed. Todd, IV, 437.

[57] See *The Romantics on Milton: Formal Essays and Critical Asides*, ed. Joseph Wittreich (Cleveland: Press of Case Western Reserve Univ., 1970), p. 334.

[58] See, e.g., M. V. Rama Sarma, *Things Unattempted: A Study of Milton* (New Delhi: Vikas, 1982), pp. 91, 93; but cf. Lynn Veach Sadler, *Consolation in "Samson Agonistes": Regeneration and Typology*, Salzburg Studies in English Literature (Salzburg: Univ. of Salzburg, 1979), pp. 72, 150; Joan S. Bennett, "Liberty under the Law: The Chorus and the Meaning of *Samson Agonistes*," *Milton Studies*, 12 (1978), 141, 142; and Camille Wells Slights, *The Casuistical Tradition in Shakespeare, Donne, Herbert, and Milton* (Princeton: Princeton Univ. Press, 1981), p. 266. John Huntley provides the now classic formulation concerning the "confident, platitudinous Chorus" of *Samson Agonistes*: "Milton does not endow his Chorus with admirable truths and emotions; much less does he put his own judgment in their mouths"; see "A Reval-

THE SAMSON STORY IN JUDGES

is also a poem that enters into a contentious and not simply a
reflective relationship with canonized morals, institutionalized
values and attitudes. Milton mediates between the old and the
new in such a way that the attitudes of the Chorus are placed
at odds with Milton's own opinions; his values require a re-
scission of theirs. In a dramatic poem like *Samson Agonistes*,
especially with regard to the Chorus and often with regard to
Samson himself, the Laurentian adage pertains: never trust
the teller, only trust the tale.

Christopher Hill is as right in his contention that, through
his representation of Dalila, Milton is challenging the reigning
attitude toward women as John Dunton, writing in 1697, is
wrong in his conviction that Milton is once again showing the
female sex "their Picture" in such a way that "they can't deny
but 'tis to the Life."[59] Two critical viewpoints are crucial here.

---

uation of the Chorus' Role in Milton's *Samson Agonistes*," *Modern Philology*, 64 (1966),
132. Huntley's comments on the unreliability of the Chorus are complemented by
Virginia R. Mollenkott's remarks on the unreliability of certain of Samson's pronouncements: "Judging everything in terms of Samson's viewpoint has been a frequent
error in criticism of the drama"; see "Relativism in *Samson Agonistes*," *Studies in
Philology*, 67 (1970), 92. The most recent interpretation (and it is highly innovative)
of the role of the Chorus is provided by Kathleen M. Swaim, "The Doubling of the
Chorus in *Samson Agonistes*," *Milton Studies*, 20 (1984), 225-45. And the remark of
G. K. Hunter—that the emphasis on the Chorus is an emphasis on commentary
rather than action—is suggestive here; see "*Paradise Lost*" (1980; rpt. London: George
Allen and Unwin, 1982), p. 80. Indeed, Hunter's observation begs to be placed
within the theoretical context afforded by Roland Barthes, who views choral commentary in Athenian tragedy as "essentially an interrogation" of narrative actions,
forcing accepted mythological answers to yield up new questions. For Barthes, the
interrogative thrust of tragedy issues from the Chorus; see *The Responsibility of Forms:
Critical Essays on Music, Art, and Representation*, trans. Richard Howard (New York:
Hill and Wang, 1985), p. 68. Milton's Chorus strikes a complicated relationship
with this tradition, now interrogating and now affirming commonplaces; it adheres
to the deadening literalism of orthodoxy, to what was regarded by nonconformist
writers, for two centuries now, as the speech of lost souls.

[59] See Hill, *Milton and the English Revolution* (New York: Viking, 1977), p. 443,
and Dunton, *The Challenge, Sent by a Young Lady to Sir Thomas or the Female War*
(London: Printed by E. Whitlock, 1697), pp. 233-34 (see also p. 210).

First, the harsh remarks made by the Chorus, as Watson Kirkconnell urges, "are part of an ancient tradition in Samson literature" and are still an aspect of thinking in Milton's own age.[60] The remarks of the Chorus are historically determined, then, with Milton's own ambivalence toward them being personally and psychologically determined. The second follows from this latter point. *Samson Agonistes*, in the words of Hill, provides an "escape from seeing Dalila as an outlet for Milton's misogyny":

> Once he had decided to use the Samson myth, how could he have avoided the hostility towards Dalila shown by his sources? He hardly chose the story for this reason. . . . Milton gave Dalila the best arguments he possibly could. . . . He made her Samson's wife—a status the Bible did not give her. . . .[61]

Milton may not go far enough, but here as in *Paradise Lost* he is busy subverting universally held ideas about male supremacy.

In the eighteenth century, George Frederick Handel understood as much and understood, certainly, that the target for Milton's ridicule in this poem is not women but rather Samson who has twice succumbed to their allurement. Dunton may have thought that Milton took one parting (and deserved) shot at women before he died, but Handel came to think otherwise. In keeping with the poem of which it is an interpretation, Handel's *Samson: An Oratorio* (1749) represents Dalila as Samson's wife but, even more tellingly, as if to focus sentiments harbored by Milton himself, presents a Samson who

---

[60] *That Invincible Samson: The Theme of "Samson Agonistes" in World Literature* (Toronto: Univ. of Toronto Press, 1964), p. 152.

[61] See *Milton and the English Revolution*, p. 443, and more recently Hill's *The Experience of Defeat*, p. 184. Unlike Thomas Goodwin Milton seems to have worked out, if not perfectly, the implications of his representation of women.

admits to error in marrying a second time. Second choices are important to Milton (see *Tetrachordon*, II, 613); yet the point he seems to be making is rather like the one urged by John Trapp: "Marriage is like a Stratagem of war . . . where one can err but once."[62] In his marriage choices, Samson has erred a second time as Milton's Samson himself admits: "my feet again in to the snare / Where once I have been caught" (931-32). Here we should be reminded of a proof-text Milton cites in *De Doctrina Christiana: "I have found something more bitter than death: a woman whose mind is full of traps and snares, and her hands of bonds. The man who seems good in God's eyes is freed from her, but the sinner is caught"* (VI, 783). *Samson Agonistes*, in one of its aspects certainly, is a poetic essay on what Samson himself calls "wedlock-trechery endangering life" (1009). Samson has still not learned that marriage should never be a bondage, curse, or snare, only a gift and blessing; that marriage has only one motive—*love*.

Tayler maintains that it would be a convenience for some critics to find a point in *Samson Agonistes* where Milton's protagonist "is portrayed as un-regenerate"; but the simple fact is, according to Tayler, that "the text of the play resists this kind of argument."[63] On the contrary, in defying his source text in order to represent Samson and Dalila as married, Milton opens his text to just this kind of interpretation. For he does more than violate the scriptural text; he undermines, by omitting the usual explanation for this marriage, the hermeneutic tradition that sanctions it in the understanding that a once lustful Samson has become loving and now knows, through the experience afforded by a mistaken first choice, that conversion is to be won before marriage. Whatever the circumstances, only after conversion is such a marriage allowable. Where tradition comprehends the Samson-Delilah relationship

---

[62] *Annotations upon the Old and New Testament*, I, 84.
[63] *Milton's Poetry*, p. 106.

as a marriage, it does so not to advance the point of divine inspiration, but to adduce an argument for a regenerated Samson on the grounds that a now wiser Samson, instead of spurning the law, observes it to the letter. Milton's point is otherwise, and is made for him by Samson himself, who makes no claim about having won Dalila's conversion before marriage but maintains, to the contrary, that Dalila possessed no more "Faith" than his former wife (387-88), that like the Woman of Timna she remained zealous in her heathen religion: "Zeal mov'd thee," Samson says scornfully, "To please *thy* gods thou didst it" (895-96; my italics).

Fish answers his own question of whether there is a relationship between the middle of a play supposedly figuring Samson's spiritual regeneration and its ending relating the temple holocaust, and answers it hedgingly, "none, necessarily."[64] What should now be apparent is that the middle of the play (a reflection upon Samson's marriages) and its ending (a reflection of the temple catastrophe), instead of disconnected by opposing patterns of regeneration and generation, are connected through the common motive, thrown into question by Milton, of divine intention and impulse. Middle and end are connected, intimately and indeed causally, by patterns of generation subduing the expected but, apparently for Milton, uncertain patterns of regeneration.

Given the usual reading of *Samson Agonistes* as a drama of regeneration and hence the usual inferences concerning Milton's reading of the Samson narrative in Judges, it is odd that he does not use this story, or for that matter this scriptural book, as a screen on the historical moment recorded in either

[64] "Question and Answer in *Samson Agonistes*," in *"Comus" and "Samson Agonistes,"* ed. Lovelock, p. 209. Fish follows in the line of interpretation established by Walter Clyde Curry, who answers the same question without hesitation: "No critical acumen can find any causal or logical relation between that simple incident [at the pillars] and the other episodes of the play"; see *"Samson Agonistes* Yet Again," *Sewanee Review*, 32 (1924), 339.

version of *The Readie and Easie Way*. This prose work enjoys pivotal status as an epilogue to Milton's career as political pamphleteer and as a prologue to his major poems and like them, in its revised version, casts the current political situation within a biblical, mythological context. Each version of *The Readie and Easie Way* begins by assaulting Matthew Griffith as among those "deceivers" who nourish "bad principles and fals apprehensions among too many of the people" and thereby would return them to bondage (VII, 407-08). One of those false apprehensions may well have been Griffith's representation of Samson as one of God's swordbearers and his remembrance of "how God renewed *Samsons* strength, to revenge himselfe at last."[65] Had Milton read the Judges narrative as many of his critics read *Samson Agonistes*, as the celebration of Samson as a deliverer of a wayward and reluctant people, that story would have provided him with a crucial lens on this particular historical moment. The fact that Milton does not here invoke the Judges narrative may also indicate that he read the Samson story within the spirit of the Judges version, as an embryonic representation of the tragedy of the Israelites, as a portrayal through an individual of the ruin of a whole people. The Samson story presents in miniature, and in terms of an individual history, what the complete Book of Judges presents as a national history. Samson's tragedy *is* the tragedy of Israel. Milton does not allow us to forget, nor does the Judges narrator, that its moral biographies have political implications and historical ramifications.

Samson, no less than his people, is impeachable for backsliding: he falls into the snare not once but twice; his role as deliverer "voutsaf't from heaven" since his birth, he "fall[s]

[65] *The Fear of God and the King* (London: Printed for Thomas Johnson, 1660), pp. 3, 9. Here the king is Samson; later the Presbyterians are Samson. Here the king as Samson is asked to revenge himself; later such zeal directed toward the setting up of the right is said to be a zeal that will pull it down (cf. *The King's Life-Guard: An Anniversary Sermon* [London: Printed by William Godbid, 1665], p. 23).

back or rather . . . creep[s] back . . . to . . . once abjur'd
and detested thraldom," in this way preparing himself and his
people for new slavery (VII, 422). Like his people, miraculously delivered many times before, he rushes back into bondage, runs his own neck and their "necks again into the yoke
which . . . [had been] broken" (VII, 428), rendering useless
the blood of thousands that he had already spilt in the cause
of liberation. The spirit of God, says Milton, may depart from
his chosen ones, "never to be voutsaf't . . . if by our ingratefull
backsliding we make these fruitless" (VII, 423). Milton, of
course, does not tie these various formulations to the Samson
story, but these formulations from *The Readie and Easie Way*
have a pointed relevance to that story as it is unfurled in
Milton's tragedy. Moreover, Milton's task, in political tract
and poem, is to succeed where Samson failed: "to . . . raise
. . . these stones to become children of reviving libertie
. . . , though they seem now chusing them a captain back for
Egypt"; his objective is to raise, not dampen, the spirits of a
defecting, because "misguided and abus'd [,] multitude" (VII,
463). His strategy, here and in his later poetry, is to situate
contemporary history within a biblical framework to which
he adds, but also from which he subtracts, in such a way that
superimpositions, as well as evasions, instead of altering scriptural meanings accentuate them.

The seals that a long history placed upon the Samson story are
loosened by the crowbar of Milton's prose writings and, in
Samson Agonistes, are opened in a drama that captures the
rhythms of history as they are embodied in the Book of Judges.
There is fighting and slaying accompanied by much brutality:
"they . . . caught him, and cut off his thumbs and his great
toes" (1:6). The Lord delivers his people from their foes only
to find them making new league with the conquered enemy

and thus entering into still another period of servitude. The anger of the Lord becomes hot, he moves against his people but also raises up judges who again deliver the people from their enemies; yet no sooner does a judge die than the people revert to their corrupt ways and become more corrupt than their predecessors had been. The people "ceased not from their own doings, nor from their stubborn way" (2:19); and once they are again corrupted, God strengthens the hand of the enemy against them. His people are made to serve false gods and also made to become their own deliverers. The pattern is always the same: "And the Children of Israel did evil in the sight of the LORD" (2:11; 3:7, 11; 4:1; 6:1; 10:6, 13:1); again they are oppressed, and again, after a great lapse of time, they are sent a new judge—now Deborah, now Gideon, now Samson. But the judges themselves have failings at times, just as do their people; and if the Judges narrative harbors a judgment on the Philistines it seems to offer an equally severe judgment on God's own people, that is, on Samson's people and the tribe of Dan, who, setting up "the graven image" subsequent to Samson's death, find themselves in a situation where now there is "no deliverer" (18:28, 30).

Northrop Frye makes the point sharply, stingingly:

> In the Book of Judges, the account of Samson is immediately followed by another story about the Danites in which, after appearing in a most contemptible light as idolaters, thieves, and murderers, they vanish from history. In Jacob's prophecy of the twelve tribes at the end of Genesis, Dan is described as a treacherous "serpent in the way," and in the list of twelve tribes in the Book of Revelation the name of Dan is omitted. For Milton this would practically mean being erased from the book of life.[66]

[66] *Spiritus Mundi*, p. 222.

Samson has been standing in his own way; and his people, subsequent to his death, are their own worst enemy. It is just another of the proliferating ironies of Judges that the narrator's harsh judgment of Samson is echoed—in fact seems to be sanctioned—by God's no less harsh judgment on Samson's people. They are exterminated as Samson had exterminated the Philistines. Thus Samson and his people are summoned to judgment in much the same fashion as the Levite who slays his concubine: "all that saw it said, There was no such deed done nor seen from the day that the children of Israel came up out of the land of Egypt unto this day: consider of it, take advice, and speak *your minds*" (19:30), Milton seems to be saying with the Judges narrator.

These are times, we are told persistently, when "every man did *that which was* right in his own eyes" (17:6, 21:25); or as an annotation to a seventeenth-century Bible puts it, "In the time of the Judges the people presumed more to do *that semed to them selves right*, or good, though it was nought."[67] The Israelites lived in God's land but not according to God's law; they had no truly superior magistrate to govern them, according to Trapp, and therefore "all was out of order, and their *Anarchy* begot a general *Ataxy*."[68] The anarchy of the times is reflected within the planned anarchy of the Judges narrative.

The Book of Judges, it has been said, is "edited to present the appearance of a history of a united Israel going through a series of crises, all of much the same shape. . . . The heavy emphasis on the structure . . . indicates that the individual stories are being made to fit that pattern," which, for Northrop Frye, "is roughly U-shaped . . . the standard shape of comedy," and for Frye of the entire Bible.[69] Whereas Frye would

[67] *The Holie Bible*, I, 564.
[68] *Annotations upon the Old and New Testament*, I, 109.
[69] *The Great Code: The Bible and Literature* (New York: Harcourt Brace Jovanovich, 1982), pp. 40-41, 169.

subsume Judges within a comic vision, Milton, it appears, and many of his contemporaries, found there a pattern in which triumph eventuates in defeat and deliverance in further servitude; they found there the structure and mythos of tragedy. "You may discerne our times so paralelling those" of Judges, writes John Green in 1644, that it is "as if the present plot were drawne from theirs, and the modell fetcht from thence."[70] Milton held a similar view concerning the interrelationship of scriptural and contemporary history, saying of Old Testament history generally that, if "not shutting wilfully our eyes, we may see the like story brought to pass in our own Land" (III, 510). The historical books of the Old Testament (and especially the Book of Judges) were thought to be "punctually pertinent" to the current historical moment and, if sometimes a mirror on God's majesty and human glory, could also be, in the words of John Vicars, a "terrour-striking *Looking-glasse*."[71]

There are those who believe with George Steiner that "Tragedy is alien to the Judaic sense of the world" and who thus conclude that the Samson story, especially in Milton's rendering of it, is a *commedia*.[72] This was not, however, a Renaissance (or even an eighteenth-century) belief, if we are to judge by such titles as *Samson, Tragoedia Nova* (1547), *Simson, Tragoedia Sacra* (1600, 1604), or *Samson, Tragédie Lyrique* (1750), and if we remember, for example, that Vondel called *Samson, or Holy Revenge* (1660) a "tragedy" and has the Mes-

70 *Nehemiah's Teares and Prayers for Judah's Affliction* (London: Printed by G. M., 1644), p. 13; see also Arise Evans, *The Bloody Vision of John Farley* (London: n. p., 1653), where the Book of Judges is similarly correlated with contemporary history.

71 *A Looking-Glasse for Malignants: or, Gods Hand against God-haters* (London: Printed for John Rothwell, 1643), pp. 1, 2.

72 *The Death of Tragedy* (1961; rpt. New York: Hill and Wang, 1963), p. 4; see also p. 31. And cf. Northrop Frye, as cited by Galbraith Crump, ed., *Twentieth-Century Interpretations of "Samson Agonistes"* (Englewood Cliffs: Prentice-Hall, 1968), p. 108: "the tragedy ends in triumph and the carnival in catastrophe."

senger, in reporting Samson's death, refer to the "tragic end" of a life "finished in a gust of utter terror."[73] These plays do not allow us to forget that "the tragic myth," in the words of Nietzsche, is an "image of all that is awful, evil, perplexing, destructive, ominous in human existence." Tragedy projects illusions not to sustain but to shatter them, with the consequence that "At first blush the tragic myth appears as an epic event having to do with the glorification of the hero and his struggles"; but, says Nietzsche, we are then made "to account for the fact that the hero's sufferings, his most painful dilemmas—all the ugly, discordant things" are a part of such representations and are, finally, what tragic representations would transcend.[74] Tragedy, that is, would transcend the very world in which its protagonist is mired and the very values of which he is a manifestation. Tragedy, whether it be exemplified by *King Lear* or *Samson Agonistes*, is like a sentence not fully predicated: part of its history is written, yet the part of history it prognosticates is yet to be lived and only then to be recorded.

Milton is emphatic about the generic category to which his play belongs: *Samson Agonistes* is "OF THAT SORT OF DRAMATIC POEM WHICH IS CALL'D *Tragedy*" (my italics), and "The Argument" to this dramatic poem ends by calling it a "Tragedy." Yet *Samson Agonistes* is also a tragedy of a special sort: one whose audience, but not "hero," has the potential for snatching spiritual victory out of natural defeat, because it breaks free from the values of the defeated protagonist. In Milton's dramatic poem, Old Testament myth is brought into terrific clash with New Testament doctrine so that the poem's very essence is compounded out of the good of one climate of opinion and the evil of another. The ending of this poem is not retrospective but prophetic. As J. B. Broadbent remarks,

[73] See Kirkconnell, *That Invincible Samson*, p. 137.

[74] *The Birth of Tragedy and the Genealogy of Morals*, trans. Francis Golffing (New York: Doubleday, 1956), pp. 8, 142.

in *Samson Agonistes* "unheard-of, unprecedented verse clashes against the ancient authority of the form; their clash echoes the collision of the terrible Old Testament myth with Christian doctrine."[75] That is, Broadbent describes a tragedy that does exactly what Henry Alonzo Myers says tragedy cannot do: "Obviously . . . a tragedy cannot be compounded out of the good of one climate of opinion and the evil of another," and just as obviously the culminating scenes of tragedy "are retrospective, not prophetic," for the spectator, rather than transcending, "surrenders himself to the standards and values of the tragic hero."[76] If there is fall and redemption in *Samson Agonistes*, the fall belongs to the players and the redemption to the playwright and, potentially, to his audience. *Samson* is less a crisis than a process poem, and the tragic process unfolds not by tying a knot but by retelling a tale.

In the Book of Judges, the Samson story, like the larger narrative of which it is a part, is a curious compound: "Samson's life and acts are described with a fulness which seems out of proportion with the actual deliverance wrought for Israel," observes A. R. Fausset; or as C. F. Burney remarks, "In the history of Samson, in particular, the conception of the hero as a divinely appointed deliverer of his people seems little suited to the narrative; since his actions, so far as his personal volition is concerned, are wholly dictated by his own wayward inclinations, and he does not in any way effect deliverance or even respite from the foreign yoke."[77] The history of the other judges begins with their entry into office; Samson's alone with his birth, in fact with the annunciation of his birth. Samson is the first hero of the tribe of Dan, the only judge anointed

[75] *"Comus" and "Samson Agonistes"* (Great Neck: Barrons' Educational Series, 1961), p. 37.

[76] *Tragedy: A View of Life* (Ithaca: Cornell Univ. Press, 1956), pp. 13, 14, 9.

[77] See Fausset's *A Critical and Expository Commentary on the Book of Judges* (London: James Nisbet, 1885), pp. 217-18, also p. 245; and Burney's *The Book of Judges with Introduction and Notes* (London: Rivingtons, 1918), p. xxxvi.

to office before his birth, but also the last of the judges, the judge also who makes kingship necessary. Yet even if the most expansive of these histories, Samson's is merely a "fragment," or "torso," of a history—an unfinished and "mutilated" story, according to Paul Carus, which at once resists closure and, preserving affinities with the earlier myth of a sun-god, deprives that myth of the glorious return of the hero and, suppressing his resurrection, silences the theme of immortality as well.[78] What has been called the Sun's tragedy, "the sunset as annihilating the visible world of day," is Samson's tragedy too: "The pillars . . . are broken and darkness comes crashing down," writes Palmer; "the place where he fell is red with the carnage of his foes! The clouds which obstructed him and exulted over him are . . . involved with him in a common ruin."[79] The final image of Samson in Milton's poem is of a man "dealing dole among his foes," treading disdainfully over heaps of their slaughtered bodies (1529-30), of a man who then "over-strong" against himself (1590) is found "Sok't in his enemies blood" (1726).

One of the many existing images of Samson, that of the militarist hero was given its fullest extension during the Renaissance by Du Bartas:

> Lo heer, another shakes his unshaven tresses,
> Tryumphing on a Lyon torne in peeces:
> O match-les Champion! Pearle of men-at-armes,
> That emptiest not an Arcenal of Armes,
> Nor needest shops of *Lemnian* Armourers,
> To furnish weapons for thy glorious Warrs:
> An Asse's Jawe-bone is the Club wher-with
> Thy mighty arme, braines, beats, and battereth

---

[78] See Paul Carus, *The Story of Samson and Its Place in the Religious Development of Mankind* (Chicago: Open Court, 1907), pp. 155, 156; 157; see also pp. 18, 135, 152, 155.

[79] See Palmer, *The Samson-Saga*, pp. 177, 180.

Th'uncircumcised Campe: all quickly skud;
And th'Hoast that flew in dust, now flowes in blood.
Heer, th'Iron Gates, whose hugenesse woont to shake
The massie Towers of *Gaza*, thou doost take
On thy broad showlders: there (in seeming jest)
Crushing their Pallace-pillars (at a feast)
Thou over-whelm'st the Howse, and with the fall
The *Philistines* blaspheming Princes all.
Heer, from ones head, which two huge coines doo
                             crush,
(As whay from Cheese) the battred braines doo gush:
Heer lyes another in a deadly swound,
Nayl'd with a broaken rafter to the ground:
Another, heer pasht with a pane of wall,
Hath lost his soule, and bodies shape withall:
Another, heer ore-taken as he fled,
Lyes (Tortois-like) all hidden but the head:
Another, covered with a heap of lome,
Seemes with his mooving to re-move his Toombe:
Even as the soft, blinde, Mine-inventing Moule,
In velvet Robes under the Earth doth roule,
Refusing light, and little aire receaves,
And hunting wormes her mooving hillocks heaves.
                             $(845\text{-}74)^{80}$

And this is an image of Samson that persists into the 1660s.
Witness Vondel's lines:

---

[80] "The Captaines: The IIII Part of the III Day of the II Week," in *The Divine Weeks and Works of Guillaume de Saluste Sieur du Bartas*, trans. Joshuah Sylvester, ed. Susan Snyder (2 vols.; Oxford: Clarendon Press, 1979), II, 612-13. For a representation of Milton as a militarist and of *Samson Agonistes* as a militaristic poem, see Robert Thomas Fallon, *Captain and Colonel: the Soldier in Milton's Life and Art* (Columbia: Univ. of Missouri Press, 1984), pp. 235-49. Fallon speaks unabashedly of Samson as "a soldier of God," "a warrior-prince," "a man of violence," and "ideal warrior" (pp. 238, 241).

When by degrees the dust-clouds disappeared,
Amid the ruins, red with oozing blood,
Were men and women, crushed or partly crushed,
Broken in neck, splintered in every bone,
Dead, or just gasping forth a choking ghost.[81]

Here we may also think of E. H. Gombrich's quip concerning representations of Samson in the visual arts where so often, as in the Medici tapestries, he is surrounded by vast numbers of dead bodies: this is not exactly the kind of art that we would expect to find hanging in a drawing room.[82] A similar image of an Iliadic Samson asserts itself powerfully, climactically in the conclusion to Milton's poem and, there, jars with the revisionist perspective on heroism afforded by Milton's epics, especially by *Paradise Regained*, the poem with which *Samson Agonistes* is paired. But *Samson Agonistes* also collides with the value system formulated by Milton in *A Treatise of Civil Power* where "fleshlie force" is "an argument that all . . . spiritual power is dead within" (VII, 257) and where, in response to the proposition, *"he beareth not the sword in vain,"* Milton proclaims: "Yes, altogether in vain, if it smites he knows not what; . . . he bears the sword not in vain only, but unjustly and to evil" (VII, 252).

That the Samson story is but a torso, or a fragment, in the Book of Judges suggests a chronicle version of history wherein, as White observes, real events appear as *"unfinished* stories" and, "break[ing] off *in medias res,* in the chronicler's own present," have no "narrative closure."[83] That Milton should

---

[81] Kirkconnell, *That Invincible Samson*, p. 139.

[82] *Norm and Form: Studies in the Art of the Renaissance*, 2nd ed. (London and New York: Phaidon, 1971), p. 48. Joseph Campbell comments suggestively: "And so we arrive at the epic date of the deeds of Homer's heroes: the date, as well, of those of the Book of Judges"; see *The Masks of God: Occidental Mythology* (1964; rpt. New York: Viking, 1969), p. 146.

[83] "The Value of Narrativity in the Representation of Reality," *Critical Inquiry*, 7 (1980), 9.

turn from a narrated piece of chronicle history, where there is no closure, to a narratized version of the same story now embedded in a drama, suggests something of his purpose as well, which is to give that story closure by imparting an ending to the too long-enduring phase of history that the Samson story came to signify. In *Samson Agonistes*, this story appears as a fully realized, fully moralized history; it is a summing up of history's significance. Milton achieves a closure that may not necessitate, but that surely facilitates, what White describes as "the *passage* from one moral order to another."[84]

In different ways, then, both the Book of Judges and *Samson Agonistes* embody the moral within the aspect of their aesthetic. The narrative embedments in *Samson* indicate that Milton's story aspires to completeness, and the implicit analysis of the received narration suggests Milton's desire to untrivialize the Samson story. Whatever status we may assign to its "middle," Milton's poem has a beginning—*and an ending*. What the author of Judges achieves through narrative Milton accomplishes through dialogic form where as analyst, almost in the psychoanalytic sense, he is able to retell the Judges history from the vantage point of different characters and sometimes through the altering perspective of a single character. In Milton's retelling, as Roy Schafer explains of psychoanalytic dialogue, "certain features are accentuated while others are placed in parentheses; certain features are related to others in new ways or for the first time; some features are developed further, perhaps at great length," and some, as we have already observed, are simply suppressed or omitted. In the process, the transformation of an episode can produce a sharper focusing of its significance and can even be construed on occasion, especially in the instance of Samson, as what Schafer, again with reference to psychoanalysis, describes as "defensive meas-

[84] *Ibid.*, p. 26.

ures adopted (out of anxiety, guilt, shame, and depression) to disguise, displace, deemphasize, [and] compromise."[85] Dialogic form, moreover, may reveal character and may even refer the tragedy less to a public action than to a private person; but typically the character of the speakers is of less concern than the substance of their speeches. When the substance, as in *Samson Agonistes*, is ethical, political, and religious, the suggestion is that such issues are debatable, even are currently under debate in the culture; and the dramatist's strategy is often to challenge, through dialogue, the commonly held tenets of society, which, if sometimes affirmed, are more often subverted. The dialogue between characters, then, at its profoundest level, is a dialogue between the poet and his culture in which he ranges his own views against commonly held opinions. The poet sings not with, but against, the collective voice of his culture.

Threaded into and around the original Samson story seem to be all the elements of epic literature; yet the story, as related in Judges and rendered anew by Milton, issues forth as a tragedy, and not the tragedy of Samson alone but increasingly of all human history. What in Judges may be but a looking glass for viewing a bygone age of history becomes in *Samson Agonistes* a window on a history still too much with us. It is not the plot *per se* that determines the Samson story, in either redaction, to be a tragedy: it is not what happens so much as the blunted moral consciousness that makes events happen— a blunted consciousness afflicting Samson no less than his people, and the people of other historical eras too, that marks this story as a tragedy.

The plot of the Judges history, reaching from the death of Joshua to the time of Eli, reveals God's people falling into "a boundless Idolatry, accompanied with an extreme depravation

---

[85] "Narration in the Psychoanalytic Dialogue," *Critical Inquiry*, 7 (1980), 35, 40.

of life and manners," and thus being punished, according to John Diodati, by "tyrannies, oppressions, violences, and desolations by war."[86] Still, as history, in comparison with Joshua, Judges is sketchy and truncated, not really extending upon Joshua as a sequel but rather intersecting here and there with it. The story of Samson is correspondingly fragmented and incomplete, making it difficult to get a real hold on the inner man, yet in its highly selective details indicating a concern with exposing a state of mind and with anatomizing the human heart. Such details, instead of aggrandizing Samson, "humanize him in such a way that we may see some of our leading features, truthfully portrayed, only on an enlarged [and hence more revealing] scale."[87] We see less virtue than vice in this mirror, and apprehend error not as a consequence of religion but as an occurence in spite of religion. We see in Samson the "gradual and secret consumption of his inner life," the brow of ruin, and take away from his history, as one commentator has remarked, "a crushing sense of religion dishonored."[88] What makes for exquisite portraiture both in Judges and in *Samson Agonistes* is that neither redactor nor poet openly meddles with character but rather like God, Robert Alter explains, "creates in each human personality a fierce tangle of intentions, emotions, and calculations caught in a translucent net of language."[89] Values are implicit, judgment is by inference: Milton ensures this will be the case by freeing the Samson story from the reign of narrative and enclosing it within the structure of drama and poetics of vision.

The Book of Judges records heroic deeds alongside human infirmities, epitomizing both in its portrayal of Samson. Judges may also be "an illustration of the christian experi-

---

[86] *Pious and Learned Annotations*, "Argument" to the Book of Judges.
[87] See Scott, *The Giant Judge*, p. 43; see also pp. 40, 52, 55.
[88] *Ibid.*, pp. 279, 284.
[89] *The Art of Biblical Narrative*, p. 87.

ence,"[90] and especially of the internal warfare between flesh and spirit; but just as importantly, Judges propounds a lesson: that human society needs purification and raising up, and so too do its leaders. The history of individual leaders and that of the people are interrelated and replete with tragedy. Indeed, the whole movement of Judges is from the local to the universal, from a central narrative of individual histories to a coda in which those histories are placed in perspective. In the process, the story of Samson, the centerpiece among the individual histories, reflects upon the condition of the country at large, and the history envisioned in the coda is made discontinuous with the history set forth in the initial chapters of Judges.

In Judges, such histories are an index to, and also a looking-glass on, national history. The very structure of the book ensures this will be the case: an introduction enunciates a philosophy of history under this or that judge; a coda following the Samson saga reveals the spirit of an age in which evil permeates all people, all acts, all history. And there are contending perspectives here, for the representation of actual history in the coda jars with the vision of history etched in the introduction. The structure of this book may organize history, but history itself is organized around contending philosophies and within contrary perspectives. What God had done to Samson when He was betrayed to Delilah, God now does to the Israelites generally: He withdraws as a player from the history that in the beginning he staged. This despairing rhythm of history is captured within Samson's own story; it is related both by the Judges narrator and by Milton. By Milton, it is related in a poem that exhibits, just as its Old Testament counterpart exhibits, "a complete interfusion of literary art with theological, moral, or historiosophical vision."[91]

[90] See Scott, *The Giant Judge*, p.41.
[91] See Alter, *The Art of Biblical Narrative*, p. 19.

Milton's own pairing of a New with an Old Testament story, and the attendant juxtaposition of comedic and tragic vision, should remind us that this is exactly how the Samson story, newly contextualized, came to be disseminated to seventeenth-century England. In the seventeenth century, an earlier set of correlations involving the Samson story is displaced by another. The effect of resetting the Judges narrative within the liturgy is to obscure the identity between Samson and Jesus and to clarify their differences by suggesting that supposed restorations of scriptural meaning owing to the Reformation are also "historically conditioned act[s] of imaginative reduction"; that, as Kenneth Gross reports, Reformation hermeneutics participate "within a dialectic of loss and gain, where often the gloss is "loss."[92]

The Book of Common Prayer, at least in Milton's century, prescribes the Samson story for March 22 and 23, correlating Judges 13 with John 9, Judges 14 with Timothy 6, Judges 15 with John 10, and Judges 16 with 2 Timothy 1. That is, the miracle of Samson's birth is paired with the miracle of Jesus' opening the eyes of a blind man and in such a way as to contrast the faithless parents of that man with the faithfulness of Manoah and his spouse. It is of no small moment that, in an exhibition of his faith, Manoa reasons that the same God who miraculously allayed Samson's thirst "can as easie / Cause light again within thy eies to spring" (583-84), and later that "since his strength with eye-sight was not lost, / God will restore him eye-sight to his strength" (1502-03). The Chorus asks similarly, "What if his eye-sight (for to *Israels* God / Nothing is hard) [is] by miracle restor'd" (1527-28)? The episode of Samson taking the Woman of Timnath as his bride,

_____

[92] *Spenserian Poetics: Idolatry, Iconoclasm, and Magic* (Ithaca: Cornell Univ. Press, 1985), p. 72-73. Broadbent is one of the few critics to associate *Samson Agonistes* with liturgical readings, but he does so without exploring the poem's relationship to those readings and also without observing the correlations that would have pertained in Milton's own time; see *"Comus" and "Samson Agonistes,"* p. 42.

only to have her given away to his friend, is coupled with St. Paul's reflections on "fall[ing] into temptation and a snare, and *into* many foolish and hurtful lusts" (1 Timothy 6:9) and his urging mankind to "follow after righteousness, godliness, faith, love, patience, meekness" (6:11). Repeatedly, Samson alludes to his marriages as a snare and allows that twice he has succumbed to temptation by a woman—"fair fallacious looks" and "venereal trains" (533), while the Chorus urges Samson now to "turn / His labours . . . to peaceful end" (708-09), and, "sight bereav'd," to choose to number himself with those whom patience eventually will crown (1294-96).

As the final chapters of Judges show, peace is but a delusion of Milton's players in the aftermath of Samson's tragedy. The story of Samson returning to his Timnian bride, of his running the foxes through the fields, of the revenge taken upon his bride and her father, and of Samson's revenge upon the revengers is coupled with the parable of the good shepherd who would lay his life down for his sheep and who himself will never perish because his sights are set on eternal life. Samson's going to Gaza, there blinded and taken prisoner, and his hurling down of the temple are harnessed to St. Paul's lesson that God's laws are made for whoremongers and manslayers, that those laws tend toward mercy and should always end in charity, that Jesus came into the world not to slay his enemies but to save sinners.

As if to emphasize this contrast between Samson and Jesus, by the 1660s the liturgical readings have undergone a slight but significant adjustment:

MARCH 22: Judges 12 and John 9
           Judges 13 and 1 Timothy 6

MARCH 23: Judges 14 and John 10
           Judges 15 and 2 Timothy 1

MARCH 24: Judges 16 and John 11

That is, because of the change Judges 16 and John 11 are now correlated with the result that the temple holocaust is conjoined to the prophecy of Caiaphas, bringing Samson and Jesus into still sharper contrast: Samson's prayer of petition is set against Jesus's prayer of thanksgiving, Samson's slaughter of the Philistines and self-slaughter are set against the prophecy: " '. . . you do not understand that it is expedient for you that one man shall die for the people, and that the whole nation should not perish.' He did not say this *of his own accord*, but being high priest that year he prophesied that Jesus should die for the nation" (John 11:50-51; my italics)—that better one man should die for the many whose deliverance is thereby achieved than that many should die and many more be delivered by such a holocaust into further, and greater, servitude. *Of his own accord* is always used scripturally to mean by one's own initiative (cf. 2 Corinthians 8:17 and Acts 12:10), and here it is used to imply a contrast between the false prophets who act of their own accord and the true prophets who act by divine commission. In precisely this way, the Messenger employs the same phrase in *Samson Agonistes*.

The story of Samson and the teachings of Jesus are also placed within the framework of Psalms 107-115, which praise God's mercy and promote the theme of deliverance. The movement of this sequence of Psalms is revelatory in that it captures the rhythms of two discrete phases of history: a period of darkness when man lives in the shadow of death and, like Samson, is bound in affliction and iron because he has rebelled against the word of God, and a period of light when God's commandments are observed and stand fast and when God, because he is gracious and full of compassion, effects the redemption of a contrite, righteous, and deserving people. The effect of this correlation of scriptural texts, and of the contextualization of those texts with these Psalms, is to underscore the disparity between Jesus and his type, between Old

Testament history and New, and is to suggest that the coming of Jesus constitutes a turning-point in history—the emergence of a new ethical system and an improved moral consciousness.

That this effect is achieved, by design, within the liturgy seems likely; for the seventeenth century displaces an earlier contextualization, a remarkably different set of scriptural correlations that pair Judges 13 and John 20, Judges 14 and Hebrews 4, Judges 15 and John 21, and finally Judges 16 and Hebrews 5. The sixteenth century, that is, chose juxtapositions that reinforced received typology by relating the miracle of Samson's birth to that of Christ's release from his tomb, Samson's going to Timnath with the gift of grace, Samson's homecoming to Christ's returning to his disciples, and the catastrophe at the pillars to the promise of eternal salvation. It was commonly acknowledged during the Renaissance that the only firm bond between the stories of Samson and Jesus is their respective passions and deaths. The security of that link is broken by the seventeenth-century prayerbook and, similarly, will be dashed by Milton in his poetic volume of 1671. The Samson story, in whatever version, is a narrative transaction between a poet-prophet and his audience. Yet not every version of the story has an identical function or meaning. This is especially true of versions separated from one another by enormous spaces of time, themselves filled in with still other versions of that story. There is, that is, the old folktale adapted to the Judges narrative, and there is that narrative now appropriated by Milton for his drama. Intervening, there are multiple versions and multiplying interpretations of the Samson story, each with its own ideological content. As the details of the story and its setting alter, so too do its function and meaning.

Initially Milton had turned the Genesis narrative into the tragedy of *Adam Unparadised*; in *Samson*, on the other hand, he lifts from the dramatized narrative of Judges the tragedy of a whole people unparadised. For some, myth flattens history into ruins from which we must segregate the mythic fragments in order to recover, quite apart from them, an outline of general truth. For others, and presumably for Milton, the ruins of myth, and specifically of the Samson myth, are themselves to be searched and reconstituted; for the fragments of this myth embody the outline of truth and the true contours of history. Embedded in myth are the profoundest truths of history; and, as Milton must have understood well in advance of Paul Carus, myth "find[s] verification in history whenever events of the same kind happen, not once but repeatedly, for the myth stands for the type and the type is realized in every concrete instance."[93]

For Milton and his contemporaries the Samson myth found its modern extension in the failure of the Puritan Revolution, a tragedy of history, but also a tragedy within a prophecy promising that history can be more than repetitions; that the cycles of history can be broken upon the block of an improved moral consciousness; that, if epic can turn over into tragedy, tragedy itself can turn over again into an epic wherein history is redeemed and paradise regained not by the sword but by the Word. Prophetic vision may not have materialized in history; the initial idealisms of the Book of Judges may still be discrepant with reality, with the realities of the present meshing too well with the actualities of that pre-Christian phase of history. For Milton the supreme irony must have been that it was the Samson story itself, rather than the prophetic history of which it was a part, that his own age brought to fulfillment. And in that there was the risk certainly that, following the way of Samson as the people of Dan had done, the Puritans themselves might vanish from history, or history vanish altogether. Yet history did not end with the disappearance of

[93] *The Story of Samson and Its Place in the Religious Development of Mankind* (Chicago: Open Court, 1907), p. 165.

the tribe of Dan, nor was it likely to end with the failure of the revolutionary effort.

If not in *Samson Agonistes* certainly in *Paradise Regained*, the poem with which it is paired, man and history are snatched out of the jaws of tragedy. Modulations toward comedy are yet to be found in the tragic rhythms of history; hope can still be wrested from defeat. Through the instrument of *Paradise Regained*, Milton would immolate the history of *Samson Agonistes* no less than of his contemporary England—would immolate that history in the name of the future. New histories are thus made, and made with the intention of releasing people from a counterfeit past and a confounding present and of stirring them into new life and creation. If in *Samson Agonistes* we see myth mutilated into tragedy, in *Paradise Regained* we envision mythology modulating into history, and prophecy, masking itself as history, moving toward fulfillment. History, once it has been perceived as prophecy, can be plotted for apocalypse, which will come once the avengers stop avenging.

CHAPTER III

THE JUDGES NARRATIVE AND
THE ART OF *SAMSON AGONISTES*

*Through the warp of all those intervening
centuries lines become blurred, contours are
distorted, colors fade; for not only have we lost the
precise shadings of implication . . . but we have
. . . forgotten the very conventions around which
the biblical tales were shaped.*

—ROBERT ALTER

The Samson story, it has been said, "demonstrates Israelite narrative art at its zenith."[1] This claim should be made for the Book of Judges as a whole, for its meaning is located not in individual tales alone but spreads out through the entire structure. The salient features of this narrative are comprehended within the body of Renaissance exegesis but were not then the preoccupation they would become for later commentators. A prospect on history, a series of inset histories, another

---

[1] James L. Crenshaw, *Samson: A Secret Betrayed, a Vow Ignored* (Atlanta, Ga.: John Knox Press, 1978), p. 149. Cf. A. Smythe Palmer, *The Samson-Saga and Its Place in Comparative Religion* (London: Sir Isaac Pitman and Sons, 1913), who speaks of "the simplicity of its [Judge's] mechanical structure: the process of its manufacture, its humble dimensions, according to the workman's rule" and thereupon concludes: "It was put together by that skill of the carpenter and metal-worker" (p. 3), and also Wolf Mankowitz, *The Samson Riddle: An Essay and a Play* (London: Vallentine, Mitchell, 1972), who praises "the beautifully plotted story-elements" in the Judges narrative (p. 11).

prospect on history that, this time, juxtaposes current actualities with earlier idealisms, the Book of Judges is also remarkable for a ruptured narrative line that makes it difficult
to sort out episodes and then situate them in a regular chronological series. Yet the Renaissance began the task of unscram-
bling, especially the Samson story, which, though a hinge-
point, is also but a fragment of the Judges narrative. By
Milton's time, it was understood that Samson was born in
1155 B.C., married in 1137 B.C., sent the foxes through the
fields a year later, and died in the temple holocaust of 1117
B.C.[2] That is, Samson married at the age of eighteen and died
when he was thirty-eight, with all events in that twenty-year
period pertaining to his judgeship.

That Milton has roughly this chronology in mind is suggested by Samson himself when he speaks of how Dalila treated
him in his "flower of youth" (938), and thereupon reasons
that, if so treated then, how much more ill-treated he would
be now that he is "In perfet thraldom" (946). That Milton
would allow himself this much latitude in interpreting an Old
Testament story is made evident in *De Doctrina Christiana*
where, arguing that the Old Testament text is "uncorrupted,"
he still allows of certain books, "particularly the historical
ones," that their chronological accuracy is suspect and so subject to revision in the interests of doctrinal clarity (VI, 588-
89). Milton makes this allowance, knowing that chronology
may be only an illusion in these narratives and having just
made clear the importance of contextualizing the biblical stories—of developing an awareness "of what comes before and
after" and of arriving at an interpretation by comparative

[2] See, e.g., James Ussher, *The Annals of the World* (London: Printed by E. Tyler,
1658), pp. 31-32, and the anonymous *Clavis Bibliorum: The Key of the Bible* (Edinburgh: Printed by Gedeon Lithgow, 1649), pp. 92-95. See also John Lightfoot,
Rules for a Student of the Holy Scriptures, in *The Whole Works*, ed. John Rogers
Pitman (13 vols.; Oxford: J. Parker, 1822-25), II, 37.

means, setting a passage here against a passage there, and finally testing the interpretation by how well it accords with faith (VI, 582). Even if the Bible has the effect of curtailing creative transmission, it leaves room for variability and improvisation; if it fosters loyalty to tradition it nonetheless allows for a limited range of flexibility. The biblical stories can be lengthened or shortened without fundamental damage; their plots can be dilated or contracted and can even be given different generic situations in order to achieve precision of detail or density of content; episodes within the plot can be cross-referenced with similar episodes in other tales or gathered together within a system of type-scenes, and the sequence of episodes within a given tale can be jumbled.

For Milton, to sabotage the chronology of an established narrative is to break the illusions it has fostered; to shatter illusions is to break in upon the truth of that narrative. Milton must have understood that *Samson Agonistes* would live by its relationship to the equivalent story in Judges and that the poem's narrative embedments would themselves live by their achieved relationship with the characters who utter them. Whether the text is the Book of Judges (a narrative) or *Samson Agonistes* (a dramatic poem with some narrative discourse), episodes are recounted in order to be interpreted; the narrative or embedded narratives, as Tzvetan Todorov intuits, will contain their own gloss.[3] If poetry is not a knowing but an embodying of truth, as Yeats thought, its objective will be not to establish a truth but to approach and give an impression of it, often through a narrative that will be as elusive, as enigmatic as the truth it searches and would serve. In those instances where there is narrative, there are both narrators and narratees validating the narrative contract, but also making it essential that we ask, as Peter Brooks has done, "not only what a

[3] *The Poetics of Prose*, trans. Richard Howard (Ithaca: Cornell Univ. Press, 1977), p. 122.

narrative is, but what it is for, and what its stakes are: why it is told, what aims it may manifest and conceal, what it seeks not only to say but to do"?[4]

In the instance of *Samson Agonistes*, there is no presiding narrator—"no narrator," as Anne Davidson Ferry reports, "endowed . . . with authority to interpret the drama for the reader."[5] But there is a narrative perspective afforded the poem by *Paradise Regained*, the poem with which *Samson* is published; and there are narrating characters, as Ferry seems to forget, who explain and interpret not only by posing counterstatements against statements in order to reinterpret proffered interpretations but also by the very strategies of narrating with which they are engaged. Drama may not allow for a commanding narrative intelligence, but it does allow for nar-

[4] *Reading for the Plot: Design and Intention in Narrative* (New York: Alfred A. Knopf, 1984), p. 236; see also p. 225.

[5] *Milton and the Miltonic Dryden* (Cambridge, Mass.: Harvard Univ. Press, 1968), p. 128. There may be no narrator, but there are narrating characters whose speeches call other of Ferry's observations into question: "No speaker intervenes between the dramatized material and the audience to shape their interpretation" (p. 131); "There are no interpretive remarks by the other characters to guide us" (p. 169; see also pp. 171-72). William Kerrigan provides altogether more searching observations: in *Samson Agonistes*, repeatedly, the characters are turned into storytellers; "the same story [is] told more than once," Milton desiring, apparently, "his readers to examine the difference between drama and narrative," and the different kinds of "illusion" these modes perpetrate. See *The Prophetic Milton* (Charlottesville: Univ. Press of Virginia, 1974), p. 225. Cf. Kathleen M. Swaim, "The Doubling of the Chorus in *Samson Agonistes*," *Milton Studies*, 20 (1984): "Because *Samson Agonistes* lacks an equivalent of the narrators of the diffuse and brief epics, the guiding principle of the value scheme it shares with them must be sought elsewhere" (p. 225). Or, as Todorov would argue, that principle must be sought by the reader, especially when a narrating character (like the Messenger in *Samson Agonistes*) has no central role in the fiction but is merely a witness to it and also when causality in the narrative discourse is kept implicit, obliging the prospective reader to perform labors the narrating characters decline to perform: "Insofar as . . . causality is necessary for perception of the work, the reader must supply it. . . . We might say that . . . the narrator and the reader supply it between them, their efforts being inversely proportional" (*Introduction to Poetics*, trans. Richard Howard [Minneapolis: Univ. of Minnesota Press, 1981], p. 46; see also p. 40).

rating characters who, in turn, become narratees and of whom we must ask, again with Brooks, "What do they recount? How do they know it? What is their motive, their investment in what they recount"?[6]

In *Samson*, without exception, the narrative passages are retrospective; they are clipped, undetailed recollections of the Samson story. We are left to ponder not only their functions but, more generally, the uses of narration, remembering that narratives are always a form of explanation and that when texts in a series interlock, as the Book of Judges and *Samson Agonistes* do, we are being provided with an explanation of a previous explanation. The use of retrospective narrative in *Samson* reinforces the poem's hermeneutic function; for as Gérard Genette explains, retrospection "confers on the past episode a meaning that in its own time it did not yet have. Indeed, this is the most persistent function of recalls . . . , to modify the meaning of past occurrences after the event, either by making significant what was not so originally or by refuting a first interpretation and replacing it with a new one."[7]

Milton's Chorus interprets Samson's marriages as evidence of his disposition to err; Samson interprets them as a sign of his divine commission, and Manoa then challenges Samson's interpretation: "thou didst plead / Divine impulse . . . / I state not that" (421-24). Later in the poem, Samson claims divine inspiration in going to the temple but also is reported as saying that, hurling down the temple, he acts of his own accord. The Chorus now associates Samson's motivation with the spirit that first rushed upon this hero and, despite the Messenger's contrary report, joins with Manoa in declaring that Samson does "all this / With God not parted from him" (1718-19). The Chorus had never previously vested its confidence in Samson's interpretation of events, and we may find

---

[6] *Reading for the Plot*, p. 297.

[7] *Narrative Discourse: An Essay in Method*, trans. Jane E. Levin (Ithaca: Cornell Univ. Press, 1980), p. 56.

it difficult now to vest much confidence in its interpretations. Indeed, to the very end, Manoa and the Chorus are found contradicting Samson and, in the end, contradict Samson into a heroism he is perhaps not meant to enjoy. Through such contradictions, Milton seems to be calling in for review all interpretations and reinterpretations of the Samson story, stringing out a re- and de-constructed Samson on the tensions of his text.

The Samson story, as it is related in the Book of Judges, has been described as "a patch" or "*appliqué*"[8] on a narrative that it ill-matches, although the incongruity seems the very point of a narrative designed to reveal what happens when the human intelligence works over primitive cultural materials and the extent to which a new and refined moral sensibility can improve upon the value system of a cruder age. Before such stories are actually recorded, they presumably move through different phases: one of oral transmission, and an equally extensive period of scribal activity when inherited stories are newly redacted through revision and amplification. Eventually the text becomes fixed, authoritative, canonical. The oral tradition entails a long period of evolution and development, both of which are continued through as long or perhaps a longer period of scribal activity until the final redaction takes place.[9] The redactor of the Judges narrative may not be creating a new story then; but he does try to penetrate to what is behind earlier redactions of the inherited story, he does create the framework in which the story will now be set, he may even revise the inherited story to fit its new setting. The redactor lifts his stories from tradition, then freezes them into form, but not without engaging in compositional activity

[8] See Palmer, *The Samson-Saga*, p. 2.

[9] Gerald L. Bruns provides an informative discussion in "Canon and Power in the Hebrew Scriptures," *Critical Inquiry*, 10 (1984), 462-80.

that may involve deletion of irrelevant or misleading material and the addition of explanatory material.

The redactors of tales such as are found in the Book of Judges probably imbued their stories with overarching structures and unifying themes; and thus, as Klaus Koch observes, " a study of redaction history first considers the beginning and end of the book, and its principles of construction and classification."[10] But such a study must also acknowledge that even as he tries to grasp the earlier significances of his inherited story, the redactor (and certainly the Judges redactor) may be reaching for a statement that the earlier material does not itself imply; that the very selection and arrangement of stories may constitute a vision of history, not personal but public, not individual but national—a vision of its totality, a revelation, as Gerhard von Rad puts it, of "the meaning and the content of a whole era in the eyes of God." The Old Testament, recording history in narrative, both dramatizes that history and deciphers in it an unfolding purpose, indeed layers of purpose. As drama, the play of history has man in the role of a principal actor and seems to be asking of him: what part has he played? what part should he play? Such a history may need commentary such as is provided in Judges by a whole sequence of stories welded together for the purpose of an interpretation that is further advanced and deepened by the importation of weighty theological apparatus. "In the cases of Gideon, Jephthah, and Samson," von Rad contends, "we have to deal not with single narratives, but with little cells of grouped narrative units":

> These histories . . . show an almost typified falling gradient. The call is followed immediately by the public proof of the *charisma* . . . ; but then the line

[10] *The Growth of the Biblical Tradition: The Form-Critical Method*, trans. S. M. Cupitt (New York: Charles Scribner's Sons, 1969), p. 59.

curves steeply downwards. . . . Thus these little narrative complexes already have as their background
a definite, pessimistic conception of the charismatic
leader. But for a moment was he able . . . to rise
above the limitations of his being, only then simply
to get himself more deeply entangled in deadly
chaos.[11]

What von Rad says of the Judges histories generally is
especially true of the Samson narrative and perhaps explains
why Milton feels compelled to stitch his own version of the
Samson story, through parenthetical aside, with the larger
Judges narrative (1:20; 4-5, esp. 5:24-27; 7:4-9; 11:12-27;
12:1-6) and even to look beyond this narrative, as editors from
Newton and Todd to Hughes and Shawcross have observed,
to Psalms and Lamentations and, more specifically, to Genesis,
Deuteronomy, Joshua, 1 and 2 Samuel, 2 Kings, Job, the
Gospel of Luke, and the Book of Revelation. This stitching
makes clear that the Samson story is at once a piece of, and
of a piece with, the whole Book of Judges, which contains, as
Robert Alter might say, "a whole network of ramified
interconnections"[12] and which is itself but a fragment of a
larger, more complex and comprehending, Scripture. Milton
understood, and in *Samson Agonistes* employs, the strategy of
forging such links between individual tales and the larger
narratives in which they are embedded. The episodes organized around the Samson story in the Book of Judges perform

[11] *Old Testament Theology: The Theology of Israel's Historical Traditions*, trans.
D.M.G. Stalker (2 vols.; New York: Harper and Brothers, 1962), I, 229, 331.
See also Bernhard W. Anderson, *Understanding the Old Testament*, 3rd ed. (Englewood Cliffs: Prentice-Hall, 1975), p. 154; W. Lee Humphreys, *Crisis and Story:
Introduction to the Old Testament* (Palo Alto: Mayfield Publishing Co., 1978), p. 32;
and Robert C. Boling, *The Anchor Bible: Judges* (Garden City: Doubleday, 1975),
pp. 252-53. Both Humphreys and Boling emphasize Samson's failings as a political
leader.

[12] *The Art of Biblical Narrative* (New York: Basic Books, 1981), p. 3.

the same function as the discrete, seemingly disparate episodes from Samson's life, which are themselves arranged around the temple holocaust in Milton's poem. Correspondingly, other scriptural books relate to, and explicate, the Judges narrative in much the same way that *Paradise Regained* is interlaced with and expounds the meaning of *Samson Agonistes*. Or more precisely perhaps: *Paradise Regained* is Milton's counterpart to the framing device in the Book of Judges, to the larger human perspective it affords on a lesser and seemingly inhumane tale.

Throughout the Judges narrative, events seem to tell themselves but, because related as history, also preclude the intervention of the narrator in the individual stories, no less than Milton's tragic form prevents his entry into the drama of *Samson Agonistes*. Yet even if effaced in individual tales, and thus for a while distanced from his narration, eventually such an author "comes to the fore and appears to be related to his writing as the prophet is to his words"[13]—not as their moralizer but as one who, once verbalizing moral insights, leaves them to the discernment of the reader. The author of Judges does just this at the end of his narration as if to void the traces of God from the events previously, and perhaps misleadingly, depicted. He emerges, finally, as a voice behind the voice of the recorded tales in much the same way that through *Paradise Regained* Milton will achieve a voice behind the voice of the actors in *Samson Agonistes*. The conclusion of the Judges narrative, "every man did *that which was* right in his own eyes" (21:25), attempts to account for the enormities represented but unapproved by a narrator who, from a posture of vexation, doubt, uncertainty, and questioning, has assumed a dramatist's relationship with his materials. And it is just this sort of formulaic conclusion that, when employed by a later redactor, signals an alternative function for the original story, the re-

[13] See Paul Ricoeur, *Essays on Biblical Interpretation*, ed. Lewis S. Mudge (London: SPCK, 1981), p. 80.

dactor "making into an etiology what originally was something else."[14]

The Samson story in its inception was probably a reflection of group consciousness; that same story, newly contextualized within the Book of Judges, reveals an expanded consciousness conditioned to a new level of ethical, religious, and cultural awareness. What we confront in Judges, then, is a double consciousness, the one current and identified with the story's redactor, the other antiquated and mythic, and identifiable with Samson and his people. We encounter here what we will meet again in an analogous form in *Samson Agonistes*—the Chorus's dim against Samson's clearer awareness, the cinched consciousness of all the play's characters against the expanded awareness of Milton and his reader/audience. In *Samson*, the narrative is divorced from the poet and invested in the characters. There is not, as in Judges, a totalized narrative—a bard's song—that speaks the truth; there are only characters who disguise or disfigure it. The narrative discourses scattered through this dramatic poem are characterizations mirroring their speakers and monitoring their thoughts; they are uttered with an express purpose, not always the same purpose, with each successive speaker thickening the discourse. Manoa, the Chorus, even Samson prove to be blocking figures in relation to a narrative that they expound and that Milton's poem would explain. Milton's tragedy is not unlike other Renaissance tragedies where there is an irreducible narrative element; yet in it we confront both "a classic narrative" and "a prophecy of the modern": a narrative that, by Frank Kermode's description, says more than it seems to know and that thus "contrives to bring into question the validity of the assumptions on which it was written."[15]

---

[14] Gene M. Tucker, *Form Criticism of the Old Testament* (1971; rpt. Philadelphia: Fortress Press, 1979), p. 34.

[15] *The Art of Telling* (Cambridge, Mass.: Harvard Univ. Press, 1983), p. 74.

Such narratives embody, but also would erode, the cultural code of common knowledge—of shared opinion and ideology. In such tales, the author's consciousness and that of his characters are usually distinguishable, as are the consciousnesses of the story's author and of its later redactor. As a relater of scriptural truth through his own biblically based fictions, Milton assumes an identity between his own consciousness and that of the Judges redactor; yet there is a difference to be observed between the Book of Judges and *Samson Agonistes* owing to centuries of disfiguring commentary on the Samson story, which must now be revoked before the meaning of the Judges narrative can, by Milton's poem, be restored.

Milton was the greatest narrative poet of his century and as resourceful in his grasp of its poetics as modern theorists like Roland Barthes, Tzvetan Todorov, Gérard Genette, Frank Kermode, and Peter Brooks. And not just Milton but others in his time, like John Lightfoot, perceived that in the Book of Judges, a *seemingly* disjointed chronicle, "there is no scruple for order," only because the individual stories are deliberately "mislaid" so that some "might be laid together for secret instruction to the reader."[16] The juxtaposition, as well as the interplay, of stories is crucial to their interpretation. If there now exists a wall between theory and interpretation, that wall was created since Milton's time by separatists who would announce as discoveries theoretical and critical insights that are actually recoveries of narrative codes that existed in Milton's own time and to which Milton himself was privy. Theoretical discourse then served, and continues to serve, interpretation.

---

[16] See Barthes, *Image Music Text*, trans. Stephen Heath (New York: Hill and Wang, 1977); Todorov, *The Poetics of Prose*, trans. Howard; Genette, *Narrative Discourse*, trans. Levin; Kermode, *The Art of Telling*; and Brooks, *Reading for the Plot*. Cf. Alter, *The Art of Biblical Narrative*, and J. P. Fokkelman, *Narrative Art in Genesis* (Amsterdam: Van Gorcum, Assen, 1975) and, more important still, see

Milton's epics are ample enough evidence that he was preoccupied with questions that are today relegated to the narratologists: what are the different kinds and functions of narrative? what conventions do narratives observe? how do they communicate and, in communicating, implicate an audience in their author's enterprise? If the Book of Judges is a narrative involving its author in the activity of narrating existing stories, *Samson Agonistes* is an abandonment of narrative, but nonetheless involves its characters in narrating what was, in the seventeenth century, an enormously popular, if often misunderstood, tale. The very fact that narrative is here subordinated to drama suggests that Milton's interest is not simply in retelling an old story but, more, in wresting meaning from it. It has been said that "Narrative is a switch point, the choice of one track rather than another."[17] To continue the metaphor, Milton may be riding the same train as the Judges narrator, but at a different time, and if that train has the same destination its cars are now in a different series and they ride another track. Implicit in this metaphoric extension is the understanding that we must identify the distinctive features of a narrative and of its situation before we can explain them, and the explanation will require finely nuanced observation that is attentive to subtle ironies in texts possessing an extraordinary density, to structures often in conflict but exhibiting nonetheless an idiosyncratic coherence, to literary shapings loaded with implications.

Obvious differences between narratives should not obscure overriding resemblances; and the resemblances, in turn, may point to a unity of purpose. The narrator of Judges and the poet of *Samson Agonistes* stand in the same relationship to the

---

Lightfoot, *Rules for a Student of the Holy Scriptures*, in *The Whole Works*, ed. Pitman, II, 37.

[17] *The Poetics of Prose*, trans. Heath, p. 140.

original Samson story and would, together, effect a transformation of that story which, as Thomas De Quincey put it, will belong "to a higher, purer, and far holier religion."[18] To that end, their own retellings are marked by deliberate hedgings, provisional formulations and patterns frustrating one another's designs. Evolutions are accompanied by devolutions, turning all talk about Samson's regeneration into discussions regarding degeneration. This is certainly one effect of the narrative repetition, "every man did *that which was* right in his own eyes" (17:6; 21:25); yet there is another such repetition, this time of image, within the Samson story itself, which works the same effect. Samson is repeatedly associated with fire—the firing of the foxes' tails, the burning alive of the Timnian bride, the cords binding Samson becoming as flax burned by fire, his breaking the withes as a tread of tow is broken when it touches the fire—so that "[b]y the time we get to the captive Samson bringing down the temple of Dagon on himself and several thousand of his enemies," as Alter remarks, "fire has become a metonymic image of Samson himself: a blind, uncontrolled force, leaving a terrible swath of destruction behind it, finally consuming itself together with whatever stands in its way."[19] Samson is that scorching fire that burns and, burning, destroys thousands throughout the Judges narrative (9:49, 52; 12:1; 20:40-41).

As C. F. Burney maintains, the narrative histories of individual judges and their exploits "cannot emanate from the author who was responsible for the framework in which they are set";[20] rather, these disconnected narratives, seemingly ill-suited to one another, derive from popular folk traditions and

[18] *The Romantics on Milton: Formal Essays and Critical Asides*, ed. Joseph Wittreich (Cleveland: Press of Case Western Reserve Univ., 1970), p. 465.

[19] *The Art of Biblical Narrative*, p. 95.

[20] *The Book of Judges with Introduction and Notes* (London: Rivingtons, 1918), p. xxxvi; see also George Bush, *Notes, Critical, and Practical, on the Book of Judges* (New York: Saxton and Giles, 1844), p. 217.

are thereupon integrated within a prophetic history. Meaning resides in the selection and arrangement, even in the juxtaposition of discontinuous narratives and in their contextualization. There is a planned relationship among the narrative parts and between the parts and the whole. The intentions of the narrator, evident in his sequence and framing devices, often collide with the presumed function of the original tales. If they were once celebratory in character, the celebration may now modulate into criticism; a nominal interest in the biography of individual heroes may mask a real interest in matters of ethics and history, in interpreting history and setting forth its meaning. One ideology dissolves into another, and the older system of values yields to one now current, or at least now being given currency. The vision of the narrator is not only intimately involved in his artistic strategies but depends upon the distance achieved from those materials, upon his objectivity, his dramatic and dialectical stance in relation to them. The teller of these tales sees differently from their original author, just as in *Samson Agonistes* the playwright sees differently from the players.

In Judges especially, to think of its writer as an author in the usual sense is impossible: he is the collector, editor, redactor of traditional material and the controlling intelligence imposing a literary order and prophetic interpretation on those materials. Here in Judges, then, we see from more than one point of view, hear more than one voice, and more than the voice of a single generation; there is assertion and counterassertion, a reinterpretation set alongside an earlier interpretation of the same story. Not only are there different voices; there are different forms embodying and conjoining those voices. A heroic tale is here transmuted into saga and legend; the personal and the private merge into matters public and political; history is elevated to the key of prophecy, and vision embedded in a narrative form. Judges hosts a conflicting system of thoughts and values and is a classic instance of the situation described by Ricoeur where narration is engulfed in prophecy, and history then menaced by the prophecy.[21]

Milton simply capitalizes on what is already implicit in the Judges narrative, picking up hints there that he follows to their logical outcome: the dramatic potential of the Judges narrative, developed through dialogic form, is realized in a formal tragedy; legend once used to explain past history is now deployed to interpret present history. In the process, scriptural history is correlated with Milton's own times and with his own personal history; issues public and political are made to reflect upon matters personal and private; prophecy issues forth as threat and warning, and claims to vision are subjected to hard scrutiny. Milton remains forever attentive to the enormous burden of prophecy.

From one viewpoint, the original Samson story might seem to embody an attitude of mind, a level of consciousness, achieved at a particular moment and typical of a moment of history that later was improved upon—would seem this were it not that the particular moment of history is all too typical and that history is *still* to be improved upon. The Book of Judges records two successive revelations, the one representative of the people and the other of its narrator; it reflects a belief, a level of moral awareness once and perhaps still held by the people but no longer shared with them by its prophetic narrator. In this way, Judges figures forth "the evolutionary process through which the religion of Israel attained its full growth"[22] and, retrospectively, reveals the way in which Christianity emerged, or should have emerged, out of Judaism. As the Judges narrator relates to his materials, the New Testament relates to the Old—is the new light under which we may

[21] *Essays on Biblical Interpretation*, ed. Mudge, pp. 78, 80.
[22] Burney, *The Book of Judges*, p. cxviii.

comprehend an earlier and persisting but still partial revelation.

In a parallel maneuver, Milton deploys the Samson legend—a prop for the existing social order and for the reigning religious attitudes, as well as a constant feature of the current political rhetoric—but in such a way as to suggest that the ideology implicit in the Judges narrative both irradiates and invalidates the now dominant ideology and in such a way as to suggest that a radical transformation of values is necessary, the extent of which is measurable by setting the received Samson story against the poet's attitude toward it. Milton's *Samson* is both an index to the current historical reality and an indictment of it, an undoing with the hope of transforming that reality. It is much to Milton's point that in a preface to the reader he should set his own version of the Samson story so emphatically within the framework of tragic literature, both classical and Christian. There is a whole school of criticism that views tragedy as antithetical to Christianity and Christianity therefore as being beyond tragedy.[23] Milton does not belong to this school, believing instead that tragedy remains, however unfortunately, the chief form of history; that the tragedy of the Book of Judges is the tragedy of his own day.

If, customarily, the plot of narrative moves from equilibrium to its disruption and finally to another equilibrium, shifting from a narrative to a dramatic mode enables Milton, on the one hand, to embody this pattern within the narrative discourse of *Samson Agonistes* and, on the other hand, to overlay that pattern with another moving from the disequilibrium of Samson's opening soliloquy to the false equilibrium of this tragedy's final choral ode: "calm of mind, all passion spent"

---

[23] See, e.g., the remarks by Roger L. Cox, "Tragedy and the Gospel Narratives," in *The Bible and Its Literary Milieu: Contemporary Essays*, ed. Vincent L. Tollers and John R. Maier (Grand Rapids: William B. Eerdmans, 1979), p. 299.

(1758). This movement corresponds exactly with Judges'. *Samson* is simply an exaggeration of the Judges transgression from paradigmatic narrative and hence a deeper etching of its tragedy. In turning from simple narrative to narrative discourse, Milton offers but a portion of the usual narrative trajectory, a concentrated version of the tragedy that intervenes between the beginning and end of history. Narrative is a form of thinking in legend and myth and its plot, a structuring operation, which, in the words of Brooks, contains "the outline or armature of the story, that which supports and organizes the rest."[24] But in Judges, as well as in *Samson Agonistes*, it is but a portion of the grand plot of history that comes under review—that portion which may be differentiated as man's plot and which opposes, and is opposed by, God's plot. If God's plot imparts a design to history, making of it a divine comedy, man's plot makes history, which is now conceived of as a series of human tragedies wherein man's hubris repeatedly calls forth the nemesis of God.

Viewing Milton's tragedy in terms of the one related in the Book of Judges is but a reminder that when they assume a fixed, canonical form myths become moribund and die. The history of myth or legend (or of myth mutilated into legend) is a history of reduction, truncation, and simplification.[25] Milton is able enough to make sense of the Judges story; it is just that he must cut through centuries of reductionist interpretation before he *can* make sense of it. In the process, he must have come to see the Samson story as, if only a part of the Judges narrative, a part with a particularly privileged relation to the whole and to have seen in that story a tragedy distilled from the scattered fragments of a myth epical in its compass and concern. In the history of Samson, he must have seen epic

[24] *Reading for the Plot*, p. 11.

[25] See the fine essay by Larry D. Shinn, "Precision or Reductionism: Whence Myth Studies?", *Religious Studies*, 17 (1981), 369-76.

erupting into tragedy and could trace the curve of his own canon, a formation in which history turns perceptibly into tragedy in the movement within *Paradise Lost* and within the movement from *Paradise Lost* and *Paradise Regained* to *Samson Agonistes*. The same wrestling between drama and epic that characterizes Milton's last poems is evident in the Judges narrative. Just as the meaning of the Samson story in Judges unfolds from the narrative placement of it within the context of an idealized history, *Samson Agonistes* derives much of its significance from the poet's contextualization of his tragedy, from his situating *Samson* within the ideological framework of tragedy and, more generally, the idealisms of *Paradise Regained*.

If it can be said that "a narrative is a long sentence, just as every constative sentence is in a way the rough outline of a short narrative,"[26] it must also be allowed that sentences—and indeed narratives—can assume very different forms, that they can be differently ordered and inflected. For example, the broken line of the Judges narrative finds an analogy in *Samson Agonistes* which encompasses most episodes in the Samson story, but now in a dislocated narrative sequence. Milton surely recognized (and his epics are the testimony) that linear narratives representing events in chronological order tend to be concerned with the events themselves, whereas scrambled narratives are less concerned with events *per se* than with functional relationships between them. Such narratives are investments in character and motives but also give their attention to the relationship between and hence the meaning of events. It is as if Milton were saying, along with the Judges redactor, that seemingly hallucinatory narratives are better than illusory ones, that fractured narratives are an invitation to intellectual labor, that broken story lines and strenuous intellectual activity

---

[26] Barthes, *Image Music Text*, trans. Heath, p. 84.

go hand in hand. If *Samson Agonistes* contains a projection and transposition of an original series of events as they are recorded in the Book of Judges, it is also a poem that conducts us back to the original series by laying out the ambiguities in the Judges tale.

Samson Agonistes intersects with the Judges narrative, and for the most part occupies the white space between 16:24 and 25. The first two thirds of the poem, with the blind Samson standing before the prison house at Gaza, are a scanning and rescanning—present an arrangement and rearrangement—of the events in Samson's life. The Judges narrative provides Milton's characters with a grid for their retrospective narrating wherein some episodes are suppressed and others subordinated so that still others may be coordinated. Individual characters in the act of narrating may slur over, or even hide, contradictions; Milton as artificer of the whole, through juxtaposed narrations, can expose and examine those same contradictions. Characters may be plotters in this dramatic poem, but Milton is its masterplotter. The remainder of the poem is Milton's revisionary elaboration of Judges 16:25-31, the verses that center in the temple holocaust and its aftermath.

Now a prisoner, blinded and in chains, Samson thinks back to the double annunciation of his birth, to Manoa's sacrifice, to his commission as a deliverer who is now in a situation from which, ironically, he himself requires deliverance (1-46). Reminded by the Chorus of his unhappy marriages, of the deception practiced upon him by both his wives, Samson proceeds to justify each of those marriages in terms of his divine commission: they were prompted by God. The movement of Samson's first soliloquy is from his present condition to the conditions set for his life by the angel of the annunciation, then back again to his present condition. The movement of the speech (219-36) in which he responds to the complaints of the Chorus concerning his marriages is, likewise, from conditions Samson presumes to be set for his life by promptings from God to his present condition of extreme suffering, with God now departed from him.

The initial speeches of Samson and the Chorus establish what will become the preoccupation of the first two thirds of the poem: Samson's marriages. The perils of such marriages, their potentiality for stirring up tragedy, had been a chief concern in Milton's plans for various biblical dramas and, later, in his envisioning of British history. Arrayed around Samson's marriages, yet subordinated to them, are other episodes in Samson's life, some of which achieve emphasis through repeated recollection. Episodes in narrative are not equally important and, like elements in a sentence, submit to different inflections. Narrators are engaged in a process of selection that enables them to suggest through a sequence of episodes relationships between them and to achieve through repetition of some episodes certain focalizations. Not only additions to and deletions from an existing narrative, but repetitions of certain of its details enable us to disinter meanings buried in narrative discourse. In Todorov's formulation, "There are points of focalization—axes and nodes—which, strategically, dominate the rest" and which exist because narrative thrives on repetition and is, as Brooks explains, a constant "going over again of a ground already covered."[27] Very simply, events acquire meaning through repetition, which is simultaneously an effect of forward and backward motion within the narrative and a way of generating significance by imparting inflections to, and thus centering, those events. Brooks says it best: "Repetition toward recognition constitutes the truth of the narrative text."[28] Repetition is not only a

[27] See Todorov, *The Poetics of Prose*, trans. Howard, p. 239, and Brooks, *Reading for the Plot*, p. 97, and also p. 100.

[28] *Reading for the Plot*, p. 108. Brooks observes that "Repetition is one of the few factors of the text that allow a reader to see patterns of coherence, and thus at least

plotting device in narrative but a way of prognosticating its outcome.

Samson Agonistes deviates from its source, detours around certain of its episodes, but dwells on others, in this way not only reiterating but thematizing the plot of Judges. In the process, this poem turns an iterative into a reiterative narrative; it stammers with repetitions and in a way that exhibits a rhetorical organization of its narrative elements. The following episodes, many of them interconnected, appear in the poem, in this sequence:

Speaker		*Narrative Detail*	*Repetitions*
SAMSON:	1.	The annunciation of Samson's birth (23 ff)	*8*
	2.	The offering of a sacrifice by Samson's parents and the angel rising in flames (24 ff)	*2*
	3.	Samson confides God's secret to Dalila (50 ff)	*7* cf. #9
CHORUS:	4.	Samson's slaying of the lion (128 ff)	*1*
	5.	Samson's slaying of the men at Askalon (138 ff)	*3*
	6.	The jawbone episode (142 ff)	*3* cf. #24
	7.	Samson's carrying away the gates of the city (146 ff)	*1*
SAMSON:	8.	Samson confides God's secret to Dalila (201 ff)	

the incipience of meaning, and to perceive how modification works, how the idea of repetition is linked to the idea of variation, indeed how an entire narrative might be constructed on the minute variations within repetition" (p. 316), and then concludes: "repetition . . . prolongs and formalizes the middle, and also prepares the end" (p. 320).

Speaker	Narrative Detail	Repetitions
CHORUS:	9. Samson's marriages (211 ff)	9 cf. #3
SAMSON:	10. Samson's marriages (219 ff)	
	11. Samson's retiring to the rock at Etham (253 ff)	2
	12. Samson bound by the men at Judah (256 ff)	1
	13. Samson delivered to the Philistines (259 ff)	2
	14. The jawbone episode (262 ff)	
CHORUS:	15. Samson's marriages (318 ff)	
MANOA:	16. The annunciation of Samson's birth (361 ff)	
	17. Samson confides God's secret to Dalila (364 ff)	
SAMSON:	18. Samson confides God's secret to Dalila (377 ff)	
	19. Samson's marriages (382 ff)	
MANOA:	20. Samson's marriages (420 ff)	
SAMSON:	21. Samson confides God's secret to Dalila (491 ff)	
	22. The annunciation of Samson's birth (525 ff)	
	23. Samson confides God's secret to Dalila (535 ff)	
MANOA:	24. The jawbone and water miracle (581 ff)	1 cf. #6
SAMSON:	25. The annunciation of Samson's birth (634 ff)	
CHORUS:	26. Samson's marriages [Samson and Dalila] (710-1060)	
SAMSON, DALILA, CHORUS:	27. Samson's riddle (1016 ff)	3

Speaker	Narrative Detail	Repetitions
SAMSON:	28. Samson's riddle (1064)	
HARAPHA:	29. The jawbone episode (1095 ff)	
SAMSON:	30. Samson's marriages (1114 ff)	
HARAPHA:	31. The annunciation of Samson's birth (1134 ff)	
SAMSON:	32. The annunciation of Samson's birth (1140 ff)	
HARAPHA:	33. Samson delivered to the Philistines (1183 ff)	
	34. Samson's slaying of the men at Askalon (1186 ff)	
	35. The Philistines going to Etham in search of Samson (1189 ff)	
SAMSON:	36. Samson's marriages (1192 ff)	
	37. Samson's riddle (1200)	
	38. Samson's slaying of the men at Askalon (1203-04)	
	39. The annunciation of Samson's birth (1212, 1217)	
	40. Samson's confiding God's secret to Dalila (1354 ff)	
CHORUS:	41. The annunciation of Samson's birth (1431 ff)	
	42. The Spirit first rushing upon Samson (1435 ff)	1
MANOA:	43. Samson's marriages (1742 ff)	

Samson Agonistes is a poem fraught with background, with the Book of Judges providing it with compositional elements emboldened in the background of Milton's poem through repetition. Through repetition, those background elements are given clear, meaningful articulation. The murder of the thirty men at Askalon is mentioned twice and then twice drawn back into focus by the references to Samson's riddle; the slaying of a thousand men with the jawbone of an ass is alluded to three times, but is also implicit in those references to the jawbone miracle, to Samson at the rock of Etham, and to the binding and delivering of him to the Philistines. These repeated references, together with disruption of sequence to give certain of them special emphasis, suggest that the tragedy of *Samson Agonistes* subsumes, along with the tragedy of Samson's marrying, that of Samson hybristes. Indeed, this interweaving of tragedies, seemingly identified separately in Milton's Trinity manuscript, indicates that, not separate tragedies at all, these are the different aspects of a single tragedy enveloping individuals and nations alike. It is also tragedy that sits squarely on the shoulders of divine inspiration: does Samson really act by divine commission? how does he, how do we, know? These are also the questions that stand behind the reiterated episodes from Judges and that harbor an answer to the equally riddling question: why are certain episodes like Samson's firing of the foxes' tails not iterated at all, and why are others like Samson's prayer alluded to only to be eluded?

These separate citations of discrete episodes in Samson's life are emphasized still further by those generalized reflections on Samson's life as a warrior hero:

> . . . is this the man,
> That invincible *Samson*, far renown'd,
> The dread of *Israel's* foes, who with a strength
> Equivalent to Angels walk'd thir streets,
> None offering fight; who single combatant
> Duell'd thir Armies . . .
> Himself an Army . . . (340-46)

Manoa describes Samson as one "who slew'st them many a

slain" (439); Samson himself refers to such activities as "mightiest deeds / Above the nerve of mortal arm / Against the uncircumcis'd, our enemies" (638-40); and Harapha, upon encountering Samson, remembers those same deeds as defining Samson as "A Murtherer, a Revolter, and a Robber" (1180), pointing especially to Samson's

> Notorious murder on those thirty men
> At *Askalon*, who never did thee harm,
> Then like a Robber stripdst them of thir robes?
> The *Philistines*, when thou hadst broke the league,
> Went up with armed powers thee only seeking,
> To others did no violence nor spoil. (1186-91)

These verses are doubly significant, for though spoken by the blustering Harapha, his words are nonetheless a faithful rendering of the Judges story, faithful even to the inflection that story gives to the jawbone episode as casting Samson in a particularly disreputable posture in as much as it follows upon a great slaughter which Samson has already promised will end his activities as an avenger (15:7). His riddling days are supposedly past, and so too should be his days as a revenger. *Samson Agonistes* does not allow us to forget that this is a cosmos in which punishments are levied for breaches of promise. Moreover, these verses not only juxtapose two mass murders, separately but insistently referred to throughout the poem; but bringing to a period the scanning and rescanning of earlier events in Samson's life, these verses have the additional effect of juxtaposing these slaughters with the one about to be reported when Samson will hurl down the pillars, killing most of the Philistines. We are not allowed to forget, either, that man's relationship with God is figured through his relationships with other men, especially in those biblical stories about crimes and punishments.

The same set of events admits to various selections and to

different structurations, both of which depend upon the concerns of not only narrating characters but the authors who themselves produce the narrative transformations that imply, in turn, "a transformation of supposition."[29] The Judges narrative may have submitted to the construction: Samson is moved by God to do this or that. But Milton's recording of the Judges sequence, and resort to repetition of certain of its episodes, suggests a rather different construction of meaning: Samson *thinks* he is moved by God to do this or that. Such complex transformations, as Todorov remarks, are an indication of "psychic operations or the relation between an event and its representations."[30] Samson himself gathers his marriages into focus by twice alluding to his confiding God's secret to Dalila; the Chorus thereupon uses those marriages to emblematize Samson's failings; Samson then rationalizes his marriages and, in turn, accuses his countrymen of failing him. The marriages become the focus of attention, thematically as well as structurally; they are set, both at the beginning and end of the poem, within the context of divine commission and, in the end no less than in the beginning, are subjected to disapproval, even derision.

If the matter of divine sanction makes Samson's marriages a piece with the temple holocaust, the same matter interrelates three other events: the slaying of thirty men at Askalon, the slaying of a thousand more at Ramathlehi, and the slaying of many thousands—of more than he had in his life ever slain before—at the temple. The Judges narrator places the whole issue of divine authority for the temple holocaust under the seal of silence. Repeatedly we hear of the spirit of the Lord "at times" coming upon Samson—when he slays the lion for instance, or when he goes to Askalon (13:25, 14:4, 14:6, 14:19, 15:14). After "the Spirit of the LORD came mightily

[29] Todorov, *The Poetics of Prose*, trans. Howard, p. 232.
[30] *Ibid.*, p. 225.

upon him" to unbind Samson (15:14) and Samson, despite his earlier vow to engage in no more slaughtering, thereupon slays a thousand, we hear no more of divine motions leading Samson. We hear only that Samson "wist not that the LORD was departed from him" (16:20). The Judges narrator remains silent about divine motions, utters not a word about inspiration, in his reporting of the temple catastrophe and in its aftermath allows only that "In those days *there was* no king in Israel, *but* every man did *that which was* right in his own eyes" (17:6) and "*there was* no deliverer" now for Samson's people (18:28).

It has been supposed that because Samson was previously inspired he must be inspired now; it is likely that the narrator's silence here is significant, that the silence means that though once God's agent Samson acts now only as his own agent. The Judges narrative invites precisely this interpretation by having Samson recall, in the moment prior to his second fall and just before the spirit of the Lord departs from him, that "There hath not come a razor upon mine head: for I *have been* a Nazarite unto God from my mother's womb" (16:17). The irony, of course, is that he will not, as Manoah's wife expects, remain "a Nazarite to God from the womb *to the day of his death*" (13:7; my italics) but, before his death, will "become weak, and be like any *other* man" (16:17). In the Book of Judges, the angel of the annunciation is notably silent about Samson's remaining a Nazarite unto his death (cf. 13:5); and, in turn, its narrator is silent about God's returning to Samson once he has experienced his second fall.

In *Samson Agonistes*, Milton breaks the silence but not to deny the significance of the Judges account. Whatever Samson's "sense of Heav'ns desertion" (632), his last day begins with his "feel[ing] amends, / The breath of Heav'n fresh-blowing" (9-10). With prophetic irony, the Chorus now pleads that on this day God will turn Samson's "labours . . .

to peaceful end" (709). When Samson ventures to the temple, he speaks of "feel[ing] / Some rouzing motions" (1381-82); the Chorus, for its part, then remembers the time when "that Spirit . . . first rusht" on Samson (1435); and in the aftermath of the tragedy the Semichorus remarks that Samson performed his final act "With inward eyes illuminated" (1689). That is, the Samson story invites, and it had amply received, the interpretation that the Chorus and Semichorus place upon this episode; but also in his own final words, as reported by the Messenger, Samson himself disavows that interpretation:

> At last with head erect thus cryed aloud,
> Hitherto, Lords, what your commands impos'd
> I have perform'd, as reason was, obeying,
> Not without wonder or delight beheld.
> Now *of my own accord* such other tryal
> I mean to shew you of my strength, yet greater;
> As with amaze shall strike all who behold.
> This utter'd, straining all his nerves he bow'd. . . .
> (1639-46; my italics)

Samson's own words join in the pressure created by his earlier, now suspect, deeds—especially his unsanctioned second marriage and previous, and surely unauthorized, killings—to silence the notion that he here acts in his public person and in accordance with divine command. Both what Samson is made to say, and the manner in which Milton has made this poem, testify against what had become, especially during the heyday of the Civil War years, the reigning interpretation of the climactic episode in Samson's life. "Of my own accord"— these are code words, as it were, for "A private, extrajudicial arrangement"; and as the *Oxford English Dictionary* explains still further, these words mean "by one's own unsolicited assent; of one's own spontaneous motion" (61.3, 5b).

Milton worried sufficiently over Samson's motivation at the pillars that he caused earlier readers to brood over the same matter—a matter that, in the words of one of them, *"demands examination"*:

> The death of Samson I need not describe; it is a sudden, momentary, event; what can hasten or delay it, but the will of the person, who by an exertion of miraculous strength was to bury himself under the ruins of a structure . . . ? To determine that *will*, depends upon the impulse of his own spirit, or it may be upon the inspiration of Heaven: If there be any incidents in the body of the drama, which lead to this determination, and indicate an impulse, either natural or preternatural, such must be called leading incidents; and those leading incidents will constitute a middle, or, in more diffusive terms, the middle business of the drama.[31]

Richard Cumberland, the critic here cited by Todd, obviously has in mind not only Dr. Johnson's stricture, that *Samson Agonistes* has a beginning and end but no middle, but the principles of poetic architecture that lay behind Johnson's stricture:

> Whoever purposes . . . "to build the lofty rhyme," must . . . take care that his edifice be solid as well as beautiful; that nothing stand single or independant, so that it may be taken away without injuring the rest; but that from the foundation to the pinnacles one part rest firm upon another.[32]

---

[31] See *The Poetical Works of John Milton*, ed. Henry John Todd (7 vols.; London: Printed for J. Johnson, 1801), IV, 354 (my italics). Albert S. Cook observed long ago that apocalyptic tragedy refuses to be bound by the laws of the Western stage and, further, that it is less a drama than a narrative of scenes; see "Milton's View of the Apocalypse as a Tragedy," *Archiv für das Studium der Neueren Sprachen und Literaturen*, 129 (1912), 74-80.

[32] *Ibid.*, IV, 345. Dr. Johnson was not alone in thinking that *Samson* lacked a

What Johnson did not understand is that the principles of poetic art and architecture in *Samson Agonistes* derive not from Aristotle but from the narrative art of the Book of Judges— its cryptic concision, its tight structuring and paradigmatic patterning, the enormous freight of its background detail, its studied reticences, equally studied contradictions, corroding ironies, and calculated ambiguities. We are thus compelled to decipher matters of character and motive in just the way that we get at such matters in Old Testament narrative art, as Alter explains, "through a process of inference from fragmentary data, often with crucial pieces of narrative exposition strategically withheld, and this leads to multiple or sometimes even wavering perspectives on the characters."[33] This is just the sort of narrative that, if we may judge from his correspondence, Milton most admired—narrative forcing comprehension, fostering judgment but free of heavy-handed moralizing. Milton is not beyond breaking the chain of events in a historical narrative, but he also belittles doing so in order to impose maxims and judgments on the exploits recorded (VII, 501).

It should come as no surprise that in the great age of narrative art, its exegetes observe, and ascribe to Judges, a principle like that recently formulated by Peter Brooks: "prior events, causes, are so only restrospectively, in a reading back from the end." Narratives, Brooks argues, often construct their meaning "*from* that end, moving back to recover markings from the past, reconstructing the outposts of meaning along the way."[34] It is precisely this principle that guided interpretation of the Samson story through the ages, interpretation that typically reads backward from the temple holocaust to events in the midst of Samson's life, especially his marriages: whatever construction was placed upon the terminal

---

"middle"; Wordsworth concurred with him (see *The Romantics on Milton*, ed. Wittreich, p. 138).

[33] *The Art of Biblical Narrative*, p. 126.

[34] *Reading for the Plot*, pp. 29, 323.

event in Samson's life determined the interpretation given to anterior events, according to the principle, again in the words of Brooks, that narrative art at its end is always pushing us back into its middle: "to the web of the text [in order] to recapture us in its doomed energies."[35] Nor should it come as any surprise that an eminent narrative poet, even when turning to drama, should assimilate to it certain principles of narrative design, especially when that drama is itself a recasting of a narrative book. The Book of Judges is replete with repetitions whose place is the middle. Insofar as a conception of "beginning-middle-end" structures the Samson story, it does so by assuming the shape of a human life, which begins with an annunciation, continues into a middle phase of repeated failures in relationships and of repeated slayings of others, and ends (as those relationships all ended) in catastrophe. In the process, a prophecy of deliverance inaugurating Samson into life modulates into a prophecy of disaster that, issuing from the end, is anticipated by all those events locked into relationship in the midst of Samson's life. What in Judges were only distant symmetries are telescoped by Milton's poem into immediate correspondences and, more, into causal relationships.

Samson's marriages are the *leading incidents* constituting "the middle business" of Milton's poem; those marriages, the middle they constitute, are buttressed by the mass slaughters which are their consequence. These are the episodes, accentuated in *Samson Agonistes* by repetition, that must have led Milton, and should lead us, to some determination concerning Samson's impulse, whether it be "either natural or preternatural." These little cells from the Judges narrative are embedded in Milton's tragedy in such a way as to assume interpretive importance and significance. Why *they* are there—why they and not others—is suggested by Hayden White as he acknowledges that histories are not so much about events as about relation-

[35] *Ibid.*, p. 110.

ships between events, "relationships . . . not, however, im-
manent in the events themselves; . . . only in the mind of the
historian reflecting on them."[36] Milton assigns valences
through creative arrangement and repetition, with the intention not of undoing the Judges narrative but of bringing out
of concealment what is hidden therein, of rendering explicit
what is there perhaps only implicitly. After all, in the Judges
narrative infidel marriages provide a frame, an envelope, for
the individual stories. What is at the beginning and end of
the scriptural narrative is transferred to the middle of Samson's
story and occupies the middle of Milton's poem—becomes the
center of its drama. In revising the Judges narrative, resolutely
excising nonessentials, Milton creates another one, in *Samson
Agonistes* affording the Book of Judges a revisionary epilogue.

Milton omits certain details from the Judges narrative (the
foxes episode, for example) and adds others (the saving of the
vulgar from slaughter); he marginalizes some events (those
involving Samson and his Timnian bride) and centers others
that are a part of his own fiction (Samson's marriage to Dalila);
he also scans the Judges narrative first in, then out of, sequence.
Well before Roland Barthes, Milton seems to have comprehended the principle of "the chronological illusion," as well
as the "elliptic power" of narrative. Lyric poems may not lend
themselves to summary, but narrative works do: they are
"*translatable* without fundamental damage"; it is possible not
only to rupture narrative sequence but to "reduce a sequence
to its nuclei . . . without altering the meaning of the story."[37]
There may be a plurality of narratives in the Bible, and the
Samson story may itself have the capacity for generating a
plurality of narratives, but these narratives, or messages, are
also conveyed through common structures and codes.

[36] *Tropics of Discourse: Essays in Cultural Criticism* (Baltimore: The Johns Hopkins
Univ. Press, 1978), p. 94.
[37] *Image Music Text*, trans. Heath, pp. 99, 120, 121.

One effect of adding new materials to a story is to reinforce its significance, to draw out into the open what previously was hidden in the tale. Where there is a shrinking of narrative, a scrambling of its sequence, and silence about certain of its episodes, there is a correspondent juxtaposition, a new alignment of episodes now brought into proximity. Relationships are now structured into a text and imbued with meanings perceived by another (and in this instance later) historical consciousness. There is inevitably distortion here, of one text by another; but it is a distortion fashioned to disclose latent meaning. In White's words, this is positive, not negative, distortion producing an "*arrangement* of events . . . different from the chronological order of their original occurrence, so as to endow them with different functions in an integrated pattern of meaning."[38] Or put more simply: the Book of Judges presents a *plot*—that is, a chronological order to events— rearranged by Milton into a *fable*, a disordered order in which Milton presents many of the same events. The Judges arrangement of episodes becomes in *Samson Agonistes* a rearrangement, with Milton thus allowing his characters to assume, and through them assuming himself, the role of "creative narrator" over that of "passive preserver."[39]

The nonsequential, scrambled narrative embedded within *Samson Agonistes* subverts a consensus reading of the Samson story by opening it to, indeed by summoning, a fresh interpretation, and thereby reveals what a sequential reading con-

[38] *Tropics of Discourse*, p. 111. Or as White explains further: the movement is "*from* the welter of facts which have the meaningless structure of mere seriality *to* the disclosure of their putatively true or real significance as elements of a comprehensible process" (p. 112).

[39] This distinction is elaborated by Robert C. Culley in *Studies in the Structure of Hebrew Narrative* (Philadelphia: Fortress Press; Missoula: Scholars Press, 1976), p. 11, and is especially evident when we place Milton's version of the Samson story, carefully adjusted to his own politics and religion, against that of, say, Mary Astell where discrepancies abound; see *The Christian Religion as Profess'd by a Daughter of the Church of England* (London: Printed for R. Wilkin, 1705), p. 213.

ceals. "Secrets" of narrative, Kermode instructs us, "are at odds with sequence"[40]—are unfolded by an imaginative distortion of a story, by deliberate revision of it. As the order of telling shifts between the Judges story and Milton's, and as the story line becomes twisted and blurred, in the words of Nelson Goodman, "Narrative gives way to exposition."[41] *Samson Agonistes* may be cast as a tragic drama but is not, by Milton's own declaration, intended for performance. That declaration may alert us to the then current problems with censorship, but it also tells us something about the tempo of this poem, alerts us to a retardation of movement effected by an undoing of the Judges chronology and by regular repetitions. In the disordered order of Milton's poem—in what was once called its "insufficient coherency, or dependence of part on part"[42]—is a system of parenthetical reference that, moving over the events of Samson's life, and often scanning those events through a backward motion, results in the layering over of the moment when Samson goes to the pillars with a recollection of the annunciation of Samson's birth, an event insistently recalled in Milton's poem (e.g., 22-23, 361, 635, 1431), and a memory of the time when the "Spirit . . . first rusht" on Samson (1435).

The effect of such a narrative strategy, as Ricoeur explains, may be to produce a "recapitulation of the initial conditions of a course of action in its terminal consequences. In this way, the plot does not merely establish human action 'in' time, it also establishes it in memory. And memory in turn repeats— re-collects—the course of events according to an order that is the counterpart of the stretching along of time between a beginning and an end." And a concept of narrative repetition

---

[40] "Secrets and Narrative Sequence," *Critical Inquiry*, 7 (1980), 87.

[41] "Twisted Tales; or Story, Study, and Symphony," *Critical Inquiry*, 7 (1980), 119.

[42] Robert Southey, in an imaginary conversation with Walter Savage Landor, in *The Romantics on Milton*, ed. Wittreich, p. 330.

implies still more for Ricoeur: "it means the 'retrieval' of our most fundamental potentialities, as they are inherited from our own past."[43] However, as Milton uses repetition to create an alignment between the beginning and end, the past and present, of Samson's life, the effect is not of revealing a Samson realizing his potentiality as a minister of his deity but of reinforcing the point that, because of his persistence in error, Samson falls short of that potentiality.

Through his scrambling of the Judges sequence, Milton produces unexpected and emphatic juxtapositions, attendant shifts of emphasis, and jarring dramatic ironies. The beginning and end of Samson's life, his birth and death, his coming hither as a divinely anointed hero and going hence as a "secular bird" (1707) anointed in his heroism by his people—such juxtapositions rivet attention to what Samson was and now is, to what might have been fulfilled but for Samson's default. The concerns of the prologue thus persist, and are accentuated, in the epilogue to Milton's poem; those concerns, as well as Milton's strategy for representing them, are identical with those of the Judges narrator. As Milton will do, he lays "strong emphasis . . . on the call and the setting apart as a Nazarite, a special instrument which Jahweh intends to use." Yet as von Rad discerns, "this prehistory of Samson's life puts to the reader what is the real problem of the Samson story; for anyone who comes from the pious story of the call . . . must be astounded by the whirlwind of very unspiritual adventures in which Samson gets lost. . . . the stories about Samson . . . show the failure of a charismatic leader, and divine powers wasted. . . . Samson himself perishes in the chaos which he spreads out around himself."[44]

Milton gathers up the separate and sometimes distorted fragments of the Samson story by way of reconstituting that

[43] "Narrative Time," *Critical Inquiry*, 7 (1980), 183.
[44] *Old Testament Theology*, I, 333-34.

story, and does so in such a way as to subordinate the gathered parts to the reconstructed whole. New to Milton's version of the Samson story, which arrays all other episodes of Samson's life around a supposed second marriage and the temple holocaust, such juxtapositions also establish a causal relationship between that marriage and the final catastrophe. As G. Wilson Knight notices, "*Comus* studied sexual energies; *Paradise Lost* and *Paradise Regained* the power impulse. *Samson Agonistes* relates the one to the other."[45] Indeed, Milton magnifies both these elements by presenting Samson, in contradiction to Scripture, as wedded to Dalila and by his then withholding the revenge motive from Samson until the Philistines are slain so as to underscore that motive. In *Samson Agonistes*, Milton has interwoven personal and political matters so completely, and so effectively, that Samson's marriages are made to be a piece with the hurling down of the pillars—are made so by virtue of the fact that each discrete episode had been explained, and could be excused, as a prompting from God. Yet, as Christopher Hill observes, once we begin to question if Samson's marriages are divinely sanctioned, we must also ask, "how certain [can we] be that the destruction of the Philistines at the end of the play was really inspired by God?"[46] *Samson Agonistes* provokes just this kind of questioning, repeatedly inviting us to see divine intention subordinated to private desire.

Samson's own community, represented by the Chorus, was

---

[45] *The Golden Labyrinth: A Study of British Drama* (New York: W. W. Norton, 1962), p. 126. With reference to *Paradise Lost*, Maureen Quilligan speaks of "interconnections between sexual intimacy and political destiny—interconnections that are causal"; see *Milton's Spenser: The Politics of Reading* (Ithaca: Cornell Univ. Press, 1983), p. 152.

[46] *Milton and the English Revolution* (New York: Viking Press, 1977), p. 433. Kermode comments appositely: *Samson Agonistes* is "an heroic examination of all such intimate impulses," although Kermode's conclusions concerning that examination are different from my own; see "Milton in Old Age," *Southern Review*, 11 (1975), 529.

no less dismayed than Manoa by his marriage choices, which, according to Samson, were "motion'd . . . of God; I knew / From intimate impulse, and therefore urg'd / The Marriage on" (222-24). Moreover, Samson argues the lawfulness of his second marriage in terms of the lawfulness of his first, a matter that Manoa disputes: ". . . thou didst plead / Divine impulsion . . . / I state not that" (421-24). No one who remembers Gideon's caution concerning divine inspiration, his repeated testing of God to determine its validity, can help but join Manoa in questioning Samson here, or later in his feeling some rousing motion and thereupon going forth to the temple.

In the Book of Judges, Gideon establishes a standard of mindful deliberation concerning divinely sanctioned deliverance:

> And Gideon said unto God, If thou wilt save Israel by mine hand, as thou has said,
>
> Behold, I will put a fleece of wool in the floor, *and* if the dew be on the fleece only, and *it be* dry upon all the earth *beside*, then shall I know that thou wilt save Israel by mine hand, as thou hast said.
>
> And it was so: for he rose up early on the morrow, and thrust the fleece together, and wringed the dew out of the fleece, a bowl full of water.
>
> And Gideon said unto God, Let not thine anger be hot against me, and I will speak but this once: let me prove, I pray thee, but this once with the fleece; let it now be dry only upon the fleece, and upon all the ground let there be dew.
>
> And God did so that night: for it was dry upon the fleece only, and there was dew on all the ground. (6:36-40)

Samson's "this once" prayer differs decidedly from Gideon's. Nowhere in Judges, or in Milton's poem, does Samson, like

Gideon, reflect upon his commission or attempt, again like Gideon, to validate it. Samson presumes what Gideon, only after much affliction, is able to assume and, furthermore, seems to be taking his lead from a god both petty and jealous whose "important cause" (1379) is Samson's forte, human slaughter.

The allegedly regenerate, or partly regenerate, Samson remains even at the end committed to "the trial of mortal fight" (1175)—is unpossessed of the truth that contradictions of their own deity, the gods cannot be. Here especially, as Stanley Fish remarks, "the reader who remembers the history of Samson's 'rousing motions' may be wary of labelling these new motions 'of God'. Samson himself is a conservative on the question. If there is aught of presage in the mind, he says, allowing for the possibility that there is not; and his parting words are a forest of qualifications."[47] Yet it is less what Samson says than what he does that matters in this poem, a principle of valuation articulated by Samson himself: "The deeds themselves . . . [speak] loud the dooer" (248).

The protagonist in this tragedy does not speak univocally; his words, too often perhaps, are "found contradicting" (301). Samson justifies his questionable marriages to the Chorus in terms of a single motive: neither marriage is a manifestation of real love; both provide but an occasion against the Philistines and thus are a devious means to an honorable end. Samson knows full well, and later tells Dalila, that love provides "other reasonings" and brings forth "other deeds" from marriages (875); he even suggests that motives in marrying provide a means for distinguishing among, and valuing, different moral characters. Samson now claims to marry honorably—out of love—and attributes to Dalila the ignoble motive, the false and unnatural pretext, of marrying to further her country over Samson, her God over Samson's (882-902). Dalila here argues

---

[47] "Question and Answer in *Samson Agonistes*," in *"Comus" and "Samson Agonistes": A Casebook*, ed. Julian Lovelock (London: Macmillan, 1975), p. 233.

as earlier Samson had done, "that to the public good / Private respects must yield . . . / Vertue . . . , truth, duty so enjoyning" (867-870), with Samson this time putting forth the case for "Private respects" (867-70). Encountering Harapha, he will revert to his initial posture, putting forth Dalila's arguments this time as his own: "I was no private . . . person" (1211). Perceived by the Messenger in the poem's catastrophe as "a public servant," Samson himself claims to act "of my own accord," as a private person, in hurling down the pillars (1615, 1643). Earlier, Samson had excoriated the Woman of Timna for proving false and being a traitor (382-91); only in the exchange with Harapha do we learn, again from Samson, of the extenuating circumstance, that "ill-meaning Politician Lords / . . . threatening cruel death constrain'd the bride / To wring from me and tell to them my secret" (1195, 1198-99). The Timnian bride is not so much false as corrupted by others to be false to Samson. In their form, and in their substance, the two marriages are made to mirror one another even as they reveal Samson's own true character.

From commentators on Judges, we hear that Samson's acts are authorized only if they are performed in his public person; from Milton's Samson we hear doubletalk. In the same breath that he remarks, "I a private person . . . presum'd / Single Rebellion and did Hostile Acts," he also reports: "I was no private but a person rais'd / With strength sufficient and command from Heav'n / To free my Countrey" (1208-1213). *Strength sufficient* here cuts against the *grace sufficient* of Milton's truly heroic poetry; and the implicit suggestion that he may act as a public person curls into irony when we remember that this is the explicit reason cited by Dalila for her betrayal of Samson: "to the public good / Private respects must yield . . . duty so enjoyning" (867-70), and remember further that the operative phrase in Samson's own explanation for what he finally does to the Philistines is *of my own accord*. Samson goes to the temple feeling "Some rouzing motions" which dispose his thoughts to something extraordinary (1382). He is perceived by others as a hero who, "With inward eyes illuminated," acts after "His fierie vertue [has been] rouz'd" (1689-90); yet he perceives himself, and so forces us to perceive him, as hurling down the pillars of his own accord. In *Samson Agonistes*, no less than in Judges, there is awkward interplay between verbal formulas and situations they do not fit, between claims made by, and for, Samson and the counterclaims by which such earlier claims are stilled. There is in Milton's poem "a tension," even perhaps "an absolute contradiction," such as Alter finds in Old Testament narrative, "between election and moral character"; yet as Alter explains, "it is important for a writer to leave this tension under a shadow of ambiguity in order to suggest a complex sense of . . . the private person and public man."[48] It is just this complex sense of character, at the very heart of *Samson*, that has eluded its interpreters.

Not only are voices found contradicting one another in *Samson Agonistes*, but there are contending perspectives here as well: Manoa's and the Chorus's with Samson's view of his marriages, Samson's avowal of divine instinct with their questioning it, their wresting a comic pattern from a life represented by Milton as a tragedy, and this story of Samson's tragic defeat vying with that of the triumphant Jesus in *Paradise Regained*, a poem published between the same covers as *Samson* and as a companion piece (of sorts) to this tragedy. Not what happens but our managed perception of what happens declares this poem to be a tragedy, and Milton manages our perception in such a way as to implicate not only himself but us in Samson's

---

[48] *The Art of Biblical Narrative*, pp. 117-18. Omitting crucial details from Milton's poem, Joan S. Bennett, addressing this very issue, attenuates it; see " 'A Person Rais'd': Public and Private Cause in *Samson Agonistes*," *Studies in English Literature*, 18 (1978), 155-68.

tragedy. In this version of the Samson story, we are made to see that things are not exactly as our previous experience may have led us to suppose, that Milton's version of this story *is* different from that of certain of his contemporaries and different, too, from the version of tragedy attributed to Milton's story by most of our contemporaries.

One way of managing our perceptions is through type-scenes which can be invoked or aborted, deflected or developed, either for purposes of characterization or for rhetorical advantages. By way of illustrating how such scenes can be both deflected and aborted, can be used both to further character development and to advantage an argument, Alter cites two examples—the annunciation scene and the betrothal scene—from the Samson narrative in Judges. At a time when the Samson typology was crumbling, when other correspondences between Samson and Christ were becoming increasingly suspect, the similarity evident in their respective annunciation scenes continued to attest to "how exactly parallel"[49] these figures actually are, although this similarity also contained a difference: Samson commences the deliverance that only Christ, the true deliverer, can complete. Samson's annunciation scene, that is, exemplifies "the slight, disturbing dissonance produced when in a pattern of repetition some ambiguous phrase is substituted for a more reassuring one":

> When, for example, Manoah's wife (Judges 13) is told by the angel that she will conceive and bear a son, she repeats almost all the terms of the divine promise word for word to her husband, but she significantly changes the final phrase of the annunciation. The angel has said, "The lad will be a Nazarene to God from the womb, and he will begin

[49] Thomas Goodwin, "Of Christ the Mediator," in *The Complete Works of Thomas Goodwin*, ed. John C. Miller and Robert Halley (12 vols.; Edinburgh: James Nichol; London: James Nisbet, 1861-66), V, 152-53.

to save Israel from the Philistines" (Judg. 13:5). In her repetition, the future mother of Samson concludes, "The lad will be a Nazarene to God from the womb to the day of his death" (Judg. 13:7). It is surely a little unsettling that the promise which ended with the liberation—though, pointedly, only the *beginning* of liberation—of Israel from its Philistine oppressors now concludes with no mention of "salvation" but instead with the word "death." From the womb to the day of death is, of course, a proverbial and neutral way of saying "all his life." In context, however, the woman's silence on the explicit promise of political salvation and the counterpoising of the three-word phrase, *'ad-yom moto*, to the day of his death, against the echo of the whole clause on the lad's future career as a liberator, turn the substituted phrase into an implicit commentary on the prophecy and restore to that final "death" a hint of its independent negative force. The absence of salvation in the wife's version would seem to be underscored when Manoah subsequently questions the angel about "what will be the regimen for the lad and his deeds." The angel, after all, has already given the answer to both parts of the question in his words to Manoah's wife, but the crucial information about the child's future deeds was deleted from her report to Manoah. In sum, the dissonance of a single phrase subtly sets the scene for a powerful but spiritually dubious savior of Israel who will end up sowing as much destruction as salvation.[50]

Milton capitalizes on this supposition by doubling the repetitions as if to reinforce just this interpretation.

[50] *The Art of Biblical Narrative*, p. 101.

In *Samson Agonistes*, however, the dissonance of phrase is also of another sort. In Judges, the angel of the Lord apprises Samson's mother that her son "shall *begin* to deliver Israel out of the hand of the Philistines" (13:5; my italics). In *Samson*, on the other hand, remembering that his birth was twice foretold by an angel, Milton's protagonist aggrandizes the message accompanying that annunciation: "Promise was that I / Should *Israel* from *Philistian* yoke deliver" (38-39). The promise of a partial deliverance is represented by Samson, at least initially (cf. 225), as a full one; he and others insistently observe the irony of "this great Deliverer . . . / Eyeless in *Gaza* at the Mill with slaves" (40-41) himself being in need of deliverance: "For this did the Angel twice descend" (361), Manoa asks bitterly. Only in the first and seventh of the eight references to the annunciation is Samson's birth explicitly and, as it happens, exaggeratedly, associated with his mission of deliverance. In the other references, the emphasis falls initially upon the irony of the deliverer's requiring deliverance (361), and thereupon on the likely reasons for Samson's failure as a deliverer (525-26, 634-35)—on his feigning a role that only tardily does the Chorus think may be legitimate (1135 ff. and 1431 ff.). What comes into focus here is not so much Samson's misconception of the extent of the deliverance he should accomplish, but his more radical misconception of how any such deliverance will finally be accomplished, in Samson's opinion through the "acts indeed heroic" of an earthly warrior who is "admir'd of all and dreaded / On hostile ground" (530-31; cf. 638-40). In comparison with *Samson Agonistes*, interestingly, the Book of Judges says very little, within his story proper, about Samson as a deliverer. Not until 15:18 is the theme of deliverance reintroduced to the Samson story, and then in such a way as to focus the irony that Milton's own poem expounds: that Samson himself is continually in need of some great deliverance.

Milton not only plays his own themes and variations upon biblical type-scenes, but out of the biblical materials he creates his own type-scenes which analogously, by alteration or suppression of detail, communicate with his audience. For example, there is the episode, three times repeated in *Samson Agonistes*, involving Samson's slaying of a thousand men with the jawbone of an ass, an episode that in the Judges narrative succeeds Samson's act of retaliation against the Philistines for murdering his wife, no less than his promise, "yet will I be avenged of you, and after that I will cease" (15:7). This "great slaughter" (15:8) is nevertheless followed by the slaying of a thousand men with a jawbone—an episode, again in the Judges narrative, that is inextricably involved with a miracle. After this great slaughter, Samson, "sore athirst," calls upon God for water, and God, in turn, "clave an hollow place that *was* in the jaw, and there came water thereout" (15:18-19). The miracle, which in Judges seems to provide sanction for this second massacre, though referred to in Milton's poem, is never mentioned within the context of that slaughter. We only hear from Manoa, with no reference to the circumstance, that "God . . . caus'd a fountain at thy prayer / From the dry ground to spring, thy thirst to allay / After the brunt of battel" (581-83). To the consternation of some commentators, Samson's prayer here, which, given the miracle in which he has just participated, ought to be one of thanksgiving is instead one of petition. Milton's divorcing of the water miracle from the jawbone miracle becomes an artful form of questioning, of raising suspicions in *Samson Agonistes*. In this way, Milton makes of the jawbone episode his own version of the type-scene, driving it into consciousness through the frequency of repetition and using the very repetition to divest the episode of the moral authority previously used to sanction it.

Yet even as Milton brings together a number of episodes such as the slaying of the lion and then the men at Askalon,

Samson's murdering of a thousand and then of many thousand more, to form his own version of a type-scene, he does so in such a way as to make those type-scenes a piece with the miracle type-scenes in the Bible. All these episodes share the motif of a divine commission, which makes of the ensuing action a miracle. But what is striking about the miracle type-scenes as they are advanced in the Judges narrative, and then accentuated in Milton's poem, is that they constitute so obvious a transgression from the usual miracle story and its paradigmatic structure, wherein a seemingly insurmountable problem is resolved through divine intervention, often through a human agent. As Robert Culley defines this pattern: a problem is delineated and, owing to divine intervention, resolved.[51] Sometimes the miracle brings help and other times punishment; it may alleviate suffering, or impose it as retribution on those who would subvert the divine plan. The miracle may be private, enabling a blind man to see or bringing a dead man back to life but, more typically, is performed to advance a public cause and achieve a public good: the feeding of the hungry multitudes, the cleansing of the waters or a diseased land. The type-scenes in *Samson Agonistes* are of a wholly different order. They record an unprovoked, unnecessary destruction that instead of alleviating problems multiplies them; instead of being executed against those who defy God's laws, they are executed by one who is regularly defying those laws, the consequence of which, always, is that Samson and his people are moved into greater servitude, with Samson himself at the end of his story standing before his people as a prisoner, blind and in chains.

Equally relevant to Milton's strategies in *Samson Agonistes* is the way in which he aborts the betrothal scene, again in the manner of the Judges narrator:

---

[51] *Studies in the Structure of Hebrew Narrative*, pp. 69-115.

At the beginning of his adventures, Samson goes down to Philistine Timnath, and so we have a young hero on foreign soil, but there is no well, no ritual of hospitality. Instead he sees a woman he wants, promptly returns home, and brusquely announces to his parents that he expects them to arrange the marriage for him. Grudgingly, they accompany him back to Timnath for the betrothal negotiations, and on the way he encounters a lion that he tears limb from limb. The awesome destruction of the lion, and the subsequent scooping out of honey from the lion's bleached carcass, may even be a pointed substitution for the more decorous and pacific drawing of water from the well. In any event, the impetuous rush of Samson's career is already communicated in his impatient movement from seeing a woman to taking her without the ceremonious mediation of a betrothal type-scene, and we all know what calamities the marriage itself will engender.[52]

In *Samson Agonistes*, there is the pointed transference of the detail of Samson tearing the lion to his encounter with Dalila, whom Samson now threatens to tear limb from limb. The set of expectations created by such type-scenes is frustrated in the Judges narrative and altogether broken in Milton's poem.

Milton must have recognized what his critics often fail to notice, that the aborting of the inspiration theme when Samson goes to the temple is consonant with the analogous strategy in the Judges narrative of aborting, once the Samson story commences, the large structural pattern into which individual stories have hitherto been woven. Samson's story begins with the frequently repeated words, "And the children of Israel did evil again in the sight of the LORD" (13:1; cf. 2:11; 3:12; 4:1;

[52] Alter, *The Art of Biblical Narrative*, pp. 61-62.

6:1; 10:6). For the first time, however, the other repeated elements in the original formula are disregarded, expunged:

(1) And the anger of the LORD was hot against Israel.
   . . . (2:14, 3:8, 10:7)
(2) . . . they were greatly distressed . . . the children of Israel cried unto the LORD. . . . (2:15, 3:9, 4:3, 6:6, 10:10)
(3) . . . the LORD raised up judges, which delivered them out of the hand of those that spoiled them. (2:16; 3:9, 15; 4:4; 6:8-13; 10:11-18; 11:1).

This or that element is occasionally eliminated from the formula, and progressively the last item, which provides the assurance of a deliverer, is expanded to include a rebuke:

> I brought you up from Egypt, and brought you forth out of the house of bondage;
> And I delivered you out of the hand of the Egyptians, and out of the hand of all that oppressed you. . . .
> And I said unto you, I *am* the LORD your God . . . but ye have not obeyed my voice. (6:8-10)
> And the LORD said unto the children of Israel, *Did* not *I deliver you* from the Egyptians, and from the Amorites, from the children of Ammon, and from the Philistines?
> . . . ye cried to me, and I delivered you out of their hand.
> Yet ye have forsaken me, and served other gods: wherefore I will deliver you no more. . . .
> And the children of Israel said unto the LORD, We have sinned: do thou unto us whatsoever seemeth good unto thee; deliver us only, we pray thee, this day. (10:11-15)

The Lord responds to this plea first with Jephthah, later with Samson; now the pattern commencing, "And the children of Israel did evil again in the sight of the LORD" (13:1), initiates the Samson story. But here there is no mention of the Lord's becoming hot with anger: he simply departs from Samson but not before unbinding him. No longer the people, now it is Samson who cries out to the Lord, always pleading without ever repenting, and who promises that he will mend his ways, cease from slaughtering the enemy, if only granted the pleasure of vengeance one more time. The prayer of the Israelites, "deliver us only, we pray thee, this day" (10:15), is replicated in Samson's prayer at the pillars, "only this once" (16:28). Delineating and redelineating God's plot for history, the Book of Judges demonstrates how that plot is repeatedly subverted by man's plot—how the divine comedy is made to roll over again and again into human tragedy.

The prophetic books of Scripture tend to highlight the pattern of fall and redemption, destruction and creation that would later be inscribed within the church liturgy; that is, they foster the idealisms that the historical books, even those with a prophetic purpose, often frustrate. In the Book of Judges, and especially in its Samson story, we witness Samson's fumbling of his redemptive role. It has been said that "Restoration, not blind repetition, was the proper direction for history to take, a linear route that ended in Zion and that depended entirely on man's contractual agreement with God"[53]—a remark that, incidentally, enables us to view repetition in *Samson Agonistes* as a symbolic, thematic device as well. Through the stammering repetitions in this poem, Milton enunciates the aberrant movement of history figured in the Samson story and elucidates the history of his own times through the Judges paradigm, thus showing the extent to which secular history still accords with sacred paradigms.

[53] David Roskies, *Against the Apocalypse: Responses to Catastrophe in Modern Jewish Culture* (Cambridge, Mass.: Harvard Univ. Press, 1984), p. 22.

In the figure of Samson, we see all of Israel "knit together as one man" (20:11). There is in *Samson Agonistes*, no less than in the Book of Judges, the Foucauldian perception that the histories of various cultures contain "another, more radical, history, that of man himself—. . . . At a very deep level, there exists a historicity of man which is itself its own history but also the radical dispersion that provides a foundation for all other histories."[54] The plot of collective history exhibits a dependency upon the plotting of individual biographies. The Samson biography gathers into itself Israelite history—the ironies of that history, its broken patterns and dispiriting failures. His is a life that repeats not the cycle of petition, intervention, and deliverance, but the breaking of such a circle by revealing the reasons for God's departure from history— by explaining why, in the aftermath of Samson's tragedy, the Israelites find themselves with "no deliverer" (18:28). It is this aborted history—personal and social—that constitutes the tragedy of Milton's poem, a poem that, instead of miring history in tragedy, seems to cry out to mankind, as the Judges narrative earlier cries out, "Awake, awake . . . : / awake, awake, utter a song: arise . . . and lead thy captivity captive" (5:12).

The Book of Judges, it appears, holds certain keys for unlocking the artistic strategies of *Samson Agonistes*. Within its context we may view Milton's transgressions of his source as a way of transcending its letter in order to observe its true spirit. Like the Judges narrator, Milton strikes a dramatic relationship with his materials, putting his own against a more primitive value system, and further stresses the implications of this strategy by juxtaposing an Old against a New Testament

[54] Michel Foucault, *The Order of Things: An Archeology of the Human Sciences* (New York: Pantheon Books, 1970), p. 370.

story, Samson's tragedy against the triumph of Jesus, the story of a partial or failed against that of a full deliverance. What is figured in Judges as the evolution of religion is formulated in Milton's tragedy, and through the juxtaposition of that tragedy with *Paradise Regained*, as an evolution of consciousness that Milton hoped to effect in the aftermath of a failed Revolution. The brief epic and tragedy together show the idealism and the actuality facing one another, in a volume that would adjust Milton's Englishmen to broken expectations by anatomizing their failures and in a way that distances apocalypse into the future without denying the prospect and promise of a better future. If *Samson Agonistes* shows the world closing down in tragedy, *Paradise Regained* shows how life may rise up again from those ruins, reminding us that tragedy played beyond the fifth act can modulate into comedy, that the dark and cheerless world of tragedy, its world of death, is played out under the blaze of the noonday sun. What so complicates *Samson Agonistes* is its dramatic form, which denies the opportunity for an authorial viewpoint like that afforded by Milton's epics. There is a consequent tendency to confuse the participants' "vision" and "point of view" with Milton's, to identify as one viewpoints that ought to be held at a distance. Samson continually rationalizes his behavior in the very terms used by some of Milton's contemporaries to legitimate that same behavior. The relationship between Milton and Samson, so often perceived as an identity, is perhaps better conceived of in terms of the relationship between analyst and analysand. As Genette remarks, "The role of the analyst is not to be satisfied with the rationalizations, nor to be ignorant of them," but to examine the personality and motives implicit in them.[55]

Paradise Regained and *Samson Agonistes*—the one an epic narrative, the other a dramatic poem—by virtue of their ge-

[55] *Narrative Discourse*, trans. Levin, p. 158.

neric difference afford and reward decidedly different claims to truth. The prophetic narrator of epic can cajole and guide, is an expositor of meanings that in drama come only inferentially, and then must be expounded by the audience—or this is usually the case. Here though, Milton pairs poems and, by a startling subordination (PARADISE REGAIN'D . . . To which is added *Samson Agonistes*), brings the one poem within the perspective of the other for the purpose of interpretation. *Paradise Regained* parses the meaning of, affords interpretive glosses on, *Samson Agonistes*, its prophetic narrator and prophet-hero imparting a finer tone to the claims and counterclaims of the fallen participants in Milton's tragedy. That is, *Paradise Regained* and *Samson Agonistes* relate to one another as do the narrative and dialogic elements in the Old Testament where, as Alter explains, "the perspective of the narrative . . . directs our attention back to the speakers, to the emphases they choose, the ways their statements may diverge from the narrator's authoritative report of what occurs."[56] The catastrophe at the pillars is *narrated* by a Messenger whose report differs markedly from the constructions placed upon it by Manoa and the Chorus. What Manoa and the Chorus may say of Samson is at odds with what they were saying earlier; they now credit him with divine inspiration, Samson's earlier claims to which they were once busy discrediting. In turn, attitudes assumed, values expressed by Samson, as well as by the Chorus, collide with those articulated by Jesus, as well as by the narrator in *Paradise Regained*. The brief epic confirms suspicions raised by the dialogue within the tragedy; it confounds, even contravenes, certain of assertions in *Samson*, and thus functions in relation to this tragedy much as narrative analogues—let us say as the respective stories of Gideon and Samson—do in Judges, with one part of the text jostling with another part,

[56] *The Art of Biblical Narrative*, p. 65.

as is the case in the 1671 poetic volume where one poem offers a corrective voice to the other.

When viewed in relation to its sourcebook, *Samson Agonistes* exhibits superimpositions and silences, a multiplication of certain episodes through repetition and a muting, sometimes even a mutilation of others, all of which strategies draw out meaning from, without damaging, the scriptural text. The narrative reports by characters in *Samson* yield to the authority of the Judges narrator as they also yield to the authority of Jesus in *Paradise Regained*. It may be sheer coincidence that the emergence of a new, immensely refined biblical hermeneutic is contemporaneous with the rise of the novel; and the emergence of that hermeneutic, as Kermode proposes following Hans Frei, is certain evidence that biblical scholarship had to invent such a hermeneutic: *it became necessary*, because "scriptural narrative could no longer be regarded as simple historical report, nor as simply 'given'." A theory of interpretation was now required, a consequence perhaps of poems like *Paradise Regained* and *Samson Agonistes* which reveal the paucity of existing, often typologically determined, interpretations of both Old and New Testament narratives—of interpretations rendered inadequate by restrictive hermeneutic codes that speak paradoxically of the inexhaustibility of the same text's meanings. In his early prose writings, Milton had challenged the Church; in his last poems, he challenges the Church's institutionalized readings of Scripture. Milton's last poems amply illustrate Kermode's statement that "poets continue the more inventive tradition of the apocryphal gospels. They rewrite stories, as the evangelists did and as the exegete must not. They place them in new contexts of story . . . , making them fit other genres."[57] Milton's poems at once unfold the secrets of biblical narrative and pluralize its meaning.

[57] *The Art of Telling*, pp. 124-25, 160, 191.

What we have seen, moreover, is that the secrets of narrative are enfolded not only in its reticences but in its repetitions—in its reiteration of verbal elements, its rehearsal of episodes, even in its redaction of motifs from one episode within another or from one plot within another. Thus Samson's threat to Dalila, that he will tear her limb from limb, recalls his earlier rending of the lion; and the atrocities he visits upon his enemies[58] recall those with which the Judges narrative begins (the men of Judah cutting off the thumbs and toes of their enemies) and those with which it ends (the dismemberment of the concubine)—events that make Jahweh's intervention in history necessary, not to aid and abet the Israelites but to make them cease and desist. Not just reticences but repetitions are deeply involved in biblical narratives and hence in the fictions of Milton's poem.

With regard to repetition, J. Hillis Miller traces its history in Western culture to the classics and to the Bible, especially to the latter's typological hermeneutic, which sees in the New Testament a repetition, in a finer tone, of the events and persons of the Old. Opaque similarities, hidden differences—Christian tradition postulates the former; classical tradition, the latter. And yet these very different forms of repetition often converge upon the same text, often with the objective of displacing similarities with differences. As Miller explains, "Each form of repetition calls up the other. . . . The second is not the negation or opposite of the first, but its 'counterpart,' in a strange relation whereby the second is the subversive ghost

[58] John M'Clintock and James Strong include this telling note on Samson's revenge against the Philistines once his wife and father-in-law have been burned alive: "The original, strictly rendered, runs, 'he smote them leg upon thigh'—apparently a proverbial expression, and implying, according to Gesenius, that he cut them to pieces so that their limbs—their legs and thighs—were scattered and heaped promiscuously together; equivalent to saying that he smote and destroyed them *wholly, entirely*" (*Cyclopaedia of Biblical, Theological, and Ecclesiastical Literature* [12 vols.; 1880; rpt. Grand Rapids: Baker Book House, 1970], IX, 313).

of the first, always already present within it as a possibility which hollows it out." We witness just this process of subversion in the shifts that occur within the Samson typologies of the sixteenth and seventeenth centuries, which, in turn, are reflected in Milton's poem, where identities are observed only to mark differences whether in the predicated relationship between Samson and Christ or in the postulated identity of Samson and Milton. As Miller goes on to say, repetitions may recoil upon themselves, suggesting not that history, individual and otherwise, repeats itself but that, actually, nothing really repeats itself: "each person, event, or thing remains stubbornly closed in on itself, as itself."[59] Milton is no more Samson than Milton's England is the world of—and under—the Old Dispensation. Repetition that marks differences is a device for demystification and eventuates in the exposure of illusion.

It is only after we have reviewed the historical record—the flattened legend of Samson, its very different versions and contextualizations during the Renaissance, and that age's efforts to render this story ambiguous—only then are we able to understand that Milton undertakes in *Samson Agonistes* to restore the jagged edges to the Samson story. He does so in the belief that such legends, stubbornly irreducible finally, have many aspects (social and psychological, religious, ethical, and political) all of which are integral parts of their meaning. The history of exegesis, Jewish and Christian—and especially the history of exegesis accruing to the Samson legend—mirrors the tendency to twist Scripture in order to reinterpret and accommodate it to emerging beliefs and new realities. As exegesis becomes increasingly preoccupied with the study of transmission it also becomes progressively removed from the

[59] *Fiction and Repetition: Seven English Novels* (Cambridge, Mass.: Harvard Univ. Press, 1982), pp. 9, 13.

text itself which, in the seventeenth century, would be for many no more than a transparency through which to look at the story of Jesus. Milton reverses hermeneutical practices and exegetical premises, in *Samson Agonistes* contributing to the deconstruction of the Samson legend of his own time, with the intention apparently of restoring that legend to what it was in the Book of Judges—with the intention of reconstituting it and of then using it to reconstruct history. *Samson Agonistes* is, though not in the sense that Georgia Christopher means, "an 'opened' version of Old Testament history."[60] Through his poem, Milton would disentangle from the scriptural text, as Ricoeur might say, its "implicit 'project' for existence" and "indirect 'proposition' of new modes of being."[61]

Samson Agonistes shows Milton pushing beyond the minimal scriptural narratives of his own time that had been generated out of different Samson typologies. The narrative discourse in *Samson Agonistes* is created by the expansion, transformation, and sometimes effacement of elements in the Judges story. As early as Josephus, the account in Judges, which represents Delilah as summoning others to cut off Samson's locks, is altered so that now Delilah herself clips Samson's hair. It has been argued, quite cogently, that Delilah is the real subject of the Judges narrative, which, charting "a paradigm of woman's wickedness" subsequently accentuated by children's versions of this story, "is a *mise en abyme* . . . , an iconic sign of tensions in the whole Bible."[62] Milton's version of this story magnifies those tensions while, in a turn of the lens, it also focuses on the character of Samson, the ambiguities of his character now accentuated through implanted contradictions.

If such tensions are hidden in the Judges narrative by Sam-

---

[60] *Milton and the Science of the Saints* (Princeton: Princeton Univ. Press, 1982), p. 230.

[61] *Essays on Biblical Interpretation*, ed. Mudge, p. 35.

[62] Mieke Bal, "The Rhetoric of Subjectivity," *Poetics Today*, 5 (1984), 347, 371.

son's silence, by his unaccountability for the events in which he participates, in *Samson Agonistes* his silence is broken and, as the narrative discourse turns upon him, he is made accountable for his actions through the contradictions implanted within contending perspectives on, alternative versions of what Samson does and why he does it. The weight of tradition may be felt in the repeated contention that divine commission prompts Samson to hurl down the pillars, but that tradition also comes under challenge in the Messenger's contention that what Samson does he does of his own accord. In reporting the catastrophe at the pillars, the Messenger introduces, as another messenger has introduced to the Oedipus story, an unresolved and unresolvable contradiction. In the story of Oedipus, the burden of guilt he carries for murdering his father is incompatible with the Messenger's report (and he is the only witness) that Laius was murdered by a band of thieves. Correspondingly, in *Samson Agonistes* the divine instinct that supposedly impels Samson to hurl down the pillars (the usual construction placed upon this crucial episode) is incompatible with the report of the Messenger (again the only witness to the action) that Samson acts of his own accord. As with the Oedipus story, so with Milton's redaction of the Samson legend: the only witness proffers an interpretation of events incompatible with the interpretation toward which the protagonist directs us. More than just throwing into question "the possibility of a coherent, noncontradictory account of narrative," the narrative embedments in *Samson Agonistes* affirm Jonathan Culler's proposition that narrative art sits on contradiction, and the contradiction manifests itself "in a moment that seems either superfluous—a loose end . . .—or too neat."[63] By Milton,

---

Barbara Herrnstein Smith very kindly insisted that I read this essay before publishing this chapter.

[63] Jonathan Culler, *The Pursuit of Signs: Semiotics, Literature, Deconstruction* (1981; rpt. Ithaca: Cornell Univ. Press, 1983), pp. 175, 178.

seemingly *neat* readings of the Samson story are exposed as having altogether too many loose ends.

In the complicated relationship it assumes with the Judges narrative, *Samson Agonistes* is a challenge to thought and rams the Samson story with life. Yet as Mary Ann Radzinowicz allows, "when Milton recast the biblical story," projecting in form what he perceived to be latent in content, he did so not only to confirm the biblical narrative but "to challenge the preconceptions of his day."[64] Many biblical stories persisted in their popularity during Milton's time; but some of them, like the Samson story, carried an enormous freight of often various—and variously restricted—interpretation. Milton seizes upon the Samson story at a crucial moment in the history of its transmission: when, however popular this story may have been, because of trite interpretation it was also in a phase of deterioration, engaged in a process of "stuttering forgetfulness," its meaning now undergoing further corruption.[65]

Milton may create a counter-narrative—not to destroy but to subvert and thereby open an existing one. In the process, what Roland Barthes calls "the obtuse" is allowed to rise up against what had come to seem "the obvious" meaning of the Samson story.[66] Milton's scrambling of the Judges narrative, his scanning and rescanning of certain of its elements, the attendant repetitions, as well as the focalization of the tableau with Samson at the pillars—these are all devices for jamming the inherited meaning of the Samson story, especially its political meaning, and for transferring that meaning into "a *different* politics." Milton's new script registers its own truth, even while representing what others had construed to be the

[64] *Toward "Samson Agonistes": The Growth of Milton's Mind* (Princeton: Princeton Univ. Press, 1978), pp. 3, 6.

[65] The process, captured in a phrase borrowed from Gyula Ortutay, is finely delineated by Culley, *Studies in the Structure of Hebrew Narrative*, p. 2.

[66] *The Responsibility of Forms: Critical Essays on Music, Art, and Representation*, trans. Richard Howard (New York: Hill and Wang, 1985), pp. 45-59.

truth of the Judges narrative. Within this sort of "dramatic dialectic," as Barthes explains, the "layering of meanings . . . always allows the previous one to subsist, as in a geological formation; to speak the contrary without renouncing the thing contradicted." This strategy is especially important, Barthes continues, in a society "which, unable to resolve the contradictions of history without a long political process, draws support (provisionally?) from mythic (narrative) solutions."[67]

Samson Agonistes represents different strata of interpretation that had, over the ages, accrued to the Samson legend. Samson in the Book of Judges is one story; that Samson as viewed through the eyes of Renaissance commentators is another and altogether more vexing story. Milton's *Samson*, in turn, engages in dialogue with both the biblical and Renaissance Samsons and, as a poem of mediation, is both a validation of the Judges narrative and a correction of the crooked versions of that narrative current in Milton's own time. Milton's version of the Samson story may pull against the weight of tradition, but only to validate the Word, and is a singularly apt illustration of a situation described by Kermode: "There may be a constellation of texts, of which the new one is the essential illuminant, that which confers an ultimate, unexpected meaning."[68]

[67] *Ibid.*, pp. 92, 49, 58.

[68] *The Genesis of Secrecy: On the Interpretation of Narrative* (1979; rpt. Cambridge, Mass.: Harvard Univ. Press, 1982), p. 86.

CHAPTER IV

THE RENAISSANCE SAMSONS
AND SAMSON TYPOLOGIES

*[There is] a compulsion to clarify what typology,
in its "strict sense," may mean. . . . like
theological exegesis itself, literary practice
commonly adapts the strict sense to freer ends. The
nature of the adaptation involves a response by a
writer to the literary as well as religious
understanding possible to a given age. . . . It
would be a mistake . . . [though] to assume that
the mere use of typology or of types in other senses
determines high literary quality. John Milton is a
great poet who uses typology in ways necessary to
his poems, but those poems are not great simply
because they incorporate typology. In all these
matters, the enduring caveat must be some version
of "Reader, beware."*

—EARL MINER

If the Samson story had been decontextualized in order to pave
the way for New Testament contextualizations, two versions
of which are afforded by the sixteenth- and seventeenth-century
prayer books, there was during the Renaissance, especially
among typologists, a parallel effort to offer recontextualizations from materials that had been repressed by Reformation
theologians but that now acquired new importance and relevance, particularly in the world of politics. By the seventeenth
century, the Samson story had achieved the status of myth in
a double aspect, its patterns and images providing fictions and

metaphors for literature and its conceptual ideas receiving their full extension into theology, philosophy, and political theory. As myth, the Samson story came to express the ideology of Renaissance culture, or rather contending ideologies, encoding their values and assumptions. New contextualizations, and recontextualizations, of the Samson story are now legion. What had been perceived by an earlier Samson hermeneutic as liabilities to overcome—artful equivocation, a legend with mythic traces, richly textured meanings, metaphysical complexity and range—were now regarded as gifts to be treasured and, once revived, were appropriated by Milton and became the defining characteristics of *Samson Agonistes*. Here Milton "extends the myth beyond a Metaphysical metaphor" and, as J. B. Broadbent perceives, "treats it in a distinctly unpopular medium"[1]: the Samson story is presented as a tragedy and in such a way that the biblical subject matter is made to clash against the ancient authority of its form.

Milton's text not only pushes us back to the Book of Judges but pulls us forward again into the Renaissance when received interpretation of the Samson story, undergoing "revisionary adulteration,"[2] is complicated and extended. One cannot afford to ignore, as so often has been done, the unique place in time occupied by Milton's interpreting consciousness; for as Hans Frei observes, "one's 'historical horizon,' and the transmission process by which a text comes to the present consciousness, make a difference in the understanding of a text's meaning; they transform the text's original horizon."[3] This transfor-

---

[1] *"Comus" and "Samson Agonistes"* (Great Neck, N.Y.: Barrons' Educational Series, 1961), p. 34.

[2] Watson Kirkconnell, *That Invincible Samson: The Theme of "Samson Agonistes" in World Literature* (Toronto: Univ. of Toronto Press, 1964), p. 167.

[3] *The Eclipse of Biblical Narrative: A Study in Eighteenth and Nineteenth Century Hermeneutics* (New Haven: Yale Univ. Press, 1974), p. 312; but see also *Literary Uses of Typology from the Late Middle Ages to the Present*, ed. Earl Miner (Princeton: Princeton Univ. Press, 1977). Or as F. Michael Krouse states the case in *Milton's Samson and the Christian Tradition* (Princeton: Princeton Univ. Press for the Univ.

mation, this revisionism, is the work of exegetes, and literary figures as well, but especially of Milton; it proceeds from the understanding that the hermeneutics of suspicion that had always surrounded the Samson story, not to be detoured, was rather something to pass through—and then perhaps beyond.

Historically, this detouring operation occurs most notably when literal and figurative reading, once interdependent, become independent:

> When the pattern of meaning is no longer firmly ingredient in the story and the occurrence character of the text but becomes a function of a quasi-independent interpretive stance, literal and figural reading draw apart, the latter gradually looking like a forced, arbitrary imposition of unity on a group of very diverse texts. No longer an extension of literal reading, figural interpretation instead becomes a bad historical argument or an arbitrary allegorizing of texts in the service of preconceived dogma.

The phenomena Frei describes—the "subjection of hermeneutics to dogmatic theology," "the split and the beginning of reintegration between historical claims and the explicative sense"[4]—are evident in the sixteenth and seventeenth centuries

---

of Cincinnati, 1949): "Even the view that the principal source of *Samson Agonistes* is the Book of Judges must be more sharply focused to allow for the intervention of a cloud of tradition between any seventeenth-century reader and the skeletal story told in those brief chapters of the Old Testament" (p. 81).

  [4] *The Eclipse of Biblical Narrative*, pp. 37, 38, 41. Krouse argues that, during the Renaissance, exegetical habits in dealing with the Samson story shift to rationalistic literalism and emphasize tropological and anagogical interpretation; then comes along the complicating example of Milton: "There is in *Samson Agonistes* no trace at all of anagogical . . . interpretation; and, although the poem is full of moral significance, there is no specific suggestion of what is known as tropological interpretation. . . . One can say that Milton's interpretation of the Samson story is ostensibly an example of rationalistic literalism" (*Milton's Samson and the Christian Tradition*, pp. 88-89, but see also pp. 64, 66, 70). This argument is curious given the attention Krouse fixes on implicit assumptions. In Milton's century, the Book of Judges was the Old

and strikingly evident in the hermeneutic that engages the Samson story, with Milton's tragedy constituting the most impressive gesture toward such reintegration.

Typology had become the chief culprit in disfiguring and eclipsing the Judges narrative, for its interest was in neither the substance of the narrative nor the implications of the narrative shape. The typologist, as Frei has said, was interested, finally, "not in the text as such" and so "does something other than narrative interpretation with a narrative because he looks for what the narrative refers to or what reconstructed historical context outside itself explains it. He is not wrong when he does this, but unfortunately he is also not apt to see the logical difference between what he does and what a narrative interpretation might be or what it might yield."[5] What Milton would have understood as being of real issue here is that typology, becoming increasingly independent of the biblical text and, in the process, muffling awareness of it, was subverting biblical narrative as narrative, was silencing the particularities of a history within the vagaries of a new mythology.

Typology was becoming, though it need not necessarily be so, a device of mythology and as such was being programmed to eternalize, not transform, the present moment. As it became increasingly independent of the biblical texts from which it issued, typology displaced their complexity with a blissful clarity and even participated in depoliticizing those narratives by universalizing individuals and generalizing patterns. As typology became ingrained in the "casuistical habit of mind,"

Testament Apocalypse, as it were, and Samson's hurling down of the pillars, a signally important evocation of that event. Furthermore, Milton's earlier citations of Samson in his prose works—Samson's locks as the law in *The Reason of Church-Government* (I, 858-59); Samson as the strong man rousing himself from sleep in *Areopagitica* (II, 557-58)—reveal, respectively, tropological and anagogical habits of thought. Rather than locating *Samson Agonistes* on "the split," as Krouse would do, I would treat the poem as an important gesture toward "reintegration."

[5] *The Eclipse of Biblical Narrative*, p. 135.

it "tend[ed] to fragment the narrative line" of scriptural books.[6] Still, Milton would have comprehended that no typology hides anything really, although it does distort, disfigure, and distance what it cannot hide and, in the process, devises new inflections. Still further, Milton would have perceived that, once brought back into contact with biblical books, and thus newly aligned with them, typology could be used against itself. A partisan invention and hence a polemical instrument, typology would necessarily be a focal point in any ideological critique. Typology could be used to expose typologies, enabling us to see through them; it could be made to reveal what earlier it had concealed—the ambiguity and complexity of the Samson narrative in the Book of Judges. Typological tradition, as it happens, provides more than one grid for interpretation.

A review of the Samson typologies current in, and emergent during, the sixteenth and seventeenth centuries suggests that the drama of *Samson Agonistes* derives not from one but from a multiplicity of Samsons, from the conflicts and discrepancies that exist within a story that is now a tangle of ideologies. Ideological critiques are customarily, and appropriately, mounted not on one but on a variety of images that pertain at the time such critiques are conceived and such investigations conducted. It is usually assumed that Milton anchors his poem in the same sort of typological perception as we find a century later in the poems of Edward Taylor. In "Meditation. Jud. 13.3," Taylor presses the point that all the saints wear Christ's colors, and the choicest of them are, like Samson, pictures of him—revelations of his glory: "Thus all the shine that Samson wore is thine, / Thine in them the Type . . . / Be thou my Samson, Lord, a Rising Sun" (37-38, 51). Taylor records only similitudes: the annunciation scenes accompanying their

---

[6] Camille Wells Slights, *The Casuistical Tradition in Shakespeare, Donne, Herbert, and Milton* (Princeton: Princeton Univ. Press, 1981), p. 292.

births, their battling of heretics and enemies and also rising up to tear down the gates, their respective betrayals by friends and betrothals to gentiles, each dying "With arms stretct greatly out" (28).[7] In his elaboration of typological connections, Taylor's procedure is reminiscent of the one followed by Francis Quarles, but with one difference: Quarles's representation of Samson includes the dissimilitudes in order to dispose of them.[8]

Quarles's procedure, not Taylor's, is characteristic of Milton's own century, when even in the most favorable representations of Samson there is mixed in some reticence, a nervous hesitation—a need to catalogue, along with similitudes, all the disparities. And in the latter half of the seventeenth century, even when similitudes are the center of concern, they often are that because of a felt need to overcome the burgeoning disparities which had the effect of diminishing, not enhancing, Samson's heroism. Like those modern-day Miltonists who tell us that *Samson Agonistes* is "a pastiche of medieval materials" and thereupon urge us to correlate Milton's Samson with medieval and early Renaissance conceptions of Samson rather than with those current in mid to late seventeenth century, certain Renaissance exegetes proclaimed:

> Hear Saint *Jerom*: Sampson was a Type of Christ.
> . . . Hear Saint *Austin*. . . . Hear *Prosper*: Having
> mentioned the Birth of *Sampson*, he concludes thus:
> Every action [by Samson] . . . sounds out the Lord
> Christ in a figure. . . . Hear *Wotton*. . . . Hear
> *Scharpius* . . . hear *Weemse* making the Comparison:
> *Sampson* . . . was a Type of Christ, as in his Con-
> ception, so in many of his Actions, and in his Death.[9]

---

[7] Taylor's meditation on Samson is quoted from *The Poems of Edward Taylor*, ed. Donald Stanford (New Haven: Yale Univ. Press, 1960), pp. 99-101.

[8] See *The Historie of Samson* (London: Printed for John Marriott, 1631).

[9] See Lynn Veach Sadler, *Consolation in "Samson Agonistes": Regeneration and Ty-*

The very fact that such strident assertions of similitude issue forth not as elaborations of obvious parallels between Samson's life and Christ's, but as exonerations of Samson's actions which seem most un-Christlike—his marrying of infidels, his slaying of the lion, his firing the tails of foxes—suggests that these are not innocent exercises in ingenuity but ones conceived as responses to the general tendency to deride Samson for these actions. Like Edward Topsel, Samson's defenders have apparently "heard some . . . speak against the History of *Sampson*" and are thus aware that some "do presently condemn" him.[10] In response to such detractors, Samson's defenders present their typological case, often as Henry Vertue does, not by reasserting obvious parallels between Samson and Christ but by eliding the most awkward and suspicious episodes in Samson's life with events of dignity and moment in the life of Christ.

Samson Agonistes appears in the immediate aftermath of such debates; and its protagonist, contrary to what is often supposed, accords not with this or that Samson available to Milton or his audience but with a variety of Samsons available to both. These differing and divergent images of Samson are synchronized in Milton's tragedy and in such a way that, instead of simply representing existing ways of seeing this figure, it alters mental habits so that Samson can now be seen anew. A vehicle for creative moral insight, Samson can now be seen not divorced from but within the full context of the political world, at the very center of its arena. Milton is not simply resurrecting an old typology for a new age and thereby silencing the debate that gathered around the Samson legend in

---

pology, Salzburg Studies in English Literature (Salzburg: Univ. of Salzburg, 1979), p. 82; cf. Henry Vertue, *Christ and the Church: or Parallels in Three Books* (London: Printed by Thomas Roycroft, 1659), pp. 45-46, 54-55.

[10] *The History of Four-footed Beasts and Serpents*, 2nd ed. (1607; London: Printed for G. Sawbridge, 1658), unpaginated dedicatory epistle.

his own time; he is not using the old typology to invest this legend with stale affirmations, but instead fires the debate by calling the old typology into question, in the process challenging the affirmations previously embedded within it. In *Samson Agonistes*, Milton brings the Samson legend under his demythologizing scrutiny, subjecting Renaissance generalizations about this story to a relentless testing. He probes the ideological content of the story to its foundations in the understanding that what the scriptural stories offer culture is not ecclesiastical and political structures, nor moral codes, but, as Herbert Schneidau remarks, "an unceasing critique of itself."[11] In the process, *Samson Agonistes* emerges as an unsettling poem, not meant to put us at ease with the world, and Samson himself, who for so long seemed to be the glory of Israel, is shown to be her grief.

Today, it is generally assumed that the Renaissance adopted, without contributing to, Medieval attitudes toward Samson and, in turn, that those attitudes are adopted by Milton and advanced uncritically within his tragedy. In the words of F. Michael Krouse, "When Milton wrote *Samson Agonistes* he might have expected his readers to have all, or most, of these conceptions in their minds. For during Milton's own lifetime Samson was remembered . . . as a tragic lover; as a man of prodigious strength; as the ruler and liberator of Israel; as a great historical personage whose downfall was caused by the treachery of a woman and therefore as an example of the perils of passion; as a sinner who repented and was restored to grace; as the original Hercules; as a consecrated Nazarite; as a saint resplendent . . . ; as an agent of God . . . ; and as a figure of Christ." Even if Krouse tells us that "By the beginning of

[11] *Sacred Discontent: The Bible and Western Tradition* (Baton Rouge: Louisiana State Univ. Press, 1976), p. 16.

the seventeenth century Samson meant a bewildering variety of things" and that "This variety must . . . be ordered and displayed for the purpose of defining,"[12] we are not told by him that in Milton's time the Samson story, regarded as a mirror of current history, acquired a political aspect and eventually became a lens through which to glimpse the Revolution's failure; or that progressively many of the Medieval suppositions concerning Samson's character came under review. Indeed, such a review was itself a Medieval phenomenon as is suggested by the fact that, whereas St. Augustine believed Samson was moved by the Spirit of God, St. Bernard registers uneasiness: "if he had not a Motive of the Holy Ghost, what he did was sinful."[13]

We are not apprised by Krouse's book nor, what is more surprising, by any of the hermeneutic analysis this book has spawned, that the Samson story undergoes a sea-change during the seventeenth century, that reference to and use of this story is ubiquitous, and that the range of significance attached to Samson himself is at once extended and becomes increasingly

[12] *Milton's Samson and the Christian Tradition*, pp. 72, 78-79. Early on in his study, Krouse says that he is concerned with "the implicit assumptions made about Samson and his story by Milton and his readers," with "what, in other words, was the shape of the seventeenth-century conception of Samson" (p. 17). As it happens, Krouse evades the assumptions that I examine, and thus our profiles of the seventeenth-century Samson are decidedly different. Krouse does allow for an inherited political element in *Samson Agonistes* and for Milton, "with a nice appreciation of contemporary applicability, . . . keep[ing] that element intact in his poem." But Krouse disallows any "political allegory" to the poem—any suggestion that Milton might have highlighted this element (p. 93)—nor does Krouse ever expound the political element he does allow to the poem. E. Wright comes closer to the mark when, arguing that "Milton did tend to seek the past—Biblical, Classical and Medieval—whose forms and modes of thought were congenial to his creative imagination," he also acknowledges: "*But* [in *Samson Agonistes*] Milton was writing a political and religious commentary," which necessitated that he engage the forms and modes of thought current in his own time; see "Samson as the Fallen Champion in 'Samson Agonistes'," *Notes and Queries*, 205 (1960), 224 (my italics).

[13] Quoted from the anonymous *Two Dissertations: The First on the Supposed Suicide of Samson* (London: Printed for W. Innys and J. Richardson, 1754), p. 45.

ambiguous. Once regarded as a plague to the uncircumcised, Samson now appears to be a plague to his own people. His story, previously cast as a saint's life, continues to figure in such literature, but now to mark the fall and mortification of various saints, not their recovery and exaltation.

Samson is a man of strength with feet of clay, is in body strong but in mind effeminate, slack, and so oftentimes apparently a fool; he is a reformed, regenerate magistrate but also a judge unworthy of his judgeship; he is now of the elect and now of the reprobate; a spiritual body but a natural man; a man here joined with Christ and there alienated from him; he is a symbol of the Church, true or false, of the Roman church some of the time and other times of Episcopacy. Samson is a hero of faith and of the Good Old Cause, but also a man of sin; he is the hero as king or as Puritan saint, or a fallen version of either—now a Royalist and now a Cromwellian soldier. He is one of the sons of God but also a son of Adam, so much so that at times he seems to be no longer a hero but just another man and even at times finds his type in Satan and is represented as a limb of Antichrist. He is an actor both in his public and private person, performing now by divine impulsion and now of his own accord—is here a true and there a false prophet. An angel or an apostate, Samson is also a vessel of anger, a minister of vengeance—sometimes of God's anger and vengeance; he is a successful or failed deliverer, a liberator or a mauler of people, and sometimes just a selfish and self-fashioned deliverer. He is a purveyor of God's word and of the divine vision, an image (real or counterfeit) of God himself; he finds his type in both Nisus and Hercules and is a type of David and of Christ—if not of Christ in his second then in his first coming, if not of Christ in the wilderness then on the cross, a type of the King of Kings in overcoming *but not* in being defeated by his enemies. Samson is a principle within—of good or evil, order or rebellion—now creative and now destructive. Here he is an agent of unity, there of division. Now he is a symbol of the English Nation or of Christian nations generally, and now a beast in the jungle—one torn, in words from the Book of Judges, "with the thorns of the wilderness and with briers" (8:7). *Samson Agonistes* comes in the wake of renewed interest in the Samson story, at a time when inherited conceptions of Samson, both allegorical and typological readings of this character, are being scrutinized anew and substantially revised and, more generally, at a time when conventional typology begins to yield to a typological symbolism, when once positive are being converted into negative types.

On the one hand, Samson continues to be equated with God's ministers of vengeance and, in this connection, is used to illustrate the proposition that "It is no good dealing with one that is mightier than our selves. . . . Wee were not best make sport with *Sampson* [nor provoke the Lord to anger], least he pull down the house about our eares, and so make us pay dearlie for our pastime."[14] On the other hand, by the end of the sixteenth century, the stories of Jesus in the wilderness and Samson imprisoned at Gaza had been allied for purposes of contrast: Samson's defeat at the pillars is opposed to Jesus' triumph on the pinnacle; Samson who slays his enemies, and perhaps inadvertently himself, is opposed to Jesus who is slain that his enemies might be saved; Samson, blinded by his rage, falling from the divine vision, is contrasted with Jesus in the moment on the pinnacle when he partakes of the divine vision. By Jesus things once bitter are made sweet: an upside-down history is turned right side up. Samson, on the other hand, reverses such a progression, exemplifying the wise man be-

[14] Lancelot Andrewes, *The Wonderfull Combate (for Gods Glorie and Mans Salvation) betweene Christ and Satan* (London: Printed by John Charlwood, 1592), p. 69; see also pp. 22-23, 31, 74.

coming foolish, and remaining foolish, as well as man's beginning in the spirit but ending in the flesh.[15] Samson's
strength may finally be renewed; but the fact that it was lost
at all, according to Heinrich Bullinger, reveals "how great
the sin of Samson was" and accounts for the fact that, "bending
the pillars of the theatre," Samson, blindly led by self-love,
is "himself slain with the fall of the palace."[16] Samson may
awaken from "spirituall lethargie," but only to fall again,
because not strengthened "to resist the spirituall Philistines"
who, through Delilah, lull him back into the "lap of carnall
pleasures."[17]

These reservations give rise to still others so that, by Richard
Hooker, Samson is numbered among those who should be
pitied for their errors, among those self-fashioned deliverers
who, displaying zeal toward God, appropriate unto themselves
the promises of Scripture; and because all they do is based on
"a certain figurative resemblance" such men are mistaken for
the true prophets. These men, says Hooker, "drew in a sea
of matter, by applying all things unto their own company,
which are any where spoken concerning divine favours and
benefits":

> . . . as Israel was to root out the idolatrous nations,
> and to plant instead of them a people which feared
> God; so the same Lord's good will and pleasure was
> now, that these new Israelites should, under the con-
> duct of other Josuas, Samsons and Gedeons, perform
> a work no less miraculous in casting out the wicked

[15] *Ibid.*, pp. 72, 98; cf. Henoch Clapham, *A Briefe of the Bible* (Printed by Robert
Walde, 1596), p. 69, for a less jaundiced view of Samson.

[16] *The Decades*, trans. H. I., ed. Thomas Hardy (4 vols.; Cambridge: Cambridge
Univ. Press, 1849-52), III, 209-10; see also I, 312.

[17] See John Downame, *The Christian Warfare*, 2nd ed. (London: Printed by Felix
Kyngston, 1608), p. 34.

from the earth, and establishing the Kingdom of Christ with perfect liberty.[18]

In actuality though, these men are the false prophets, agents of tyranny and perverters of the Word. With the emphasis falling so heavily upon contrasts, oppositions, and differences, it is unsurprising that at the turn of the century Samson should be remembered not as one acting in accord with divine command but as one of those who "did usuallie . . . strive with God, as Iacob did wrastle with the Angell." And it is understandable, moreover, that such commentators will resist any effort to allow Samson to image God by saying of Christ that he is God's "owne and *onelie* naturall Image."[19]

The seeds are sown at the beginning of the seventeenth century for the interiorization of the Samson story that emerges full-blown by mid-century. Edward Hutchins uses Samson's jawbone to emblematize the power of prayer, his point being that the jawbone of prayer must be deployed against the spiritual Philistine within all of us, that we must rely upon this jawbone to protect ourselves.[20] At the same time, however, commentary on the Samson story becomes notable for its widening discrepancies. In the one substantial commentary on Judges produced during the seventeenth century and published in 1615, Richard Rogers distinguishes the wicked kings from the good judges of Israel, some of whom, like Samson, are commended in St. Paul's Epistle to the Hebrews, for even if they fell they rose up again. "Scripture . . . doth never condemne" Samson and the other judges, says Rogers, because

[18] *The Works . . . of Richard Hooker*, 7th ed., ed. John Keble, rev. by R. W. Church and F. Paget (3 vols.; Oxford: Clarendon Press, 1888), I, 188-89.

[19] Edward Hutchins, *Sampsons Jawbone against the Spiritual Philistine* (London: Printed by Peter Short, 1601), unpaginated preface to the reader and p. 55 (my italics).

[20] *Ibid.*, pp. 1, 198. Cf. *The Sermons of Master Henry Smith* (London: Printed by the Assignes of Thomas Man, Paul Man, and Ionah Man, 1631), p. 376, and also by Smith, *Twelve Sermons* (London: Printed by John Haviland, 1615), sig. Dᵛ.

"they lived in a golden age." Such special pleading for Samson and his age is nevertheless coupled with the recognition that "under the Judges, the people were sometimes oppressed grievously by strangers, and especially under *Samson* . . . (for why? we must know, their horrible sinnes deserved it, and provoked God to deale with them in that manner.)"[21] The redeeming clichés woven around the Samson story are discontinuous with the larger picture of man living in the fourth age, with the result that the Samson story comes under hard review and that Samson emerges therefrom as the actor in a great tragedy of human history.

Thus, in the initial four decades of the seventeenth century, there is a tendency to diminish Samson's supposed heroism and to find in his story the "lamentable lapses" of mankind generally, to regard his strength as "nothing . . . but fantasticall . . . to the eye: as those Kingdomes which the Divell offered to Christ."[22] There is also a tendency to see mirrored in Samson's own life of effeminate folly, the life of his people, a pattern of backsliding and defeat. Samson is now represented as a figure in whom lust reigns, and his alliance with the wicked Delilah serves as a reminder that the Israelites repeatedly made league with those whom they should have cast out and that, providentially, those whom they wrongly befriended "became goads to their sides, and thorns in their

---

[21] *A Commentary upon the Whole Booke of Judges* (London: Printed by Felix Kyngston, 1615), unpaginated Lecture 1. See also Archibald Simson, *Samsons Seaven Lockes of Haire: Allegorically Expounded, and Compared to the Seaven Spirituall Vertues* (St. Andrewes: Printed by Edward Raban, 1621): "this Historie is a faithfull Recorder, as well of the Vices as Vertues of Sancts, & a perfect mirrour wherein one may behold both the deformity & beauty of his own person" (p. 12).

[22] Edward Vaughan, *A Plaine and Perfect Method, for the Easie Understanding of the Whole Bible* (London: Printed by T. S., 1617), pp. 2, 3; see also pp. 68-70 for Vaughan's placement of the Samson story within "The Age of the fourth Observation." Cf. Vaughan, *An Introduction into the Bookes of the Prophets and Apostles* (London: Printed for William Holme, 1598), unpaginated "An Introduction to Booke of Judges."

eyes."[23] Samson now illustrates the proposition that even those who are seeming "phoenixes among men" possess infirmities, display failings, and fall; we all inhabit "houses of clay, our breath goes away, and we all perish: *Mathuselah* with his yeares, *Samson* with his strength."[24] An ordinary man, "the fly, the deluded young foole: . . . the fly strong-womanish weake *Samson*" finds his match in the devilish Delilah, "the spider," whose "deceits and delusions [are] the webbe."[25]

Samson continues to be a type of Christ but even among avowed typologists loses his earlier stature. Now to speak of Christ as "the true *Sampson*," as does Thomas Taylor, involves the assertion of a difference:

> . . . although *Sampson* the type was at last overcome by his enemies: our true *Sampson* [presumably unlike his type] is invincible, and hath gloriously triumphed over them all. Both of them were great deliverers; the one from great thraldome and temporall misery: the other from a greater spirituall and eternall thraldome under sinne, the Law, Satan, hell, &c.

Taylor thus feels obliged to proclaim "Christ a mightier and better Deliverer, then *Sampson*, in six things": Samson overcomes a liar, Christ a devil; Samson abuses his strength and grieves God by sinning, neither of which Christ ever does;

---

[23] See the anonymous *The Doctrine of the Bible: or, Rules of Discipline* (London: Printed by Thomas Pauier, 1610), ff. 40-40ᵛ.

[24] See both S. I., *Haughty Heart Humbled* (London: n.p., 1628), p. 14, and Sampson Price, *The Two Twins of Birth and Death* (London: Printed for John Hodgets, 1624), p. 29.

[25] S. I., *Haughty Heart Humbled*, p. 131. Commentators would not let go of the idea that by a woman Samson was made to sin (see, e.g., William Prynne, *Histrio-Mastix: The Players Scovrge, or, Actors Tragaedie* [London: Printed for Michael Sparke, 1633], p. 230). See also Francis Rollenson, *Twelve Prophetical Legacies: or Twelve Sermons vpon Iacobs Last Will and Testament* (London: Printed for Arthur Johnson, 1612), p. 57.

Samson is physically strong, not like Christ, cunning and wise; Samson's overthrowing of his enemies involves his own overthrowing, whereas Christ's crucifixion is his greatest victory and most glorious exaltation; Samson merely *begins* the deliverance that Christ completes.[26]

The eventual demise of the Samson typology becomes increasingly evident in the neutral terms chosen for comparison (Christ and Samson are alike in their aloneness, the one in the wilderness, the other at Gaza) and in the favoring of a spiritual interpretation which sees the Samson story as an encounter within the human soul of good and evil, reason and passion, soul and body. As the story is interiorized, Samson and Delilah come to emblematize inward principles. The collapse of the usual Samson typology is further evident in the continuing uneasiness concerning his marriage which, Taylor allows, "might seeme a sinne" if Scripture did not say "*It came of God*, Judg. 14. 4" and which finally Taylor can explain only as an anomaly, an instance of God's "strange means" since marriages are ordinarily designed to mend, not make, differences.[27] Elsewhere Taylor remarks again on this marriage as part of a more extended reflection upon marrying idolaters, the only justification for which is the conversion of a heathen

---

[26] *Christ Revealed: or the Old Testament Explained* (London: Printed by M. F., 1635), pp. 56, 61. Even Thomas Haynes, who provides the chart of tabular correspondences for Krouse's book, in addition to summarizing the Samson story in this fashion, feels obliged to submit that "Some of these passages manifestly shew Sampsons weaknesse and sins, and his unwarrantable entercourse . . . [with] the Philistines" (see Haynes' *The General View of the Holy Scriptures*, 2nd ed. [London: Printed for Henry Ockould, 1640], p. 216; the chart appears on pp. 217-18 in Haynes and is reprinted between pp. 68-69 by Krouse, *Milton's Samson and the Christian Tradition*).

[27] *Christ Revealed*, pp. 56, 59. See also Taylor's interiorization of the Samson story in *The Progresse of Saints to Full Holinesse* (London: Printed for John Bartlet, 1630), p. 72. Sampson Price wonders, "What is more common now then for the *Sonnes* of God to match with the daughters of men, and *Protestants* to conuerse with *Papists* . . .?" (*Ephesus Warning Before Her Woe* [London: Printed for John Barnes, 1616], p. 55).

woman; yet Samson's wife was plainly "not converted," his objective was "revenge against the Philistims." Taylor thus concludes that even if divinely sanctioned and thus an exception, Samson's marriage is no example: "we must *walke by the rule*, not by an exception from it," and the rule is that if the wives were not converted "the marriages were sinful, and not imitable."[28] Nor is Samson's revenge at the pillars an example. An "heroicall" act, a "publique Revenge" in Samson's "publike person," such an execution of justice upon enemies "must not be made a president or become imitable, seeing the same occasions can never concur againe."[29]

In view of Taylor's remarks, it is noteworthy that Samson does not figure importantly in Taylor's lengthy discussion of Christian combat and conquest: Samson is not mentioned among those who are led by the spirit of God to confront evil and not numbered among the worthies of the world nor among the famous tempted ones; he is not enrolled among the heroes of faith nor cited with the illustrious men who perform miraculous feats beyond human strength, nor even included among the saints in Taylor's remarks on Hebrews 11:36-39. Samson is given no place among the "speciall types of Christ"[30] but is rather reduced to the status of an ordinary man, Delilah dealing with him as Satan deals with the rest of us. Samson is typologized with Christ only twice, first by way of emphasizing that Christ overcomes as a "true man, in the flesh," and later by way of contrasting the enemies of Samson who prevail with those of the "inuincible *Sampson* . . . [who] cannot hold him."[31] The only unhackneyed piece of typology analogizes Samson with Satan, Delilah with Christ, so as to

[28] *The Progresse of Saints*, p. 162.

[29] Thomas Taylor, *The Works of That Faithful Servant of Jesus Christ* (London: Printed by John Bartlet, 1653), pp. 378-79.

[30] *Christs Combate and Conquest: or, the Lyon of the Tribe of Judah* (London: Printed by Cantrell Legge, 1618), p. 163.

[31] *Ibid.*, pp. 37, 193.

suggest that Jesus learns in the desert of Satan's strength and there "as *Dalilah*, when she knew wherein *Sampsons* great strength lay, did soone disarme him, so Christ spoyled Satan of his lockes."[32] Taylor says little of Samson in his later description of the progress of saints toward holiness, using Samson here only as a negative example; but he does, quite apart from Samson, set forth a proposition that others eventually will turn back upon Samson in the understanding that when vision fails grace perishes:

> Thou maist deceive thy selfe in thy reckoning, and think he [God] dwells in thee as one of the elect, when he is in thee but in some common graces: and then he goes quite away at length, and never comes anymore. . . . Suppose he will come againe to thee that art the Lords, yet hee will not come againe so freely. . . .[33]

It is but a step from Taylor to other commentators who will represent Samson as one of the sons of God who has matched with the daughters of men, illustrating converse between Protestants and Papists and, in turn, Delilah "as a hunch vpon a Camel's [Samson's] backe," preventing him from "enter[ing] into the narrow gate which leadeth to Ierusalem."[34] The episode at the pillars is now treated not as a triumph but as a defeat; and by some Book of Revelation commentators Samson is opposed to the true church and identified with the third angel of the apocalypse who, falling away from the divine vision, poisons the earth and its waters, defiling God's Word.[35]

Still, in these four decades there survives, although not

---

[32] *Ibid.*, p. 36.

[33] *The Progresse of Saints*, p. 39.

[34] Price, *Ephesus Warning Before Her Woe*, p. 52.

[35] See, e.g., John Trapp, *Gods Love-Tokens, and the Afflicted Mans Lessons* (London: Richard Badger, 1637), pp. 131, 141.

conspicuously, a view of Samson as representing the Elect who groan to be delivered, as one of those testifying to the importance of faith and zeal. "The world may cast these men out as the Sea doth Pearles, among mire and dirt, but they are Pearles notwithstanding," says John Preston, "Pearles excelling other men, as much as Iewels doe common stones." Preston then applies this piece of wisdom to the zealous whose prototype is Samson: "when we injury any of them, doe not wee cut off the haire from *Sampsons* head, wherein the strength of every Countrey and Nation, and every Citie and Towne consists? Yea, the cutting off of them, is like the cutting off of his lockes, which the more the[y] grow, the more strength a Kingdome hath."[36]

A type of the Christian elect, Samson is even more emphatically here a symbol of a nation in all its strength and is even sometimes placed in the lineage of St. George,[37] in which guise he is appropriated as a hero of the revolutionary cause.

If Samson was once the instrument of division in the state, that role is now assigned to Delilah with Samson emerging, at least some of the time during the 1640s, as an agent for unity. In the words of John Price, the whorish Delilah, per-

[36] *The Saints Qualifications* (London: Printed for Nicholas Bourne, 1633), p. 287. While S. I. acknowledges that "the repentance of . . . Sampson, be not expressly recorded as are . . . [his] sinnes," he nevertheless cites Samson, in the following way, under the heading, "Gods children restored to grace with God, and in their Graces revived by their repentance":

> Some Glimpses of comfort breake out euen in the darkest night of . . . sinnes . . . their souls wounded, their spirits perplexed, their consciences disquieted, their hearts oppressed . . . ; . . . their sinnes . . . expose them to the expropriation, vituperation, yea derision of the vncircumscribed, as *Sampson* was to the Philistines, and in respect of the Church, subiect them to her censure . . . (*Haughty Heart Humbled*, p. 93).

[37] See, e.g., "St. George's Commendation" (1612), in *The Pepys Ballads*, ed. Hyder Rollins Edward (6 vols.; Cambridge, Mass.: Harvard Univ. Press, 1929), I, 43. The terms of the comparison are that Samson slays with a jawbone, hurls down the temple upon thousands of Philistines, just as St. George slays the dragon.

ceiving the army's might and seeking to break its power "like Sampsons coards, is trying her tricks to finde out your strength, and the seat thereof, and well perceiving that it lies in your hair, rooted together in your head, (we mean in your Union with Christ, and each with other,) she hath applyed her self in her several Instruments, by her enticing words to cut you from him, and then to divide you each from other." Yet Price also recognizes that in the battle between Christ and Antichrist, between Samson and Delilah, while the objective may be for the one to defeat the other, the actual consequence of such physical combat is that each is bruised by the other so that the army is not always, Samson is not always, what it and he ought to be: "humble under victories, meek under injuries, patient under provocations."[38] As William Gouge implied earlier in the century, there is something curious in the fact that, unlike the prototypical heroes Gouge cites (David, Samuel, Joshua, Job, St. Peter, St. Paul, Jephthah, Moses, Jeremiah, Jonah, Elijah, and Elisha), Samson was not miraculously preserved and protected from traitors as they were, or as had been the modern-day exemplar of the spiritual warrior, Queen Elizabeth.[39]

For Samson to be reclaimed as a member of God's army required the sort of casuistical argument advanced by William Ames. Samson was often an issue when the topic was murder or manslaughter, with the commentator typically allowing, as Ames does, that, though one can kill for justice, justice requires the observance of certain criteria:

> First, That the cause bee weighty and just. Secondly,
> That it bee done by publike authority. Thirdly, That
> it bee done orderly and by just meanes. Fourthly,

[38] *Walsins Wiles* (1649), in *The Leveller Tracts 1647-1653*, ed. William Haller and Godfrey Davis (New York: Columbia Univ. Press, 1944), pp. 287-88.

[39] See *The Whole Armour of God, or a Christians Spirituall Furniture* (London: Printed by John Beale, 1619), p. 137.

That it bee done out of right intention and zeale for
Justice, not out of wrath, hatred, or desire of private
revenge, or any other inordinate passion.

Samson was not always thought to have observed such criteria,
and in his hurling down of the pillars he further complicated
matters by introducing the question of whether, and in what
circumstances, it was lawful "to expose ones selfe to such a
danger, by which death must necessarily though indirectly
follow." A soldier may keep his station, says Ames, as Samson
did "out of singular instinct" when, intending to kill the
Philistines, "hee fore saw, that his owne death must needs
follow."[40] In this way, Ames opens the way for Samson to
become the patron saint of the revolutionaries and the prototypical soldier in the New Model Army.

In the 1640s, Samson is thus redeemed for heroism—by
Puritan apologists who, through his figure, exalt the com-
monfolk as the bearers of the real strength, the true nobility,
of the nation; by the prayer book for the New Model Army
where Samson is represented as an exemplary soldier, devoutly
at prayer before going forth to battle; and by those like John
Lilburne who extol Samson as hero and patron saint of the
revolutionaries whose fate may be to follow Samson, even unto
death, in order to achieve their goals.[41] Samson would have

[40] *Conscience with the Power and Cases Thereof* (n.p.: n.p., 1639), p. 182; see also
pp. 178, 222-24.

[41] See Edmund Staunton, *Rupes Israelis: The Rock of Israel* (London: Printed for
Christopher Meredith, 1644), p. 10; *The Souldiers Pocket Bible* (London: Printed
by G. B. and R. W., 1643), pp. 2-4; and Lilburne, *The Resolved Mans Resolution*
(London: n.p., 1647), p. 1. The notion that Samson was a representative of the
common folk was elaborated earlier in the century by Rollenson, *Twelve Propheticall
Legacies*, p. 141: "the worthiest & most valiant of all the Judges of *Israel* was *Samson*
a man of a meane *Tribe*, and yet God chose him to deliuer his people out of the
handes of the *Philistines*, herein teaching vs . . . that hee himselfe is not an *accepter*
of *Persons*; for the ostentation of *Birth*, and *Parentage* in his eye, is but a *Bubble*, and
worldly *Possessions* and wealth like *Chaffe* or *dust* before the winde." Within the

been "a madde man so to have dyed if he had not a warrant from God, which without a doubt he had (though it be not expressed)," says Thomas Wilson, so that he died by executing his high calling and herein is a glorious "type of Christ, who by his death procured deliverance to his people, destroyed his and their enemies."[42] Not always, but now, "The central idea of Samson's history," sometimes thought to be the central fact

Judges narrative, this point is underscored, according to Rollenson, by representing the privileged men of Judah as the betrayers of Samson who belongs to a meaner lot. A recent attempt by David S. Berkeley and Salva Khoddam to make this tradition central to Milton's undertaking in *Samson Agonistes* has been sternly refuted by Leo Miller; see Berkeley and Khoddam's "Samson the Base Versus Harapha the Gentle," *Milton Quarterly*, 17 (1983), 1-7, and Miller's "Milton's Heroic Samson: In Response to Berkeley and Khoddam," *Milton Quarterly*, 18 (1984), 25-27. Miller is properly perturbed by the rhetorical excesses in the essay to which he responds; and those excesses, it is true, get in the way of these authors making an obvious connection between the carpenter's son of *Paradise Regained* and the commoner of Milton's tragedy. Rollenson remarks upon Samson in this manner by way of reaching toward a conception of democratized tragedy: "This world is a theater, the earth is a stage, our life a Tragedie, and every man is an actour, one man playes the Kinges part, and another the seruants, whose robes being chaunged, the seruant becomes the King, and the King is turned to be a seruant; and thus the state of man like a Planet . . . is moued circularly" (p. 142). Nor is any connection made between Dan's (Samson's) being the son of a concubine and Samson's going off, as a child of the tribe Dan, with the harlot of Gaza. On Samson as "a culture hero" during the Civil War years, see Jackie DiSalvo, " 'The Lord's Battells': *Samson Agonistes* and the Puritan Revolution," *Milton Studies*, 4 (1972), 39-62; and specifically on Samson as a symbol of the New Model Army and/or the Good Old Cause, see Christopher Hill, *God's Englishmen: Oliver Cromwell and the English Revolution* (London: Weidenfeld and Nicolson, 1970), pp. 190-91, and also by Hill, *The Experience of Defeat: Milton and Some Contemporaries* (New York: Viking, 1984), p. 311. See as well Mark A. Kishlansky, *The Rise of the New Model Army* (Cambridge: Cambridge Univ. Press, 1979), p. 252. In hurling down the pillars, Samson is viewed by William Carter as bringing down "the whole structure of the Romish Babel" (*Israels Peace with God, Beniamines Overthrow* [London: Printed for Giles Calvert, 1642], p. 43), and by Nathaniel Fiennes (1640) as bringing down the whole structure of the English Church Government (*Private Papers of State*, in *Historical Collections*, ed. John Rushworth [8 vols.; London: Printed for D. Brown et al., 1721-22], IV, 180).

[42] *A Complete Christian Dictionary*, 6th ed. (London: Printed by E. Cotes, 1655), annotation to Hebrews 11:32.

of Milton's poem as well, "is the idea of a national champion, first victorious, then abased, then finally triumphant in a national cause."[43] Samson is a common point of reference among the Cromwellians, a feature of their rhetoric, cropping up even in the chatter of their conversation and correspondence.[44] If there is reason to suppose that the Jesus of *Paradise Regained* "is drawn on the lines on which Milton had already sketched Cromwell in the hour of Cromwell's greatest ascendancy,"[45] there may also be grounds for conjecturing, as we shall see later on, that the Samson of *Samson Agonistes* is etched in such a way as to recall Cromwell, and through him the entire revolutionary cause, in the moment of his and its failure. Even in the hours of their greatest hope, Roger Williams would depict God's Englishmen as, Samson-like, "drunk with the cup of the Whore's fornication" and "fast asleep in Antichristian Delilah's lap."[46] More commonly during the 1640s though, Samson figures the hope of England, not her waywardness—the hope, as Milton states it in *Areopagitica*, of "a noble and puissant Nation rousing herself . . . [from] sleep" (II, 558) and now being readied for the millennium by "a mighty and puissant, victorious army."[47] By 1660, the hope

[43] See Sir Richard C. Jebb, *"Samson Agonistes* and Hellenic Drama," in *"Comus" and "Samson Agonistes": A Casebook*, ed. Julian Lovelock (London: Macmillan, 1975), p. 181.

[44] See David Underdown, "Cromwell and the Officers, February 1658," *English Historical Review*, 83 (1968), 101-07. The Catholics had used the Samson story similarly so that in Fabricus' play, says Kirkconnell, "The Bavarian duke, Albrecht, is cited as a second Samson, a mighty champion of the Catholic faith" (*That Invincible Samson*, p. 163).

[45] See Herbert J. C. Grierson, *Milton and Wordsworth, Poets and Prophets: A Study of Their Reactions to Political Events* (London: Chatto and Windus, 1950), p. 134.

[46] *The Bloody Tenet of Persecution* (1644), in *Puritanism and Liberty*, ed. A.S.P. Woodhouse (1938; rpt. London: J. M. Dent and Sons, 1950), p. 270.

[47] Richard Overton, *An Appeal from the Commons to the Free People* (1647), in *ibid.*, p. 328. It is nevertheless noteworthy that, in this context, Milton does not name Samson, nor does Overton who had every opportunity to include Samson in his catalogue of names: "Never let any English spirit be taxed with . . . dishonour. You

figured by Samson will be different, not of a nation awaking into a glorious regeneration but into a moment of terrible yet gratifying vengeance.

An old typology is revived wherein Samson is likened to Christ, not now to a fallen, sleeping Adam, and Delilah to Antichrist; wherein Samson is part of a carefully plotted historical and typological progression: "*Samson* did never quite free the people from the *Philistims* yoke," says John Diodati, "that being reserved for *David* to do, who was the figure of Christ, who shall accomplish the delivery of his Church, at the last glorious appearing of his kingdom." Diodati allows Samson to retain his status as "a figure of Christ" executing God's vengeance upon accursed and tyrannical nations, "a figure of Christ the true Nazarite in . . . strength and power," while diminishing Samson's stature somewhat by having him typify the Christ of the First Coming in contrast to David who typifies Christ in his Second Coming.[48]

This distinction derives from the contention that judges should bear no sign of violence or pride and should remain wholly dependent on God's election and guidance, aiming only at the public good and safety of the people. Where others saw Samson as a profile in reverse of a true judge, Diodati affirms Samson's claim to that title by insisting that he acts by divine instinct and for the public welfare, and so concurs with those commentators who see in Samson "a faithful man, humbling himself to the very death, that he might do God and his people service."[49] Samson may not always be cited as an exemplary judge; but there is, nevertheless, a certain urgency on the part

have Othneils, Ehuds, Baraks, and Gideons, before you, even a mighty and puissant, virtuous army."

[48] *Pious and Learned Annotations upon the Holy Bible*, 4th ed. (London: Printed by Thomas Roycroft, 1664), annotations to Judges 14:6, 14:18, 15:20, 16:17.

[49] See John Downame et al., *Annotations upon All the Books of the Old and New Testament* (London: Printed by John Legatt and John Raworth, 1645), annotation to Judges 16:30.

of some to return to judgeship. As Henry Parker states their case, without specific mention of Samson:

> Man being depraved by the fall of *Adam* grew so untame and uncivill a creature, that the law of God written in his breast was not sufficient to restrayne him from mischiefe, or to make him sociable, and therefore without some magistracy to provide new orders, and to judge of old, and to execute according to justice, no society could be upheld.[50]

Like Diodati, John Trapp exonerates Samson's prayer at the pillars as coming from a man of faith, "a fruit of his repentance," and extols Samson for hurling down the pillars out of zeal for God's glory.[51] Unlike Diodati, however, Trapp will not cover over the blemishes in Samson's character that had arrested the attention of commentators from Luther onward. Samson merely begins the deliverance that David perfects and Christ completes. Trapp does not approve of Samson's marriage choices and remembers, only to discredit, those traditions which would excuse Samson by holding that he wins conversion from the Woman of Timnath and takes Delilah not in adultery but as his wife. Unqualified examples of strong faith and conjugal love, from Trapp's point of view, are provided not by Samson but by his parents, who were nevertheless overcome, as Luther believed, by Samson's importunity and, "being loth to cross his desires, yielded to him, though against their own judgements."[52] Although a type for Ovid's Nisus and also a greater Hercules and "an heroick spirit" and "*a little Sun*, a type of Christ," both in the wilderness and on the cross, Samson cannot be altogether excused.[53] He is among

---

[50] *Observations upon Some of His Majesties Late Answers* (1642), in *Tracts on Liberty*, ed. Haller, II, 179.

[51] *Annotations upon the Old and New Testament* (5 vols.; London: Printed by Robert White, 1662), I, 93.

[52] *Ibid.*, I, 84; see also pp. 82, 85, 90-91, and *Luther's Works*, ed. Pelikan et al., IV, 226; XLV, 382; XLVI, 269; LII, 219.

[53] *Annotations upon the Old and New Testament*, I, 83-84, 92. See also *The Holie*

those "Ill guides" in Scripture who are lustful, jealous, and martial, who forget God and their high calling, and who vow revenge. Blindness is a fit punishment for a man whose sin is lust, a sin of the eye, and who sees neither what he is called upon to do nor what he is expected not to do.[54] Just as "The Prophets . . . had not alwayes the gift of Prophecy," so Samson had not always "extraordinary impulses of the spirit" to sanction his acts.[55] Samson probably did not act by divine instinct in marrying the Woman of Timnath and went to Gaza, certainly, "Not by a call from God, but of his own mind . . . presuming upon his strength, and therefore justly deserted, and foiled."[56] Most a type of Christ in his death, Samson finally acts not in his private but in his public person to take, for the first time, a revenge that is creditable.

Although Samson is still remembered as an agent of division and an instrument (though not necessarily God's instrument) for destruction, more often, in this decade when Samson is redeemed for heroism, he is seen hurling down the wall that stands between this world and Paradise, opening for his people the gates of life. The example of Samson elicits the observation, "what mervailous deliverances God wrought for his people"; and his own private history, in turn, is a micro-history in-

---

Bible, I, 550; John Donne, *Biathanatos*, ed. Ernest W. Sullivan II (Newark: Univ. of Delaware Press; London and Toronto: Associated Univ. Presses, 1984), pp. 135, 235; Thomas Jackson, *The Works of Thomas Jackson* (12 vols.; Oxford: Oxford Univ. Press, 1844), I, 99; Thomas Fuller, *A Pisgah-Sight of Palestine* (London: Printed for John Williams, 1650), p. 214; the anonymous *Two Dissertations*, p. 63; and Robert Burton, *The Anatomy of Melancholy*, ed. A. R. Shilleto (3 vols.; London: George Bell and Sons, 1893), III, 176. Eugene M. Waith uses the Hercules myth to interrelate *Samson Agonistes* and *Paradise Regained*: "Milton assigns to the chorus of *Samson Agonistes* a comparison with Hercules, and in *Paradise Regained* he compares Christ's struggle with Satan to that of Hercules with Antaeus" (*The Herculean Hero in Marlowe, Chapman, Shakespeare, and Dryden* [New York: Columbia Univ. Press; London: Chatto and Windus, 1962], p. 39).

[54] *Annotations upon the Old and New Testament*, I, 84.

[55] *Ibid.*, I, 86.

[56] *Ibid.*, I, 90; see also pp. 84-85.

suring, in the words of Paul Knell, that though "the Prologue have been Tragicall, yet the Catastrophe shall be Comicall, God will make good to us that promise."[57]

Still, we continue to hear of Samson as a fallen hero who, in the very moment when he is stripped of his strength and might, had "become *as another Man*" with no "occupation too base for him"; and in his fallenness Samson is now seen "portraying forth . . . our *British* Union, fast knit and bound, soon dissolved." Great Britain rent in pieces, according to Lady Eleanor Douglas, is "shadowed out in Samsons exploits,"[58] a view of Samson already implicit in *King Lear*. Samson is a more congenial figure for those who believe that "God the avenger of blood, wil require it of the obstructors of justice and freedom. Judges 9.24" than for those who refer to the "killing and slaying of men . . . [as] the most horrid worke to Nature and Scripture,"[59] or who believe that while "the best of men may erre, yet they are the worst of men, that persist in error, after the discovery."

Once the discrepancy is highlighted between Samson as a symbol of the elect and emblem of the true church and Samson by his activities calling this supposed election into question, Samson himself may seem a better illustration of those men who "doe such things as the holy Scriptures abhorre; and yet could never rest till they had done them."[60] Samson's activities, having the effect of casting doubt on the divine authority used

[57] Paul Knell, *Israel and England Paralelled* (London: n.p., 1648), pp. 5, 18. See also Featley et al., "Sermon III: A Christians Victorie; or, Conqvest over Deaths Enmitie" (1639), in *Threnoikos*, p. 273.

[58] See, e.g., Lady Eleanor Douglas, *Samsons Fall, Presented to the House 1642* (London: n.p., 1642), pp. 3, 7, 10.

[59] See George Masterson, *A Declaration of Some Proceedings* (n.d.), pp. 93, 107; William Walwyn, *The Bloody Project* (1648), p. 136; and the anonymous *The Vanitie of the Present Churches* (1649), p. 274, all in *The Leveller Tracts*, ed. Haller and Davies.

[60] See *The Vanitie of the Present Churches*, in *The Leveller Tracts*, ed. Haller and Davies, p. 259.

to legitimate them, will eventually align him with such men as are described in the anonymous "Vanitie of the Present Churches," with those who "presume to be so Goded with God, and Christed with Christ." This is the "sad condition," according to this author, to which men in these times are brought "by this fals presence of a Spirit, which once taken up, & insisted on, their credit becomes so ingag'd . . . in being thought the darlings of God, that it is the hardest thing in the world, to make them see their mistake."[61]

Until the end of the century, Samson continues to be a topic whenever such matters as "Whooredome or Fornication" or "Whether it be lawful for children to mary without the con- sente of theyr parentes" are under discussion.[62] And whatever political purposes the Samson legend had been put to by the Puritans, it continues through the century to supply political rhetoric now being used against traitors and rebels in the realm as pointedly as once it had been employed to advance the revolutionary cause.[63] It is the currency of the Samson story in the arena of politics that lies behind Bunyan's transposition of that story into the spiritual realm of his fiction where, when the captains or high commanders in the town of Mansoul learn that they are about to be beleaguered, they rise up "like so many Samsons, . . . shake themselves, and come together . . . to defeat those hellish contrivances . . . of Diaboles and his fiends."[64] Like Christ and Satan (and with both of them Samson achieved a measure of identity during the seventeenth century), Samson himself, and not without an earlier precedent, has become allegorized and internalized, an ordering principle

[61] *Ibid.*, p. 260.

[62] See, e.g., Samuel Mather, *The Figures or Types of the Old Testament* (Dublin: n.p., 1683), p. 214. Cf. Peter Martyr (P. Vermigli), *Most Fruitfull and Learned Comentaries* (London: John Day, 1564), f. 214ᵛ.

[63] See both *Samsons Riddle* (1678) and *Dagon's Fall* (1680).

[64] *The Whole Works*, ed. George Offor (3 vols.; London: Blackie and Sons, 1862), III, 340.

within that quells another, Delilah-like principle of rebellion within.

The Book of Judges continues to be regarded, as it was in the previous century, as the Old Testament book of God's judgments and mercies, its individual stories alternately revealing God rebuking obstinate sinners and rewarding the penitent. In this sixth period of Old Testament history, according to Edward Vaughan, the Judges were "stirred vp to be deliuerers of the poore oppressed people of God. They were men of great faithfulnes and courage"[65]—at least some of them were, some of the time. For the Judges themselves, and chief among them Samson, could be seen as imaging the failings of their people and the tragedy of their nation. Thus the Book of Judges is also referred to as "a Glasse [for] discovering *Israels* calamity" and is viewed as a revelation of her "barren Common."[66] In this scriptural book, we are asked to observe parallels—Israel corresponding to England, Sodom and Gomorrah to London and Westminster—and are made to see contrasting patterns with the people continually returning evil for evil and God rewarding their evil with good.[67] There is a repeated pattern of apostatizing accompanied by the promise that there will always be a deliverer for those who return to God, for as he did with Samson God repeatedly shows mercy in the midst of his severest judgments.[68] Though composed by some prophet,

[65] *Method, or Briefe Instruction; Verie Profitable and Speedy, for the Reading and Understanding of the Old and New Testament* (London: Printed by T. Orwin, 1590), p. 70.

[66] See the anonymous *Clavis Bibliorum: The Key of the Bible* (Edinburgh: Printed by Gedeon Lithgow, 1649), p. 95.

[67] Knell, *Israel and England Paralelled*, pp. 1, 14. For a later example, see John March, *A Sermon . . . on the 30th of January 1676-7* [Judges 19:30] (London: Printed for Richard Randell, 1677).

[68] *Clavis Bibliorum*, pp. 92-95.

Judges is derived from records and registers and its prophecy applied to the present times.

Whether the plot of the Book of Judges is salutary depends upon the commentator. For John Greene it is not. He allows the opponents of the king their favorite analogy (they are *Samsons*) but also turns the analogy against them: they are more "like *Sampsons* foxes turned taile to taile and firebrands betwixt them."[69] For Henry Robinson, the plot is hardly more salutary, as he makes evident by analogizing Presbytery with Delilah and Episcopacy with Samson. Although the Presbyters may "cut the Bishops Locks, a little regulate them," Samson-like their hair will grow again, enabling them, if they wish, to "pull down the house of the Common-wealth about us all."[70] Yet even here, the Samson analogy is used guardedly; for "in reality," says Robinson, Presbytery is "a tyrannicall Episcopacy . . . a regulated Episcopacy," and he thereupon argues that "man can do nothing religiously without the perswasion of his conscience" but must simultaneously resist any acts of "blinde obedience."[71] Robinson is thus acutely aware of the potential error in following individual conscience, urging that before one obeys what are presumed to be divine commands, one should be convinced first of their lawfulness, "for *whatever is not of faith is sinne*," whatever contradicts the fundamentals of religion or is repugnant to the Word should not be obeyed: to act with a rod of iron instead of a golden scepter "is to separate the soul from the body, and bid the body act."[72] It is just this sort of understanding that underlies Joshua Sprugge's contention that "we die with the Lord, into the Lord, as all the Lords of the *Philistines* did with *Sampson*."[73]

[69] *Nehemiah's Teares and Prayers for Judah's Affliction* (London: Printed by G. M., 1644), pp. 12-13.

[70] *A Moderate Answer to Mr. Prins Full Reply* (London: Printed for Benjamin Allen, 1645), p. 15.

[71] *Ibid.*, pp. 36, 38, 42.   [72] *Ibid.*, pp. 19, 37.

[73] *Christus Redivivus, The Lord Is Risen* (London: Printed for Giles Calvert, 1649), sig. A4^v.

That is, we die into Christ's spiritual body, as the Philistines died into Samson's natural body; we possess within ourselves both the natural and the spiritual image, the former figured by Samson, woman, Eve, and the tree of knowledge, and the latter by Christ, man, Adam, and the tree of life. Here Samson the alienated man contrasts with Christ, or man in union with God.

If an old typology is revived early in the 1640s, by the end of the decade that typology is again under challenge and, when not completely scuttled, is wrought into a symbolism. Reverting to in order to develop a distinction between private and public principles of action, carnal interests as opposed to "common and publick principles, . . . the outward liberty and freedom of the Nation," Joseph Salmon says of the former, "This is your Dalilah," and of the latter, this is your "Lord, *our* spiritual *Sampson*" whom "I see . . . hath laid his hands of almighty power upon (you) these Pillars of this wooden Farbrick":

> . . . he will dis-joynt you, and shake you all to pieces in you the whole edifice of this swordlie Power shall be annihilated; the Lord will die with it, in it (or rather out of it, and from it) and in his death will destroy more then you have done all your lives time. The Lord will *here* take you napping, and you are eating and drinking, marrying, and giving in marriage to strange flesh, and the like of divine burning shall consume you. Oh, it will be a glorious day: wait for it.[74]

The private-public distinction is first cast in terms of Delilah and Samson, the carnal versus the public spirit, but is there-

---

[74] *A Rout, A Rout; or Some Part of the Armies Quarters Beaten up* (London: Printed for G. C., 1649), pp. 14-15.

upon recast in terms of the carnal, historical Samson and the spiritual Samson who is Christ; the former goes awhoring, exercises swordly power, and is consumed because Christ flees from and dies out of him. If the Lord remains within the vengeful Samson (or Cromwell's army), we can only assume that he hides himself in foul habit and then must countenance the prospect of "the Lord . . . besmear[ing] himself with blood and vengeance, deform[ing] his own beauty, hid[ing] his amiable presence under a hideous and wrathful form."[75]

Those who have slain the king have played the role of Samson "acting under a fleshly discovery of things . . . are led forth in a way of vengeance upon . . . [their] adversaries; . . . sentence and shoot to death at . . . [their] pleasure; it little moves . . . [them] to trample upon the blood of . . . [their] enemies; This is . . . [their] Victory, Glory and Triumph. All this well," Salmon concludes, but "you must tarry here till God moves higher amongst you."[76] And for Salmon, finally, to think of the whore or the avenging angel only as Pope, Presbyter, or Episcopacy is to know them "in History, but not in the Mistery." The whore, the avenging angel, even the true deliverer find only their "carnall conceptions" and "fleshly appearance" in Delilah, Samson, and Christ, all of whom are really "in thee." Michael and Satan, the insurrection and the rebellion, the heaven and earth, "are *Mystically* in man"; and he must "expect Jesus to come in Judgment . . . and the end of the world" to be within as well.[77]

In the 1650s, as the failure of the Revolution seems imminent and the causes for its failure undergo scrutiny, these hermeneutic tendencies persist and even are intensified. Among the revolutionaries, the pressing question is "How

[75] *Ibid.*, p. 30.
[76] *Ibid.*, p. 21.
[77] *Antichrist in Man* (London: n.p., 1649), pp. 2, 47.

could the God who willed 1649 also will 1660? And how could he sacrifice his servants then even if others had let down his Cause?"[78] These questions elicit an array of sometimes unexpected answers, even from among the ranks of the revolutionaries. It is not far from John Greene who sees current history writ in the Book of Judges to Joseph Salmon who sees the rhetoric of the Revolution, much of it derived from the Samson story, as a defilement of God's word. Arise Evans similarly correlates contemporary history with the Judges narrative, squaring all supposed visions and revelations, inspirations and promptings, with the word and dismissing all those which do not exalt God or accord with his teachings. In keeping with this tendency, Thomas Fuller, describing Samson as a mauler of people, argues that it is "easier . . . for me to be consumed to ashes, then to quench the last spark of lust in our soul" and further that Samson's silence in not telling his parents about killing the lion is "no less commendable then his valour."[79] Anyone who presumes on his might, says Fuller, has not strong brains.

Samson continues to typify Christ, principally in his might and strength; but the comparison is never far off from the realization that "Gods dispensations are so chequer-wrought with blacks and whites, that many times a Saint hath cause to rejoyce, but yet with trembling; at other times to tremble, but yet with rejoycing," nor far off from the awareness that "To revenge a wrong, is to do wrong to God," making that man "guilty of that which he complains of, . . . unjustly complains of," for it is not other than what he himself does.[80] The attitude

[78] Christopher Hill, *The Experience of Defeat: Milton and Some Contemporaries* (New York: Viking, 1984), p. 307.

[79] *A Pisgah-Sight of Palestine*, pp. 215, 216. In *An Eccho to the Voice from Heaven* (London: n.p., 1652), Arise Evans sets forth rules for "squar[ing] and try[ing] all the Visions and Revelations": first, "ye that take Visions and Revelations for your guide, and leave the Scripture, ye feed on husks and chaff, and ye shall be burut with them," for "every true Vision and Revelation is subordinate to the Scripture, and is for the exaltation of the Scripture" (pp. 102, 103).

[80] Ralph Venning, *Canaans Flowings* (London: Printed for John Rothwel, 1658),

may persist that the judges, coming first, are better than kings; but it persists in the realization that there are kings because the judges themselves failed God and their people and became corrupt—and in the paradox that if judges are better than kings[81] Judge Samson is nonetheless inferior to King David; is in relation to David, his antitype, as much a flawed image as is David in relation to his antitype, who is Christ. As these Christian typological connections begin to crumble, others of classical derivation become more secure: "*Hercules* the *Pagan-Samson* in some sort may seem, by the luxury of Poets wits, to *ape* this *Iewish Hercules*," says Fuller; yet "both of them very like for their valour" are also "too like for their wantonness. . . . As Samsons lustre did rise, so it did set in this Tribe."[82]

The crude political rhetoric that enveloped the Samson story in the 1640s is refined by both sides, each of which eventually uses the Samson story to anatomize its own failures. A story that was a window during the 1640s, with one side looking through it at its adversary, becomes a mirror, with each side now glimpsing itself in the reflection. The Royalists comprehended that a king must be a great judge and that the ultimate pattern for both offices is provided by Christ whose nobleness of mind raised him above revenge, "or executing . . . anger upon the many," and taught him that there is "more inward complacency in pardoning one, then in punishing a thousand." Within this context, Arise Evans credits Charles I with being an improvement upon all former kings: "none . . . came

---

pp. 171, 187-88; see also *Mysteries and Revelations* (London: Printed for John Rothwel, 1657), where Samson, in his strength and might, is presented as Christ's type (p. 57).

[81] See John Brayne, *The New Earth* (London: Printed for Richard Moon, 1653), p. 1; Diodati, *Pious and Learned Annotations*, annotation to Judges 16:17; Trapp, *Annotations upon the Old and New Testament*, I, 81; Downame et al., *Annotations upon All the Books*, annotation to Judges 13:5; George Wither, *Epistolarum-Vagum-Prosa-Metricum: or, an Epistle at Random* (1659), in *Miscellaneous Works of George Wither* (5 vols.: London: Spenser Society, 1872), I, 27-28.

[82] *A Pisgah-Sight of Palestine*, p. 214.

nearer to Christ in word and deed then he did." Yet "the kingdom was turned upside down" by certain of Charles's failures: like Samson, he was a lapsed judge, God became angry with him and his people and hence anointed Cromwell as the instrument of his wrath and vengeance "to fight Christ's battels."[83] If the first Charles was regarded in the similitude of Samson, another Charles, learning from the first one's mistakes, will reign in the similitude of David. Samson is the only figure in Scripture who, laying a wager, loses it; and he loses it "through his own folly" in making others pay for it so dearly, this being a lesson for those who have not lost their profaneness and want to return the king by arms.[84] Samson and those who model themselves after him misconstrue the spirit of true warfare and also of true prophecy; "God sends a Prophet to pronounce disaster to a people, and sets a time for it, if upon it they repent and mend their evil wayes, they should not be destroyed at that time . . . [and] if that people . . . do not repent and mend their evil wayes," they are not destroyed in consequence but simply "shall not be delivered."[85]

A fanatical monarchist like Arise Evans, no less than a revolutionary sympathizer like Robert Norwood, wants a peaceful settlement, and so pleads with his people to be Samsons—but not *fallen* Samsons. Their resurrection is at hand, they must not now go down to Egypt and into the house of bondage. "Take heed of *Dalilahs*," Norwood urges, "for though thou be a *Samson*, yet if thou sufferest thy seven locks to be shaved off, the *Philistines* will take thee, yea and *put out*

[83] *The Voice of King Charles the Father, to Charles the Son; and the Bride Say, "Come"* (London: Printed for the Author, 1655), sigs. A4ᵛ, A6ᵛ, B2, and p. 13. Outspoken in his criticism of both the Anabaptists and the Presbyterians, Evans has sometimes been numbered among the Independents. In fact, he was regularly the king's spokesman; he always supported the Church of England as the true church and was notorious for warning the king through his prophesyings and for prophesying repeatedly the Restoration.

[84] *Ibid.*, p. 23.   [85] *Ibid.*

both thine eyes also, *binde thee in fetters*, and *cause thee to grinde in the prison-house.* The wise will know this saying, and understand this Parable." Norwood continues with this parable later on, urging that we must not be fallen Samsons, we must avoid idols, lest "We . . . go down into *Egypt*, into *the house of bondage*":

> We will not (for we may not, being all and every one of us Nazarites unto the Lord) suffer our seven locks to be shaved off our heads by any *Dalilah* whatsoever, lest we be taken by the *Philistims*, and by them have both our eyes put out; and so be led . . . and bound in fetters, to grind in the prison-house. We have kept and preserved them hitherto; we have defended and maintained our Liberties against Kings and Parliaments, with the hazard of our lives . . . and blood also. Those who have lost their locks, let them grinde in the Prison-house, if it must be so, until they be grown again.[86]

During the 1650s there are still those, like Theodore Haak, who continue to look upon Samson as one of God's "valiant Champions," as an "excellent and transcendent . . . Champion," who view him in his public, never his private, person and regard Samson at the pillars as "a type and figure of our Lord Jesus Christ, who conquered all his and our enemies chiefly by his death."[87] But Haak's are also anomalous views in the 1650s when more insistently than ever the Book of Judges is being viewed as a history, the record of which shows, and certainly Samson's record shows, the corruptibility of the judges themselves—their frailty, their inconsiderateness. Sam-

[86] *An Additional Discourse* (London: Printed for Richard Moon, 1653), p. 57.
[87] *The Dutch Annotations upon the Whole Bible* (London: Printed by Henry Hills, 1657); see "The Argument" to Judges and the following annotations: 15:7, 16:16, 16:31.

son's case can no longer be argued without extensive and some-times embarrassing special pleading. If Delilah is still cast in the role of the Great Whore, Samson now seems to resemble the Great Beast. He who seemed a type of Christ is revealed as an arm of Antichrist. There is uneasiness still with Samson's first marriage, alleged by Samson to be motivated by God but probably actually motivated by Samson's private desire for revenge; with his stripping dead bodies of their apparel, some-thing strictly forbidden by the Nazarite code; and with Sam-son's going off to Gaza and, instead of rising out of sin, "sink[ing] deeper and deeper into this whirl-pool, and re-laps[ing] again into the same sin."[88] About judges and judg-ments, this scriptural book elicits judgments concerning its judges so that we may learn "by their example to imitate such things in them as are worthy of imitation, and shun the con-trary."[89] As Norwood puts the case, "even those of the house of *David* in special were to be judged, as well as to judge."[90] Or as Thomas Fuller now urges of this scriptural book, the last part of which is "mournfull with murther, a murther most strange, most true," and which as a tragedy ends in "weeping and bleeding": "let us read histories that we be not made an history . . . let us tell *Judah* of their sinnes, and *Israel* of their transgressions."[91] Let us also remember, the commentators

[88] See Downame et al., *Annotations upon All the Books*, annotation to Judges 16:4; but see the following annotations to Judges as well: 14:13 ("God had straightly forbidden his people to make marriages with these cursed nations, of which the Philistines were a part"); 14:19 ("How could Samson do this, seeing he was a Nazarite, unto who it was unlawfull to touch a dead body?").

[89] *Ibid.*, see "The Argument" to Judges.

[90] *An Additional Discourse*, p. 18. Or as Thomas Fuller puts the case: "Do thou as *Samson* did, and it shall be forgiven thee: Pluck down at once two fundamental pillars of a Church. His action shews his commission extraordinary and is no warrant for others to drown, stab, poyson, and murther themselves" (*A Comment on the Eleven First Verses of the Fourth Chapter of S. Matthew's Gospel* [London: Printed by James Cottrel, 1652], fifth sermon, p. 91).

[91] "Strange Justice: Judges 19. 30" (1655-56), in *The Collected Sermons of Thomas Fuller*, ed. John Eglington Bailey and William E. A. Axon (2 vols.; London:

seem to be saying still, that Judges is the Old Testament counterpart to the New Testament Revelation: it is another map of providence, "the book of the VVrath and Mercy of God."[92]

Any political faction could deploy the Samson story, and many did after the Restoration, as a warning to its adversaries—"let them remember how God renewed *Samsons* strength, to revenge himselfe at last"—but usually not apart from the principled awareness that to pretend zeal to set up Jesus Christ is none other than to pull him down, that because religion and politics are twins they should not be allowed to contradict one another. Matthew Griffith, whose words I have just quoted and many of whose positions Milton abhorred, stands at one end of the political spectrum: the king and his men are Samsons, looked upon with scorn and contempt by a nation of Philistines whose schisms and sects are rather like, and so should be subjected to the same fate as, Samson's foxes. They and their parliament "did professedly maintain that we may do Evil that good may come thereof; and they had no other ground but . . . their *Utopian Reformation*."[93]

The Book of Judges taught many besides Griffith that the sins of a nation and its weaknesses move God to put a nation in the hands of her enemies. For the king's men, this proposition entailed their accepting the view that God, once on the side of the Cromwellians, had switched sides—was now liberating the nation from the yoke under which earlier He had placed it:

> During which Inter-regnum Almighty God had a
> Controversy with this Nation, for our Ingratitude,

Gresham Press, 1891), II, 527, 529, 537. The notion that Samson is an actor in a tragedy is implicit certainly in Prynne's *Histrio-Mastix*, p. 230.

[92] See Vaughan, *An Introduction into the Bookes of the Prophets and Apostles*, unpaginated "An Introduction to Booke of Judges."

[93] See Griffith, *The Fear of God and the King*, pp. 9, 68, 91-92, and his later remarks in *The King's Life-Guard*, pp. 22, 32.

Schism, Sedition, and Rebellion; which he severely
punished by sheathing that Sword in our own Bow-
els, that was so causelessly, and unlawfully, drawn
against his Annointed. . . .

The martyred Samson, no less than the martyred Christ, was
in a line leading to "our Kingly Proto-martyr" Charles I, "the
livelyest representation of God's Majesty," whose horrid death
reminds us of the efficacy in following the laws of nature. For
"even nature . . . abhors all Murther, and Blood-shed."[94]

Subscribing to the same providential view of history, believing equally that God's hand was forever shaping the course
of human history, the Puritans would simply reverse this
argument: God could now be seen abandoning the Good Old
Cause and again punishing a backsliding nation, which pre-
ferred tyranny to freedom, with another yoke of kingship—
God's greatest plague. God places a nation in such a situation
by way of forcing it to free itself, urging upon it the duty of
using the dagger against the tyrants who have made all laws
fruitless and helpless, as well as the responsibility of summoning the tyrants to the court of justice as Samson did with
the Philistines. Edward Sexby, who argues in just this way,
avers:

> In the story of *Samson* 'tis manifest, that the denying
> him his wife, and after the burning her, and her
> Father, which though they were great, yet were pri-
> vate injuries, he took for sufficient grounds to make
> war upon the *Philistins*, being himself but a private
> man, and not onely not assisted, but opposed by his
> servile Countreymen. He knew what the Law of
> Nature allowed him; where other Laws have no
> place, and thought it a sufficient Justification for
> smiting the *Philistines* hip and thigh, to answer for

[94] *The King's Life-Guard*, unpaginated "Epistle Dedicatory," and pp. 1, 14, 15.

himself, that as they did unto him, so had he done unto them.

Now that which was lawful for *Samson* to do against many Oppressours, why is it unlawful for us to do against one? Are our Injuries less? Our Friends and Relations are daily murdered before our faces. Have we other ways for reparation? Let them be named, and I am silenc'd. But if we have none, the Fire-brands, or the Jaw-bone, the first Weapons our just Fury can lay hold on, may certainly be lawfully employed against the uncircumcised *Philistin* that oppresses us. We have too the opposition and discouragements that *Samson* had, and therefore have the more need of his courage and resolution. As he had the men of *Judah*, so we have the men of *Levi*, crying to us out of the Pulpit, as from the top of the Rock *Etam*, Know you not that the Philistin is a ruler over you? The truth is, they would fain make him so, and bind us with *Samson* in new Cords; but we hope they will become as Flax, and that they will either loose from our hands, or we shall have the Courage to cut them.

Thereupon Sexby proceeds to dispose of two objections, each of them likely to be grounded in Scripture, that might be brought against his argument:

The first is, That these examples out of Scripture, are of men that were Inspired of God, and that therefore they had that Call and Authority for their Actions, which we cannot pretend to, so that it would be unsafe for us to draw their actions into examples, except we had likewise their Justifications to alledg.

The other objection, says Sexby, is that the people are no

longer in opposition to the king and so give their "tacit consent to the Government":

> To the first I answer with learned *Milton*, that if God commanded these things, 'tis a sign they were lawful and commendable. But secondly, as I observed in the Relations of the examples themselves; Neither *Sampson* nor *Samuel* alleged any other cause or reason for what they did, but retaliation, and the apparent justice of the actions themselves. Nor had God appeared to *Moses* in the Bush when he slew the *Egyptian*; nor *Jehafàda* alledg any Prophetical Authority or other Call to do what he did, but that common Call which all men have, to do all actions of Justice that are within their power, when the ordinary course of Justice ceases.[95]

Milton's own ethics do not accord well with those of Sexby; what further complicates, and compromises, Sexby's argument is his insistence that killing a tyrant is lawful only when the people are ready to benefit from it. Judging from Milton's remarks in *The Readie and Easie Way*, the people are ready rather to be led back into bondage.

A sanction for very different political programs, and sometimes a warning, the Samson story is also a reminder, significantly in 1659, that would-be Samsons "must first have occasion given, by an outward [not as in the biblical Samson's case, a private] injury, before he could be rowzed up to execute GOD's Vengeance upon the enemies of his *Country*"—a vengeance that more appropriately is wielded by words, or the spiritual sword, as the true means of man's deliverance. It is of some significance that, having uttered this statement, George Wither proceeds to identify himself with David, not Samson, as "a Type of the Messias."[96] Here Wither presses grievances,

---

[95] *Killing, No Murder* (London: n.p., 1659), pp. 9-10.

[96] See *Epistolarum-Vagum-Prosa-Metricum*, in *Miscellaneous Works*, I, 27-28.

petitions for redress, and issues a warning prophecy, appropriating the spiritual sword (or word) as the proper means for delivering himself and his people from bondage.

The Samson legend was the property of no single political party and the promoter of no one ideology. During the Civil War years and in their immediate aftermath, this extraordinarily supple story, exhibiting a capacity for serving a variety of purposes, also enjoyed a wide range of applicability. In view of John Shawcross's contention that Griffith "did not recognize Samson as a metaphoric figure who stood for change and sedition against the established (albeit evil) state,"[97] it is interesting that Griffith should have previously used the Samson story as both a positive and a negative example. Predictably, Griffith will say "of the enemies of the Church, that they may kill us (if God permit) but they cannot conquer us: For (like *Sampson*) we shall be victorious, even in death it self; at which time, . . . we shall *see the heavens open*." But in the same treatise, and perhaps surprisingly in the light of Shawcross's remark, Samson is also represented as putting into disarray what ought to be "tyed together"—as perverting rather than promoting the objectives for establishing Jerusalem, a city of unity and peace. Samson is now identified with the Parliament, which would "set all in combustion, and bring all to confusion" and which, moving against law and conscience, would also "palliate all, by pretending the spirit, as having some extradininary Inspirations, Illuminations, Revelations of the spirit for all they do." Griffith then proceeds to place Samson before a set of allegorical pillars:

> One use of pillars, is to preserve the remembrance of things past . . . A second use of pillars, is to expose to open view such things as are fastened upon them . . . A third use of pillars, is for the suppor-

[97] See "A Survey of Milton's Prose Works," in *Achievements of the Left Hand: Essays on the Prose of John Milton*, ed. Michael Lieb and John T. Shawcross (Amherst: Univ. of Massachusetts Press, 1974), p. 337.

> tation of the fabrick which is built upon them: and
> such a pillar is the Church to the truth; Gods true
> Religion, . . . which doth indeed support the Com-
> mon-wealth; and therefore they which (with *Sampson*
> . . .) thrust at this pillar with all their might, will
> ere they be aware bring the whole fabrick about their
> eares, to the certaine ruine of themselves and others.

Samson here emblematizes a people fallen into grievous anarchy who, devoid of all charity, "speak what they think not,
and also do what they approve not,"[98] scattering with war all
of what in peace they had gathered.

Elsewhere, and still earlier in Griffith's writings, Samson
represents the Protestants who must stave off repeated attacks
by "holy-hollow-hearted Catholikes" like Delilah; he is a measure against which men intoxicated by their own self-importance
are wont to estimate themselves; he is an illustration of bad
marriages, both in his liaison with the Woman of Timnath
("Will no Tree please thee but that which is forbidden?") and
in the marriage which Griffith, like Milton, presumes to have
taken place with Delilah: "Oh that there were no such husband
to whom the wife may justly say as *Dalilah* did to *Sampson;
How canst thou say I love thee, when as thy heart is not with
me?*"[99] Though Griffith may here speak of the "strong
Sampson," like Goliath Samson is nevertheless said to be mas-
tered by *"Death* [which] gave him a fall"—a fall that repeats
what he had experienced in his own lifetime:

> . . . doe not *smooth*, and *sooth* up your selves in the
> *lusts* of the *flesh*; doe not countenance them, no not
> so much as connive at them: nor is it enough to give

[98] *A Patheticall Perswasion to Pray for Publick Peace* (London: Published for Richard Royston, 1642), pp. 45, 28, 29, 37, unpaginated "Epistle Dedicatory."
[99] *Bethel; or a Forme for Families* (London: Printed by Richard Badger, 1633), pp. 170, 250, 283, 457, 477; see also pp. 87, 136, 250, 253.

> them two, or three faint denials, as *Sampson* did to
> *Dalilah*; for, as the *Ramme* goes back, but 'tis to
> returne with the greater birre: and as *Dalilah* de-
> luded, so wil our *lusts* make the stronger on-set till
> they prevaile, and we perish.[100]

Much later, in the aftermath of the Restoration, instead of
finding his identity in the king, Samson will find it in the
Presbyterians whose brothers, says Griffith, are the Jesuits.[101]

This diverse usage of the Samson story had the effect sometimes of shattering the legend and scattering its pieces and
other times, especially in the post-Restoration years, of trivializing the legend and reducing it to mock satire. This or
that strand of the story could be laced through a literary text
rather as the different components of a topic are strewn through
a commonplace book. By the middle of the seventeenth century, an array of commonplaces had accrued to the Book of
Judges, the largest number of which were anchored to the
Samson story. Yet the commonplaces of one century are not
always those of the next, as is made evident by the fact that,
though the Samson legend in both the sixteenth and seventeenth
centuries is cast as a saint's life or spiritual biography, the
inflections of the story shift from century to century. In the
sixteenth century, the Samson story dramatizes the period of
regeneration, whereas increasingly in the seventeenth century
it provides analogues for the saint's fall—for mortification,
suffering, and degeneration. And within the realm of imaginative literature, there were available alternatives to mining
the Samson story for commonplaces or to trivializing it. This
legend, as *Samson Agonistes* exemplifies, could be deployed
inventively within a work that instead of trivializing could
thematize such commonplaces by way of interrogating them.
Moreover, if there are shifting accents observable when the

---

[100] *Ibid.*, pp. 457, 477, 170.   [101] *The King's Life-Guard*, p. 23.

Samson story is subjected to century-by-century scrutiny, there are similarly different implications discernible when the usage of this legend by the Puritans comes under surveillance, especially in the crucial decades of the 1640s and 50s.

During this stretch of time, Samson does not lose his political identity with the Puritan Revolution but, maintaining that identity, becomes a mirror for gazing upon its failures. Just those qualities that we are told a contemporary of Milton would never have discerned in Samson—his continual backsliding, his retaliatory spirit, his wanton lust, his becoming inured to blood and violence, his quick beckoning to what he presumes to be divine promptings—just these qualities, whether they are cause for celebration or censure, come to be stressed—and I say *stressed* because these attributes had always been glimpsed in Samson, indeed were made his conspicuous character traits by Reformation theologians. Such ambiguities in Samson's character were particularly evident to those like John Price who came to recognize early on the extent to which both sides are injured in "the great contentions between Christ and the Devil" where, instead of the one side defeating the other, both sides are likely to be bruised in the battle; or to those like Humphrey Brooke who articulated the difficulty in "distinguish[ing] between things that are and but seem to be, between Truth and Falsehood: insomuch that this vain world frequently mis-calls Good, Evil; and Evil Good."[102]

Samson Agonistes is a poem of, and partly about, the Puritan Revolution: it has its deepest roots in that experience and is, in the largest sense, an emanation of the spirit of its age. Criticism of Milton's tragedy has too often been written by interpreters who have effected a ruthless separation of poetry and politics, politics and religion, and who, in turn, have spawned a criticism attentive to commonplaces, yet insensitive

---

[102] See Price's *Walwins Wiles*, p. 286, and Humphrey Brooke's *The Charity of Church-Men*, p. 346, both in *The Leveller Tracts*, ed. Haller and Davies.

to the extent to which those very commonplaces are being eroded in Milton's own time. A criticism that fosters such separations, whatever its pretensions, is not ideologically innocent—is, in fact, evading the critic's job. It retains its merit as criticism only when we remember that its contextual conception of *Samson Agonistes* may be different from Milton's own, that critical advances are nevertheless to be made by taking into account the gaps and splits. Some poets submit to, and become dominated by, this or that version of a myth or archetype; by this or that portion of some field of knowledge; by this, not that, ideology. Milton is rarely this kind of poet. He is no upholder of norms and certainly no upholder of the norms of a criticism still gathering to *Samson Agonistes*, a poem that conducts a polemic with the *topoi* of seventeenth-century politics, theology, and ethics. *Samson Agonistes* is a poem that pushes norms into abeyance and that, in the process, signals its own resistance to codified wisdom and consensual belief. Milton writes this poem not as a purveyor of "popular tosh" but, as Broadbent remarks, in order to replace such tosh with a literature of "better ethical and political effect."[103]

It continues to be said, in our own time, that among the English Puritans Samson enjoyed a steady immortality, "his 'copious Legend' becoming part of the word of God to the Christian era as a prefiguration of the Messiah and the Apocalypse," and more, that this literary immortality "as a puritan saint overcomes the dramatic irony most immediate to the story: that the hero's coup of liberation is undone and the Israelites soon taken captive. However ephemeral Samson's political achievement," says Georgia Christopher, "the *story* of his faith perseveres, useful over the ages."[104] It is true that in the sixteenth century Samson's story was forever being cast as a saint's legend and continued in this same casting in the

[103] *"Comus" and "Samson Agonistes,"* p. 35.
[104] *Milton and the Science of the Saints,* p. 248.

writings of Joseph Hall. But early in the seventeenth century, the Judges story is also given a new setting in the church liturgy, one that would explode instead of exploit the received typology. By the time that *Samson Agonistes* is published, even if Samson continues to figure in saints' lives and spiritual biographies, it is to provide an analogy to the saint's fall, not to the saint's exaltation. A once positive has become a negative example; a Reformation tradition stemming from Luther is recovered.

Hebrews 11 is still thought to contain "*a little Book of Martyrs*"; Christians are still being instructed to be "the Saints Apes"—to "*Dwell upon the* Exemplary Lives of *these Transcendent* Saints," until they metamorphose into "the Image." Yet the life of Jesus now provides the essential analogies for the saint's regeneration and the life of Samson, certain analogues to his fall. In Samuel Clarke's "Life of Tertullian," for example, Christ is said to liberate the people from the very idolatries into which the Samson story had led them. In the same author's "Life of Origen," there appears the following lamentation:

> *I bewaileth sometimes the fall of* Sampson, but now have faln worse my self: . . . Sampson had his hairs cut off; but the Crown of glory is faln off my head. Sampson lost the carnal eyes of his body; but my spiritual eyes are put out. It was the wilyness of a Woman that brought confusion upon him: but it was my tongue that brought me into this sinful condition: And as he afterwards wanted the comfort of his Earthly possessions: so my tongue by this wickedness hath deprived me of those spiritual gifts, which sometimes have flowen into me with heavenly riches: And as he endured those things by leaving the Israelites and cleaving unto forreiners; So I going

about with some notorious sinners, made my self
Captive to Captives, and a bondslave unto sin.[105]

Criticism of *Samson Agonistes* has given us a false consciousness of Milton's text. It has done so by confusing its own
ideology with Milton's and then by conspiring to give us as
Milton's Samson a figure who is simply a saint, a hero of
faith, and thus a positive example to all the ages. Such is the
delusion that Christopher shares with many readers of Milton's
poem, with many of its critics, even with various of the deluded
persons in that poem; it is their delusion, not Milton's:

> Nothing is here for tears, nothing to wail
> Or knock the breast, no weakness, no contempt,
> Dispraise, or blame, nothing but well and fair,
> And what may quiet us in a death so noble.
>
> (1721-24)

Not only has Manoa twisted these observations away from
reality, but he has surrounded them with erroneous declarations: that Samson's legacy to Israel is freedom (1715), that

[105] See the unpaginated prefaces by Edmond Calamy and John Wall, as well as
the lives of Tertullian and Origen in Samuel Clarke's *The Marrow of Ecclesiastical
History*, 3rd ed. (London: Printed for W. B., 1675), pp. 15, 21. In the former
Clarke says that, in fact, Christians do not, as is sometimes held, "Worship an Asses
Head, the occasion of which slander arose from the *Jews* worshipping the Jaw bone
of an Ass, from the story of *Sampson*, which therefore was falsely and wrongfully
charged upon the Christians" (p. 15). See also John Marbeck's *The Lyues of Holy
Saints* (London: n.p., 1574), pp. 284-86—an obvious influence on Hall's *A Plaine
and Familiar Explication* (London: Published by Miles Flesher, 1633), pp. 95-101.
The source of this idolatry, mentioned by Clarke, seems to derive from the worry
over Samson's prayer at Ramathlehi, a hymn not to God but to the jawbone; see
Simon Patrick (1626-1707), *A Commentary on the Books of the Old Testament*, in *A
Critical Commentary and Paraphrase of the Old and New Testament*, comp. Simon
Patrick et al. (4 vols.; Philadelphia: Carey and Hart; New York: Wiley and Putnam,
1844-45), II, 71. Cf. Richard Bernard's insistence, despite the lack of any evidence,
that Samson always acknowledges and praises God after his victories (*The Bible-
Battells; or the Sacred Art Military* [London: Printed for Edward Blackmore, 1629],
pp. 240-41).

his accomplishments have been "to the end" aided and abetted by God (1720). (Earlier in the poem Manoa himself thought otherwise.) These are precisely the propositions that the historical record calls into question and that by Milton's tragedy are undone. They are, very simply, principles of *Samson* criticism that are unprincipled.

It is one of the many ironies of Milton criticism that those it has accused of reading anachronistically have actually been reading historically and those it thought were reading historically have been reading idiosyncratically. On this matter, Stanley Fish is near enough the truth that he can be allowed to make an initial point for me: "For present-day readers Christ is 'in the text' of *Samson Agonistes*, for others he is not, and before the typological interpretation of the poem was introduced and developed by Michael Krouse in 1949, he was not 'in the text' for anyone."[106] No less than those who argue that the consolation in *Samson Agonistes* is regeneration, that the

---

[106] *Is There a Text in This Class?: The Authority of Interpretive Communities* (Cambridge, Mass.: Harvard Univ. Press, 1980), p. 274. It is important to remember here what Krouse actually says: "It is impossible to suppose that any of Milton's literate contemporaries could have thought of Samson without thinking also of Christ. And yet," he continues, "in *Samson Agonistes* one finds almost no vestige of this aspect of the tradition. There is but one shred of palpable internal evidence to suggest that Milton intended the poem to call to mind the age-old correspondence between Samson and Christ . . . , although there are passages in which one whose ear is attuned to the tradition can hear echoes of the many allegorical analogies between Samson and Christ" (*Milton's Samson and the Christian Tradition*, pp. 120, 122). Krouse's followers, admittedly, have been less circumspect in their formulations; see, e.g., T.S.K. Scott-Craig, "Milton's Tragedy and Christian Vision," in *The Tragic Vision and the Christian Faith*, ed. Nathan A. Scott (New York: Association Press, 1957), who contends that "The final Samson is a figure of the death of Christ" (p. 108), and A. R. Cirillo, "Time, Light, and the Phoenix: The Design of *Samson Agonistes*," in *Calm of Mind: Tercentenary Essays on "Paradise Regained" and "Samson Agonistes,"* ed. Joseph Wittreich (Cleveland: Press of Case Western Reserve Univ., 1971), pp. 209-33.

mode for that consolation is typology, and at this late date that "the link between tragedy and regeneration . . . has not been fully [enough] explored,"[107] Fish illustrates the proposition that much literary history has still to be written for the first time. Hazarding an historical guess, Fish makes a false surmise. Handel's *Samson: An Oratorio* (1749) suggests that, a full two centuries before Krouse's speculations, Milton's Samson was perceived, and hence presented, as a type of Christ, an image of him in all his strength. Handel's allusion to the sun's pillowing its chin upon an orient wave places Milton's nativity ode in juxtaposition with *Samson Agonistes*, hinting at a typological connection that Handel will make explicit in the death scene where, like Christ, Samson's body is bathed and anointed. Handel's *Oratorio* ends with a fulfillment of the promise harbored in its first act: with Samson transported into eternity, his glorious name vindicated, where he now receives the crown of life, basks in an endless blaze of light, and thus typifies the hero who falls "Thro' Sorrow to Felicity."[108]

Or later in the same century, there is the example of Blake's "Samson," which, adhering assiduously to Milton's *Samson*, as Robert Gleckner observes, "exploits the terrible irony of Samson's birth and prophesied destiny by casting it in the commonly accepted typological guise of the birth of Christ," presumably because Milton himself was expert in such typological play and pressed it into service in his own poem in order to link Samson and Dalila not to the story of the resurrected Christ but to that of the fallen Adam and Eve.[109] A century later, W. A. Scott says that he "will not dwell on Samson as a type of Christ" because Milton has already dwelt

[107] Sadler, *Consolation in "Samson Agonistes,"* p. 57.

[108] See *Samson: An Oratorio as Performed at the Theatre in Oxford* (1749), pp. 19, 23, 24; see also p. 8.

[109] See *Blake's Prelude: "Poetical Sketches"* (Baltimore: The Johns Hopkins Univ. Press, 1982) p. 142.

too much on the subject in *Samson Agonistes*. In this typological drama, failing to recognize that "Samson's last prayer is not the prayer of a dying christian—that it breathes the spirit of revenge," Milton, Scott argues, "wholly fails to apprehend his character . . . fall[ing] far below our idea of Samson in that awful moment" where again "Retaliation was his catechism."[110] When in his pioneering essay, *"Samson Agonistes* and Milton in Old Age," James Holly Hanford urges that, for Milton, the Samson story has "an independent human value, neither implying nor prefiguring the life of Christ,"[111] the critic is doubtless protesting against a sometimes unspoken premise of *Samson* criticism now nearly two centuries old.

Fish's uncompromising literalism bears its own yoke of servitude, its own snare of error, and no less than the mystifiers' talk about types and figures, risks, as Fredric Jameson fears in another context, "fixing the mind in external trappings," thereby fostering institutional guardians of interpretation.[112] No less than the typologists, Fish aspires to a monopoly on an exegesis that would assign to *Samson Agonistes* a meaning not very different from that already claimed for it by previous exegetes. Fish's *Samson*, by virtue of its deft design and artistic

[110] *The Giant Judge: or the Story of Samson, the Hebrew Hercules*, 2nd ed. (San Francisco: Whitton, Towne, and Company, 1858), pp. 41, 303, 310. See also *Remarks on Samson, as a Type of Christ* (Leamington: Printed by C. H. Fox, 1850). Robert A. Watson holds a similar view, arguing that Milton's "apology" for Samson derives from a typological tradition which, forcing parallels where none exists, disfigures the true meaning of the Judges narrative; see *Judges and Ruth* (New York: A. C. Armstrong and Son, 1903), p. 331.

[111] Hanford's essay is conveniently reprinted in *John Milton: Poet and Humanist* (Cleveland: Press of Case Western Reserve Univ., 1966), p. 268. Similarly, when Denis Saurat declares, "No allusion, no prophecy on the subject of Christ [is] in *Samson* . . . ! The Son is not mentioned in *Samson*," he is probably not speaking in a vacuum but rather speaking against a supposition that was, even when not openly acknowledged, sitting deep in the structure of *Samson* criticism; see *Milton: Man and Thinker* (1944; rpt. Hamden: Archon Books, 1964), p. 199.

[112] "Religion and Ideology," in *1642: Literature and Power in the Seventeenth Century*, ed. Francis Barker et al. (Univ. of Essex, 1981), p. 320.

complexity, is more interesting and inviting than that of his precursors; but, even more than theirs, it is a poem of rigorously programmed orthodoxy. Fish's Samson, more ambiguous in his heroism than theirs, is their Samson nevertheless— a figure exculpated in his final act of "heroism," in a poem that is not so much a drama of regeneration as the phenomenology of faith recovered, "an experience structured so as to leave unanswered the questions it itself raises,"[113] and so complexly structured as to be more riddling than Samson's own riddles.

What stability *Samson Agonistes* possesses is, for Fish, the function of criticism which, as it changes, allows for the text to change. New ways of reading are founded upon new interpretive assumptions which may or may not bring about new interpretations. As it happens, Fish's way of reading prevents him from admitting to certain kinds of interpretive possibilities—as John Reichert points out, often to those which are theoretically the most interesting and pertinent: the circumstance never addressed by Fish "is that of the interpreter, either on his own or with help, noticing something in the text that makes his former reading seem implausible and hitting upon a new reading that makes better sense of the whole and its parts."[114] Writing about a poet who repeatedly makes second choices, Fish himself avoids the second choice—resists the alternative reading, paradoxically, it would seem, because while distancing himself from typological readings of *Samson Agonistes*, Fish achieves no distance at all from typologically determined interpretations of the Samson story. The problem is endemic to criticism of this poem and is evident, in still more exaggerated form, whenever we hear Milton's critics speak, as Anne Davidson Ferry does, of our *"knowing* the

[113] "Question and Answer in *Samson Agonistes*," in *"Comus" and "Samson Agonistes*," ed. Lovelock, p. 209.

[114] "Making Sense of Interpretation," *Critical Inquiry*, 6 (1980), 748.

promised end of the story . . . we *know* that the poem will end with Samson's triumphant death as God's chosen champion."[115] Ferry here makes explicit what Fish and others assume: we know how Milton's poem will end because we know a version of its story's ending that derives from typological readings of the Judges tale. We *know* only to the extent that we can assume that Milton subscribes to, rather than scrutinizes, an interpretation of the Samson story with which his own century was uneasy. Indeed, this sort of easy knowing threatens to make of us all, as Kenneth Gross might say, "scholiasts of illusion" rather than "purveyors of revelation."[116]

Fish's method for reading, not his reading of *Samson Agonistes*, is different from what obtains in Milton criticism. Ostensibly Fish's argument with the typologists is that they appropriate from Renaissance hermeneutics a device for reading and interpreting that *Samson Agonistes* itself resists. In actuality, what Fish would displace is a critical method of latter-day Miltonists but not the interpretation which is its yield; he would substitute the historical surmise for historical scholarship which, because it has been mistaken, is judged to be a mistake—a failed, fallen form of criticism. The fact is that *Samson Agonistes* flirts with the typological method only to distance itself from the interpretation of the Samson story that has been its yield. Milton, that is, deploys typology against itself. Apart from method, there is little difference between Fish and the typologists: their respective *Samsons* are informed by the same wizened theology and have as their issue the same drama of faith.

The real difference between Milton's critics is evident in

---

[115] *Milton and the Miltonic Dryden* (Cambridge, Mass.: Harvard Univ. Press, 1968), pp. 171, 155 (my italics); see also p. 170.

[116] *Spenserian Poetics: Idolatry, Iconoclasm, and Magic*. (Ithaca: Cornell Univ. Press, 1985), p. 28.

the widening gulf between interpretations themselves: those that represent the poem as conforming to, indeed as codifying, a select part of the Samson tradition and those that discern in the poem a jostling of disparate elements from that tradition, a representation of the conflicting attitudes toward Samson that became increasingly prominent during the seventeenth century. The real difference is between those who see Milton brushing with and those who see him brushing against the grain of history; between those who see Milton representing a Samson from tradition and those who see him representing the Samsons of tradition. For the latter, *Samson Agonistes* is less the presentment of an action than the representation of societal attitudes and conditions; it is a poem that, instead of recapitulating, recreates the Samson story by wresting it away from a conformism threatening to overpower it; it is a poem that exhibits rather than conceals the contradictions of Milton's society and that is a perfect showcase of its dialectics. It is as if Milton determined to say through his Samson that "every image of the past that is not recognized by the present as one of its concerns threatens to disappear irretrievably."[117] *Samson Agonistes* brakes against the disappearance of the Samson story.

Once some allowances are made for the reactionary thrust of Fish's interpretation and for the distractions attendant upon his persistent privileging of a rhetorical flourish over historical accuracy, we can begin to appreciate his uneasiness with the typological method—an uneasiness, as it happens, that does not extend to the contours of the interpretation which that method has yielded. When Fish errs, it is always on the side of relentlessly orthodox and ideologically conservative readings. At the same time, it is evident that, because his own deconstructionist tendencies are layered over the premises of New Criticism, Fish is unresponsive to certain forms of con-

[117] Walter Benjamin, *Illuminations*, ed. Hannah Arendt (1968; rpt. New York: Schocken Books, 1978), p. 255.

textualization. The deconstructive urge should (but in Fish's case does not) refuse subservience to established orders and codified wisdom, and the failures of New Criticism should have taught Fish that certain texts are immune to New Critical and, at times, even to Fishean premises. Christ may not be "in the text" of *Samson Agonistes*—critics are surely mistaken who contend that "Samson Agonistes is really Christus Ago-nistes";[118] but Jesus is inescapably present in the 1671 poetic volume. Through the placement of poems, even through the front-matter to his tragedy, Milton secures that presence. Fish's question concerning what is in the text implies others, of course: not only what is *in* the text but what, even if not specifically mentioned, is predictably within the consciousness of its characters? and not only what is within the purview of the play, but what is present in the mind of the poet and within the consciousness of his audience? The crucial question is not what is in the text of the play, but what lies within the consciousness of a play whose horizon of awareness is set now by its characters and now by its author and his audience. The distinction is one that Milton himself feels obliged to formulate, in *A Treatise of Civil Power*, as he addresses the argument that the first kings and, earlier, the judges authorize the use of force in matters of religion:

> . . . the state of religion under the gospel is far
> differing from what it was under the law: then was
> the state of rigor, childhood, bondage and works;
> now is the state of grace, manhood, freedom and
> faith; to all which belongs willingness and reason,

[118] See, e.g., T.S.K. Scott-Craig, "Concerning Milton's Samson," *Renaissance News*, 5 (1952), 46, and also Krouse, *Milton's Samson and the Christian Tradition*, p. 124: "In the very title of this tragedy Milton invited his readers to think of Samson as a model of virtue, as a hero, as a champion of God, as a saint, a martyr, and a counterpart of Christ." Neither critic is sensitive to the ironies tumbling forth from this invitation.

not force: the law was then written on tables of stone,
and to be performed according to the letter, willingly
or unwillingly; the gospel, our new covnant, upon
the heart of every beleever, to be interpreted only
by the sense of charitie and inward perswasion. . . .

(VII, 259)

When Fish proposes "a demonstration that in Milton's other
works Samson is always treated as a political rather than a
theological example,"[119] he insinuates what is not "always" the
case as evidenced by certain of Milton's plans in the Trinity
manuscript for a tragedy centered in the Samson story and by
the Samson allusion in *Paradise Lost*; and more, Fish mistakes and therefore mis-states the argument likely to be made
by a serious contextualist, one that would take into account not
only explicit references but hidden allusions, significant silences, and singularly relevant discussions of issues raised by
the play and previously reflected upon by Milton, but often
outside the boundaries of the Samson story. Or when Fish
speaks of "the absence in contemporary responses to *Samson
Agonistes* of any reference to typological significances,"[120] he
evades what must have been within the mind of any contemporary reader of the play and what, most assuredly, was on
the mind of Andrew Marvell whose dedicatory poem on *Paradise Lost*, in certain of its verses, is credibly a response to
Milton's tragedy. Most surprising of all, given the orientation
of Fish's criticism, he glosses over *Samson* as a play addressing
an audience whose consciousness may be different from, and
more capacious than, that of the play's characters and whose
minds would be uninhibited by the typological decorum that
necessarily controls the range of consciousness in the play itself.
Fish forgets, very simply, that the absence of a conventional

[119] *Is There a Text in This Class?*, p. 294.
[120] *Ibid.*

typology does not preclude the use of typological symbolism, nor does it necessarily militate against typological irony. What is in a play, finally, is a function of the "discrepant awareness" that exists between the players, as it were, and the playwright; or as Bertrand Evans puts it, "Between the awareness that packs our minds and the ignorance that afflicts the participants lies a crucial—and highly exploitable—discrepancy."[121]

In *Samson Agonistes*, no less than in *King Lear* perhaps, the drama derives from just this sort of twin consciousness where characters restricted to a pre-Christian world interact with an audience imbued with Christianity. It is customary for tragedy to achieve its powerful ironies, according to Northrop Frye, by placing its characters in a state (pagan or Old Testament) from which its audience has been theoretically redeemed. What Frye remarks of *King Lear* he could just as easily have applied to *Samson Agonistes*: "The events . . . are supposed to be contemporary with those of the Old Testament, and the sense of life under the law is present everywhere"; the audience that receives the play, on the other hand, belongs to another phase of history—exists under the new dispensation.[122] Shakespeare's strategy is identical with the one Milton employs: to use an episode drawn from pre-Incarnational history to reflect upon current history; to imply a knit of identity between the past and the present only to force a distinction between history under the old and new dispensations. Prophecies of former times can now be brought to fulfillment; fictive history written as prophecy can now become actual history. An upside-down world can be turned right-side-up again.

[121] Bertrand Evans, *Shakespeare's Comedies* (Oxford: Clarendon Press, 1960), p. vii. Ferry brings the point to bear on *Samson Agonistes*: "Because we are familiar with the metaphorical use in Scripture of certain clusters of words . . . as Milton repeats these over and over . . . we recognize their metaphorical meanings even when those meanings are not intended or understood by the speaker who utters them" (*Milton and the Miltonic Dryden*, p. 155).

[122] *Anatomy of Criticism: Four Essays* (Princeton: Princeton Univ. Press, 1957), p. 222; see also p. 221.

Samson Agonistes is a Christian tragedy, which is to say that its hero's fault is not Christianity but rather that primitive Hebraic element which persists in Renaissance Christianity. Wordsworth understood something, but not all, of this—and certainly not the complexity of Milton's dramaturgy—when he remarked that by the time Milton wrote *Samson Agonistes* his "mind was Hebraized. Indeed, his genius fed on the writings of the Hebrew prophets. This arose, in some degree, from the temper of the times; the Puritan lived in the Old Testament, almost to the exclusion of the New."[123] Apparently, when Milton wrote *Samson Agonistes* he was no star who dwelt apart from the main currents of his age; he was instead weltering within them. As it happens, what Wordsworth says so matter-of-factly about Milton's own involvement with his age is *in* Milton's poem and constitutes the basis of Milton's own critique of that age. To speak of Samson's fault is to say not that his Philistine oppressors, including Dalila, are faultless, only that in turning their evil into his own motive, Samson becomes what he beholds, visiting upon others the same evil that is visited upon him, always loathing another's evil rather than his own. The same code of vengeance is shared by Samson and the Philistines, making it difficult to distinguish between the two on moral grounds and, from the vantage point of *Paradise Regained*, a poem of positive non-action, making it necessary that we entertain Samson's final action as a negative, as a foolhardy embracing of self-destruction, while he is engaged in the slaying of others. This juxtaposition of poems does not allow us to forget that Milton is again "contrast[ing] the fallen ways of men in society with ideal images,"[124] but it also presses us into seeing the ideal images in *Paradise Regained* rather than in the various representations of Samson in Milton's tragedy. Moreover, to describe *Samson* as a "Christian

---

[123] *The Romantics on Milton*, ed. Wittreich, p. 136.
[124] Ferry, *Milton and the Miltonic Dryden*, p. 221.

tragedy is to establish an important inflection; for while a human tragedy, Milton's poem is equally a theological tragedy, not because Samson accepts a theological model, but because he accepts a *mistaken* theological model as a justification for his behavior.

Calvinist conceptions of election and reprobation, for example, cannot reside within the consciousness of Milton's characters, although they would surely reside within the consciousness of Milton and his audience. By allowing these conceptions to be coded into the play and hence anticipated by it, and by reinforcing the anticipation with a description of the three classes of men among the Philistines, without ever breaking typological decorum or allowing his play to become anachronistic, Milton can nevertheless suggest that Calvinist categories of thought, still too much with us, are a throwback to the Old Dispensation; he can suggest that Calvin understood Samson all too well and can link his own tragic Samson to modes of thought, both Calvinist and militantly Protestant, that have effected the tragedy of the modern world. Such modes of thought, their rhetorical terms and conceptual categories, are what Jameson might call "distorted anticipations" of the dialectic that plays itself out in Milton's 1671 poetic volume.[125] Here the dialectical motion is not between the type and its antitype but between the antitype and its parodies, with the relationship between these poems asserting itself as a difference, in the words of Balachandra Rajan, "between perfection and fallibility, between the pattern possessed and the pattern stumblingly groped for, between the clarity of the completed understanding and the darkness through which the design is seen in fragments, illuminated by the lightning of the 'great event.' "[126]

---

[125] "Religion and Ideology," in *1642*, ed. Barker et al., p. 319.

[126] "To Which Is Added," in *The Prison and the Pinnacle: Papers to Commemorate the Tercentenary of "Paradise Regained" and "Samson Agonistes,"* ed. Balachandra Rajan (London: Routledge and Kegan Paul, 1973), p. 98.

It is perhaps a still greater irony of Milton criticism that the Samson critical orthodoxy finds in Milton's play is the Samson, save a few particulars, preserved for the seventeenth century in the eccentric writings of Joseph Hall—that learned fool mentioned in the preface to *Animadversions*, whose "haughtinesse" Milton would send home "well bespurted with his owne holy-water" (I, 662). "I never read that Samson slew any, but by the motion and assistance of the Spirit of God," writes Hall, who thereupon cites as evidence his belief that Samson's "dying revenge" is a manifestation of divine wisdom, that Samson is conducting God's quarrel, not his own.[127] Inspiration coming from God justifies Samson's apparent wickedness, making "obedience" of Samson's "very cruelty," in an account that finally redeems him for heroism by aligning Samson and his God, and not the Philistines, with a theology of cruelty:

> *Samson*, being not mortally wronged by one *Philistine*, falls foul upon the whole nation: the *Philistines*, heinously offended by *Samson*, do not fall upon the whole tribe of *Judah*, but, being mustered together, call to them for satisfaction from the person offending. The same hand of God, which wrought *Samson* to revenge, restrained them from it. It is no thanks to themselves, that sometimes wicked men cannot be cruel.[128]

This hero, Hall emphasizes, is wily (he gets the Philistines to perform murderous acts for him); and he is the agent of an admittedly vindictive god who, stooping to cruelty, is nevertheless one on whom mankind can "cheerfully depend."[129] Hall's Samson is the answer to those, like Broadbent,

---

[127] *Contemplations on the Historical Passages of the Old and New Testaments* (3 vols.; Edinburgh: Willison and Darling, 1770), I, 346, 360-61.

[128] *Ibid.*, I, 347, 349.

[129] *Ibid.*, I, 353. See also Hall, *A Plaine and Familiar Explication*, pp. 95-101.

who believe "It is a failing of Christian mythology, that its vital parts do not include violence, physical prowess"; and Hall himself, an example of those who would "humanize" Christianity by "roughening it up."[130] We might imagine Milton hurling his words from *De Doctrina Christiana* at both these commentators: "for God's sake let us not come to any rash conclusions about God!" (VI, 219)

Samson is rebuked by Hall on only one account: "I Can no more justify *Samson*, in his leaving of his wife, then in the chusing her. . . . Slight occasions may not break the knot of matrimonial love; and if any just offences have slackened it on either part, it must be fastened again by speedy reconciliation"; besides, says Hall, Samson ought to be fighting with his father-in-law, not with the Timnian bride. Marriage choices, flaunted by Samson, are important for Hall, as they will be for Milton: "If religion be any other than a cypher, how dare we not regard it in our most important choice." Yet Samson disregards it, in marrying the Woman of Timnath is "sensual and brutish," and in this disregards his parents too, who are properly "unwilling to call a *Philistine*, daughter." If God had any part in this marriage, it was only "to make a treacle of a viper; and rather appointed to fetch good out of *Samson's* evil, than to approve that for good in *Samson*, which in itself was evil."[131]

In this one conception, Hall's thoughts lock arms with Milton's poem; otherwise there is not much in Hall that invites, or even allows for, comparison with *Samson Agonistes*. In "Samson's End," Hall will ask "who can pity the loss of that strength which was so abused!" and thereupon will explain that, whereas Samson's acts "are for wonder, not for imita-

---

[130] *"Paradise Lost": Introduction* (Cambridge: Cambridge Univ. Press, 1972), p. 94.

[131] *Contemplations on the Historical Passages of the Old and New Testaments*, I, 338-39, 345-46; see also pp. 337-45.

tion," they are also prompted by "zeal . . . not malice" and culminate in a "revenge . . . no less sweet to him, than the liberty of his former life."[132] Hall's account of Samson, and of Samson's God especially, presses upon us the realization that we all substitute monstrous, and monstrously depraved, fictions for the true God, thus loosing an immense flood of error upon the world; that Milton's poem assails and would finally scuttle just that religious system which perpetrates the fiction of a God careless of mankind and sometimes tormenting him and which, with Hall's God as a model, sanctions rather than subverts earthly tyranny.

Hall practices the same sort of pernicious casuistry on the Samson legend that certain of Milton's critics will practice on both this legend and Milton's poem. For A.S.P. Woodhouse, Renaissance commentators "had transfigured the barbaric tribal hero in various ways . . . they had read into Samson himself what is wholly lacking in the Old Testament account . . . the desire for forgiveness and restoration to God's service . . . . Thus the latest experiences of Samson become a study in regeneration, and his act of fierce revenge the seal of repentance and restoration. . . . The righteousness of Samson's revenge troubles Milton not at all. . . . To Milton this seems self-evident: at least he assumes it in silence."[133] And for John Ulreich, "if we fail to rejoice at God's and Samson's triumph, our apathy probably bespeaks some deep-rooted hypocrisy in us, a refusal to acknowledge our own capacity for violence."[134]

Yet Hall's account also remains of singular interest not because his Samson is coincident with Milton's, nor even because Milton's play squares off against this account. Rather,

---

[132] *Ibid.*, I, 358, 360-61; see also pp. 354-61.

[133] *The Heavenly Muse: A Preface to Milton*, ed. Hugh McCallum (Toronto: Univ. of Toronto Press, 1972), p. 296.

[134] " 'Beyond the Fifth Act': *Samson Agonistes* as Prophecy," in *Composite Orders: The Genres of Milton's Last Poems*, ed. Richard S. Ide and Joseph Wittreich (Pittsburgh: Univ. of Pittsburgh Press, 1983), p. 312.

Hall is alert to all the proliferating paradoxes in the Samson story: Samson's strength begins in infirmity: not drinking wine he is nonetheless drunk with the cup of fornication; the number of weaknesses attributed to him is surpassed only by the number of miracles ascribed to him; the deliverance from the Philistines begins in Samson's alliance with them; Samson instead of overcoming the Philistines is rather overcome by Philistian women—is fettered by the invisible bonds of a harlot and, in this, feeds his sexual passions rather than nourishing his strength. Finally Samson is more blind when he saw than he is having lost his eyes and more a slave when serving his affections than when grinding at the mills of Gaza. A confirmed typologist, Hall also looks to Jesus, the real source of Samson's strength, as "our better *Nazarite*," concluding that when Samson rises up from Delilah's lap he is no Nazarite and "scarce a man"; that Jesus is "our better *Samson*," who "conquer[ing] in dying; and, triumphing upon the chariot of the cross, didst lead captivity captive" rather than himself becoming a captive of death.[135] The Samson legend, as rendered by Hall, has some mythic elements, with Samson's rending of the lion being catalogued among "initiatory encounters" and with the lion itself, a lion within, typifying an internal battle and victory just as later Delilah will be represented as a principality and power "lodge[d] in our bosoms."[136] Alert to these paradoxes and to these mythic traces in the Samson story, Hall manages to focus the issues—man's duty to his wife and his God, the nature of that God and the motives for man's actions, whether they derive from divine compulsion or tragic impulse—that will come under review in Milton's poem.

[135] *Contemplations on the Historical Passages in the Old and New Testaments*, I, 351, 358, 361.

[136] *Ibid.*, I, 340-41, 356. Cf. Featley, *Clavis Mystica*, p. 769, who speaks of men not fully repentant keeping "a *Dalilah* in their bosome."

But more, Hall's interpretation of the Samson story draws attention to the superimpositions of ideology upon that story. The original Samson story reveals mankind confined by a primitive ethical system from which the Judges narrator would release it; analogously, Renaissance versions of the same story display the mind imprisoned by dogmatic systems, both ethical and theological. Hall's account of this story may assert the truth of one ideology over another, but in this serves as a contrast to Milton's poem, which, attentive to different historical and ideological layerings over the Samson story, sifts them for the truth or falsehood of this or that order, subsumes them all as the components of an interpretation newly discovered and now to be asserted. Milton's redaction absorbs all earlier ones, but analytically, within a new version and thoroughly revisionist interpretation of the Samson saga. It encapsulates what might be called "the dramatic truth"[137] of his own emerging religious, political, and ethical commitments—of a system designed to deliver us, not by neglect but only after careful analysis, from all earlier systems of thought, from earlier, partial, and hence inadequate ideologies that had accrued to the Samson story.

In fine, the poetics of *Samson Agonistes* correspond with what has been called a "poetics of idolatry" and with the iconoclastic enterprise Kenneth Gross attributes to such a poetics.[138] What the Renaissance inherited and began to dismantle, only to witness its being remantled during the Civil War years, was the image of Samson as an idol, an idol created through an evasion of the paradoxes and ambiguities surrounding the Samson story in the Judges narrative. Renaissance allegorizings

[137] I borrow the phrase—and the concept—from Jerome McGann, *The Romantic Ideology* (Chicago: Univ. of Chicago Press, 1983), p. 67.

[138] *Spenserian Poetics*, pp. 27-77.

and typologizings of this story were legion; and both were devices for overcoming the presumed scandals of the biblical text, were also ways of ridding that text of its supposed absurdities. Allegory and typology, operating within the realm of illusion, as Gross astutely observes, operate according to the logic that to lie about a text—to de-ambiguate it—is to tell its essential truths. Paradoxically, what that logic produces is a mythology of religious error, a snare for the reader. The "idolizing" of Samson involves the reader in taking the lie for the truth. Milton's iconoclastic enterprise, on the other hand, would collapse such "truth" back into a lie by revealing the essential vacancy of allegorizings and typologizings of the Samson story. Gross says it best when he writes that such iconoclasm "help[s] us recover a difficult power, a revelation, an otherness, an openness, in the face of blockage, reification, and reduction."[139]

[139] *Ibid.*, p. 41.

CHAPTER V

SAMSON
AMONG THE NIGHTINGALES

> *Perhaps the duties of the poet have been the
> same throughout history: Poetry was honored to go
> out into the street, to take part in combat after
> combat. When they called him rebel, the poet was
> not daunted. Poetry is rebellion. The poet is not
> offended if he is called subversive. . . .*
> *We poets hate hatred and make war on war.*
> —PABLO NERUDA

Joseph Summers has reminded us of how C. S. Lewis taunted
both students and friends: "Don't you rejoice with that chorus
[in *Samson Agonistes*]":

> While their hearts were jocund and sublime,
> Drunk with idolatry, drunk with wine
> And fat regorged of bulls and goats,
> Chanting their idol, and preferring
> Before our living dread who dwells
> In Silo, his bright sanctuary,
> Among them he a spirit of frenzy sent,
> Who hurt their minds,
> And urged them on with mad desire
> To call in haste for their destroyer . . . ?

"The young friend would protest, 'No! No! It's unchristian,'

and Lewis would reply, 'Oh, come now! Rejoice! You're supposed to, you know'."[1]

This story provides Summers with an occasion for counseling that even if "many modern readers reject Samson, along
with other military and national figures in the Old Testament,
as spiritually alien and ethically benighted, most Christians of
Milton's time seem to have accepted him as an authentic hero
of the Chosen People's divinely guided history before the
Christian revelation, and to have perceived significant relations
between pre-Christian and post-Christian histories." Such
musings are meant to substantiate Summers's claim that Milton's contemporaries (and indeed all subsequent readers)
should "recognize in Samson a heroic servant of God who
seemed to have lost and then to have won everything,
'Triumphing over Death, and Chance, and thee O Time'."[2]
Summers is not alone among Miltonists in leaving untested,
untried, his thesis concerning the Renaissance Samson; nor is
he alone in positing a spiritually triumphant Samson at the
end of Milton's poem. Yet against Summers's thesis we might
place this alternative formulation: that Summers's (and what
he supposes to be Milton's) Samson survives within the sweet
lyric song of Milton's century; but at the same time the Samson
of the religious lyric is continually being diminished by the
Samson of secular literature and, more, by the copious legend
still accruing to this supposed hero and *sometimes* celebrated
type of Christ.

Ever since the publication of F. Michael Krouse's *Milton's
Samson and the Christian Tradition*, there has been an alarming,
and misguided, tendency to elide the Renaissance Samsons with
the Samson of the Middle Ages and, through this elision, to
collapse the very different Samsons of the Renaissance into one
Samson or, in the instance provided by Krouse, into *two* Sam-

---

[1] "Response to Anthony Low's Address on *Samson Agonistes*," *Milton Quarterly*,
13 (1979), 106.
[2] *Ibid.*

sons, the one belonging to religious and the other to secular literature. The saint of religious poetry, says Krouse, stands in marked contrast with the sinner of secular literature:

> In nearly all the secular literature of England during the sixteenth and seventeenth centuries, Samson was treated exactly as he had been treated during the medieval period. . . . The poets of the Renaissance, almost without exception, adopted the medieval literary conception of Samson as a great man brought low by woman's treachery.[3]

It is true that the restraints especially of the religious lyric engendered reductionist tendencies, eliminating the opportunity for including certain kinds of representations of Samson; yet the forms of reductionism commanded by the celebratory character of the religious lyric seem to have been countermanded in a secular literature that arrayed around the saintly image of Samson his various fallen forms—and not just that of a lustful hero snared by female charm. The religious lyric of the seventeenth century may be a zone of contentment; but the secular literature of the same period is a zone of unrest where commonplaces are being dismantled and conventional images destroyed. It is as if Samson as a man of virtue, popularized in the seventeenth century by Josephus ("we cannot too much admire his vertue"[4]) is finally exposed as one of those who "with thir freedom lost all vertu loose" (*PL* XI.798)— who

> . . . having spilt much blood, and don much waste
> Subduing Nations, and achieved thereby
> Fame in the World . . . ,
> Shall change thir course to pleasure, ease, and sloth,

---

[3] (Princeton: Princeton Univ. Press, for the Univ. of Cincinnati, 1949), p. 72.

[4] *The Works of Josephus*, trans. Thomas Lodge (London: Printed for H. Merringman et al., 1683), p. 142. Lodge's translation went through eight editions between 1602 and 1640.

Surfet, and lust, till wantonness and pride
Raise out of friendship hostil deeds in Peace.

(XI. 791-96)

Let us recognize, first of all, that Samson's history was popular
enough to have been the subject of two different plays in
Renaissance England, both of them now lost, the one dating
from 1567 and the other from 1602.[5] Moreover, the details
of his history were sufficiently disseminated that they could be
referred to casually, even flippantly, as in these lines spoken
by Quick-silver in *Eastward Hoe*:

I *Sampson* now, haue burst the *Philistins* Bands,
And in thy lappe my louely *Dalila*,
Ile lie and snore out my enfranchisde state.[6]

By both Thomas Dekker and Shakespeare, the Samson story
is referred to without explicit citation. In Dekker we read:

Humble mee . . . that . . . my heart may not swell
up with pride. . . . As thou hast placed mee, to bee
a Pillar to uphold others, so grant that I may not
proove a weake Pillar, to throw my selfe downe; and
with my fall to bruise others that stand under me.[7]

Or in Shakespeare: Lear has just embraced Cordelia and thereupon tells her, "He that parts us shall bring a brand from

[5] See *Annals of English Drama 975-1700*, comp. Alfred Harbage, rev. S. Schoen-
baum (London: Methuen, 1964), pp. 40, 84; see also the catalogue of Samson plays
in *That Invincible Samson: The Theme of "Samson Agonistes" in World Literature* (Toronto: Univ. of Toronto Press, 1964), pp. 145-215.

[6] See George Chapman et al., *Eastward Hoe* (London: Printed for William Aspley,
1605), sig. C.

[7] *Four Birds of Noahs Arke* (1609), ed. F. P. Wilson (Oxford: Basil Blackwell,
1924), "The Eagle," p. 35. Samson is probably behind Dekker's lines concerning
the pulling down of vengeance on our heads ("The Dove," p. 3) and the driving
away of all foxes ("The Eagle," p. 20).

heaven, / And fire us hence like foxes. Wipe thine eyes; / The
good years shall devour them, flesh and fell" (V.iii.22-24).[8]
In the example provided by Dekker, the speaker is the antitype
of Samson, the strong, not the weak pillar. In the Shake-
spearean example, however, he is Samson's antithesis, regenerate instead of degenerate, wiping away tears rather than
occasioning them, pouring a balm upon the world instead of
devastating it. And Samson is here invoked both to emblematize the agent of division and fragmentation and to illustrate
the proposition that evil is self-consuming.

Annabel Patterson is surely right in her surmise that Shakespeare's muted reference to the Samson story derives resonance
from, indeed depends for its significance upon, John Thornborough's similar citation of Samson.[9] Thornborough's theme,
like Shakespeare's, is disunion in the realm created by those
who "seeke to stay the maine & mighty Streame of great
Britaine by dividing it, and in dividing, to make it of sundry
kindes, vnlike it selfe."[10] The English and the Scottish, Thornborough continues, are "as a people disionted one from the
other? Or as Sande without Lime? Or scattered straw without
binding? Or as *Sampsons* Foxes running divers and contrary
waies, with fire-brands of dissention among them? Nay here
in the glory of great Brittaine is renowned, that King *Iames*,
and his Royal issue doe gather togither that, which *was* scattered and unite that, which was divided, and restore that,
which was endangered . . . vniting al in one name of Brittaine."[11] Igniting the tails of the foxes, Samson is viewed, like

[8] Quoted from *King Lear*, The Arden Shakespeare, ed. Kenneth Muir (London:
Methuen, 1972).

[9] *Censorship and Interpretation: The Condition of Reading and Writing in Early
Modern England* (Madison: Univ. of Wisconsin Press, 1984), pp. 69-70.

[10] *The Ioiefvll and Blessed Revniting of the Two Mighty & Famous Kingdomes,
England & Scotland into Their "Ancient" Name of "Great Brittaine"* (Oxford: Joseph
Barnes, 1605), p. 32.

[11] *Ibid.*, pp. 32-33.

Lear and his unkind daughters, as an instigator of dissension and disunion: he is like Nebuchadnezzar who similarly performs acts of division and like those sons of Adam who, never learning from their wrongs but practicing disobedience and dissension, dualism and division, produce the "ruine of al."[12] What others had previously divided James I unites in accordance with Ezekiel's declaration, "I will make them one nation" (37:22). James is thus the good shepherd, keeping Israel together like a flock of sheep; he is a new Alexander joining what had been torn asunder. James is a peacemaker, a bearer of the olive branch, who "sheweth that the vvaters are abated, anger appeased, dangers escaped, sorrows fled, and that salvation, and joy entereth the Arke of great Brittaine"; he is of God, manifesting truth, peace, fortitude, and perfection.[13] James is also the opposite of Adam and his sons, of Nebuchadnezzar, Constantine, Brutus, Lear, and the meaner of Lear's children—the opposite of Samson, one of Adam's sons—who divides and demolishes, bringing forth "falshood, war, feare, dishonor, & confusion." If James is of God, Samson is, with other of Adam's sons, "of the deuil."[14] Under the former, history becomes a comedy; under the latter, it continues as a tragedy.

In view of these observations and these figurings of the Samson story, certain propositions should be set forth immediately. Retellings of the Samson story pale against the proliferation of allusions, often implicit or muted, to that story; the allusions themselves are evidence of the popularity of the Samson story, of its being fixed, in all its details, within the Renaissance mind, of its being a significant part of the mental furniture of the age. Such allusions suggest that the Samson story, by the beginning of the seventeenth century, had acquired an overlay of political significance and further that it had become netted within a typological scheme, both secular and sacred, that exhibits a tarnished Samson—a Samson who,

[12] *Ibid.*, p. 31.   [13] *Ibid.*, p. 80.   [14] *Ibid.*, p. 14.

nurtured in blood, delights in vengeance and whose enterprise entails the wretched interchange of wrong for wrong. The Samson typology, once used to establish an identity between Samson and Christ, is now being used, in the happy formulation of Raymond Waddington, to mark "the modulations of difference."[15]

In the seventeenth century, biblical narratives, no less than the Bible's in-lays of wisdom, are sometimes translated into lyrical effusions:

> O What a number more there are,
>   time will not serve to tell,
> Of Barac, Samson, Gideon,
>   Jephte, Dauid, Samuel.
> P Rophets also, which all through faith
>   kingdomes subdu'd and gain'd,
> Wrought righteousnesse, stop't Lyons mouthe,
>   and promises obtain'd.
> Q Vench'd violence of flaming fire,
>   escap'd the sword in fight.
> Of weake, made strong and valiant,
>   great Armies turn'd to flight.[16]

The Old and New Testaments brought an extraordinary collective inspiration to the religious lyric of the Renaissance, a poetry often fueled by biblical paraphrases such as the one just cited.[17] Still, such poetical fancies, or scriptural epitomes, whatever their gains for art may be, exhibit the customary losses of translation: narrative probity and nuance, ambiguity

[15] "Milton among the Carolines," in *The Age of Milton: Backgrounds to Seventeenth Century Literature*, ed. C. A. Patrides and Raymond B. Waddington (Manchester: Manchester Univ. Press; Totowa: Barnes and Noble, 1980), p. 352.

[16] Simon Wastell, *Microbiblion or the Bibles Epitome* (London: Printed for Robert Mylbourne, 1629), pp. 467-68, but see also pp. 52-53.

[17] For elaboration, see Ernest Rhys, *Lyric Poetry* (1913; rpt. London and Toronto: J.M. Dent and Sons; New York: E. P. Dutton, 1933), p. 221; and Barbara Kiefer Lewalski, *Protestant Poetics and the Seventeenth-Century Religious Lyric* (Princeton: Princeton Univ. Press, 1979), p. 144.

and complexity are sacrificed to lyrical simplicity and intensity; ideological rifts opened in biblical narratives, more often than not, are concealed within the restraints, ideological and aesthetic, of the religious lyric; analytical power gives way to typological play; modulations of difference modulate into similitudes. The presence of the Samson story, its infiltration of the religious lyric, provides a striking example.

Typological parallels, *express similitudes*, are highlighted in the religious lyric. Witness the example provided by George Herbert in "Sunday": "As Samson bore the doores away, / Christs hands, though nail'd, wrought our salvation, / And did unhinge that day" (47-49).[18] Or witness the complicated, and complicating, instance offered by Thomas Traherne in *The First Century* (I, 90):

> In Death it self, will I find Life, and in Conquest Victory. This Samson by Dying Kild all His Enemies: And then carried the Gates of Hell and Death Away, when being Dead, Himself was born to his Grave.[19]

Artful accommodation of theological commonplaces, through the device of typology, is a part of the story told by lyric and prose-poem alike. But another, more interesting, part of the same story involves the extent to which a typology that had proved binding to scriptural texts and that had effectively sealed their fictions, largely through the counterthrusts of secular literature, often had the effect of sabotaging the commonplaces of religion and, with them, the conventional typologies. One of the blurring effects of the Samson typology was achieved by identifying Samson and Christ in the perception that both figures, in their respective deaths, slew God's

---

[18] *The Works of George Herbert*, ed. F. E. Hutchinson (Oxford: Clarendon Press, 1941), p. 76.

[19] *Poems, Centuries, and Three Thanksgivings*, ed. Ann Ridler (London: Oxford Univ. Press, 1966), p. 208.

enemies and thereby opened the gates into paradise. Their deaths, that is, were construed as births, with each of these heavenly champions being a resplendent image of "earth's bright *Glory*"[20]—a bright shoot of everlastingness.

Herbert's formulation, and to a certain extent the one by Traherne, may be correlated with Daniel Featley's "Sermon III: A Christian Victory: or, Conquest over Death's Enmity" (1639), where we read that when Christ "rose againe, then he spoyled him of his power, and tooke his weapons away, and triumphed over him intoken of conquest, as Sampson took *the Gates of Gaza on his shoulders, and carried them to the top of the hill.*"[21] Correspondingly, the formulations by Herbert and Traherne call to mind Matthew Griffith's declaration that, like Samson, "we shall be victorious, even in death it self; at which time . . . we shall *see the heavens open.*"[22] In triumphing over their enemies, Samson and Christ alike bruise the head of the serpent, defeat Antichrist and all his limbs. Samson's carrying off of the gates of the city and especially his hurling down of the temple are the episodes sanctioning and securing the typological connection between him and Christ. In taking the gates of Gaza, Samson was recognized as "A figure of Christs glorious resurrection"; and at the pillars, he was perceived as one who "humble[s] himself to the death, that he might have his people out of the hands of all their spiritual enemies."[23] In his death, Christ is a second mighty Samson

[20] *The Historie of Samson* (London: Printed for John Marriott, 1631), p. 140.

[21] In *Threnoikos: The House of Movrning* (London: Printed by John Dawson, 1640), pp. 272-73.

[22] *A Patheticall Perswasion to Pray for Publick Peace* (London: Published for Richard Royston, 1642), p. 45.

[23] See John Trapp, *Annotations upon the Old and New Testament* (5 vols.; London: Printed by Robert White, 1662), I, 90; and John Downame et al., *Annotations upon All the Books of the Old and New Testament* (2 vols.; London: Printed by Evan Tyler, 1657), annotation to Judges 16:30. But see also Thomas Taylor, *The Works of That Faithful Servant* (London: Printed by John Bartlet, 1653), pp. 378-79, and Theodore Haak, *The Dutch Annotations upon the Whole Bible* (London: Printed by Henry Hills, 1657), annotation to Judges 16:31.

SAMSON AMONG THE NIGHTINGALES

overcoming his enemies, and at a time when he seems most overcome by them, says Thomas Taylor; and in rising from the dead, Christ is another mighty Samson who in his might, carried away the gates of death. In virtually the same breath, however, Taylor will use these episodes, through which typological identification had often been achieved, to underscore typological distance and difference. Only Christ is never "ouercome" by his enemies: "The Philistims desired but to get *Sampson* into their hands, and preuailed: but here is an inuincible *Sampson*, his enemy cannot hold him."[24] Invincibility, it appears, may not be an attribute of Samson or, for that matter, of any man.

Implicit in such comparisons is the realization that, finally, the heavenly Samson is qualitatively different from the earthly Samson; and from that realization issues a host of comparative formulations intended to mark their differences: "our better Samson," "our better Nazarite" truly conquers in dying; Christ alone leads captivity captive—is "the true *Sampson*, who by his death brake the bands of death, and destroyed his and our enemies."[25] To these comparative formulas could be added

[24] *Christs Combate and Conquest: or, the Lyon of the Tribe of Judah* (London: Printed by Cantrell Legge, 1618), pp. 37, 193, and see also p. 273; cf. *The Works of Thomas Goodwin*, ed. John C. Miller and Robert Halley (12 vols.; Edinburgh: James Nichol; London: James Nisbet, 1861-66), III, 96. Elsewhere Taylor writes: "although *Sampson* the type was at last ouercome by his enemies: our true *Sampson* is inuincible, and hath gloriously triumphed over them all" (*Christ Revealed: or the Old Testament Explained* [London: Printed by M. F., 1635], p. 56; see also p. 60). In the sixteenth century, Henoch Clapham was compelled to distinguish between Samson "A Nazarite" and "our Nazaret Annointed, who by his death on the Crosse, overcame Death, and destroyed all power infernall, to the Faithfull" (*A Briefe of the Bible* [London: Printed by Robert Walde, 1596], pp. 68-69). The tag of invincibility placed on Samson by Martin Luther is gradually detached from him in the seventeenth century; see *Luther's Works*, ed. Jaroslav Pelikan et al. (55 vols.; St. Louis: Concordia Press; Philadelphia: Fortress Press, 1955-76), VIII, 281.

[25] See Joseph Hall, *Contemplations on the Historical Passages of the Old and New Testaments* (3 vols.; Edinburgh: Willison and Darling, 1770), I, 351, 361; and Trapp, *Annotations upon the Old and New Testament*, I, 89.

others: our mightier Samson, our stronger Samson, our spiritual and celestial Samson, this better and mightier deliverer, this invincible Samson. Whatever the formula, its purpose is always to make the same point: if "Samson was sanctified from the womb: So was Christ much more. . . . And herein beyond *Sampson*, for in Christ are all sanctified"; if Samson is a strong-armed man, Christ is still stronger, "the true *Sampson*" triumphing over all his enemies, not through wrath but patience.[26] Even the Milton of *Samson Agonistes*, it seems, would score such differences. The quality of invincibility is assigned to Samson by Manoa and the Chorus: "That invincible *Samson*" (341). Yet that very phrase reverberates with irony when it is read within the context of Milton's other writings.

Manoa's description of Samson as invincible and the Chorus's later explanation that "God into the hands of thir deliverer / Puts invincible might / To quell the mighty of the Earth, th' oppressour" (1270-72) may seem to be authorized by the God of *Paradise Lost* who declares, "lead forth to Battel these my sons / Invincible, lead forth my armed Saints" (VI.46-47), yet is actually complicated by the Son's "this day from Battel rest" for you have "don / Invincibly" (VI.802, 805-06). The fact is that the saints have conquered no one in Book VI of *Paradise Lost*, and thus the Son must enter the battle on the third day. Invincibility is an attribute only of Godhead: the victory is the Son's. And as we learn from the Satan of *Paradise Regained*, this attribute manifests itself in patience, in "temperance invincible" (II.408), although there is a brutal irony here for Satan had once maintained that the rebel angels in mind and spirit remain invincible (*PL* I.139:40).

The irony of ascribing invincibility to Samson is doubled by the recollection of how Milton uses this term in *Of Reformation* and by the attendant recollection that by this time

[26] Thomas Taylor, *Moses and Aaron, or the Types and Shadows of Our Saviour* (London: John Williams, 1653), pp. 49, 53.

Samson had been iconized as a divider and destroyer: "joyn your invincible might to doe worthy, and Godlike deeds," Milton urges of those now charged with joining together a disjointed world, with uniting what had become disunited and broken (I, 597). The notion of an invincible Samson, a measure of both Manoa's and the Chorus's obtuseness, collapses into full irony when it is juxtaposed with Milton's own pronouncement in *Eikonoklastes*, which comes under the subheading, "Upon . . . raising Armies, & c":

> *But he had a soule invincible.* What praise is that? The stomach of a child is ofttimes invincible to all correction. The unteachable man hath a soule to all reason and good advice invincible, and he who is intractable, he whom nothing can perswade, may boast himself *invincible*; when as in some things to be overcome is more honest and laudable than to conquer. (III, 151)

What Milton says of invincibility here, when situated within the context of his tragedy, becomes a stinging indictment of Samson; and the concept of invincibility unfolded here is crucial to any typology founded upon differences between Samson and Christ.

In the previous illustration provided by Herbert, Samson and Christ are similitudes; but in the one afforded by Traherne that typology begins to crumble as a speaker becomes the third term in a comparison wherein he associates himself with not the type but its antitype and thus represents himself not as a recapitulation but as a fulfillment. As it happens, Herbert's easy associationalism is less characteristic of the seventeenth century than Traherne's dissociationalism, which in a similarly mild form is evident in Robert Southwell's poem "At Home in Heaven," where "our heavenly *Samson*" (13) is compared with his earthly counterpart, and in a more extreme form typical of secular literature is evident too in the stress John Donne places, in "The Calme," on Samson's essential fallenness and hence effeminate slackness: "like slack sinew'd *Sampson*, his haire off, Languish our ships" (34-35).[27] The pressure exerted by secular literature early in the seventeenth century becomes so considerable that later in the century hermeneutic texts, no less than religious lyrics, can no longer formulate parallelisms between Samson and Christ without formalizing disparities. What can be presented as tabloids of differences by the commentators are coded into the religious lyric where, as in the examples afforded by Traherne and Southwell, there is a straining toward such formulations. In this way, unexpected meanings may be seen breaking through the surfaces of poems with which those meanings also seem incompatible, indecorous, or simply irrelevant.

Like all lyrics, the religious poem is constrained by demands for abbreviation and abridgment; such poems are still-lifes in comparison with the expansive canvases of narrative and drama where there is leisure for detailed exposition. Even so, the religious lyric does not destroy itself, as Ira Clark argues, by overlooking typological discrepancies or by blurring differences;[28] rather, it accommodates them by introducing as a middle term in its typological comparisons a speaker/persona and, if only implicitly, a readership that will itself be measured by resemblance now to type and now to antitype, here to Samson and there to Christ. The religious lyric, as Sharon Cameron has so astutely remarked, had been acting as a vise on certain fictions, housing them "within the walls of their own limitations."[29] Through the introduction of a middle term

---

[27] See *The Poems of Robert Southwell*, ed. James H. McDonald and Nancy Pollard Brown (Oxford: Clarendon Press, 1967), p. 56, and *The Complete Poetry of John Donne*, ed. John T. Shawcross (Garden City: Anchor Books, 1967), p. 193.

[28] *Christ Revealed: The History of the Neotypological Lyric in the English Renaissance* (Gainesville: Univ. Press of Florida, 1982), p. 139.

[29] *Lyric Time: Dickinson and the Limits of Genre* (Baltimore: The Johns Hopkins Univ. Press, 1979), p. 22.

to typological comparisons, the hold of that vise is effectively broken. The hold of that vise is loosened, certainly, by a
secular literature that thrusts against similitudes in order to
brandish not a regenerate but a fallen Samson into whose
heart, according to Phineas Fletcher, women "So finely
steale themselves":

> That strongest Champion, who with naked hands
> A Lyon tore, who all unarm'd and bound
> Heap't mounts of armed foes on bloody sands;
> By womans art, without or force or wound
> Subdu'de, now in a mill blind grinding stands.
> That Sunne of wisedome, which the Preacher crown'd
>   Great King of arts, bewitch't with womens smiles,
>   Fell deepe in seas of folly by their wiles.
> Wit, strength, and grace it selfe yeeld to their
>   flatt'ring guiles.[30]

Samson's is a lechery, suggests George Gascoigne, that dwells
"Not outwardly, but inwardly," that "marreth and corrupteth
every age, . . . every sect, . . . every order, and . . . over-
throweth every degree. For it invadeth young and olde, men
and women, wyse and foolish, higher and lower, unto the
laste generacion . . . [it] cursed *Ruben*, seduced *Sampson*, and
perverted *Salomon*."[31] The secular parries with the religious
lyric in such a way as to capitalize on the drama, not the
dogma, inherent in the Samson story and does so, at least
initially, by problematizing the supposedly triumphant close
of Samson's life.

Donne allows that Samson dies with the same zeal as Christ
and that, if Hercules is a type of Samson, in his death Samson

---

[30] See *Giles and Phineas Fletcher: Poetical Works*, ed. Frederick S. Boas (2 vols.;
Cambridge: Cambridge Univ. Press, 1908-09), I, 169 (*The Apollyonists* by Phineas
Fletcher, IV.xxii-xxiii).

[31] *The Complete Works of George Gascoigne*, ed. John W. Cunliffe (Cambridge:
Cambridge Univ. Press, 1907-10), II, 247-48.

is a type of Christ, but in the context of *Biathanatos* where the murdering of Christ is contrasted with Samson's "self-killing" and where contending traditions of exegesis are brought into play: some argue that Samson's principal desire is for the death of the Philistines, not his own death; others, that the responsibility is God's for he inspires Samson's acts. Donne seems to have little regard for the "particular inspiration or New Commission" that exegetes "are forced to purchase for Samson,"[32] and the scrutiny he and others give to Samson's final days eventually has its consequences for the religious lyric which, in the instance of Bunyan, will cancel the events of the entire sixteenth chapter of Judges from consideration, emphasizing not the supposedly heroic feats of Samson's life but the problem-ridden times of a now domesticated figure whose sanctuary is his parent's home: "unto his father's house returned."[33] That special form of "Vertue transcendent and heroycall," which the scriptural commentators had sometimes ascribed to Samson, was already under challenge by Donne and would come under challenge often, especially by those who recognized that the spirit of revenge sometimes borrows the visard of fortitude and that its only sanction, in the instance of Samson, seems to be his claim of divine instinct.[34]

Whether or not he approves of the situation, Joseph Wybarne describes it accurately: "The deedes of *Sampson* are scoft at by many," especially by poets, who misunderstand what Wybarne believes is the scriptural intent, "which was to describe a man indued . . . with eminent Vertues, yet not exempt from humaine passions." When described by the poets, Sam-

[32] *Biathanatos*, ed. Ernest W. Sullivan II (Newark: Univ. of Delaware Press; London and Toronto: Associated Univ. Presses, 1984), pp. 18, 135-37; see also pp. 33, 134, 138, 141, 143, 235, 238.

[33] *The Whole Works*, ed. George Offor (3 vols.; London: Blackie and Son, 1862), III, 393.

[34] See Joseph Wybarne, *The New Age of Old Names* (London: Printed for William Barrett and Henry Fetherstone, 1609), p. 72.

son's peculiar brand of heroism is seldom "free from all tinc-
ture of folly," as Wybarne well knows, because such "bloody
couenants are commonly drawn with Sathan."[35] Especially in
their dealings with the Samson story, poets review and, from
Wybarne's point of view, revile the commonplaces of theology
valorized by scripture. Even epic poets assault the cult of
heroism in the belief that heroes, none of them faultless, should
be represented in their various and contradictory aspects; this
is true not only of feigning poets like Homer and Virgil but
of modern ones like Spenser who, less prone to err, "have set
downe men of heroycall vertues, yet darkened like the Moone
with some blot; therefore as well the sinnes as the vertues of
Moses, Sampson, David are registered with the point of a
Diamond in the glasse of true history"[36]—and registered in
such a way as to exalt present over past history and modern
heroes over their antecedents. Typology, in the seventeenth
century, has become a kind of subterfuge for including, especially in religious poetry, what might otherwise have to be
excluded. And it is in just this way, with just this objective,
that Wybarne himself speaks of Henry VII as "that second
Salomon" who rises like "a new Phoenix" from "out of the
ashes of the olde Nobility."[37] Typology is now being used not
to deny but to diminish earlier heroism and, at the same time,
to promote the idea that true heroism is being fully realized
in the modern age by a new breed of protagonists. There are
twists and turns in such poetry to which we are only now
beginning to pay proper attention.

  Another way of presenting Wybarne's objections to the poets
would be to say that they resist the special pleading of certain
tradition-bound commentators who would ignore cruxes in the
Samson story and thus halt further inquiry into the Samson
legend. If we turn to the end of the seventeenth century, we
find in the biblical annotations of Matthew Poole the hesitations

---

[35] *Ibid.*, 27,67, 72.   [36] *Ibid.*, p. 73.   [37] *Ibid.*, p. 79.

and contradictions that plagued commentators throughout this
century and the one before. The motions that begin to move
in Samson early in his story are meant "To stir him up to
Heroicall Designs," which always seem to involve the suspension of common rules of behavior—his marrying an infidel
without parental consent; his handling of dead bodies, animal
and human, and in the latter instance stripping them of their
apparel; his taking private revenge when he fires the tails of
the foxes; his going off "accidentally" with a harlot; his being
filled with the strength to carry off the gates of the city after
one of his foulest sins; his "marrying" Delilah whether out of
"Conjugal . . . or lustful love"; his prayer of personal injury
and malice; his betrayal of his word in contrast with the Philistines who, whatever their faults, are faithful to what they
promise: they humble Samson but will not kill him.[38] But
there is often special pleading; and it results, usually, in the
acceptance of a god who subverts his own laws, tampers with
his own values, inhabits even foul forms, employing whatever
means are at hand to justify his vengeful ends. Such special
pleading invariably excuses Samson, whose concerns are allegedly contrary to appearances and must be construed as public
not private ones; who becomes only "accidentally . . . ensnared" by infidel women; who, despite any evidence, must
have "in some measure repented of his Sin, and begged of
God Pardon and Assistance."[39] The Samson story is riddled
with problems that for some do not warrant attention and that
are diminished by them just as Poole dismisses the matter of
Samson's foxes: "it is not worthy of our inquiry what became
of these Foxes afterward."[40] Not only the Samson story but
Samson, himself a riddler, proves to be a riddle.

[38] See *Annotations upon the Holy Bible* (5 vols.; Printed by Robert Roberts, 1688);
annotation to Judges 13:25, but see also annotations to Judges 14:3, 14:9, 15:3, 16:1,
16:3, 16:4, 16:28.

[39] *Ibid.*; see annotations to Judges 16:1, 16:3.

[40] *Ibid.*; see annotation to Judges 15:5.

Donne resists just this sort of special pleading as both Shakespeare and Spenser had done before him. In *Love's Labor's Lost*, where wenches "prove plagues to men" (IV.iii.385) and great men become gnats, and within a context in which great spirits grow melancholy and lose the light of life by going blind, Samson is numbered among love's fools.[41] Samson is here a revenger revenged for submitting to the mockery of women who, having proved false to him, cause Samson to prove false to himself. Armado asks, "What great men have been in love?" (I.ii.67-68), and is informed by his page Moth of two:

> Hercules, master . . . Samson master. He was a man of good carriage, great carriage, for he carried the town gates on his back like a porter—and he was in love. (I.ii.69, 74-76)

Armado thereupon responds:

> O well-knit Samson! Strong-jointed Samson! I do excel thee in my rapier as much as thou didst me in carrying gates. I am in love too. Who was Samson's love, my dear moth? (I.ii.77-80)

"A woman, master," Moth tells him, whose complexion is "sea-water green" and who has "a green wit" (II.ii.81, 86, 95). Through this exchange, Shakespeare conjures up several different faces of Samson: that of the lustful lover, that of the strong man scant on wit who had "small reason" for loving Delilah (I.ii.92), a man deformed by love and because of that refashioning his obligations, thus betraying them just as he himself has been betrayed. Contrary to Shakespeare, and perhaps accounting for the anti-Shakespearean sentiments in the

---

[41] Quotations from this play, given parenthetically within the text, are from *Shakespeare: The Complete Works*, ed. G. B. Harrison (New York and Burlingame: Harcourt, Brace and Company, 1952).

preface to *Samson Agonistes*, Milton seems to have thought that the Samson story is no matter for a "Christmas comedy" (V.ii.462) but instead the stuff of tragedy. And it is with Milton that Spenser seems to have concurred.

In Book V of *The Faerie Queene*, Artegall is linked typologically to earlier mythic and historical figures, among them Samson. Echoes from the Book of Judges reverberate throughout Spenser's Book of Justice, where Samson's effeminate slackness illustrates the "wondrous powre [of] . . . wemens faire aspect, / To captiue men, and make them all the world reiect" (V.viii.2). "[T]hat mighty Iewish swaine," with hardened heart "enur'd to blood and cruelty," says Spenser, did "lay his spoiles before his lemans traine" (V.viii.1-2).[42] Artegall is numbered with those men—not just Samson but also Hercules and Anthony—who have been beguiled by women; yet once Artegall is dissociated from his types in terms of his outer strength, the Hercules and not the Samson analogy is developed by way of revealing Artegall's inner strength and newly acquired wisdom.

The aura of prophecy and millennial expectation once associated with Samson now comes to surround Artegall as if to suggest that, whereas Samson represents an extreme of injustice, Artegall embodies the mean of justice. Samson, not Ar-

[42] Quoted from *The Works of Edmund Spenser*, ed. Edwin Greenlaw et al. (11 vols.; Baltimore: The Johns Hopkins Press, 1932-45), V, 89. The following critics offer particularly incisive commentary on this passage: Jane Aptekar, *Icons of Justice: Iconography and Thematic Imagery in Book V of "The Faerie Queene"* (New York and London: Columbia Univ. Press, 1969), p. 180; Angus Fletcher, *The Prophetic Moment: An Essay on Spenser* (Chicago: Univ. of Chicago Press, 1971), pp. 147-50; and James Nohrnberg, *The Analogy of "The Faerie Queene"* (Princeton: Princeton Univ. Press, 1976), p. 374. Reflecting upon Milton's Samson as "knightly champion," Wright finds in *Samson Agonistes* a subtle manifestation of Spenser's influence; see "Samson as the Fallen Champion in 'Samson Agonistes'," *Notes and Queries*, 205 (1960), 222. It was noted long ago that *Samson* may owe something to a parallel description of Artegall in *The Faerie Queene;* see *The Poetical Works of John Milton*, ed. Henry John Todd (7 vols.; London: Printed for J. Johnson, 1801), IV, 372.

tegall, emblematizes those times, described by Eudoxus in *A View of the Present State of Ireland*, when "swordes are in the handes of the vulgare," and never really out of their hands, for even when they seem wearied by war and are "broughte downe to extreame wretchedness . . . they Creepe a little . . . sue for grace" and, recovering their strength, go forth to slaughter still others.[43] Spenser may affirm the proposition that arms occasionally further the divine purpose, but only in those instances when they are employed to maintain the public right over private ends. Those who judge others, Spenser seems to be saying, must themselves be just; and their justice stands in marked contrast to such injustices as cruelty, barbarity, and savagery. In Book V of *The Faerie Queene* identity is forged between Samson and Artegall by way of forcing a distinction.

Not just Samson's fall but the consequences thereof—the hardening of his heart, his becoming inured to violence—are gathered into focus by Spenser, and in such a way as to give priority to Artegall, Spenser representing Artegall, by no means a perfect hero, as superior to his type, the bringer of justice to a world (as Samson never quite managed to do) where laws do not exist, or perhaps have failed to work. In its largest extension, this typology reaches beyond the poem to envelop the poet and his queen as well, and in the process the sacred is secularized: typology invades history in order to explicate it, envelops its protagonists to elucidate their objectives and accomplishments. If in times past, history was crossbred with mythology, with Spenser typology comes to be crossbred with current history and in the process becomes an agent by which present is exalted over past history, the neotype over the type.

Wybarne may believe that poets, even if unwittingly, are dismantlers of myth and deconstructionists of the Samson legend; yet it is equally true that in the seventeenth century poets

---

[43] *The Works of Edmund Spenser*, ed. Greenlaw et al., X, 55.

participate in the rehabilitation of this story, but still a typology
of difference prevails. In "On Iesus and Sampson," included
in *Divine Fancies*, Francis Quarles sets forth the typological
associations between these scriptural figures and their respective stories, starting with the annunciation scenes that forecast
their births: both are Nazarites and deliverers, both marry
(one a Gentile, one the church), speak riddles, exhibit ire,
slay lions, befriend harlots, and eventually burst their bonds.
Yet Jesus also purchases a higher fame than Samson did:

> *Iesus*, the first, and second day, could be
> The *Graves* close pris'ner; but, the third, was free:
> In this they [i.e., Jesus and Samson] differ'd:
> > *Iesus* dying Breath
> Cry'd out for Life; but *Sampson* cald for *Death*:
> *Father forgive them*, did our *Iesus* crye;
> But *Sampson*, *Let me be reveng'd and dye*:
> Since then, sweet *Savior*, tis thy *Death* must ease us,
> We flye from *Sampson*, and appeale to *Iesus*.[44]

This typology of difference emerges out of Quarles's more
sustained meditation, *The Historie of Samson*, published the
year before. That poem ends, as Milton's tragedy will also
end, with a celebration of Samson's name and fame, both
lasting and flourishing until the end of time:

> [Samson's] name shall flourish, and be still in prime,
> In spight of ruine, or the teeth of *Time*:
> Whose fame shall last, till heaven shall please to free
> This *Earth* from Sinne, and *Time* shall cease to be.[45]

[44] See *The Divine Fancies: Digested into Epigrammes, Meditations, and Observations*
(London: Printed for J. Marriott, 1632), pp. 55-56; see also p. 54.

[45] See *The Historie of Samson*, p. [140]. Quarles affords a valuable perspective on
Milton's poem, although the one argument in behalf of indebtedness is unpersuasive
and strained; see ch. VIII of George Wesley Whiting's *Milton's Literary Milieu*
(1939; rpt. New York: Russell and Russell, 1964).

The celebration of Samson one year becomes more measured the next, we may suppose because of the sorts of tortuous reflections, and tortured reasonings, that Quarles had already pored over in his studied review of Samson's checkered history.

The Historie of Samson commences with the announcement: "I sing th' illustrious, and renowned story / Of mighty Samson; the eternal glory / Of his Heroicke acts: His life, His death."[46] The poem proceeds by anatomizing that history in a series of episodes, each accompanied by sober reflections which are themselves a valuable index to what in the Samson story had become so troubling to its seventeenth-century readers: the "haughty spirit" and "wandring eye" of this "greedy Lover," as well as the unexemplary marriage of this "Revengefull *Samson*,"[47] the wages of whose sins are blindness and eventually death and whose history is explicable only in terms of the mysterious, and sometimes mysteriously vengeful, workings of providence. The most troubled broodings here concern Samson's marriage, which occasions a debate between Reason and Passion, and later the revenge he will take first upon the people of Timnath and subsequently upon Delilah's countrymen.

In the debate between Reason and Passion, Reason argues that " 'Tis vaine, to make a choice, / Where parents have an over-ruling voice," and thereupon Samson's parents advise their son to "Make a wiser choice."[48] Nevertheless, Samson continues to appeal to his parents, explaining that he is bent upon winning this woman's conversion and thereby turning her to his own God. Samson is being rehabilitated here by subliming his motives (he returns to his bride in a gesture of forgiveness) and then by tracing his decision to marry, along with his parents' unexplained acquiescence in that marriage, to the ways of God: man does not choose, rather heaven dic-

---

[46] *Ibid.*, unpaginated proem.   [47] *Ibid.*, pp. 33, 36, 45, 86.
[48] *Ibid.*, pp. 37-38.

tates, when to love; and though this is not an "exemplar" marriage it exhibits the mysterious ways of God who orchestrates all events in order to execute through Samson that higher vengeance which is *the secret pleasure of his sacred* will."[49] Samson's only serious failing, according to Quarles, lies in his misconstruing the purpose of his marriage as effecting conversion instead of executing vengeance, and since the earthly authority for his marriage is Samson's parents, not Samson himself, they are seen as the real culprits. " 'Tis too severe a censure" to say that Samson marries without his parents' consent—to say, in effect, that *"He lives, a* Fornicator; *She, a* Whore: / *Too hard a censure! And it seemes to me, / The parent's most delinquent of the three."*[50] Samson is not only exonerated in choosing to marry but is then exalted by the portrayal of him returning to the Woman of Timnath, imputing guilt for her liaison neither to himself nor to his bride but to her people and thereupon urging forgiving and forgetting what has happened between his bride and paranymph in the interval of his absence.

Behind Samson's marriage Quarles sees a vindictive, vengeful deity. That marriage, and the consequences thereof, occasion a series of meditations on such matters as "May these revenge their wrongs, by blood? May these / Have power to Kill, and murther where they please?":

> Is God the God of vengeance? And may none
> Revenge his private wrongs, but he alone?
> What meanes this franticke Nazarite to take
> Gods office from his hand . . . ?
> . . . Who warranted his breath
> To threaten ruine, and to thunder death?[51]

[49] *Ibid.*, pp. 40-53.

[50] *Ibid.*, p. 46. Luther had argued similarly; see *Luther's Works*, ed. Jaroslav Pelikan et al. (55 vols.; St. Louis: Concordia Press; Philadelphia: Fortress Press, 1955-76), IV, 222; XLIV, 12; XLV, 382; XLVI, 269; LIII, 219.

[51] *The Historie of Samson*, pp. 77, 83.

Nazarites are forbidden to do such things, Quarles argues; but he then allows that in this instance God has mixed his own quarrels with Samson's and suspended his own laws, in this way limiting his glory for our good and showing himself to be more human than hitherto we may have supposed. Samson is God's avenging angel, "A lawfull Prince . . . Gods Lieutenant, here," into whose hands is placed the Sword of Justice. [52] In his dealings with the Timnian people and later with the Philistines, Samson's rage increases, vengeance becomes his preoccupation, so that he is finally standing at the pillars and there praying to glorify God in a final slaughter and simultaneously to end his own misery by dying along with the Philistines. Samson's blindness is here construed as God's punishment and his death, as God's reward; for a just God punishes sin in every member where he finds it, whether among the Philistines or in Samson himself. The Samson story thus becomes a sustained comment on God, the justice of his ways and the secret workings of his providence. A tragic figure, Samson, in that "glorious Fray," is both the executioner of God's justice and one executed by it. [53]

God's justice—precisely, God's distributive not retributive justice—becomes a principal theme of the Samson story as it is mused over by commentators and even poets during the 1650s. Samson's own retributive justice, occasioned by his rage and anger, provides Elias Ashmole, in his poetical pieces, with a foil for God's own merciful distribution of justice. "Thynke how *Adam* lost hys wysdome," urges Ashmole, and "*Sampson* hys myght that was soe strong":

> But see how others that livyd well,
> And to their God did none offence,
> Such Chastysment did never fele,
> But God shewed ever to them benevolence;

[52] *Ibid.*, p. 84.   [53] *Ibid.*, p. 85.

Enok and *Ely* were caryed hence,
To Paradyse, and other good livers were
Of God rewarded in dyvers manner. [54]

Within this broad context, which charts the gradual erosion
of parallels between Samson and Christ, the demise of an old
typology, Samuel Pordage's post-Restoration representation of
Samson as Christ's type, bursting the bonds of death and
throwing open the bar standing between this world and paradise, may seem but a throwback to an earlier and by now
outmoded typologizing of the Samson story. But it is more
than that and, in this, an unexpected prefiguration of Milton's
last poems. Pordage's "Sacred Poem" reaches from the loss of
paradise by Adam to its apocalyptic restoration by Christ, but
is also preeminently concerned with the redemptive process in
history resulting from human effort rather than divine intervention, with the way in which man himself repairs the ruins
of the Fall and wrests comedy from tragedy. Thus Samson
and Jesus are typologically coupled by way of reinforcing the
point that heaven is reached not by divine but by human effort:
"O Noble Work! O mighty strength of the / Blest Son of
God's glorious Humanity! / 'Twas his Humanity this work
did do, / Or else no passage here had been for you, / Not for
an' humane Soul." [55] Samson appears here, with all his typological trappings, but now as a foil less for the heroism than
for the humanity of Jesus. Still, the most important reflection
upon Milton's Samson by a contemporary is contained within
a Marvellian parenthesis whose implications depend upon
Marvell's own perception of what by now is, at least as a
literary tradition, nearly a century-old practice of typological
differentiation.

[54] *Theatrum Chemicum Britannicum: Containing Several Poeticall Pieces* (London:
Printed for Nathaniel Brooke, 1652), pp. 118-19.

[55] *Mundorum Explicatio . . . A Sacred Poem* (London: Printed for Lodowick Lloyd,
1661), pp. 233-34.

Typological differences are registered increasingly as the Samson story comes to be treated less and less reverently. Samuel Butler's Sir Hudibras is promptly identified with "that stubborn Crew / Of Errant Saints, whom all men grant / To be the true Church *Militant*":

> Such as do build their Faith upon
> The holy Text of *Pike* and *Gun*;
> Decide all Controversies by
> Infallible *Artillery*;
> And prove their Doctrine Orthodox
> By Apostolick *Blows* and *Knocks*;
> Call Fire and Sword and Desolation,
> *A godly-thorough-Reformation*,
> Which alwayes must be carry'd on,
> And still be doing, never done. . . . (I.i.190-202)

Thereupon, this errant Knight's tawny beard is likened to "*Sampson's* Heart-breakers":

> . . . it grew
> In time to make a nation rue;
> Though it contributed its own fall,
> To wait upon the publick downfall. (251-54)[56]

Scornful allusions of this sort, stressing (as John Dryden will do in *The Medall*[57]) that Samson is the betrayer and destroyer of a nation, provide an ambience for Andrew Marvell's unflattering reference to Samson by way of flattering Milton in "On Mr. Milton's *Paradise Lost*."

The "Argument" to *Paradise Lost* causes Marvell, for a while, to doubt Milton's intentions and to fear that Milton might

[56] *Hudibras*, ed. John Wilders (Oxford: Clarendon Press, 1967), pp. 7, 9.

[57] See *The Medall* (73 ff.), in *The Works of John Dryden*, ed. Edward Niles Hooker and H. T. Swedenborg, Jr. (19 vols.; Berkeley and Los Angeles: Univ. of California Press, 1961), II, 45.

"ruine (for I saw him strong) / The sacred Truths to Fable and old Song, / (So *Sampson* groap'd the Temples Posts in spight) / The World o'rewhelming to revenge his Sight" (7-10).[58] Marvell's hesitations recall similar ones registered by H. L. Benthem, who was led to believe, both by Theodore Haak and by his own reading of Haak's translation of the first three books of *Paradise Lost*, that Milton's epic was really about politics in Restoration England. "So far as I understand from what Haak told me and what I read for myself," says Benthem, "this very wily politician" used the myth of the fall as a veil for exactly the kind of lament his friends feared he would write.[59] Supposing that Marvell, even more than Haak, would be privy to Milton's intentions, Christopher Hill would have us bear this story in mind when we read Marvell's dedicatory poem, "On Mr. Milton's *Paradise Lost.*" In that poem, of course, Marvell goes out of his way to aver that his doubts were groundless; for omitting "all that was improper," Milton "hast not miss'd one thought that could be fit" and has interpreted Scripture without violating it: "things divine thou treatst of in such state / As them preserves, and Thee inviolate" (27-28, 33-34). Marvell presses this argument, moreover, by invoking Samson only to explode an older typology wherein Samson is numbered among the chief precursors of Christ and touted as the patron saint of the Puritan revolutionaries.

"A curious thing" about this poem, says Hill, "is its reference to Samson," which, more than any other allusion in the poem, as Hill might have gone on to say, has frustrated interpretative efforts.[60] If we turn to the best of Marvell's

[58] *The Poems and Letters of Andrew Marvell*, 2nd ed., ed. H. M. Margoliouth (2 vols.; Oxford: Clarendon Press, 1952), I, 131-32. All other citations of this poem, given parenthetically within the text, derive from this edition, and other of Marvell's poems cited in this chapter are likewise from this edition.

[59] See Christopher Hill, *Milton and the English Revolution* (New York: Viking Press, 1977), pp. 391-92.

[60] "Milton and Marvell," in *Approaches to Marvell: The York Tercentenary Lectures*, ed. C. A. Patrides (London: Henley; Boston: Routledge and Kegan Paul, 1978), p. 22.

critics—or even to Milton's critics who have taken cognizance of these lines—we confront a bewildering array of contradictory observation, a critical dispute staggering in its claims and counterclaims: the poem is, or is not, reflective of the contemporary political situation; either does, or does not, exonerate Milton from Marvell's suspicions concerning his intentions. The Samson of Marvell's poem is now the spiteful Samson of the Book of Judges, and now the presumably regenerate Samson of *Samson Agonistes*; and through the Samson allusion Marvell is said here to assert a comparison and there a contrast, for some forges an identity between Milton and his biblical counterpart and for others forces a distinction between them. For one critic, the lines are concrete testimony that Marvell knew of and surely read Milton's tragedy and, for another, are certain evidence that Marvell could not possibly have read this tragedy.[61]

Before we worry further over Milton's intentions, we should review Marvell's. His poem is an encomium which would rescue Milton from his detractors and *Paradise Lost* from prospective censors. We should allow to Hill that "literary historians . . . do not always bear sufficiently in mind the subterfuges which writers necessarily had to adopt in order not to expose themselves to danger"[62]—subterfuges now detailed by Annabel Patterson in her study of the hermeneutics of censorship. Here Patterson proposes a principle of inexact analogy that, asserting difference, actually urges the perception of likeness. In such poetry there is, according to Patterson, a felt tension between the authorized message and its author's

[61] For a full review of this matter, see my "Perplexing the Explanation: Marvell's 'On Mr. Milton's *Paradise Lost*'," in *Approaches to Marvell*, ed. Patrides, pp. 280-305. See also Judith Scherer Herz, "Milton and Marvell: The Poet as Fit Reader," *Modern Language Quarterly*, 39 (1978), 239-63, and Kenneth Gross, " 'Pardon Me, Mighty Poet': Versions of the Bard in Marvell's 'On Mr. Milton's *Paradise Lost*'," *Milton Studies*, 16 (1982), 77-96.

[62] "Milton and Marvell," in *Approaches to Marvell*, ed. Patrides, p. 14.

actual feeling; though there may be "disclaimers of topical intention," they "are not to be trusted, and are more likely to be entry codes to precisely that kind of reading they protest against."[63] These are the unacknowledged suppositions that seem to underlie those readings of Marvell's poem which would ascertain sameness between Samson and Milton despite the stated difference, and that would correlate Marvell's Samson with the supposedly regenerate Samson of Milton's play without regard for the invitation Marvell's poem makes to relate its Samson to the spiteful figure in the Book of Judges. The impression left by Haak upon Benthem, coupled with the fact that Marvell *would* have been more likely than Haak to know Milton's intentions, may very well discourage the belief that Marvell's "doubts are . . . submerged in . . . approval," encouraging instead the view of J. B. Broadbent, that Marvell's "retraction of . . . doubts is not quite whole-hearted, and his statement of the excellencies of *Paradise Lost* continues to hint at . . . difficulties."[64] Yet there are perhaps even more compelling reasons to dismiss such speculation, not the least of which is that Haak's only meeting with Milton dates back, at the latest, to the early 1650s.

Marvell's principal objective is to redeem Milton from his critics, most notably Samuel Parker and Richard Leigh, both of whom had belittled Milton's theological radicalism, Samson-like tactics, and blindness. His poem is an *apologia*, al-

[63] *Censorship and Interpretation*, p. 57.

[64] See James Holly Hanford, *John Milton, Englishman* (New York: Crown Publishers, 1949), p. 252, and Broadbent, *Some Graver Subject: An Essay on "Paradise Lost"* (London: Chatto and Windus, 1960), p. 64. In the eighteenth century, it was being argued in certain quarters that poets like Marvell and Milton must often use curtains to shade over certain parts of their history and to shield certain of their sentiments: "Whatever he [Marvell] might say to obviate the invideous reflections of his antagonist, there is no doubt that he thought, at the very time, that neither himself nor Milton had been on the wrong side" (*Memoirs of Thomas Hollis*, comp. Francis Blackburne [2 vols.; London: Printed by J. Nichols, 1780], I, 369).

laying fears about Milton that were in part raised by his supporters. In another time, in another century, and in an imaginary conversation between Marvell and Parker, Walter Savage Landor has Parker chastize Milton as a Samson who shook the pillars of the church and "subverted . . . the better form of Christianity."[65] This is but a reminder that in his own time Milton came to be regarded as an enemy of orthodoxy and already had been celebrated (or perhaps chided) in terms of the Samson story: "I answer with learned *Milton*," says one of the poet's contemporaries, "that if God commanded these things, 'tis a sign they were lawful and are commendable . . . Neither *Sampson* nor Samuel alleged any other cause or reason for what they did, but retaliation, and the apparent justice of the actions themselves."[66] Landor's imaginary conversation may derive from Parker's complaint against the "wretched and horrible abuses of Religion" among the Puritan pamphleteers who would effect the apotheosis of Samson and who, by such efforts, may have prompted Parker's exclamations: "What horrid work did they make with the word of God? How

---

[65] *The Complete Works of Walter Savage Landor*, ed. T. Earle Welby (16 vols.; London: Chapman and Hall, 1927-34), IV, 216.

[66] William Allen [i.e., Edward Sexby], *Killing No Murder* (1659), as quoted by William Riley Parker, *Milton's Contemporary Reputation* (Columbus: Ohio State Univ. Press, 1940), p. 97. But see Richard F. Hardin, "Milton's Radical 'Admirer' Edward Sexby, with a Note on Samson's Revenge," *Milton Quarterly*, 15 (1981), 59-61. Hardin restores the passage cited above to its proper context where, urging that the nation get rid of Cromwell, Sexby contends that Samson's was a private revenge and, moreover, that the law of nature allows private men to take revenge:

> In the story of Samson tis manifest, that the denying him his wife, and after the burning of her and her father, which though they were great, yet were but private injuries, he took for sufficient grounds to make warre upon the Philistins, being himself but a private man, and not onely not assisted, but opposed by his servile countreymen. He knew what the law of nature allowed him. . . .
>
> Now that which was lawfull for Samson to doe against many oppressours, why is it unlawfull for us to doe against one?

shamefully did they urge the Prophecies of the Old Testament, in defiance of the Precepts of the New."[67] The poet who believed, as Marvell remarks in *The Rehearsal Transpros'd*, that the causes behind the Puritan Revolution were "too good to have been fought for,"[68] clearly would resist any attempt to associate Milton with Samson. To do so would be to erode the ideological base, to counter the rhetorical thrust of an entire poem in which the Samson allusion is a chief supporting device.

If it can be said that Marvell's Samson is Milton's Samson, as is so often done, it can just as reasonably be postulated that Milton's Samson is Marvell's Samson. And Marvell's Samson need not be inferred (as Miltonists are inclined to do) from the dedicatory poem on *Paradise Lost*: he can be extrapolated from Marvell's reference to "the fear'd Hebrew . . . the public scorn" (935-36) in *The Last Instructions to a Painter*. Here, when Marvell "compares England in its state of decline to the bound Samson," says Warren Chernaik, "there is no suggestion of a possible regeneration, no sense that the dark ways of providence will suddenly be illumined, that suffering will turn by unforeseen ways into triumph. Instead," Chernaik argues, "the lines suggest only ignominy, in evoking the former greatness and potential for good which have been laid waste by man's folly and venality. . . . The 'Black Day' of England's humiliation, so different from the 'blest Day' for which Marvell had seen presages under the reign of Cromwell, is made more painful by the memory of past glories and blighted promise." This allusion, for Chernaik, emphasizes the late "magnanimous despair" of both Marvell and Milton, their "ultimate solitude," their questioning whether man can know

[67] *A Reproof to the Rehearsal Transprosed* (London: Printed for James Collins, 1673), p. 396.

[68] *The Rehearsal Transpros'd and The Rehearsal Transpros'd The Second Part*, ed. D.I.B. Smith (Oxford: Clarendon Press, 1971), p. 135.

with certainty that his actions are sanctioned and that he will be saved.[69]

Better perhaps than any poet of the seventeenth century, Marvell reveals the extent to which Samson, once a figure around whom to spin witty conceits, gradually became one inducing sober reflection. Behind the "iron gates of life" (44) in "To His Coy Mistress" may lie a playful allusion to the gates burst by Samson in anticipation of Christ's later opening of the gates into Paradise; and more probably, the Mower's "Revenge" in "The Mower's Song," reducing the world to a "Common Ruin" (30), harbors an allusion to Samson's revenge in hurling down the pillars, itself an anticipation of the great ruin at the end of time. Samson who could once be, as here, a figure in "a comic Apocalypse,"[70] after the failure of the Revolution, becomes an image of that horror; previously a figure in sweet lyric song, he now emerges as a principal protagonist in the tragedy of history. Allusions that once were evidence of a poet's typological skill and mode of thought are now replaced by ones in which the poet not only withholds but resists such typological play.

Typology is still, for Marvell, a strategy for enveloping historical personages in an enduring pattern of significance; yet in his poem on Milton it is honed into an analytical instrument of extraordinary precision. In *The First Anniversary*, Marvell had netted Cromwell within a typological system involving Noah, Gideon, Elijah, and an angel of the Apocalypse, but in such a way as to make Cromwell seem inferior to his types.[71] The inexact analogy here tempers heroism as, through a reverse strategy, in the poem on Milton it will

[69] *The Poet's Time: Politics and Religion in the Work of Andrew Marvell* (Cambridge: Cambridge Univ. Press, 1983), pp. 147, 148.

[70] Bruce King, *Marvell's Allegorical Poetry* (New York and Cambridge: Oleander Press, 1977), p. 143.

[71] See Annabel M. Patterson, *Marvell and the Civic Crown* (Princeton: Princeton Univ. Press, 1978), pp. 68-69, 74, 80-82, 84.

heighten it. Milton gains stature in the typological comparison with Samson just as Cromwell loses stature in the earlier comparison with Elijah, whose achievements for Israel were won by prayer, not force. The poet who reflects upon history may alter its course by the sword of the Word, may dispel the dark cloud that violence always seems to bring between the would-be prophet and the hoped-for apocalypse. It is certainly significant, as Annabel Patterson has argued, that "whenever he has something important to say" Marvell alludes to Milton's poetry, quotes from Milton, or employs one of Milton's poetic procedures, "a process brought to fulfillment in . . . 'On Mr. Milton's Paradise Lost'," which is at once "the summative statement" of Marvell's values and a provocative reflection on Milton's own.[72]

All we know of the Marvell-Milton relationship during the years of the Restoration suggests that, if *Samson Agonistes* had been published before the writing of Marvell's dedicatory poem, Marvell would have known about and probably read it. Indisputably, Marvell's poem was composed subsequent to the publication of *Paradise Regained*, to which was added *Samson Agonistes*, and the verses in that poem referring to Samson appear to derive from a studied reflection on Milton's tragedy. Standing behind Marvell's poem, and insinuated by Marvell as a context for Milton's tragedy, is the understanding of the Samson story current in the late 1650s and 60s but also a mainstay in the literary tradition now for nearly a century. Pre-revolutionary reservations about Samson emerge again, and with them emerges a new concern with the political implications of the Samson story. What initially had seemed a foreboding of apocalypse is now construed, in analogy with the Samson story, as a broken apocalypse. Milton's Samson, Marvell implies, is the fallen hero of Judges: Milton's Samson

[72] *Ibid.*, p. 30.

is Marvell's vengeful Samson, and the fallen Samson of *Paradise Lost*.

It may well be that Marvell is not alone among his contemporaries in rendering this sort of judgment on Milton's Samson. Dryden clearly had read *Samson Agonistes* and echoes it in *Aureng-Zebe* (1676), as was acknowledged in his own century by Gerhard Langbarne.[73] There may even be a reminiscence of *Samson* in *Absalom and Achitophel*, as Stephen Zwicker suggests by paralleling lines 279-80 in Dryden's poem with lines 33-34, 68-69 of Milton's.[74] In fact, Dryden's decision to parallel Old Testament and contemporary history in *Absalom and Achitophel*—to use 2 Samuel as a screen on current history—may be evidence of Milton's influence reaching beyond echo and allusion into the realm of poetic conceptualization. In *Samson Agonistes*, no less than in Dryden's poem, history seems to get swallowed up in the biblical metaphor because of the very complexity of the analogy being drawn: "The poem . . . is neither Jewish history nor English history," Arthur Hoffman writes of Dryden's poem, "but a *tertium quid*, an action somewhere between or above both histories and commenting on both."[75]

---

[73] *An Account of the English Dramatic Poets* (Oxford: Printed by C. C., 1691), p. 157. For another example of the possible influence of *Samson Agonistes* in its own century, see the anonymous *A Vindication of the State* (London: Printed for John Weld, 1698); and for actual citation of the poem in the seventeenth century, see John Dunton, *The Challenge Sent by a Young Lady to Sir Thomas* (London: Published by E. Whitlock, 1697), pp. 210, 233-34. The most thorough and suggestive study of Dryden's indebtedness to Milton's poetry, especially to *Paradise Lost* and *Samson Agonistes*, is provided by Anne Davidson Ferry, *Milton and the Miltonic Dryden* (Cambridge, Mass.: Harvard Univ. Press, 1968). See esp. pp. 125-218, where Ferry argues that *Samson* is the crucial text intervening between Shakespeare's *Antony and Cleopatra* and Dryden's *All for Love* and a principal determinant of the latter text's final shape.

[74] *Dryden's Political Poetry: The Typology of King and Nation* (Providence, R.I.: Brown Univ. Press, 1972), p. 94.

[75] *John Dryden's Imagery* (Gainesville: Univ. of Florida Press, 1962), p. 80; see also Earl Miner, *Dryden's Poetry* (Bloomington: Indiana Univ. Press, 1967), esp. pp. 106-43.

Both poems envision a moral order beyond what is actually supplied by their biblical contexts and even beyond what survives in their own time as a moral order; both swerve in their preoccupations from matters of history to concerns over value, with Milton's two epics affording important contexts for both *Absalom* and *Samson*, a point of reference for each poem, a perspective for valuation. What Hoffman says of Dryden's poem is equally true of Milton's: that England is a paradise that may be lost or regained depending upon whether assaults upon it are successful or successfully resisted and upon whether historical personages are true or false sons of God.[76] Dryden's measure of true sonship—man's vesting of value in earthly kingship—is not shared by Milton, of course, although Dryden and Milton alike arrive at their definition of values, however different, through the glance they cast upon the figure of Samson. Here is Dryden:

> Kings are the publick Pillars of the State,
> Born to sustain and prop the Nations weight:
> If my Young *Samson* will pretend a Call
> To shake the Column, let him share the Fall:
> But Oh that yet he would repent and live! (953-57)[77]

However different their idealisms, Milton and Dryden, no less than Marvell, can perceive Samson's final call as a pretense, a fall, and can perceive Samson himself, because he is a pretending Messiah, as an obstacle in the very different paths each poet would take in his effort to recover the lost paradise in history. Dryden would press down upon the opponents of kingship the image of Samson, as well as of Satan; Milton, allowing the same biblical images to merge into one another, would press the image of Samson on royalists and revolutionaries alike (a plague on both their houses!) and would register

[76] *John Dryden's Imagery*, pp. 88-89.

[77] *The Works of John Dryden*, ed. Hooker and Swedenborg, II, 33-34 (ll. 953-57).

in that image, as with the fine point of a diamond, the very different vices of both parties. What has been said of Dryden's allusion here to Samson pertains as well to such allusions in Milton's writings: each poet may refer to Samson, and play with Samson allusions, but always with "typological distance."[78] In the instance of Milton, however, the ambivalence registered toward Samson is not only historically but biographically and psychologically determined.

Since the seventeenth century, Samson has not fared well among either poets or biblical commentators. In the eighteenth century, from the anonymous author of *The History of Samson*, we hear that "it is difficult to say which was greatest, the folly and stupidity of Samson, or the impudence of Delilah . . . the folly of Samson [was not] less than Delilah's wickedness. . . . It is scarcely possible to imagine a man so besotted and void of all consideration."[79] In the nineteenth century, attendant upon the realization that "after the death of Samson we find the people again in idolatry, accompanied by social crimes of horrible character," comes the following observation from the anonymous *Song of the Prophets*: "Samson . . . did not, for all his strength, deliver his countrymen from the Philistines. Strength is the only extraordinary quality which he is revealed as possessing. He was not very moral or very wise."[80] And in our own century, James Ackerman declares

---

[78] George McFadden, *Dryden the Public Writer 1660-1685* (Princeton: Princeton Univ. Press, 1978), p. 251. In Milton's century, the notion of typological distance is finely articulated by Daniel Featley: "A glasse sheweth the lineaments and proportion of a man, but at a distance; so wee may see Christ in the predictions, visions, and figures of the Old Testament, as so many glasses, but at a distance, according to the words of that *Seer, I shall see him, but not neare"* *(Clavis Mystica: A Key Opening Divers Difficult and Mysterious Texts of Holy Scripture* [London: Printed for Nicolas Bourne, 1636], p. 172).

[79] (London: Printed by John Marshall, 1797), pp. 11-12.

[80] (London: Orr and Smith, 1835), pp. 72, 91-92.

that Samson "does not emerge as a great hero. . . . He is instead a tragic failure whose selfish impulses led to his destruction. . . . Samson's demise illustrated man's lonely weakness once Yahweh's spirit had departed."[81]

This post-Miltonic Samson captures the tragic rhythms of history—captures, that is, what Milton in his own portrayal of Samson sought to capture. Indeed, this post-Miltonic Samson may be said to exist by virtue of Milton's Samson; he emerges from the understanding that resorting to violence to establish the rule of the saints is not a feature of millenarian thought but rather a feature of thought imposed upon millenarianism during the revolutionary era in England; and the lineaments of this Samson find their surest delineation in the words of J. H. Hexter. In the 1650s and 60s, Hexter contends, Puritanism becomes introspective and, in its introspection, discovers that "it was the saint who at every turning point blocked the erection of the *regnum Christi* by the saints." At the very heart of Puritanism during the Civil War years was an explosive illusion, that the few could impose the will of God on the many—and an illusion even more unsettling, "that any human agent or instrument willing and able to establish the Holy Commonwealth was divinely authorized to do whatever need be done to that end, that such ability and willingness was in fact the sign of God's special choice. . . . This is the heroic tragedy," says Hexter:

> It is tragedy because circumstance and event provide only the setting in which Puritanism, through its own inner flaws and failings, thrusts itself down the path to disaster. It is heroic because Puritanism itself in the days of its triumph and its catastrophe was no trifling, hole-in-the-corner affair—because Puritanism was indeed heroic, magnificent in its virtues and

[81] *On Teaching the Bible as Literature* (Bloomington: Indiana Univ. Press, 1967), p. 105.

force, magnificent even in its failings: Samson Agonistes, but Samson still.[82]

This is the tragedy that Marvell points to in his famous declaration that the cause was too good to have been fought for.
   This is also the tragedy that Henry Oldenburg wished Milton to record:

> Nor would it be unwelcome to learn whether you
> are preparing a history of the English revolution.
> If only it would subside and the cultivation of peace
> and justice succeed all war and injustice. Men squan-
> der men all too prodigally. (VII, 513)

And that Milton, responding to Oldenburg's urgings, for a
time resisted:

> I am far from writing a history of our political
> troubles, which you seem to urge; for they are wor-
> thier of silence than of publication. What we need
> is not one who can compile a history of our troubles
> but one who can happily end them. (VII, 515)

With the purpose of ending those troubles Milton presents
his poetic volume of 1671, with *Samson Agonistes* anatomizing
the tragedy of "Blood, death, and deathful deeds . . . / Ruin,
destruction at the utmost point" (1514-15). As Milton would
state his case in *A Treatise of Civil Power*, "the kings of *Juda*
and those magistrates under the law might have recours . . .
to divine inspiration"; but he also stipulates that those operating
under the Gospel have no such recourse, "and so, instead of
forcing the Christian, they force the Holy Ghost; and, against

---

[82] *Reappraisals in History: New Views on History and Society in Early Modern
Europe*, 2nd ed. (1961; rpt. Chicago: Univ. of Chicago Press, 1979), pp. 247-48.
Cf. William Haller, "The Tragedy of God's Englishmen," in *Reason and Imagination*,
ed. J. A. Mazzeo (New York: Columbia Univ. Press; London: Routledge and Kegan
Paul, 1962), pp. 201-11.

the wise forewarning of Gamaliel, fight against God" (VII, 260). *Samson Agonistes* reflects upon the Puritan Revolution, indeed portrays that revolution in just the way that truly revolutionary art should, according to Herbert Marcuse: "[in] critical, if not hostile presentations, hostile to the actual revolutionary practice and its exigencies" and in the interest of producing "a cosmic transfiguration of the revolution."[83] In *Samson Agonistes*, we see Milton pausing "Betwixt the world destroy'd and world restord'd" (*PL* XII.3).

The world goes on, of course. But it is a world that is to the good malignant and to bad men benign, now "under her own Waight groaning" (*PL* XII.39); yet this is also a world from which Milton expects for "new hope to spring" and eventually "Out of despaire, joy" (XI.138-39). It is from the Samsons that, in the past, God has averted his eyes, leaving such men to their own corrupt ways; but God has also regularly provided for the just men in history (such as Milton clearly imagines himself to be) who, eminent and wise, speak "much of Right and Wrong, / Of Justice, of Religion, Truth, and Peace, / And Judgment from above" (XI.666-68). In moments of darkness, these are the men who admonish friends and countrymen, "denouncing wrauth to come," and before them set "paths of righteousness, how much more safe, / And full of peace" (XI.814-15).

Marvell plainly asserts a contrast between Samson and Milton and, through that contrast, would have us distinguish Samson, the false prophet and destroyer, from Milton, true prophet and creator—the one figure falling away from the divine vision, the other in old age achieving something like the prophetic strain; the one figure ignominiously losing his life, the other being providentially spared his. That is, Marvell uses typology (rather as Milton does in *Samson Agonistes*) to

---

[83] *Counter-Revolution and Revolt* (Boston: Beacon Press, 1972), pp. 103-04.

acknowledge discrepancies, to assert a difference, both poets, it appears, wishing to divest Samson of his usual place in typological systems. Cryptic and not so cryptic references to the ransom theory of the Atonement, to Christ's betrayal, and to Christ suffering in Milton's tragedy, or in its front matter, suggest that Samson simply does not measure up to the heroic norms delineated in Milton's epics nor, as I suspect Marvell would add, to the heroic attributes exemplified by Milton himself and exhibited in his lifetime. Following Milton, Marvell detaches the usual typology from Samson, yet proceeds to attach that same typology to Milton.

As an old typology crumbles, a neotypology emerges, with Milton at its center. *Samson Agonistes* is not an autobiographical poem but a poem that derives an important dimension of meaning from the inclusion of the kind of autobiographical detail which invites a comparison of Samson and Milton—and eventually a contrast. In his poem on *Paradise Lost*, then, Marvell simply capitalizes on a poetic strategy deployed by Milton himself. When Marvell acknowledges a knit of identity between Samson and Milton, he points toward an abstract, secular typology such as he had employed earlier both to define Cromwell and to describe his followers; he points toward a mode of typology that, popularized by the seventeenth-century lyric, was by no means restricted to it, and that as it became assimilated to other genres underwent significant shifts in emphasis.

Reformed theology had already come to emphasize "the disparity between type and antitype" as Ira Clark observes, thereby underscoring the independent value, as well as the failure of types, and hence their "ultimate need for the saving antitype."[84] Poets became involved in such typological systems, representing themselves and sometimes being represented by

[84] *Christ Revealed*, pp. 1, 2.

others, as neotypes or failures, inadequate in comparison with earlier types and like their types requiring redemption by the antitype. Moreover, as poets became mired in typological schemes, so too did the stretch of history in which they participated, typology thus affording both "a psychic framework for self-examination and portrayal" and a handle on the history of the poets' own time and on their involvement, for good or bad, in that history.[85] In the process, typology becomes a political language progressively touched by irony.

The period from 1640 to 1660 is a crucial turning-point in the re-formation of this symbolic vocabulary, which already had enveloped poets, their audiences, and both the private and public history of each. Now, though, there is not only a typologizing of history but a politicizing of theology; and increasingly in the latter half of the century, when there is a decided turn toward ambivalent types, even a displacement of positive with negative types, typology, once a device in panegyric, becomes a device for chastisement and lamentation. Individuals, no less than nations, now embody typological paradigms that frustrate, as once they had furthered, the providential design of history. Barbara Lewalski contends that "Milton turned to brilliant dramatic account the characteristic Protestant use of typological reference to explore the psyche and to analyze the spiritual progress of a particular individual."[86] I agree—but in terms different from those set forth by Lewalski.

[85] *Ibid.*, p. 29. See also *Protestant Poetics and the Seventeenth-Century Religious Lyric*, pp. 111-44, where Lewalski acknowledges "the Reformation emphasis upon the application of all scripture to the self" and the attendant "shift from Christic antitype to a focus upon the individual Christian" (pp. 131, 135.).

[86] "Typological Symbolism and the 'Progress of the Soul' in Seventeenth-Century Literature," in *Literary Uses of Typology from the Late Middle Ages to the Present*, ed. Earl Miner (Princeton: Princeton Univ. Press, 1977), p. 103. In this same essay, Lewalski remarks on the seventeenth-century tendency "to examine personal experience and the human condition in relation to certain recognized typological paradigms" (p. 113); in another essay in the same volume Paul Korshin comments

In *Paradise Lost*, for instance, Milton analyzes himself as the neotype of Moses and England as a neotype of the Chosen People. A comparable analysis is provided in Milton's tragedy, where the poet finds his counterpart in Samson, and the English people find theirs in the Israelites. However, whereas *Paradise Lost* promises success instead of failure, *Samson Agonistes* anatomizes the causes for failure in the first place, in terms of both the individual and the community, and thus presents tragedy in both its private and public aspects. Autobiographical detail reinforces the point: just as Mary Powell returns to Milton, Dalila returns to Samson, but only to be spurned by a husband who does not allow her to repent; Samson and Milton are both blind, but whereas Samson's blindness emblematizes his past failings and failures of vision, Milton's is the badge of his prophetic office. Samson's early speeches in Milton's tragedy recall Milton's entries into *Paradise Lost* through strategically placed prologues: Samson's "How many evils have enclos'd me round" (194), one of which is his blindness, recalls Milton's "fall'n on evil dayes, / On evil dayes though fall'n, and evil tongues; / In darkness, and with dangers compast round" (VII.25-27). Yet within the similarity of their situation—both are "Blind among enemies" (68)—is the difference that Samson's blindness is a curse, evidence of his own spiritual blindness, whereas Milton's is a blessing, enabling him, through "Celestial light," to "see and tell / Of things invisible to mortal sight" (III.51, 54-55).

---

incisively on the politicizing of theological contexts, especially in the latter part of the century ("The Development of Abstracted Typology in England, 1650-1820," pp. 147-203). The anonymous *Samsons Riddle, or, a Bunch of Bitter Wormwood, Bringing Forth a Bundle of Sweet Smelling Myrrah* (London: n. p., 1678) is as good an example as any of the way in which the Samson story gets netted within the political rhetoric of the age; another example is *Dagon's Fall: or the Knight Turn'd out of Commission* (London: n. p., 1680); and yet another, "A Letter to Satisfy All Persons" (1692), *The Pepys Ballads*, ed. Hyder Edward Rollins (6 vols.; Cambridge, Mass.: Harvard Univ. Press, 1929), VI, 311.

Finally, Milton's disappointments are quieted into a heroic patience, whereas Samson's eruptions into a spiteful rage culminate in violence. Patience is extolled to Samson "as the truest fortitude" (654), "the exercise / Of Saints . . . / Making them each his own Deliverer" (1287-89) and, thus extolled by the Chorus, is glimpsed by them in Samson as he departs for the temple: "He patient . . . where they led him" (1623), only to be swallowed up in the irony that Samson's is a patience resulting in devastation and death, in the deliverance of no one. In contrast, Milton hurls down the temple on no one, is undaunted, and with true patience would, through poetry, deliver both himself and his nation from defeat and despair. The fault for a failed mission, which Samson will not take upon himself but instead places squarely on the shoulders of his people, is shared by Milton with his people, and in the understanding that there are no innocent people in a guilty nation—not Samson and not Milton himself. In these ways, despite obvious similarities with Samson, Milton differentiates himself from and thereby eclipses his type. Milton's (and Marvell's) subversive submission is different from Samson's brawling bravado.

The poet himself applies types to self and self to types, as is customary in the seventeenth-century lyric, but with an effect here that, however uncharacteristic of earlier poetry, is a hallmark of Milton's: instead of exalting the type over the neotype in order to identify his own failings, Milton measures his advances against the failures of the type, assuming the role of an antitype in relation to that type. To dismiss autobiographical and political content from criticism of *Samson Agonistes* according to the argument of William Riley Parker—"Milton had no thought of creating a personal or political allegory . . . He was an artist"[87]—is to misconstrue the nature of his art, especially in this highly personal and political poem. Northrop

[87] *Milton: A Biography* (2 vols.; Oxford: Clarendon Press, 1968), I, 314.

Frye is nearer the mark when he says that "the link between Samson and Milton does not mean that *Samson Agonistes* is an autobiographical poem: it simply means that Milton was the only man who could have written it."[88]

Surely the reigning reading of this poem in the two centuries immediately after its publication touches its very pulse. The fundamentally personal content of the poem was then thought to involve Milton's reflections on bad marriages with the Samson story, more generally, serving as a metaphor for his own life in its final stages. Politically—and *Samson Agonistes* was always thought to have been a profoundly political poem—the tragedy was read as a dramatization of the death and predicted resurrection of the Good Old Cause. What have we here, asks David Masson, but "a representation of the Puritan and Republican Milton in his secret antagonism to all the powers and all the fashions of the Restoration":

> There were moments, I believe, in Milton's musings by himself, when it was a fell pleasure to him to imagine some exertion of his strength, like that legendary one of Samson's, by which, clutching the two central pillars . . . he might tug and strain till he brought down the whole fabric . . . upon the heads of the heathenish congregation, perishing himself in the fact, but leaving England bettered by the carnage.[89]

According to this argument, Milton identifies with Samson

---

[88] *Fearful Symmetry: A Study of William Blake* (Princeton: Princeton Univ. Press, 1947), pp. 325-26.

[89] *The Life of John Milton: Narrated in Connexion with the Political, Ecclesiastical, and Literary History of His Time* (6 vols.; 1880; rpt. Gloucester, Mass.: Peter Smith, 1965), VI, 676-77. Elsewhere Masson remarks: "The story of Samson must have seemed to Milton a metaphor or allegory of his own inner life in its later stages"; see *The Poetical Works of John Milton*, ed. David Masson (3 vols.; London: Macmillan, 1874), II, 91.

rather as Luther once did: "I hope that it also happens to me that I, like Samson, bring them more misfortune with my death than with my life."[90] The question for criticism is whether Milton's poem is an assimilation of, or an assault upon, this ideology, whether this theology and ethics underpin or are undermined by the poem.

An earlier criticism erred, not in discerning personal and political mirrorings in *Samson Agonistes*, but in deciphering the nature of Milton's statement through too easy and too simple correlations. Milton may be *like* but he is *not* Samson. There is a distancing maneuver within the poem, whose operations are evident in Milton's prose writings and finally rendered within this poem through implicit differentiations. In the process, the bite of Samson's militancy is displaced by the humanity of Milton's prose writings. Through the figure of Samson, then, Milton weighs past failures, his own and those of his nation, against present achievements, differentiating his own historical consciousness from the more primitive one of Samson still too much in evidence among the English people. Samson represents a state of mind in which men become inured to cruelty and war, "that state of mind which Puritanism created and introduced into the political arena"[91] and which, for Marvell, has to be transcended—was

[90] See *Luther's Works*, ed. Pelikan et al., XXXIX, 135; cf. XXXVIII, 233:

> These are the two pillars on which the papacy rests, like the house of the Philistines in Samson's time. . . . Now what if God had made Luther a Samson who would take hold of and tear down both pillars so that the house would collapse and they would all perish? Who could hold this against him? He is God and, therefore, beyond our comprehension. They gouged out both of Luther's eyes because according to them I hold that both the worldly and the spiritual authorities are opposed to each other. And the whore Delilah . . . is the holy, beautiful monkery which shaved off the hair that had grown for me as a Nazarite. . . .

[91] Michael Walzer, *The Revolution of the Saints: A Study in the Origin of Radical Politics* (Cambridge, Mass.: Harvard Univ. Press, 1965), p. 299.

transcended by Milton in the years following the Revolution's failure. Samson's failure is that, by employing force, he perpetuates the very patterns of history that he would reverse; Milton's success, that by not failing poetry he opens the gates into a paradise of the future. In this way, *Samson Agonistes* responds to a program for a new biblical hermeneutics deriving from Martin Luther and finely detailed by Georgia Christopher as she observes that Old Testament stories were becoming "lattices" into the sense of which exegetes and even poets began "to weave [themselves] . . . by filling in the interstices with details of situation and psyche from . . . [their] own experience."[92] In accordance with such a program, through the Samson image Milton figures what he himself once was and what many in his nation still are. Those who have not cast Samson off, as Milton has done, are his recapitulation, whereas Milton has become an oracle of fulfillment. He may not now be able to locate the fulfillment in himself but nonetheless situates himself in proximity to the antitype, carving out for himself a special place in the line leading toward apocalyptic fulfillment. He is a harbinger of that event, no less than an agent in effecting it. Once a correlative type, he stands not as, but close to, the antitype. We can almost hear Milton proclaiming with Abiezer Coppe (and with a large measure of self-reference):

> Arise out of *Flesh*, into *Spirit*; out of *Form*, into *Power*; Out of *Type* into Truth; out of the *Shadow*, into the *Substance*; out of the *Signe*, into the thing *Signified* . . . All *Forms*, appearances, *Types*, *Signes*, *Shadows*, *Flesh*, do, and shall *melt away* . . . into *power*, reality, *Truth, the thing Signified, Substance*, Spirit.[93]

[92] *Milton and the Science of the Saints* (Princeton: Princeton Univ. Press, 1982), p. 68.

[93] *A Fiery Flying Roll* (1649), in *A Collection of Ranter Writings of the Seventeenth Century*, ed. Nigel Smith (London: Junction Books, 1983), pp. 47-48, 71.

We have been told by Leslie Tannenbaum that the Book of
Judges inaugurates a new phase in biblical history and reminded that Protestant commentators came to regard this book
as "a paradigm of the 'tragedy of the apocalypse' that would
be broken only by replacing those imperfect Old Testament
deliverers with the apocalyptic Christ as the true deliverer."⁹⁴
In Milton's writings, the poet himself becomes the new deliverer, and his potential success is gauged by the degree to
which he eclipses his types, whether they be Moses (as in
Paradise Lost) or Samson (as in Milton's tragedy). The reference to the Book of Revelation in the preface to Milton's
play is another reminder that *Samson Agonistes* follows that
scriptural book in its premises that theater is mental and tragedy historical, and in its basic objective: the creation of a new
historical consciousness. The Reformation is a New Creation,
as it were—an extension of new spiritual light and marks the
emergence of a new consciousness. But as Lord Brooke explains, "it was not perfect at first dawning, but encreaseth still
by degress, till it have quite chased away the darkness, and
there be not more Night."⁹⁵

It has been said that when Samson hurls down the temple/
theater, he destroys not only himself and others but drama as
well, and that in this demolition of drama (and more notably
of tragedy), Milton, through the final speech of Manoa, insinuates a poetic anticipatory of "another [poetic] mode, 'legend' and 'lyric song.' The claim that the work never was
intended for the stage," argues Nicholas Jose, "is a tactical
move in the interests of higher truth," with the modes of
narrative and drama now giving way, by virtue of their inferior truth claims, to the reign of lyric.⁹⁶ The question lurking

⁹⁴ *Biblical Traditions in Blake's Early Prophecies: The Great Code of Art* (Princeton:
Princeton Univ. Press, 1982), p. 269.
⁹⁵ Robert Greville, Lord Brooke, "A Discourse Opening the Nature of That
Episcopacie," in *Tracts on Liberty in the Puritan Revolution 1638-1647*, ed. William
Haller (2 vols.; New York: Columbia Univ. Press, 1933-34), II, 159-60.
⁹⁶ *Ideas of the Restoration in English Literature 1660-71* (Cambridge, Mass.: Har-

behind Jose's observation may be stated thus: what do poets hear when they listen to the song of a nightingale, its song or a myth? Or thus: what do readers of *Samson Agonistes* hear in Milton's poem, a song of joy or a tragic lament? what do they see therein, the phenomenology of faith which is the province of lyric[97] or some other phenomenology that ordinarily comes within the purview of tragedy? What is implicit in Jose's argument was rendered explicit early in our own century: that whatever Milton accomplished in *Paradise Lost* and *Paradise Regained* it is less than he had already achieved on the plane of lyric song; that lyric effusions intervene insistently in the narrative mode of these epics, especially *Paradise Lost*; that *Samson Agonistes* is a progressive regression—"a very deliberate attempt at lyric drama" by way of recovering "the irrepressible song of the man's own soul."[98] Such an argument presses the questions upon us: what did Milton intend for us to hear? do narrative and drama reign over lyric or not?

As others have done, Jose presumes that "or" means "and" in *Samson Agonistes*, especially when Manoa promises that Samson's "Acts [will be] enroll'd / In copious Legend, *or* sweet Lyric Song" (1736-37; my italics), when, in fact, those lines seem to participate in the gathering cloud of prophetic irony that settles over the concluding verses of Milton's tragedy. Manoa's remark, more probably, anticipates the double form of the Samson story, his contrarious fame, which in its negative aspects will find conveyance in legend and in its positive aspects, in lyric song. Manoa's lines are genuinely prophetic of

---

vard Univ. Press, 1984), p. 158; cf. Earl Miner, "The Reign of Narrative in *Paradise Lost*," in *Composite Orders: The Genres of Milton's Last Poems*, ed. Richard S. Ide and Joseph Wittreich (Pittsburgh: Univ. of Pittsburgh Press, 1983), pp. 3-25.

[97] See William Elford Rogers, *The Three Genres and the Interpretation of Lyric* (Princeton: Princeton Univ. Press, 1983).

[98] Rhys, *Lyric Poetry*, pp. 223, 227.

Samson's "double-fac't . . . double-mouth'd" fame (971), but ironic, too, inasmuch as Milton, contrary to most of his contemporaries, will embed his version of the Samson legend not in sweet lyric song but in stately tragedy and, contrary to Shakespeare, his chief Renaissance rival in dramatic form, will judge that story to be the stuff of Christian tragedy, not Christmas comedy.

Harbored in Manoa's lines is a profound critique of lyric poetry, of its propensity for simplifying and thereby mutilating myth and legend, and thus a recognition of the poet's need to move beyond lyric if he is going to restore dramatic ambiguity and narrative probity to the Samson story, the very qualities of which it had been divested by the religious lyric, where poets are inclined to strong-arm temporal sequence and where, so often, they conquer the space between this world and the next, themselves and God, by collapsing, even annihilating, that space altogether. As Barbara Hardy explains, "the advantage of lyric . . . is its concentrated and patterned expression of feeling"; and she continues, "This advantage is negatively definable: the lyric does not provide an explanation, judgment, or narrative; what it does provide is feeling, alone and without histories and characters." That is, lyric poetry is, by definition, a poetry of exclusions, "more than usually opaque because it leaves out so much of the accustomed context." The very fact that lyric poems are an embedment in larger schemes or more encompassing genres, that often they encroach on other genres, is one indication, says Hardy, that the poets themselves "are sometimes aware of the limitation of lyrical declaration" and hence of the need for expanded vision.[99] Far from reverting to lyric in *Samson Agonistes*, Milton, who had earlier strained at its boundaries, now strains to get beyond lyric, not through an act of annihilation but through a gesture

[99] *The Advantage of Lyric: Essays on Feeling in Poetry* (Bloomington: Indiana Univ. Press, 1977), pp. 1, 2, 6. Cf. Cameron, *Lyric Time*, pp. 244-245, 248, 257.

involving the accommodation and absorption of lyric. The Samson legend, Milton seems to be saying, captures disparate orders, different facets of human experience. Politics and history, religion and psychology, must all come into play in any faithful rendering of that legend and, coming into play, will be the mythopoeic displacements so characteristic of such renderings in the seventeenth century. Yet it is just this multifacetedness against which the lyric of the seventeenth century, with its religious fervor and often facile typologizing, militates.

The typological lyric could acknowledge but not anatomize ambiguity: it could expose discrepancies and differences through a linguistic code but not explore them as dramatic and narrative forms might do. In lyric poetry, the writer beholds the ground of his own being; he becomes one with the images under contemplation. In the words of Nietzsche, the lyric poet "discover[s] his own image in a state of turmoil: his own willing and desiring, his groans and jubilations." In tragedy the situation is very different; for here, again as Nietzsche explains, we encounter the poet in "serene, wide-eyed contemplation gazing upon its images." It is not now the character of the hero *per se*, his luminous shape projected on to a dark wall, that matters so much as "penetrat[ing] into the myth which is projected in these luminous reflections." Now we come up against a phenomenon quite different from appearances, "the exact opposite of a familiar optical one," says Nietzsche: "After an energetic attempt to focus on the sun, we have, by way of remedy almost, dark spots before our eyes when we turn away."[100] The noble images of the religious lyric modulate into the ambiguous ones of tragedy. And there is studied irony in Milton's using his dramatic form to interrogate the commonplaces walled within its lyric embed-

[100] *The Birth of Tragedy and The Genealogy of Morals*, trans. Francis Golffing (New York: Doubleday, 1956), pp. 39, 45, 59, 78.

ments—of his then using the narrative of his epics to scuttle those commonplaces altogether.

The limitations of the religious lyric may be imposed by the restraints of genre but, in the seventeenth century, are surely intensified by a larger cultural phenomenon. In the realm of hermeneutics, typological readings displace allegorical readings and figural are displacing literalistic interpretations. In these displacements, there is loss, obliteration, especially when the narrative books of the Bible are made a concern: scriptural narratives, if not altogether ruined, become disfigured; cumulative patterns, doubling perspectives, chronological sequence, narrative shape (the foci of literal reading) fall by the wayside. The ascendancy of typological reading throws biblical narrative, even drama, into eclipse.[101] When typological reading ceases to work in concert with literal interpretation, it begins to subvert biblical narratives as narrative. Such concepts as "typological evolution" and "typological continuity" reveal more about the preconceptions of modern-day interpreters than they do about the texts those concepts are devised to explain.[102] Insofar as they imply a concern with unity, it is the extrinsic unity of dogma, not the intrinsic unity of art; and insofar as they are hosts to an ideology, it is that of a rationalistic age which, as Hans Frei remarks, saw fit "to alter the ending of *King Lear* in order to bring it into harmony with more advanced moral ideas";[103] it is one that would obliterate the original Hebrew tale, because of its supposedly false consciousness, and replace it with the reigning Christian consciousness of the Samson story. Let us face it: typology was being used to patronize the Hebrew religion. In the process,

---

[101] See Hans Frei, *The Eclipse of Biblical Narrative: A Study in Eighteenth and Nineteenth Century Hermeneutics* (New Haven: Yale Univ. Press, 1974), p. 134.

[102] See, e.g., Lynn Veach Sadler, *Consolation in "Samson Agonistes": Regeneration and Typology*, Salzburg Studies in English Literature (Salzburg: Univ. of Salzburg, 1979), p. 39.

[103] *The Eclipse of Biblical Narrative*, p. 313.

past history is obliterated in the interests of present history, and meaning is wrung from the mind of the interpreter, *his* historical consciousness, and not the Samson story itself. Or as Kenneth Gross would probably state the case, typological readings of the Samson story, especially in the seventeenth century, are a form of reader-nostalgia for "earlier, more secure centers of meaning," and have the effect of turning readers into stone and of making their gaze a "reflection back from a text's unbroken surface of the stoniness . . . the reader himself . . . imposed upon it."[104] Secure centers of meaning may finally have very little to do with the Samson story's real center of concern.

In the Book of Judges, Samson is less a hero than a foil for the heroism of Gideon. When Scripture does invite us to reflect upon the heroism of Samson (in Hebrews 11:32), it is by way of measuring the gulf that separates Jesus from his Old Testament types and shadows—a gulf that seems so great to seventeenth-century commentators that they are reluctant to attribute to Samson an unqualified heroism and, sometimes, to ascribe heroic character to him at all. Not Judges but Hebrews, in conjunction with Revelation, offers the text that focuses the whole question of Samson's heroism for the seventeenth century; those texts discourage—they do not encourage—the typology implicit in most efforts to read Samson's story as a drama of regeneration. Those texts, as Fredric Jameson might say, confront "figuration" with a critical eye; they confront figuration, as a text like *Samson Agonistes* will do, with an eye on "the ambiguous situation in which a figural *expression* of a cognitive truth is still little more than a picture-thought or hieroglyphic degradation of that same truth" and "is thus the source of the limits and distortions which the religious or theological master-code imposes on its political content" by

[104] *Spenserian Poetics: Idolatry, Iconoclasm, and Magic* (Ithaca: Cornell Univ. Press, 1985), p. 66.

way of concealing that content. What a theologian like Luther would conceal, many in Milton's century, and Milton among them, would reveal, and in such a way as to show how "an older hegemonic theological code," in the words of Jameson, "can provisionally be appropriated for an expression of far-reaching new social possibilities."[105]

Typology may be a peril of the seventeenth-century religious lyric and a manifestation of its limitations, but it is, likewise, a bond between different kinds of religious poets, between very different kinds of poetry, between literatures both sacred and secular. It is a functioning device in *King Lear* no less than in *Samson Agonistes*, in *The Faerie Queene* no less than in *Paradise Lost*, in Donne's *Anniversarie* poems no less than in *Lycidas*, and in *Lycidas* no less than in Marvell's Cromwell poems, although in each instance typology seems to function differently. Now it is a device for exalting the present over the past, and now for collapsing the past into the present. Here it measures a middle term in relation to a type, and there in relationship to the antitype; sometimes the middle term is advantaged, and other times disadvantaged, by the comparison. Now the middle term is the poet's persona or the poet himself, and now the poet's audience.

Typology is both a peril of, and a procedure in, the seventeenth-century lyric; and we need not transfer to a later time, as Barbara Lewalski has done, what are its conspicuous character traits at this time. According to Lewalski, "Typology is not unimportant in later [i.e., post-seventeenth-century] poetry . . . , but given the changes in consciousness and religious attitudes, good poets necessarily used it obliquely and ambiguously."[106] Good poets almost always use typology obliquely, ambiguously; and the shifts in religious attitudes, the altera-

---

[105] "Religion and Ideology," in *1642: Literature and Power in the Seventeenth Century*, ed. Francis Barker et al. (Univ. of Essex, 1981), p. 320.

[106] *Protestant Poetics and the Seventeenth-Century Religious Lyric*, p. 144.

tions in human consciousness of which Lewalski speaks, are
part of the tale of seventeenth-century culture and hence a
manifestation in that century's poetry. Even the religious lyric,
however indirectly, has the capacity for registering, if not for
explicating, advances in consciousness, alterations in attitude.
Poets simply cannot revert to the commonplaces of their ances-
tors without falsifying their newly acquired cultural awareness;
poets are the purveyors of such awareness, moreover, not
protectors against it.[107] Initially a revelation of Christian
"truths," typology would eventually be used against itself to
reveal the *truths* of the Bible. An agent in the deconstruction
of Old Testament narratives, typology would eventually be
used, as in *Samson Agonistes*, to effect their restoration.

It remains an irony of literary history that Marvell should
ever have been cast in the role, as he is by Walter Savage
Landor, of questioning whether any of Milton's contemporaries saw the poet for what he really was, and of then privileging future generations with the capacity for looking beyond
Milton's dark clothes, gray hair, and sightless eyes to the
bright light emanating from his countenance. What Marvell
is here represented as finding in a later criticism is, in fact,
the achievement of his own. His contribution to Milton criticism stands as a reminder that criticism will always fail when
its enterprise, as it has so often been with *Samson Agonistes*, is
"to square the circle of poetry"—when it fails to recognize
with Marvell that, unlike many of his contemporaries, Milton
managed to break loose from the infections of his own times.[108]
In Marvell's poem about Milton the same tendency is evident
as in Milton's poem about Samson—a movement away from

[107] See C. Day Lewis, *The Lyric Impulse* (Cambridge, Mass.: Harvard Univ.
Press, 1965), p. 23.
[108] *The Complete Works of Walter Savage Landor*, ed. Welby, IV, 178, 249.

the shadow of a figure in order to expose the reality that a figure like Samson adumbrates. If Milton is a true poet, Marvell thus reminds us, we may have to stop thinking of Samson as "a true poet in the Miltonic and Blakean sense."[109] It is better perhaps that we think of Milton as a true poet in the terms delineated by Hermann Broch: such a poet "must always embrace the totality of the world, must be the mirror of that universe, but one of full counterweight. This is felt by every true artist, but is creatively realized only by the artist of old age."[110]

What Marvell encourages in his dedicatory poem on *Paradise Lost* is what, we may suppose, Marvell thought Milton had achieved in *Samson Agonistes*: the removal of identification and sympathy from his protagonist. This is the price we pay for such calculated objectivity by which we are enabled to prepare ourselves for the profounder experience that comes from the realization that the tragedy is not Samson's only, but Marvell's, Milton's, England's, our own. The tragedy of *Samson Agonistes*—the tragedy of apocalypse and of *the* Apocalypse—is the same tragedy projected onto human history by Michael in *Paradise Lost*, in his vision of "violence / Proceed[ing], and Oppression, and Sword-Law"—a vision which leaves Adam "all in tears" lamenting:

> O what are these,
> Deaths Ministers, not Men, who thus deal Death
> Inhumanly to men. . . . (XI.671-72, 674, 675-77)

[109] For this argument, see T. Wilson Hayes, *Winstanley the Digger: A Literary Analysis of Radical Ideas in the English Revolution* (Cambridge, Mass.: Harvard Univ. Press, 1979), p. 2. But see also *Lyric Poetry*, where Rhys contends that Marvell likens Milton's strength and Samson's and then comments: "There is something Herculean in his [Milton's] struggle for mastery, something a little superhuman. His whole poetry resolves itself into heroic lyric; temperamentally and in his art, he was a Sampson" (p. 228).

[110] "The Style of the Mythical Age," in *On the "Iliad,"* trans. Mary McCarthy (1947; rpt. Princeton: Princeton Univ. Press, 1970), p. 12.

Michael thereupon responds in a way that should give him
the first word on subsequent interpretation of Milton's tragedy
and that properly gives him the next to the last word here:

> These are the product
> Of those ill mated Marriages. . . .
> Such were these Giants, men of high renown;
> For in those days Might onely shall be admir'd,
> And Valour and Heroic Vertu call'd;
> To overcome in Battle, and subdue
> Nations, and bring home spoils with infinite
> Man-slaughter, shall be held the highest pitch
> Of human Glorie. . . .
> Destroyers rightlier call'd and Plagues of men.
>
> (XI.683-97)

The last word goes to the Jesus of *Paradise Regained*, who
renders dubious the casuistical claim that "Samson responded
appropriately; [for] his revenge was not murder and robbery
but war":[111]

> They err who count it glorious to subdue
> By Conquest far and wide, to over-run
> Large Countries, and in field great Battels win,
> Great Cities by assault: what do these Worthies,
> But rob and spoil, burn, slaughter, and enslave. . . .
> . . . who leave behind
> Nothing but ruin wheresoe're they rove . . .

[111] Camille Wells Slights, *The Casuistical Tradition in Shakespeare, Donne, Herbert, and Milton* (Princeton: Princeton Univ. Press, 1981), p. 279. In a study remarkable for its sensitive, subtle observations, G. K. Hunter writes, "The Humanist disdain of war, of which Erasmus is the most famous exponent, was complicated in Milton's case by his deep involvement in an armed struggle"; yet his praise of that struggle "is regularly accompanied by clear reservations" such as are expressed in Sonnet XV: "For what can war, but endless war still breed, / Till Truth and Right from Violence be freed" (10-11); see *"Paradise Lost"* (1980; rpt. London: George Allen and Unwin, 1982), p. 21, and also p. 22.

Then swell with pride, and must be titl'd Gods,
Great Benefactors of mankind, Deliverers,
Worship't with Temple, Priest and Sacrifice;
One is the Son of *Jove*, of *Mars* the other,
Till Conquerour Death discover them scarce men,
Rowling in brutish vices, and deform'd,
Violent or shameful death thir due reward.

(III. 71-87)

CHAPTER VI

MILTON'S SAMSONS AND
SAMSON AGONISTES

> Even the best of those who argue for Samson's
> regeneration rather noticeably close their eyes to
> the nature of his last act. They focus exclusively on
> Samson as though no one else were involved and
> dismiss the victims of his wholesale murderousness
> as "God's enemies" presumably placed there by
> divine providence in order that the Chorus may
> rejoice over "thy slaughter'd foes in number more /
> Than all thy life had slain before." Some of us
> cannot without profound discomfort identify
> Milton's with the gross morality that exonerates
> every injury of others if only it be committed in
> the name of God's will. Milton himself had lived
> through a long civil war during which God's will
> was all-too-seriously called upon as sanction.
>   No, either we accuse the poet of Samson
> Agonistes of a serious moral blindness, of sheer
> bigotry, or we recognize that he called the work
> a tragedy for good reason. . . . All that
> he [Samson] says and does is appropriate to
> the protagonist of a tragedy; and as a tragic
> agent Samson does not violate the ethic that
> Milton held.
>
> —IRENE SAMUEL

It is within the context of shifting attitudes toward Samson
that Milton writes *Samson Agonistes* and that it should be in-

terpreted—or reinterpreted. Or, better, contextualization should nudge us into adjusting our interpretations of *Samson* in a way that shows it to accommodate more than one perspective on its protagonist; that reveals its tragic power emanating from the ambiguities in which the Samson story came to be lodged and which obfuscate the moral clarity (i.e., platitudinous Christianity) Milton is sometimes thought to have imposed upon that story. Not just in later centuries, but in Milton's own time, decidedly different views of Samson sit side by side. Either Samson "manifested his Courage and Valour, to a higher degree, than any *Heathen Hero*"; or his "Case was absolutely desperate, affording no Field of Courage and Valour, and allowing, no chance for Life: And only like those savage and desperate *Sea Captains*, who order the blowing up of the *Ship*, that it may not be useful to the enemy."[1] Either Samson is laudable, glorious, and heroic—or he is otherwise.

These discrepant attitudes toward Samson raise the crucial question concerning the meaning of Milton's poem: is Milton's Samson the Samson of his twentieth-century critics—a regenerate Samson; or is he instead the Samson of pre- and postrevolutionary England, the vengeful Samson of Spenser and Shakespeare, of Andrew Marvell and of many poets and biblical commentators during, and after, Marvell's and Milton's own time? Milton is not altogether silent about Samson outside *Samson Agonistes*, nor is he unreflecting on the moral considerations the Samson story had raised before, during, and in the aftermath of the Puritan Revolution. Milton's opinion of Samson may alter from decade to decade; yet the principles by which Milton values Samson, once summoning him to judgment, remain steady, even as they render dubious the claim that, with Milton, Samson becomes "a mighty Christian hero, worthy of all those prophetic embellishments with which

[1] See the anonymous *Two Dissertations: The First on the Supposed Suicide of Samson* (London: Printed for W. Innys and J. Richardson, 1754), pp. 48-49.

a thousand years of Christian exegesis had adorned him."[2]
Milton's is an art of intimation, not of bald statement or naked
assertion; and though this strategy of implication may mask
unanswerable incongruities, deployed by Milton it may also
open fissures and expose contradictions—deliberately.

Perhaps the earliest of Milton's citations of Samson appears
among his jottings in the Trinity manuscript, where we discover "a kind of *Samson Agonistes* in embryo," although *Samson*
is itself an embryonic tragedy—"the fifth act of the tragedy
of Samson's successive failures."[3] Samson's life affords various
topics for a tragedy, and other stories from the Book of Judges
provide still more such topics:

> Gideon Idoloclastes Jud. 6. 7.
> Gideon *per*suing Jud. 8
> Abimelech the usurper. Jud. 9
> Samson pursophorus or Hybristes, or
>   Samson marriing or in Ramath Lechi Jud. 15
> Dagonalia. Jud. 16
> Comazontes or the Benjaminits Jud. 19. 20. &c.
>   or the Rioters. (VIII, 556)

What these entries reveal is that for Milton the Book of Judges
is emphatically a tragedy (a gathering of tragedies) centered
in the story of Samson. The second of the Samson entries is

---

[2] Don Cameron Allen, *The Harmonious Vision: Studies in Milton's Poetry*, rev. ed.
(Baltimore: The Johns Hopkins Press, 1970), p. 82.

[3] Evert Mordecai Clark, "Milton's Earlier 'Samson'," *Studies in English*, Univ.
of Texas Bulletin 2743, 7 (1927), 154. In this essay (pp. 144-54), Clark provides
a survey of Milton's use of the Samson legend before *Samson Agonistes* but comes to
conclusions different from my own; see by the same author, in the same journal,
"Milton's Conception of Samson," 8 (1928), 88-99. But see also Paull Franklin
Baum, "*Samson Agonistes* Again," *Publications of the Modern Language Association*, 36
(1921), 357.

clear enough: the tragedy will focus upon the scene at the temple. The matter of focus is less clear in the first of the Samson entries which, rather than positing as many as four tragedies, probably proposes different inflections for a single tragedy grounded in the story of Samson's first marriage. Item by item, we move through the principal episodes reported by the Judges narrator: (1) Samson taking the firebrand to the tails of three hundred foxes (15:4-5); (2) the Philistines avenging themselves on Samson by burning alive his wife and father-in-law; and Samson, in turn, avenging himself on them, even as he promises that this will be his last act of vengeance (15:6-8); (3) the tragedy of Samson's first marriage, which presumably would subsume the foregoing topics and perhaps even the following one; (4) Samson being bound by the men of Judah, then unbound by the spirit of the Lord, whereupon he slays a thousand men with the jawbone of an ass (15:11-17).

The events of both chapters 15 and 16 of Judges are set within the framework of Samson's judgeship and thus become a means for measuring its success: "And he judged Israel in the days of the Philistines twenty years" (15:20); "And he judged Israel twenty years" (16:31). The events of either chapter could easily be gathered under the title, "Samson . . . Hybristes," for which the Yale Milton provides this telling note: "Masson translates as 'Violent'; Liddell and Scott . . . 'violent, wanton, licentious, insolent' " (VIII, 562). The title *Samson Agonistes* alters the inflection, or rather captures the new inflection of Judges 16, while it allows for the absorption of the events, as well as the Samson profile etched in Judges 15. The tragedy of his first marriage, his going to Etham, his being bound and delivered to the Philistines, his slaying a thousand men with the jawbone of an ass—all these events are represented parenthetically in the poem Milton does write.

In a gathering of passages from his prose writings, Milton

makes other significant references to the Samson story. Samson is a king among Philistines, a duped leader rendered powerless and, hence, an illustration of strength's dependence upon wisdom, a warrior-saint and tyrant-queller, and a womanizer reduced to effeminate slackness by a harlot. In *The Reason of Church-Government*, Samson is likened to a king, his locks to the law, and Delilah to the clergy who, shearing Samson's locks, would deprive the king of his strength (I, 858-59). Behind this reference is a conception of Samson elaborated by Marjorie Reeves: "The King of England is a holy prince who will reform the life of his people, . . . he is also . . . a new Samson."[4] In *Areopagitica*, although here he remains nameless, Samson seems to be identified with the strong man (the English nation) rousing himself from sleep (II, 557-58) and, in *Eikonoklastes*, represents the degradation of the national leader (III, 461, 545-46). Milton reports in *The First Defense* that "whether prompted by God or by his own valor," at least Samson "thought it not impious but pious to kill those masters who were tyrants over his country, even though most of her citizens did not balk at slavery" (IV, i, 402). Finally, in *Paradise Lost*, Milton portrays Samson and by analogy Adam and Eve, succumbing to Delilah/Satan (IX. 1059-62). In each of these instances save the last, Milton's citation of Samson is neither positive nor negative but ambivalent. No poet has a sharper sense of the power of allusion than Milton; and his allusions, explicit and especially implicit, are testimony to this fact. If we consider the latter, another from *Eikonoklastes* must be added to the list; and if we introduce another category altogether, that of significant silences, still other passages should come under scrutiny.

Of the explicit references, the one in *The First Defense* is most favorable but like all other such references is qualified.

4 *The Influence of Prophecy in the Later Middle Ages: A Study in Joachimism* (Oxford: Clarendon Press, 1969), p. 377.

Samson *thought* himself pious in hurling down the pillars, but it is not clear whether he does so because he is divinely propelled—*or* self-motivated. That has always been the crucial question in interpreting the Samson story, and Milton is steadfast in his refusal to commit himself either way. Context also qualifies any positive construction previously placed upon this reference. Samson is a warrior, the hero here of the New Model Army, though at the same time that Milton is praising the army for its effort, he is quietly exalting himself, his own effort, above the army and its activities. The greatest of all heroes, Milton will explain in *The Second Defense*, fight not with the sword but with the pen and are engaged in warfare not carnal but spiritual (IV, i, 553). Here is a classic instance of that special position of the prophetic in the political sphere which Angus Fletcher delineates by quoting H. W. Robinson: the prophet "is ready both to claim the service . . . of the armies . . . , and to assert a superior power in the word of God which goes infinitely beyond theirs."[5] Yet the position here asserted by Milton is one that he becomes increasingly reluctant to maintain.

Much earlier, in the allegory of *The Reason of Church-Government*, as we have just observed, Samson is the king and his locks are the law, identifications complicated by the fact that Milton was notoriously disrespectful of kings and here is concerned with asserting the primacy of the new over the old dispensation. Milton also concludes this account by reporting that Samson's final act brings great affliction upon him. There are, of course, the later instances when Samson is the duped leader (*Eikonoklastes*) and the duped lover (*Paradise Lost*). The use of context as a qualifying strategy, the hesitancy especially about the final moments of Samson's life (whether he is impelled from within or compelled from without), the privileg-

[5] *The Prophetic Moment: An Essay on Spenser* (Chicago: Univ. of Chicago Press, 1971), p. 5.

ing of the spiritual over the carnal soldier and Milton's worrying over the great affliction that the latter brings upon himself—all these matters have considerable bearing on the artistic strategies and intellectual concerns of *Samson Agonistes*.

As for the implicit allusions, they are more problematic and revelatory, even in the case of *Areopagitica* where the allusion may seem obvious and obviously celebratory. Here the English nation is likened to a strong man rousing himself from sleep and shaking his invincible locks. Samson is not named, it is sometimes suggested, because Milton wishes to avoid the suggestion of a holocaust, his concern being with cultural renewal, not national disaster. It should be noted, though, that 1643 is the year that Joseph Mede's commentary on the Book of Revelation got by the censor; and its preface, written by Dr. Twisse, contains several sentences that may have been an important influence on this passage. There Twisse speaks of "God awaking . . . out of a sleep . . . like a giant refreshed . . . : and the Lord Christ awaking, and stirring up his strength."[6] Here Milton may very well have omitted specific reference to the first Samson because his concern is actually with the second, greater Samson who, unlike the first, succeeds in delivering his people. In *Paradise Lost* Milton is a second Moses; England, a second Chosen People. In *Areopagitica*, most likely, England is compared not to the historical Samson but to the true and greater, the spiritual, Samson who effects not devastation but deliverance. The emphasis is on not the type but the antitype, on not the prefiguration but the postfiguration,

[6] *The Key of the Revelation*, trans. Richard More (London: Printed for Phil. Stephens, 1643), unpaginated preface. Ernest Tuveson similarly correlates the passage from Twisse's preface with the one from *Areopagitica*; see *Millennium and Utopia: A Study in the Background of the Idea of Progress* (Berkeley and Los Angeles: Univ. of California Press, 1949), p. 79. The only parallel iconographic juxtaposition I have seen appears on an early fourteenth-century cross, belonging to the Florentine School and in the Academia dell' arte in Florence (no. 436). At the top of the cross is an eagle muing its young and heralding the Resurrection.

with specific reference to Samson excised because Milton wishes to block from view the horror that the historical Samson perpetrated.

A second, equally oblique, reference to Samson occurs in *Eikonoklastes* where Milton speaks of those governors of nations who are "overswaid . . . under a Feminine usurpation" (III, 421). Judging from other such references in *Samson Agonistes* to man's—to Samson's—"foul effeminacy" (410), to his being "Effeminatly vanquish't" (562), and to the contrast here of Samson with those "not sway'd / By female usurpation, nor dismay'd" (1059-60), Samson is invoked as an emblem of all victims of such usurpation. And it is precisely this construction that is placed upon the Samson story in *Paradise Lost*, where we encounter, in unexpected quarters, another employment of the Samson story, this time in the form of a significant silence. *Paradise Lost* concludes, as Mary Ann Radzinowicz observes, with an overview of history that "includes the life of Samson"; and this overview, she allows, receives "the curtest possible treatment," she thinks because of "the pressure of time": in *Samson Agonistes* Milton "supplies . . . what was here omitted."[7] Given Radzinowicz's premises, this is a logical enough conclusion; but given another set of premises, it is just as logical to assume that the silence here is calculated—and meaningful. In a poem filled with political allusion, a reference, however abbreviated, is possible; such a reference, surely, would not snatch the thunder from Milton's later poem—no more so, let us say, than references here to Jesus's trial in the wilderness are debilitating to *Paradise*

[7] *Toward "Samson Agonistes": The Growth of Milton's Mind* (Princeton: Princeton Univ. Press, 1978), pp. 289-90. For a brilliant discussion of the heterogeneous uses to which Milton puts the Samson story by privileging the personal and the domestic, see Mary Nyquist, "Textual Overlapping and Delilah's Harlot-lap" (forthcoming), especially the reflections on the Samson allusion in *PL* IX.1059-63. It is seldom noted that in the second edition of the poem Milton fully brackets the Samson allusion by placing a period after "Shorn of his strength."

Regained. If what Radzinowicz says were a concern, Milton could have simply deleted from his first epic the extended story of recovering paradise that sprawls over Books XI and XII.

The little that Milton says in Book XII of *Paradise Lost* pertaining to Samson and the other judges is, on the other hand, indication that, while God is provoked into raising up enemies against Israel (cf. Judges 2:10), he also saves the penitent from those enemies "By Judges first, then . . . Kings" (XII.320). There will be a succession of kings, as there was previously a succession of judges, who themselves made kingship necessary; hence what Michael confides to Adam about kings would seem to be doubly true of the judges:

> Such . . . shall be registerd
> Part good, part bad, of bad the longer scrowle,
> Whose foul Idolatries, and other faults
> Heapt to the popular summe, . . . will so
> incense God . . .

as to expose them to scorn and leave their land "in confusion" (XII.335-39, 343). There are similar silences, and similarly muted or hidden allusions to the Samson story, in Milton's prose writings: in *The First Defense* where Milton speaks of "a candidate for slavery to replace an ass in a mill, under the solemn obligation of grinding . . . under some most foolish tyrant" (IV, i, 374); but also in both *The Doctrine and Discipline of Divorce* where there is reference to "grind[ing] in the mill of an undelighted and servil copulation" (II, 258) and in *De Doctrina Christiana* where there is a similar reference to "the slavish pounding-mill of unhappy marriage" (VI, 379). In the latter two instances, Samson is not specifically named, probably because the Samson story does not accord well with the ethical concerns of either treatise.

The most striking and revelatory of such passages, and one usually ignored, appears in *Tetrachordon*:

. . . evil must not be don for good. And it were a
fall to be lamented, an indignity unspeakable, if law
should becom tributary to sin her slave, and forc't
to yeild up into his hands her awfull minister Punishment, should buy out her peace with sinne for
sinne, paying as it were her so many *Philistian* fore-
skins to the proud demand of Transgression.
(II, 658)

This passage recalls the story of David's slaying two hundred
Philistines and bringing their foreskins to the king (I Samuel
18:27); it anticipates the episode of Samson's slaying a thousand
men with the jawbone of an ass: "A thousand fore-skins fell,
the flower of *Palestin* / In *Rameth-lechi* famous to this day"
(144-45). The duplication of language between prose work
and poem is crucial, suggesting Milton's own understanding
of the transgression of the law exemplified by both David and
Samson. Analogies between David and Samson in Milton's
poem, usually thought to work to Samson's credit,[8] are sometimes deployed to discredit him.

Once we tabulate all these allusions, direct and oblique,
muted or hidden, together with deliberate silences, what is
perhaps most important is that we make a fundamental dis-
crimination. The Milton of *Areopagitica*, if in fact the primary
reference is actually to Samson, is concerned with relating one
phase, the supposedly triumphant phase, of Samson's life to
English history. When Milton reinvokes the same phase in

---

[8] See, e.g., Miriam Muskin, " 'Wisdom by Adversity': Davidic Traits in Milton's
Samson," *Milton Studies*, 14 (1980), 233-55. In the seventeenth century, Samson
was often thought to be a type of David and David the true type of Christ; in this
equation, David's fight with Goliath is a type of Christ's wilderness temptation. Jesus,
says William Cowper, is our David who "in this singular combate, fights with
spirituall *Goliah* hand to hand, and overcomes him" (*Three Heavenly Treatises, Concerning Christ* [London: Printed for John Budge, 1612], p. 114). Samson's encounter
with Harapha, and challenging of him to mortal fight, parodies this understanding
and may even be construed as a parodic comment on the true nature of the wilderness
story which *Samson Agonistes* succeeds in the 1671 poetic volume.

The First Defense he is deliberately evasive and hesitant. Otherwise he reverts to an earlier stage in the Samson story, his objective being to relate man's tragedy, and England's tragedy, to the defeated Samson. What is of concern here is that both these phases are synchronized in *Samson Agonistes*, assuming a causal relationship with one another. In this regard, it should also be noticed that, whereas Milton's previous critics have sometimes been untrue to his poem, they have managed, for the most part, to remain unfailingly true to an ideological view of that poem, which, when the evidence is in, may have to be adjusted.

Milton's own reading of the Samson story swerves from allegorical to typological interpretation and, then, from a typology of sameness to a typology of difference. Eventually the figure of Samson is wrested from received typological systems and rendered by Milton as typological symbol. In virtually every citation of Samson, Milton speaks guardedly; and more, he equivocates on every accepted touchstone to Samson's heroism—his stature as national leader and deliverer, his supposedly authorized slayings of others, even his self-slaying, and most of all his ostensible promptings from God. Milton's Samson is no villain, to be sure, but he *is* deeply flawed and thus ambiguous in his heroism. Indeed, it may be that the same motives that obliged the young Milton to withdraw from poetic comparisons involving Amphion explain his handling of similar comparisons involving Samson. It may even be that the disparity between Amphion and Orpheus, elucidated by Richard DuRocher, is exactly analogous to the similar disparity between Samson and Jesus in the 1671 poetic volume: "Amphion [read Samson], . . . because he wreaked retribution on his . . . captors (rather than, like Orpheus [read Jesus], enduring violence himself), drops out of Milton's comparisons."[9] Not the Samson allusions alone, but the issues focused

[9] "Milton and Ovid: *Paradise Lost* and the *Metamorphosis*," Ph. D. dissertation, Cornell Univ., 1982, p. 40.

by the Samson story itself—the ethical imperatives—must now draw our attention, but in the full recognition that the most extravagant set of variations ever produced on the theme of ethics, in the seventeenth century, is played upon the Samson story.

An important insight into Milton's attitudes and values is afforded by *De Doctrina Christiana*, whose views are perfectly consonant with those expressed in the Divorce tracts and where it becomes clear that Milton more often challenges than confirms tradition and that, even when a traditionalist, Milton's concern is less with outlining broad contours than with etching particularities and shading in intricacies. Milton's theological treatise is important in defining issues and for developing arguments that must have been on Milton's mind when he wrote his last poems and that, even if not intended for popular consumption, were, as Christopher Hill urges, a way of "clarify[ing] Milton's own position to himself."[10] Milton's own procedure here is to examine an array of topics in the light of Scripture, thus performing an act of interpretation mounted upon a series of moral inferences. Our procedure will be the same: to examine the central concerns of *Samson Agonistes* under the light afforded by Milton's theological treatise and to press from it certain inferences about his tragedy. For a poet who believed that the ultimate test of a scriptural interpretation is, in words from *De Doctrina*, "how far the interpretation is in agreement with faith" (VI, 482), it seems reasonable to apply a similar kind of test to interpretations of his own poems: how well do they accord with the articles of Milton's own faith—with the precise, and precisely formulated, terms of his religion and ethics? "The things written," again in Milton's words from *De Doctrina*, must take precedence over "the

---

[10] *Milton and the English Revolution* (New York: Viking Press, 1977), p. 239.

things debated in academic gathering"; when they do not, we risk "mistaking the shadow for the substance" (VI, 483).

It remains a curiosity of Milton criticism that the most conservative of critics have attested to, have even sought, agreement between *De Doctrina Christiana* and Milton's epics. Oddly, few of them have acknowledged the lack of consonance between ideas developed here and attitudes allegedly assumed by Milton in *Samson Agonistes*. It has been left to more radical critics, like Andrew Milner, to articulate the position that others seem quietly to have embraced: "there is little or nothing of Christian doctrine to be found in *Samson Agonistes* . . . it is precisely the absense of certain obviously relevant Christian notions . . . which constitutes one of the most distinctive features of the poem.'[11] In the interim between the divorce tracts and *De Doctrina* and in the lapse of time between it and the publication of *Samson*, Milton's attitudes undergo no sea-change; but just as the Gospels do in relation to the Law, Milton's attitudes seem to moderate toward love and charity. The crucial questions, then, are not only what accord is there between this poem and Milton's earlier thinking but, ultimately, what harmony exists between *Samson* and *Paradise Regained*, two poems published between the same covers? I shall argue for both poems what William Hazlitt avers only of *Samson Agonistes*: that they are "a canonisation of all the high moral and religious" principles that Milton bound himself to during his lifetime.[12]

[11] *John Milton and the English Revolution: A Study in the Sociology of Literature* (Totowa: Barnes and Noble, 1981), p. 193. A.S.P. Woodhouse is one among many in his contention that "the doctrines assumed or advanced in *Paradise Lost* and *Paradise Regained* are entirely consonant with those reached in the *De Doctrina*"; see *The Heavenly Muse: A Preface to Milton*, ed. Hugh MacCullum (Toronto: Univ. of Toronto Press, 1972), p. 125. Anthony Low argues for a subtle interrelationship between Milton's theological treatise and his tragedy in "*Samson Agonistes*: Theology, Poetry, Truth," *Milton Quarterly*, 13 (1979), 96-102.

[12] *The Romantics on Milton: Formal Essays and Critical Asides*, ed. Joseph Wittreich (Cleveland: Press of Case Western Reserve Univ., 1970), p. 365.

It is true that Milton says in *De Doctrina* that "we are not forbidden to take or to wish to take vengeance upon the enemies of the church" (VI, 755), and he acknowledges that war is neither disallowed by the New Testament nor unlawful in the Old (VI, 803); he also allows for the necessity of homicide. Still, the ethical bent of *De Doctrina* does not accord well with the ethics of Samson, nor with those of most of his associates. Surely, it is noteworthy that in *Samson Agonistes* Milton has nothing to say of Samson's judgeship, very probably because a survey of the historical record reveals that "it is generally acknowledged that Samson is most improperly called 'a Judge of Israel,' since his deeds decidedly do not aim at the liberation of his tribe, much less of his nation, and that most of his deeds far exceed the bounds of credibility."[13] When Samson's judgeship is remembered by commentators on Judges, it is either to make this uncomplimentary observation or, more often, to excuse Samson from any wrongdoing by insisting that what he does is not only divinely inspired but done in his public person. To excise any reference to Samson's judgeship, as Milton does in his tragedy, has the effect, then, of placing all occurrences under the aspect of his private, not his public, person. It is equally noteworthy that Milton derives very few proof texts from the Book of Judges, presumably because Christ had very little truck with the judges and "always utterly renounced the role of a judge" (VI, 380) and perhaps because Milton himself, remembering judges both ancient and modern in *A Treatise of Civil Power*, judged them to be "far beneath infallible" (VII, 244).

When the Book of Judges is cited in *De Doctrina*, it is to make a linguistic point first, then to place Gideon in the line of David, and later to provide examples of fornication and adultery. Milton does not, despite the obvious opportunity,

[13] A. Smythe Palmer, quoting Abraham Kuenen, in *The Samson-Saga and Its Place in Comparative Religion* (London: Sir Isaac Pitman and Sons, 1913), pp. 62-63.

place Samson in the line of David either here or in *Paradise Regained*, and though the encounter between Samson and Harapha has been cited to suggest that Milton does otherwise in *Samson Agonistes*, enhancing Samson with Davidic characteristics, the blustering Harapha is not so much a foil to, as a revelation of, an equally blustering Samson who has more than a fair share of Goliath in him. Judges is not cited to illustrate the proposition that there are ministers of divine vengeance, although this is exactly how Samson is represented in the one full-length commentary on Judges produced during Milton's lifetime—as the Lord's "revenger" and one of his "worthie instruments."[14] Nor is Samson included among the heroes of faith in Milton's citation of Hebrews 11:32 (only Gideon), nor even named among the Judges of Israel (now only Gideon and Jephthah).

Samson is simply not mentioned in Milton's theological treatise, though in it there are formulations concerning issues crucial to Samson's story as it is related in Milton's tragedy—such issues, for example, as Samson's election and the Philistine's reprobation, Samson's marriage and supposed inspiration, his anger, his violence, his alleged suicide. *De Doctrina* offers an objective ideal by which standards Samson's actions are made to appear wrong; yet in *Samson Agonistes* Milton portrays his hero as a profoundly tragic figure, as a prisoner of the circumstances, hence not in any simple sense wrong and beyond the realm, certainly, of simple moral platitudes. In *De Doctrina*, Milton puts the matter succinctly: although every man is going to judge according to the light he has received, "each man will be judged according to the light which *he* has received" (VI, 623; my italics). We see and judge Samson by a standard appropriate to our own expanded revelation, but that judgment will eventually be tempered by another which

[14] Richard Rogers, *A Commentary upon the Whole Booke of Judges* (London: Printed by Felix Kyngston, 1615), pp. 611, 613.

properly takes into account the extent or limits of Samson's *own* revelation. It is this discrepancy between revelations that, on the one hand, mires Samson in tragedy and, on the other, offers us a possible release from tragedy.

Many may claim election, Milton says, but those especially called are known by their resemblance to the Son—are thus justified and made glorious. There is election in God's design, but no reprobation, with those believing in such a decree accusing God and thereby dishonoring him (VI, 197, 202). "The aim of reprobation," Milton argues, "is the destruction of unbelievers, a thing in itself repulsive and hateful . . . God wished neither for sin nor for the death of the sinner . . . , then certainly he did not wish for reprobation itself" (VI, 173). Further, Milton says that "it is disgraceful and disgusting that the Christian religion should be supported by violence" (VI, 123). And yet it is violence, self-inflicted and inflicted upon others, that we witness at the end of *Samson Agonistes* where, in his death, Samson is conjoined with "slaughter'd foes in number more" (1667) than in all his life he had slain before.

Significantly, in Milton's poem Samson represents himself, as he is represented by others, as God's agent, his "work from Heav'n impos'd" (565). This "mighty minister" (706), as he is described by the Chorus, says of himself that he is "a person separate to God, / Design'd for great exploits" (31-32), one "Whom God hath of his special favour rais'd" (273); it is said of Samson by his father that he is "Ordain'd . . . / Select, . . . Sacred, Glorious for a while, / The miracle of men" (362-64), and by the Chorus that he is of the "solemnly *elected*, / With gifts and graces eminently adorn'd" (687-79; my italics), vying with the "reprobate" Philistines (1685). This view of Samson is nevertheless called into question, even here, by Manoa's "for a while." For a while Samson is all these things, but only *for a while*. What is said here of the Philistine reprobate could just as appropriately be said (often was said) of a reprobate Samson: that he calls for his own "speedy" end, his own "destruction" (1681), that "Fall'n into wrath divine" he calls his "own ruin" upon himself, "with blindness internal struck" (1683-86).

Moreover, the Philistines, by Manoa, are divided into three classes of men:

> Some much averse I found and wondrous harsh . . .
> That part most reverenc'd *Dagon* and his Priests
> Others more moderate seeming, but thir aim
> Private reward . . .
>
>   . . . a third
> More generous far and civil, who confess'd
> They had anough reveng'd . . .
> The rest was magnanimity to remit . . . (1461-70)

Such magnanimity, if we are to believe Harapha (who fairly represents the evidence of the Book of Judges), is nowhere evinced by Samson:

> The *Philistines*, when thou hadst broke the league,
> Went up with armed powers thee only seeking,
> To others did no violence nor spoil. (1189-91)

Samson, that is, defies the very premises of a just and holy war: that it be "truly defensive" and, as Michael Walzer documents, that it be "fought at the command of a legitimate authority, and carried on in a restrained and more or less orderly fashion, without pillage . . . or unnecessary murder."[15] In *De Doctrina*, Milton gives emphatic definition to his own thinking: "As for WAR, we are instructed, in the first place, that it is to be undertaken only after extremely careful consideration . . . ; secondly, that it is to be waged

---

[15] *The Revolution of the Saints: A Study in the Origin of Radical Politics* (Cambridge, Mass.: Harvard Univ. Press, 1965), p. 268.

knowledgeably and skilfully . . . ; and thirdly, with moderation . . . ; and fourthly, in holiness . . ." (VI, 802). For all the proof-texts cited, none is from the Book of Judges, and Samson himself is never invoked as illustration or authority, not even for such precepts as "a cruel enemy should not be spared" or "we should not trust in the strength of our forces, but in God alone" (VI, 802). Anointed at the beginning of Milton's poem as a deliverer, in its end Samson is proclaimed a "destroyer" (1678).

Nor does Samson quite meet the specifications of the Chorus for either an active or a passive heroism:

> He all thir Ammunition
> And feats of War defeats
> With plain Heroic magnitude of mind
> And celestial vigour arm'd,
> Thir Armories and Magazins contemns,
> Renders them useless, while
> With winged expedition
> Swift as the lightning glances he executes
> His errand on the wicked, who surpris'd
> Lose thir defence distracted and amaz'd.
> But patience is more oft the exercise
> Of Saints, the trial of thir fortitude,
> Making them each his own Deliverer . . .
> Either of these is in thy lot,
> *Samson*, with might endu'd
> Above the Sons of men; but sight bereav'd
> May chance to number thee with those
> Whom Patience finally must crown. (1277-96)

Samson approaches the first of these idealisms; he fulfills neither. Despite the fact that he is portrayed as "Himself an Army" (346) and as in "strength / Equivalent to Angels" (342-43), the ideal of the spiritual warrior is better represented by

Christ in the victory of Book VI in *Paradise Lost*; and that of
the martyr-saint, by Christ in his victories both on the cross
and in the desert. For what in the end appears as Samson's
newly won patience is swallowed up in a torrent of rage.

In *De Doctrina*, Milton also has something to say about the
conditions of a divinely sanctioned marriage, and he says it
through the proverb, *"why, my son, do you go astray with a
strange woman?"* (VI, 782). God only joins together "things
compatible, fit, good and honorable: he has not joined chalk
and cheese: he has not joined things base, wretched, ill-omened
and disastrous. It is violence or rashness or error or some evil
genius which joins things like this, not God" (VI, 371-72;
cf. *Tetrachordon*, II, 650-51). The purpose of marriage, Milton insists, is not procreation only, but "the help and solace
of life" (VI, 355); and if one's parents are alive their consent,
free from any kind of falsehood, must be obtained, and should
be given, only when "husband and wife are of one mind in
religious matters" (VI, 368-69). This is as important under
the Law as under the Gospel, and under both a happy marriage
is at once a sign of God's sanction and his providence; but
even an unhappy or improper marriage "should not be dissolved while there still is any hope of winning over the un-
believer" (VI, 369). Good works, according to Milton, are
what "WE DO WHEN THE SPIRIT OF GOD WORKS WITHIN US"
(VI, 638), and they "never run contrary to the love of God
and of our neighbor" (VI, 640); for God wished to exclude
"no man from the way of penitence and eternal salvation" (VI,
194).

Anger is not a comely quality, Milton continues: *"better be
long-suffering than mighty"* (VI, 722); and anger often opposes
charity, is a perverse hatred of oneself and can eventuate in
suicide. On the other hand, charity involves the showing of
mercy to our neighbors, even those with cultural and religious
differences (VI, 741); and showing mercy also to our enemies:

"Our enemies are not to be excluded from our charity" as is evidenced by Christ's plea, "*Father, forgive them*" (VI, 742). Such a plea the false prophet is incapable of making; for he is the master only of wrong answers, speaking and acting "falsely, without command from God" (VI, 338) and without realizing that "an excess of . . . charity is simply impossible" (VI, 642).

A steady defender of charity from *The Doctrine and Discipline of Divorce* onward, unflagging in his commitment to the notion expressed there that all expositions and precepts are incidental to "the general and supreme rule of charitie" (II, 277), that "the Gospel enjoyns no new morality, save only the infinit enlargement of charity" (II, 330-31), Milton, in *De Doctrina*, holds that "It is quite unthinkable that Christ should have expunged from the Mosaic law any provision which could sanction the extension of charity towards the wretched and the afflicted" (VI, 379-80). Those (like Samson) who are without charity are without pity, even for animals, and are also without righteousness, unable to control their affections and forgetting that "resistance to or endurance of external evil" are nothing without "the pursuit of external good" (VI, 720). In *De Doctrina*, Milton the humanist idealizes *humanity* which, he says, "means not failing to observe the common courtesies of life in our dealings with our fellow men . . . simply because they are our fellow men" (VI, 744); to spurn the values of gentleness and forgiveness, he concludes, leads inevitably to the murdering of life. In exactly the same moment when bondage seems most inevitable, when the aggrieved party is ready to mutiny into melancholy despair, then, says Milton, "charity ought to venture much, and use bold physick, lest an overtost faith endanger to shipwrack" (II, 254). What Milton here preaches he seems, in his own lifetime, to have practiced. Edward Phillips writes tellingly of Milton's forgiveness of Mary Powell: he pardoned her from 'his own generous nature, more inclinable to Reconciliation than to perseverance in Anger and Revenge."[16] And what Phillips says here accords perfectly with Peter Heimbach's description, preserved in Milton's private correspondence, of the poet's having achieved "that union . . . of gravity with fairest humanity, . . . of a magnanimous and not the least bit timorous spirit with a solicitous love of peace, even when younger souls became disheartened—a union altogether remarkable, and beyond the deserts of the age" (VIII, 2). Moreover, what Milton writes in *De Doctrina* is perfectly consistent with what he states in *A Treatise of Civil Power*: "our whole practical dutie in religion is contained in charitie" (VII, 256).

Dalila quickly makes an issue of Samson's "uncompassionate anger" (818)—an "anger, unappeasable . . . / . . . never to be calm'd" (963-64), and much in evidence in Samson's retort: "Not for thy life, lest fierce remembrance wake / My sudden rage to tear thee joint by joint" (952-53). That anger is admitted to by Samson who describes himself as "swollen with pride," "like a petty God . . . walk[ing] about admired of all and dreaded" (529-30). Samson's is an anger that joins force with force—"force with force / Is well ejected" (1206-07); "My heels are fetter'd, but my fist is free" (1235)—and that, judging from the Dalila episode, knows no real forgiveness and never with patience will be crowned. In his death, Samson returns to an earthly father who would build him "A Monument . . . / With all his Trophies hung, and Acts enroll'd / In copious Legend, or sweet Lyric Song . . . / The Virgins also shall on feastful days / Visit his Tomb" (1734, 1736-42). That is, Samson achieves in his death what Dalila hoped for in hers: "I shall be . . . / . . . sung at solemn festivals, / Living and dead recorded . . . / . . . my tomb / With odours visited and annual flowers" (982-87). Only death

---

[16] *The Early Lives of Milton*, ed. Helen Darbishire (1932; rpt. London: Constable, 1965), p. 67.

can deliver the idolater from his idolatry, a proposition verified for Milton's own time by the Samson story: "Idolaters . . . have layd themselves downe . . . as *Sampson* did upon *Dalilahs* [lap], till they lose their *locks*, and their life as he did . . . all the light of grace, the light of knowledge; . . . cannot pull them out of her lap."[17] Milton accentuates the irony of an idolater becoming himself an idol by recording Samson's deeds not in sweet lyric song but in "a Tragedy."

The only citation of Samson in Milton's heroic poems occurs in Book IX of *Paradise Lost* where Samson, a postfiguration of the fallen Adam, appears there to elucidate the paradox: "thir Eyes how op'nd, and thir minds / How dark'nd" (1053-54). The rest is under the seal of silence. Not mentioned in the later catalogue of Old Testament types and shadows, neither is Samson arrayed among the prefigurations of Jesus in *Paradise Regained*, as if to suggest that, though Samson is a member of the First Adam, he is not a bearer of the image of the Second Adam. The point is reinforced, it seems, by Milton's citation of *Christ Suffering* in the preface to a play that itself resists association with the Crucifixion story, even as it allows certain pressures to mount up owing to the cryptic scriptural reference and to the constant pressure of doctrinal allusion. For instance, the Book of Judges says only that Samson's body, once recovered, is interred in the burial place of Manoah; but in *Samson Agonistes* those who recover Samson's body go to the stream and "With lavers pure and cleansing herbs wash

---

[17] Daniel Featley, "Saint Pauls Trumpet; or, an Alarme for Sleepie Christians" (1639), in *Threnoikos: The House of Movrning* (London: Printed by John Dawson, 1640), p. 505. To argue, as Arnold Stein does, that "Milton is here poetically sanctioning a shrine," that here Milton is "belatedly recognizing and dignifying a basic human urge," is to miss altogether the irony in this passage; see his remarks in *Twentieth-Century Interpretations of "Samson Agonistes,"* ed. Galbraith Crump (Englewood Cliffs: Prentice-Hall, 1968), p. 72. Cf. J. B. Broadbent, who finds in this passage "another of those curious *naïvetés* of Milton" (*"Comus" and "Samson Agonistes"* [Great Neck: Barrons' Educational Series, 1961], p. 58).

off / The clotted gore" (1727-28). There is hidden reference here to the cleansing and anointing of Christ's body after the Crucifixion, and yet other such allusions establish a point of similarity only to mark a difference. Jesus is made to walk through the streets and is continually humiliated on his way to Calvary, whereas Samson is content to go to the pillars only "Because they shall not trail me through thir streets / Like a wild Beast" (1402-03). Repeatedly, doctrinal pressures in Milton's text explode expected typological associations.[18]

Manoa's desire to pay a ransom for his son is alluded to parenthetically in the argument to Milton's poem and is referred to persistently within the poem itself. In "The Argument," Milton refers to Manoa's "purpose to procure . . . [Samson's] liberty by ransom"; and in the poem itself, speaking of Manoa, the Chorus allows that "Fathers are wont to lay up for thir Sons, / Thou for thy Son art bent to lay out all" (1485-86). Samson's commission was to begin the deliverance of his people; but Manoa and, more insistently, Dalila assume that their commission is to effect Samson's deliverance, either not caring about, or not knowing (as in the case of Dalila), the extent to which their concerns run contrary to Samson's charge. Manoa tells his son, "I however / Must not omit . . . / To prosecute the means of thy deliverance / By

[18] The now classic formulation of this argument is provided by William G. Madsen, *From Shadowy Types to Truth: Studies in Milton's Symbolism* (New Haven: Yale Univ. Press, 1968), pp. 181-202. In this context, it should be noted that the scoffing at and mocking of Samson and Christ often seemed to secure their typological connection: "the proud and vainglorious man . . . shoote[s] it [an arrow of mockery] against such as hee meaneth to disgrace; with his Arrow was *Samson* wounded by the *Philistims*, when they made him their laughing-stocke: & our SAVIOUR by the *Jewes*, when they platted a Crowne of thornes vpon his head"; see Francis Rollenson, *Twelve Prophetical Legacies: or Twelve Sermons vpon Iacobs Last Will and Testament* (London: Printed for Arthur Johnson, 1612), p. 244; and see also Richard Bernard, *The Bible-Battells; or the Sacred Art Military* (London: Printed for Edward Blackmore, 1629), p. 211. The literal and metaphoric blinding of Samson and Christ respectively lend further support to the connection (Rollenson, *Twelve Prophetical Legacies*, p. 218).

ransom or how else" (601-04); and Dalila tells her husband, "I may fetch thee / From forth this loathsome prison-house, to abide / With me, where my redoubl'd love and care / With nursing diligence . . . / May ever tend about thee to old age" (921-25). Samson, who survives in legend, and in history, as the agent in the redemption of others, is portrayed in Milton's poem as himself in need of redemption. Manoa thus prosecutes his endeavor, which is Dalila's too, for "*Samsons* redemption" (The Argument).

It is difficult not to recall the ransom theory of the Atonement and then not to relate theological tradition to dramatic event, both of which, in concatenation, draw attention to father-son relations and away from Dalila to the Philistines generally as the Antichrist figure in the play. The ransom payment contemplated by Manoa typologizes not only the Philistines as Satan but Manoa as earthly counterpart to the Heavenly Father. Yet such equations also subject theological tradition to parody. According to that tradition, God pays a ransom to Satan; the ransom is his Son; and God's objective is to accomplish, through his Son, the liberation of the human race. In contrast, Manoa would ransom "his things" for the liberation of his son, a requisite of which will be that Samson forego his charge to begin the deliverance of his people: "His ransom, if my whole inheritance / May compass it, shall willingly be paid" (1476-77), says Manoa; "For his redemption all my Patrimony, / . . . I am ready to forgo / And quit" (1482-84). Manoa, of course, speaks nonsense, for the whole purpose of Atonement theory is deliverance; the theory exists to explain how, alienated from God, man will become at one with him; how man will be enabled to leave the midnight of the wilderness and enter upon the dawn of a new paradise. The nonsense is punctuated by Manoa's lament that, finally, it is Death who pays Samson's ransom (1572-73), delivering him not into new life but into the grave.

Milton had already set forth his own radically new version of atonement theory in *Paradise Regained* and then, in *Samson Agonistes*, set against it the most primitive and offensive of all explanations of this mystery—one that in the Middle Ages had "deteriorated into a grotesque view of the work of the Christ" and that could only be revived by reformers, says C. A. Patrides, once they had "sensibly divested it of its most unpleasant aspects" by having Christ himself pay a ransom, not now to Satan but to God.[19] It is not just the theory, but the theory in its most offensive details, that Milton revives in *Samson Agonistes*, and reinforces, by the placement of this poem alongside but after *Paradise Regained*. Milton thus twins two very different myths of deliverance and, with them, two opposing states of consciousness, implying that part of Christ's deliverance involves delivering us from the modes of consciousness that afflicted an earlier, pre-Christian phase of history. If Jesus violates the law, it is always to exhibit charity; when Samson breaks the law, it is usually to wreak vengeance. Or as Milton formulates the difference in *The Doctrine and Discipline of Divorce*: whereas the Judges (among them Samson) speak to the vulgar, Jesus addresses the regenerate (II, 344). Accordingly it might be said that *Paradise Regained* and *Samson Agonistes* are addressed to different audiences rather like Shelley's *Prometheus Unbound* and *The Cenci*, the one poem to the select few, the other to the multitudes. *Samson*, however, without *Paradise Regained*, is sealed from the multitudes in keeping with Milton's intention of never "conceal[ing] any part of . . . [his] meaning," but acknowledgement that he retains "much more confidence" in "learned than . . . untutored readers," in those "who thoroughly understand the teaching of the gospel," and in keeping with Milton's insistence, also in *De Doctrina*, that *"the wicked shall act wickedly, and*

[19] *Milton and the Christian Tradition* (Oxford: Clarendon Press, 1966), pp. 133, 134.

none of the wicked will understand; but the wise will understand"
(VI, 122, 339).

What we witness in *Samson Agonistes* is the wrenching apart
of received typological associations, as John Ulreich observes
their being repeatedly "dash[ed] . . . against the rock of Samson's unremittingly Judaic consciousness."[20] This is nowhere
more evident than in Samson's encounter with Dalila, where
typological correlations, blistering with irony, are asserted
only to be denied. Milton's strategy here is reminiscent of one
earlier employed by Thomas Jackson (1577-1640): to invite
the recollection that Judas was commonly regarded as "an open
Delilah" and Jesus as the true Samson, or "Sun of righteousness," then to let typological differences challenge these received associations. "*No type at all*, not so much as a shadow
of Christ's humility and patience in all his sufferings," says
Jackson, Samson is "rather a foil by his impatience, to set a
lustre upon the unparalleled meekness of this true Nazarite of
God by an *antiperistasis*:

> Samson's last prayers unto the God of his strength
> were, that he would give him power at the hour of
> his death to be revenged on his enemies for the loss
> of his eyes. Jesus of Nazareth, the true Nazarite of
> God, when he came unto the cross on mount Calvary,
> the stage and theatre for his enemies' sport and
> triumph over him in this solemn feast, prays heartily
> even for those that hoodwinked him . . . and for
> the Roman soldiers . . . : he prays for both in such
> a sweet and heavenly manner, as no prophet had ever
> done for his persecutors—*Father, forgive them, for
> they know not what they do.* He did not so much as
> either lift up hand or voice, or conceive any secret

20 " 'Beyond the Fifth Act': *Samson Agonistes* as Prophecy," in *Composite Orders:
The Genres of Milton's Last Poems*, ed. Richard S. Ide and Joseph Wittreich (Pittsburgh: Univ. of Pittsburgh Press, 1983), p. 281 (a special issue of *Milton Studies*).

prayer against one or other of his persecutors, during the time of his lingering but deadly pains; or knowing this was the time wherein his body was to be made as an anvil, that he might do the will of his Father by the sacrifice of himself, and sufferance of all other indignities more bitter to a mere man than twenty deaths, though of the cross.[21]

The Variorum Commentary on *Samson Agonistes* will instruct its readers that the poem "is silent on the subject of Christ and Atonement (unless, without encouragement . . .), we interpret Samson as a figure of Christ."[22] It is true that *Samson Agonistes* resists easy typological equations, but that truth is complicated by the fact that its depth of resistance to received typology can only be measured by references to Christ and his Atonement (they appear explicitly in the preface and implicitly in the poem)—references that are enunciated only to be eroded. The significance of such references, and then of such strategies of subversion, is underscored by the fact that the only secure link between the stories of Samson and Christ was thought to reside in their respective deaths. John Bunyan succinctly summarizes a century and a half of thinking when, in the year of Milton's death, he explains that there are many types of Christ in all ages of the world and that each type is authenticated by its connection with some special phase, or specific episode, in Christ's life, the Samson story being valorized by its correspondence with the Passion story: "Adam was . . . [Christ's] type. . . . Moses was his type . . . and

[21] *The Humiliation of the Son of God* (1638), in *The Works of Thomas Jackson* (12 vols.; Oxford: Oxford Univ. Press, 1844), VIII, 82-83; cf. Archibald Simson, *Samsons Seaven Lockes of Haire: Allegorically Expounded, and Compared to the Seven Spirituall Vertues* (St. Andrewes: Printed by Edward Raban, 1621), pp. 14, 42, 46, 63.

[22] I quote from William Riley Parker's portion of the manuscript (see n. 35 for Ch. I), ms. p. 175.

so was Melchisedec. . . . Samson was his type in the effects of his death; and as Samson gave his life for the deliverance of Israel from the Philistines, Christ gave his life to deliver us from sin and the devils."[23] Unlike Bunyan, but not without precedent to be sure, Milton makes a usual point of identity into an emphatic mark of distinction.

In Milton's poem, Samson plays Jesus to his Judas-like betrayer, the recipient of "*Philistian* gold." The issue quickly becomes forgiveness—"let me obtain forgiveness . . . *Samson* / . . . At distance I forgive thee, go with that" (909, 954)— a forgiveness offered, yet gravely qualified, by one who threatens to tear his betrayer limb from limb as earlier he had torn the lion and as, earlier still, his countrymen had cut off the thumbs and toes of their enemies, or as later in the Judges narrative the concubine will be dismembered. This episode conjures up, yet stands in marked contrast to, the compassionate plea of Jesus: "*Forgive them, Father*"—the very type of generous forgiveness belittled by Samson in his contemptuous reference to those "wisest and best men . . . / With goodness principl'd not to reject / The penitent, but ever to forgive," whose sole reward is "to wear out miserable days" (759-62). Such men, Samson concludes, are rather as he himself claims to be, "to Ages an example" (765) of what *not* to do. By inviting us to correlate this episode with the betrayal scene of Jesus, Milton not only marks the disparity between the ethics of Samson and Jesus, but marks it boldly by allowing us to remember that, when Jesus is betrayed, "one of them which were with Jesus stretched out *his* hand, and drew his sword, and struck a servant of the high priest's, and smote off his ear. Then said Jesus unto him, Put up again thy sword into his place: for all they that take the sword shall perish with the sword" (Matthew 26:51-52). The practitioners of vio-

---

[23] "Light for Them That Sit in Darkness" (1674), in *The Whole Works of John Bunyan*, ed. George Offor (3 vols.; London: Blackie and Son, 1862), I, 396.

lence die by violence, "self-kill'd" even if "Not willingly" (1664-65).

Still more boldly, the disparity between Samson and Jesus is marked by the juxtaposition of *Paradise Regained* and *Samson Agonistes* in a poetic volume where any notion of typological progression is disrupted by the inverted sequence in which the poems appear and where the suggestion may very well be that it is the philosophy of Samson, not of Jesus, that persists and prevails in the modern world. Only an ethical drama derived from an Old Testament book like Judges, Milton seems to be saying, is primitive enough to approximate the moral conditions obtaining in England during the Revolution and its aftermath—is adequate to the task of anatomizing the reasons for its failure, the full extent of this tragedy. Samson's attitudes contrast strikingly with those of Jesus, who would unburden the human race of the very ethical system that Samson is intent upon upholding: "I us'd hostility, and took thir spoil / To pay my underminers in thir coin" (1203-04). It is an ethical system, in the Book of Judges, shared by Samson and his Philistian oppressors: "to do to him as he hath done to us . . . As they did unto me, so I have done unto them" (15:10, 11). Jesus, in *Paradise Regained*, would "subdue and quell . . . / Brute violence," holding it more humane, and heavenly, to "make perswasion do the work of fear" (I.218-23). Samson belongs to that class of men, so roundly condemned by Jesus, whose sports are cruelty and who make sport of blood (IV.137-40), whose fleshly arms are "argument / Of human weakness rather than of strength" (III.401-02), and who have yet to learn the value of "vanquish[ing] by wisdom hellish wiles" (I.175).

Samson and Jesus both go to the temple; but when Jesus goes, "there to hear / The Teachers of our Law" (I.211-12), it is with the intention of improving not just his own knowledge but "their own" (I.213); it is to redeem himself, and those teachers, from just that ethical system, founded upon cruelty and violence, that Samson espouses in both his life and death. The effect of such juxtapositions, but also of representing Samson here as in the epics Jesus is represented—as "The Image" of the Heavenly Father and his "mighty minister" (706)—is to fracture instead of securing received typological associations; is but to remind us, as John Shawcross would do, that here "Typological symbolism is not superimposed, but made to function dramatically"[24] in a poem where typological irony is a chief source of dramatic, even prophetic, irony and where seeming contraries emerge finally in a siege of opposition.

This war of opposites is conducted within *Samson Agonistes* no less than between this and other of Milton's poems. In the latter instance, as John Hollander has remarked, echoes of *Paradise Lost* are to be heard within Samson's opening soliloquy with the consequence that his rhetoric here comes to be associated with Satan's casuistry in the epic and his "misplaced concreteness" simultaneously reveals itself as "his own self-deluding dialectic."[25] On the other hand, within *Samson Agonistes* this war of opposites is conducted, in part, to subdue an older and recently outmoded Samson typology, which had been geared to present Samson as a martyr-hero. "Every martyr play, whether religious or secular," says Herbert Lindenberger, "works rhetorically to excite the audience's admiration for the martyr and convince it of the rightness of his cause. The greatest martyr plays," among which Lindenberger numbers *Samson Agonistes*, are said to "succeed in presenting images of heroic possibility with a convincingness and lack of ironic qualification such as we rarely find elsewhere in drama," with

[24] "The Genres of *Paradise Regain'd* and *Samson Agonistes*: The Wisdom of Their Joint Publication," in *Composite Orders*, ed. Ide and Wittreich, p. 229.
[25] *The Figure of Echo: A Mode of Allusion in Milton and After* (Berkeley and Los Angeles: Univ. of California Press, 1981), p. 95.

a convincingness achieved through a hero who "carries an automatic 'halo-effect' for those about to witness his martyrdom" and with ironic qualification eliminated by a conspicuous imitation of Christ, both his suffering and transcendence.[26]

Milton's "martyr play" is different, though, less a celebration than a censure of its hero. Furthermore, it is a tragedy struck from the plate of revolution and ambivalent in its attitude toward that revolution, so much so that the words of Herbert Marcuse could easily be Milton's:

> Martyrs have rarely helped a political cause, and "revolutionary suicide" remains suicide. And yet, it would be self-righteous indifference to say that the revolutionary ought to live rather than die for the revolution. . . . Where the Establishment proclaims its professional killers as heroes, and its rebelling victims as criminals, it is hard to save the idea of heroism for the other side. The desperate act, doomed to failure, may for a brief moment tear the veil of justice and expose the faces of brutal suppression; it may arouse the conscience of the neutrals; it may reveal hidden cruelties and lies. . . . Any generalization would be ambivalent, nay, profoundly unjust: it would condemn the victims of the system

[26] *Historical Drama: The Relation of Literature and Reality* (Chicago: Univ. of Chicago Press, 1975), pp. 44-45, 46, 49. See also Kenneth Fell for whom "the saint's death is the culmination and epitome of, and the way of release from . . . sin" ("From Myth to Martyrdom: Towards a View of Milton's *Samson Agonistes*," *English Studies*, 34 [1953], 154) and Mason Tung, according to whose reading "God's grace overpowers all of his [Samson's] resistance and converts him into a patient heroic martyr in the end" ("*Samson Impatiens*: A Reinterpretation of *Samson Agonistes*," *Texas Studies in Literature and Language*, 9 [1968], 477). On the other hand, Lynn Veach Sadler contends that "Milton decentralizes the medieval focus on martyrdom"; see *Consolation in "Samson Agonistes": Regeneration and Typology*, Salzburg Studies in English Literature (Salzburg: Univ. of Salzburg, 1979), p. 93.

to the prolonged agony of waiting, to prolonged
suffering. But then, the desperate act may have the
same result—perhaps a worse result.[27]

The "worse result" is where the Samson story concludes, both
in the Judges narrative and in Milton's poem; it is also where
the tragedy of history commences and from whence it
continues.

Samson Agonistes teases us into, then out of, arranging the
details of Samson's life in accordance with a saint's legend.
Instead of moving with, it cuts across the grain of the usual
martyr play, challenging rather than conforming to such conventions by presenting as its protagonist a figure of dubious
heroism, the rightness of whose course was regularly debated
and questioned through typological correlations that evoked
disparities and eventuated in qualification. Even as it dismantles the generic conventions of the martyr play, *Samson Agonistes* adheres to its larger objective of using old history to
create a new history. It is not Samson, though, but Milton
who, like the typical protagonist in such plays, stands both
outside and inside history, his task being "to free himself from
history in order to create a new historical consciousness"—not
by this play alone but through the twin consciousness afforded
by the placement of this play with *Paradise Regained* in the
1671 poetic volume. The presence of *Paradise Regained* in this
volume insures that there is nothing programmatically anti-
humanistic about *Samson Agonistes*. Rather, the poems coop-
erate in a final effort, as Hayden White might say, "to generate
a visionary politics on the basis of a sublime conception of the

---

[27] *Counter-Revolution and Revolt* (Boston: Beacon Press, 1972), pp. 52-53.

historical process"[28]—one which sees in the past a spectacle of confusion and moral anarchy and which offers the present a vision of a perfected society in the future, that perfection attainable through the invalidation of one set of values and the institution of another. In the 1671 poetic volume, we behold history moving through the whirlwind and back to the Word.

[28] "The Politics of Historical Interpretation: Discipline and De-Sublimation," *Critical Inquiry*, 9 (1982), 129; see also p. 128.

CHAPTER VII

SAMSON AGONISTES
IN CONTEXT

> *The fundamental requirement of interpretation is always the determination of context, that is, the principle by which the parts perform their constitutive function; and our interpretive disagreements are usually disagreements over what the relevant context is . . . To achieve greater [interpretive] precision, it is customary to choose among the syntactical systems possibly applicable the one that conforms most nearly to the author's habit of mind. . . .*
>
> —EARL R. WASSERMAN

The wisdom of putting *Paradise Regained* and *Samson Agonistes* together in the same volume, writes John Shawcross, "is the commerce which is thus established between them": "Perhaps we have misread *Samson Agonistes* so ineptly because we have not fully acknowledged the interrelationships of the two works."[1] And Balachandra Rajan comments similarly: "How little in the impressive outpouring of Milton scholarship bears explicitly on this problem" of intertextual connection.[2] The

---

[1] "The Genres of *Paradise Regain'd* and *Samson Agonistes*," in *Composite Orders: The Genres of Milton's Last Poems*, ed. Richard S. Ide and Joseph Wittreich (Pittsburgh: Univ. of Pittsburgh Press, 1983), p. 240 (a special issue of *Milton Studies*).

[2] "To Which Is Added *Samson Agonistes*," in *The Prison and the Pinnacle: Papers to Commemorate the Tercentenary of "Paradise Regained" and "Samson Agonistes*," ed. Balachandra Rajan (London: Routledge and Kegan Paul, 1973), p. 96. William Kerrigan remarks, "It is interesting to entertain (though folly to prove) the possibility

poems in Milton's 1671 volume, for a long time, seemed resistant to the sort of criticism that both Shawcross and Rajan would sponsor; for on the one hand they clearly embody radically different states of mind, in the words of A.S.P. Woodhouse are "so divergent . . . in doctrine, temper, and tone," and on the other hand, as William Riley Parker remarks, *Samson* seems "a bitter poem, a dark poem . . . a relapse" from *Paradise Regained*.[3] Still, this tired hypothesis should not be allowed to cancel out the more creative and daring one, shared by Shawcross and Rajan alike, that Milton placed these poems together because he wished to make a statement through the juxtaposition—meant for these poems to be mutually reflective and illuminating and thus interpretively significant for one another, with *Paradise Regained* providing a fractional gloss on the poem that succeeds it.

The juxtaposition of these poems and the ensuing dialogue between them suggest that they are not autonomous but dependent upon one another for their meaning. Milton's poems are always a plurality of other texts, which help to unravel their significance; their intertextuality, whether overt or covert, provides access to their meaning, with *Paradise Regained* and *Samson Agonistes* internalizing the usual presuppositions about intertextuality and then moving among themselves in the same way that texts, usually of different authorship, through the same elusive presuppositions become involved with one another. It is as if Milton were using explicit intertextuality between *Paradise Lost* and *Paradise Regained, Paradise Regained* and the Gospels, *Samson Agonistes* and the Book

---

that the publication of *Paradise Regained* and *Samson Agonistes* in one volume . . . was no accident: the two works complement each other almost as perfectly as 'L'Allegro' and 'Il Penseroso' " (*The Prophetic Milton* [Charlottesville: Univ. Press of Virginia, 1974], p. 268).

[3] See Woodhouse, *The Heavenly Muse: A Preface to Milton*, ed. Hugh MacCallum (Toronto: Univ. of Toronto Press, 1972), p. 293, and Parker, *Milton: A Biography* (2 vols.; Oxford: Clarendon Press, 1968), II, 910.

of Judges, to signal a hidden intertextuality between the poems themselves, with *Samson* relating to *Paradise Regained* as each poem relates to its biblical context and thus as text relates to pre-text. An explicit intertextuality achieved through allusion masks an elusive intertextuality, with the presuppositions governing the former now transferred to and providing the controls for the latter. Surface intertextuality, at least in *Paradise Regained* and *Samson Agonistes*, holds the reader within the confines of inferential meaning whereas, in these same poems, a covert intertextuality leads the reader into the realm of specified but subversive meanings. Interpretation of both these poems will proceed when we begin to ask, with Jonathan Culler, how a text establishes a pre-text, and then provide, as Culler urges, "an account of how texts create presuppositions and hence pre-texts for themselves and how the ways of producing these presuppositions relate to ways of treating them."[4]

The signals of a hidden intertextuality in Milton's 1671 poetic volume are various: we can point to the habit of composition evident in such precursors as Spenser and Donne, Herbert and Marvell; and, more, one can point to Milton's own habit of composition evident in his early poems and prose works alike. This method of composition engages all these poets in certain strategies devised to secure intertextual connection: typological patterning, generic organization, self-quotation and echo, imagistic and thematic repetition, a common subtext, all of which are conspicuously evident in Milton's 1671 volume. *Paradise Regained* and *Samson Agonistes* have not a separate but a shared syntax; these poems together form a totality, with the individual poems themselves becoming like fragments. The volume, that is, becomes the poem; *its* syntax, not that of the separate poems, governs the meaning; and the meaning itself derives from the concatenation. Beyond these

---

[4] *The Pursuit of Signs: Semiotics, Literature, Deconstruction* (1981; rpt. Ithaca: Cornell Univ. Press, 1983), p. 118.

shared devices for signalling and securing relationships, there is the device, distinctively Miltonic, of making arrangements mirror a dialectical interplay between poems: Milton's poems do not exist in peaceful cohabitation but are joined in strife, engaged in contention. Containing its own inner polemic, the entire volume takes energy from this opposition.

The fact that *Paradise Regained* and *Samson Agonistes* were published together tells us something about how they were intended to be read and about how they *were* read for a full century after their original publication. Not until 1779 was either poem published separately. This particular pairing of poems is sufficiently odd that the oddity itself alerts us to the ways in which normal expectations would have been dashed: first, the obvious connection, and interplay, between *Paradise Lost* and *Paradise Regained* is eschewed by the decision to separate the poems in publication; second, the natural order of works is disregarded in the decision to publish *Samson Agonistes* after, and as an appendage to, *Paradise Regained*. This frustration of expectations may, in fact, signal that Milton is employing surreptitious strategies in order to bypass difficulties with the newly institutionalized censorship; and the very effectiveness of such strategies is testified to by the fact that *Paradise Regained* regularly, but *Samson Agonistes* seldom, was perceived as a challenge and threat to orthodoxy—a challenge and threat mitigated by the apparent movement in this volume from the unconventional to the conventional, from wildly speculative theology to platitudinous Christianity. The movement is illusory, probably deliberately so; but the sheer power of the illusion is registered in the history of criticism where, for a full century, Milton is portrayed as a poet converting back to the supposed orthodoxies of his early poetry, and consequently where little attention is given to the possibility that *Paradise Regained* provides a deliberately widened context in which to read *Samson Agonistes*.

Where there is censorship, poets must circumvent its re-
strictions by devising new—and devious—means of expression. With *Paradise Regained* and *Samson Agonistes*, it is not
enough to look at mere words on a page to arrive at an interpretation and not enough, either, to segregate poems for interpretation that are themselves integrated through their publication. There are various detouring operations for poets
writing under the intimidation of censorship: the use of "safe"
genres to convey "unsafe" ideas, the concealment of radical
content within a subtext, the appropriation of biblical stories
as a screen on contemporary history, the depersonalizing of
unsettling convictions, the avoidance of responsibility for dangerous opinions by investing them in dialogue, the signaling
of heresies in the deep structure of a poem by the flickering
unorthodoxies on its surface, the severing of contexts in order
to make innocent what, if bound together, might be too provocative, the establishment of a meaningful connection between poems through casual, seemingly idiosyncratic placement of them. These very strategies for detouring censorship,
now extrapolated from Renaissance texts and so finely elucidated by Christopher Hill and Annabel Patterson, are all
operative in Milton's 1671 poetic volume.[5]

An argument for the interrelationship and deliberate coun-
terpositioning of *Paradise Regained* and *Samson Agonistes* is all
the more plausible now that Milton's critics have sensitized
us to the collective design of his poems and to the wholeness
of his canon, the impulses toward which are evident early on:
in the role accorded *Lycidas* both in *Justa Edovardo King Naufrago* (1638) and in *Poems of Mr. John Milton* (1645); in the
organizational patterns and intertextual relationships tested in

[5] See *The Collected Essays of Christopher Hill: Writing and Revolution in Seventeenth-
Century England* (Amherst: Univ. of Massachusetts Press, 1985), pp. 32-71, and
Patterson, *Censorship and Interpretation: The Conditions of Writing and Reading in
Early Modern England* (Madison: Univ. of Wisconsin Press, 1984), pp. 44-119.

the former volume, then transferred to the 1645 *Poems*; and even in that gathering of prose works which, though it be an afterthought, Milton seeks to capture within the overarching conception of freedom—domestic, civil, and religious. The other poems in *Justa Edovardo King Naufrago* are related to one another as *Lycidas* relates to them, through a carefully plotted mental and emotional progression and also through a system of echoing, as well as of corresponding yet contending images. The 1645 *Poems* are disposed in such a way as to chart the course of a rising poet, figured by generic progression within "a unifying and developing vision of the transforming power of poetry,"[6] its thrust beyond pagan toward Christian truth and its grasping for the prophetic strain. The attainment of the prophetic strain is not only the climax of the volume but the culminating moment in the companion poems, *L'Allegro* and *Il Penseroso*, which like the volume as a whole, almost the volume in miniature, arrive at the prophetic moment through an elaborate generic progression. The twin lyrics are bound together, their relationship sealed, by structural and imagistic mirroring, which allows always for the perception of difference within the apparent likeness.

The poetic volumes to which Milton contributed, or which he composed, have their own logic and rhetoric, then, and their own deliberate, distinctive architectonics. Milton's conception of the poetic volume does not alter, although the principles for intertextuality do become muted owing to the cir-

[6] William A. Oram, "Nature, Poetry, and Milton's Genii," in *Milton and the Art of Sacred Song*, ed. J. Max Patrick and Roger H. Sundell (Madison: Univ. of Wisconsin Press, 1979), p. 48. The fullest discussions of these early poetic volumes and of the crucial place of *Lycidas* in them are provided by Louis L. Martz, *Poet of Exile: A Study of Milton's Poetry* (New Haven: Yale Univ. Press, 1980), pp. 31-59; Raymond B. Waddington, "Milton Among the Carolines," in *The Age of Milton*, ed. C. A. Patrides and Raymond B. Waddington (Manchester: Manchester Univ. Press; Totowa: Barnes and Noble, 1980), pp. 338-64; and Joseph Wittreich, *Visionary Poetics: Milton's Tradition and His Legacy* (San Marino: Huntington Library, 1979), esp. pp. 79-117.

cumstances in which *Paradise Regained* and *Samson Agonistes* are published and concerning which Annabel Patterson is altogether too reticent:

> We still do not know whether Milton turned to biblical reinterpretation [in these poems] in order to transcend his political experience, now seen as failed and useless, or whether in the Restoration poems he was still operating in the tradition articulated by James I before he became king: "Ze man . . . be war of wryting any thing of materis of commoun weill, or uther sich grave sene subjectis (except Metaphorically . . .) . . . they are to grave materis for a Poet to mell in."[7]

Milton's last poems are probing, powerful political statements; they are of a piece with the 1645 *Poems* and yet a significant advance upon Milton's earlier concerns. A biblical poet, such as Milton has now become, might be expected to appropriate biblically sanctioned oppositions between positive and negative images—between prophetic idealisms and historical actualities. If the earlier poems reach for the prophetic moment, these last poems, an embodiment of that moment, turn their attention to the formation of the prophetic character, with *Paradise Regained* and *Samson Agonistes* scrutinizing the evidence for and excesses of such characters, as well as the perils of prophecy and its burden. Not only is *Paradise Regained* anticipated in the last books of *Paradise Lost*, but so too is the very problem that will be sorted out in *Samson Agonistes*: of those "feigning . . . to act / By spiritual [power], to themselves appropriating / The Spirit of God, promised alike and giv'n / To all Believers" and of all the turmoil in history issuing from that "pretense" (XII.517-20).

Milton's earlier efforts, in poetry and prose alike, are but

---

[7] *Censorship and Interpretation*, p. 20.

harbingers of what has been called the "intense inter-relatedness"[8] of his last poems which, as a trilogy, reveal the extent to which one poem reaches out to others and defines itself in relation to them. The poetic volume of 1671 specifically raises the problem of relationship on a title page where *Paradise Regained*, as Arthur Barker notices, appears in an "emphatic typeface" and *Samson Agonistes*, in a "smaller, and perhaps hesitantly insignificant, type." According to Barker, in raising the problem of interrelationship, this title page raises the whole question of intersignificance:

> . . . does the collocation represent the imperfectly resolved conflict of the later Miltonic moods which we can discern in the poetic difficulties we encounter in the two pieces? Does not the first poem express, or move toward the expression of, the tuningly harmonious vision of spirituality towards which Milton was always striving to make his way and needed all the more after being diverted into national revolutionary efforts and defeated in them? And does not the second poem chiefly represent the painfully guilty despair of defeat and the difficulty of struggling out of that towards vision? Should not Samson's fallen, if ultimately, in some sense, rescued, experience rather precede Christ's making possible the regaining of Paradise for all mankind . . . ? Or is there some deep significance in the apparently inept reversal? Can we interpret our poems in a way which will demonstrate that . . . they are properly sequential?

[8] John F. Huntley, "The Images of the Poet and Poetry in Milton's *The Reason of Church-Government*," in *Achievements of the Left Hand: Essays on the Prose of John Milton*, ed. Michael Lieb and John T. Shawcross (Amherst: Univ. of Massachusetts Press, 1974), p. 113. See also the "Postscript" to the important study by Arnold Stein, *Heroic Knowledge; An Interpretation of "Paradise Regained" and "Samson Agonistes"* (1957; rpt. Hamden: Archon Books, 1965), pp. 203-13.

> In short, are the two poems . . . to be regarded
> as companion or rather as contrasting pieces?[9]

Milton's is a poetry not only of allusion but of contexts, both extrinsic and intrinsic, with the *oeuvre* having as much "connective life" and being as fully designed certainly as the contexts of either genre or milieu.[10] Hence, both *Paradise Regained* and *Samson Agonistes* hark back to *A Masque* and *Lycidas*; and both contain richly textured, finely pointed allusion to *Paradise Lost: Paradise Regained* in its opening lines and *Samson* in its initial soliloquy. The poems are companion, but contrasting, pieces, as well as the second and third items in a trilogy, with *Paradise Regained*, by virtue of its backward glances and forward gaze, subordinating *Paradise Lost* and *Samson* to itself and thereby achieving the status of centerpiece. There is, moreover, the often avoided yet still obvious context that each of these poems provides for the other. These are poems, as Coleridge might say, that "answer and provoke each other's songs,"[11] with the pairing itself enabling criticism to unmould the essence of each poem.

The principle of opposition is essential to Milton's volume and is essentially corrective of those who see in *Samson Agonistes* a repetition of *Paradise Regained* in a finer tone instead of a more bellicose version of that poem and even to those who, aware of opposition, define it in terms of defeatism and noble defiance instead of perceiving in both poems a call for staying the course and a joint exploration of how and why that matters. In Milton's poems, as later in Byron's and Shelley's, opposites meet—find a point of convergence—in their respective en-

---

[9] "Calm Regained through Passion Spent: The Conclusion of the Miltonic Effort," in *The Prison and the Pinnacle*, ed. Rajan, pp. 13-14.

[10] See Rajan, "The Cunning Resemblance," *Milton Studies*, 7 (1975), 30, and also *The Lofty Rhyme: A Study of Milton's Major Poetry* (Coral Gables: Univ. of Miami Press, 1970), p. 10.

[11] "The Nightingale," in *Lyrical Ballads 1798*, 2nd ed., ed. W.J.B. Owen (London: Oxford Univ. Press, 1969), p. 39.

counters with apocalypse. The Apocalypse is their subtext, and the ideologies at different times attributed to that book their point of reference and concern. It has been said that "if *Paradise Regained* can be thought of as leading into the Gospels, *Samson Agonistes* leads into the Epistles,"[12] which is but to say that what we witness in both poems is Milton's effort to square scriptural myth with historical reality. For this reason especially, these poems also lead away from the Gospels and Epistles into the Book of Revelation and the alternative myths of deliverance therein, with one myth being invalidated by the other.

Interrelated by allusion and echo, and by genre (both poems are *visionary* epics, records in part of *visionary* experience), *Paradise Lost* and *Paradise Regained* are nevertheless unrelated to the usual typology that correlates the Fall in the garden with the Redemption on the cross. This is not to say that there is no typological connection between the two epics. On the contrary, the two temptation cycles are interconnected by anticipation in the penultimate book of *Paradise Lost* (XI.381-420) and through retrospection especially in the proem to *Paradise Regained* and additionally by insistent, pointed reference to the forty days both Moses and Elijah spent in the same "barren waste" (I.352-54; cf. II.266-72, 312-15) which Jesus now travels and to which Adam and Eve were exiled. The experience of the desert, in the Old no less than in the New Testament, was not historical but metaphysical, with that metaphysical experience, according to Herbert Schneidau, being far more important than any verifiable facts of history.[13]

[12] Barker, "Calm Regained through Passion Spent," in *The Prison and the Pinnacle*, ed. Rajan, p. 47.

[13] *Sacred Discontent: The Bible and Western Tradition* (Baton Rouge: Louisiana State Univ. Press, 1976), p. 135; see also p. 144.

When Calvin wonders "whether [Christ] was caried vp on high in deed, or whether it was done by a vision," or whether rest is the end of temptation or just a prologue "to newe conflicts,"[14] he focuses the concerns for a new wilderness hermeneutic, initiating a revisionary interpretation of the temptation story. Whatever Milton may say to the contrary in *De Doctrina Christiana*, it is just this view of the wilderness temptation as a visionary experience, a mental transport, that enables him to conjoin it with another such visionary episode in the conclusion of *Paradise Lost*—and in books of that poem clearly intended to provide a prospect on *Paradise Regained*. The "Hill of Paradise" from which Adam beholds the visions of future history is neither higher nor wider than the one on which "the Tempter set / Our second *Adam* in the Wilderness, / To shew him all Earths Kingdomes and thir Glory" and from which "in Spirit perhaps he also saw / Rich *Mexico* . . . / And *Cusco* in *Peru*" (XI.377-78, 382-84, 406-08). In anticipation of this later, but analogous, mount in history, Adam is "pierc'd / Eevn to the inmost seat of mental sight" and, "now enforc't to close his eyes, / Sunk down and all his Spirits became intranst" (XI.417-20). This visionary moment, in *Paradise Lost* copied as Newton and Todd both note from Daniel 10: 8 and Revelation 1:17, is conjoined by Calvin, and here by Milton, with the Gospel story of Jesus on the mountain top.[15]

Furthermore, the forty days Jesus spends in the desert, as John Evans has shown, were thought to parallel the forty days Adam spent in the garden before the creation of Eve, a par-

---

[14] Calvin, *A Harmonie upon the Three Evangelists*, trans. Eusebius Page (London: Printed by Thomas Adams, 1610), pp. 131, 134. Cf. Daniel Dyke, *Michael and the Dragon, or Christ Tempted and Satan Foyled*, in *Two Treatises: The One of Repentance, the Other of Christs Temptations* (London: Printed by John Beale, 1635), p. 275; Thomas Taylor, *Christs Combate and Conquest; or, the Lyon of the Tribe of Judah* (London: Printed by Cantrel Legge, 1618), p. 188.

[15] See *The Poetical Works of John Milton*, ed. Henry John Todd (7 vols.; London: Printed for J. Johnson, 1801), III, 369.

allelism deriving from the Book of Jubilees and developed by Iraneus and Gregory the Great. Moreover, according to Evans, "the Pelagian view of the Fall as the first example of sin implies a view of the Redemption as the first example of goodness." In such a scheme, resistance to temptation dwarfs the remedy of the Cross, or as Evans argues, Adam's Fall is "neutralized not on the Cross but in the desert. It is in this typological tradition that *Paradise Regained* had its origins."[16] Exactly one decade before the publication of *Paradise Regained*, Samuel Pordage observed that Adam and Eve did not so much leave paradise: "Paradise / Rather departs from them." While Jesus is also represented as "a Pattern, by whose foot-steps ye / May view the way unto Aternity," it is equally clear that for Pordage the real issue is not one of searching out a paradise beyond history but rather of retrieving it within history, which, although it may be fraught with temptations, is fraught with temptations of a special sort and perfectly analogous to experiences Adam has in the final books of Milton's epic where he takes in a vision of the future. The last books of *Paradise Lost* and *Paradise Regained* are equally visionary in that temptations coming upon man in the wilderness are pictures in the mind.[17]

[16] *"Paradise Lost" and the Genesis Tradition* (Oxford: Clarendon Press, 1968), pp. 92n, 104. On Adam's forty days in Eden, see also Christopher Hill, *The Experience of Defeat: Milton and Some Contemporaries* (New York: Viking, 1984), pp. 297-303, and for Hill's political application of the wilderness myth, see these same pages.

[17] *Mundorum Explicatio . . . A Sacred Poem* (London: Printed for Lodowick Lloyd, 1661), pp. 233-34. According to some, says Thomas Fuller (who believes this possibility must be taken into account by all), the kingdoms provide but a "seemingly" outward temptation—one seen in vision. This hermeneutic tradition, then, has the effect of stressing the importance of the eye in the temptation process: "this *Pageant* was but *the shadow* of a *shadow*. . . . The whole Text is but a *Dumb-show*, wherein nothing is spoken, but onely all things presented to the sight of our Saviour" (*A Comment on the Eleven First Verses of the Fourth Chapter of S. Matthew's Gospel* [London: Printed by James Cottrel, 1652], pp. 134-35). In view of Richard Capel's description of Adam's Fall as an overruling of him by lust and an attendant loss of sight—"*Adam* did then put away from him his original righteousnesse, put out his

A similarly unexpected typology forges a link between Milton's brief epic and tragedy. What Barbara Lewalski has said of another poet, and another poetic volume of Milton's century, is even more true of Milton's poems of 1671: "Typology . . . affords a loose unity to the volume, helping to distinguish and relate the two parts in terms of the level of spiritual experience rendered in each."[18] The forty days spent by Jesus in the wilderness are made to preface an Old Testament story, but one with which the Passion story was consistently paired and through which the drama of the Crucifixion was regularly glimpsed. Viewed in terms of the two Testaments, *Paradise Regained* and *Samson Agonistes* may seem discontinuous and disjunctive; viewed in terms of a crucial phase in the liturgical calendar, the poems are perfectly continuous. A story with obvious connections to the Lenten season is paired with a story often correlated (as in early editions of the Book of Common Prayer) with Holy Week. Both poems, containing temptation cycles, are also centered in the tradition of good temptations, with the Father's words in *Paradise Regained* providing an equally apt epigraph for either poem:

> . . . this man born and now up-grown,
> To shew him worthy of his birth divine
> And high prediction, henceforth I expose
> To Satan. . . . (I. 140-43)

Although a good temptation is intended to "proveth" a man,

---

own eyes, and so came in original sin, *viz.* this Lust, that ever after tempts all meer men that are tempted"—it is noteworthy that Milton analogizes Samson and Adam in Book IX of *Paradise Lost* in order to make just this point, to emblematize the darkening of vision that comes with the fall and to expound the relationship between vision and temptation; see Capel, *Tentations: Their Nature, Danger, Cure,* 4th ed. (London: John Bartlet, 1650), p. 5. I am grateful to Alinda Sumers-Ingraham for this citation.

[18] *Protestant Poetics and the Seventeenth-Century Religious Lyric* (Princeton: Princeton Univ. Press, 1979), p. 142.

as William Cowper remarks, it may have the opposite effect
of "snar[ing] him, or manifest[ing] some weaknes in him."[19]
It may in fact be used to unmask hypocrisy. Thus out of their
shared experience emerge decidedly different heroes: one who
is "wiser far" than to be lured "to the bait of Women" (II.
204-05), the other who is tempted and twice succumbs to their
allurements; one who conquers through weakness, the other
by strength; one whose forte is mental, the other's mortal fight.
The sense of discrepancy between the heroes of the two poems
is much stronger than any sense of analogy so that, instead of
thinking that "the central theme of *Samson Agonistes* is the
reconstruction of . . . Samson's *heroism*,"[20] we should begin
to talk about that poem as engaged in the deconstruction of
Samson's *supposed* heroism. And because *Samson Agonistes* is
a poem, it will not do to argue that if Milton had meant to
break with convention, he should have made his intentions
clearer. Poetry is the medium of the delicate and subtle insight,
and Milton's poem represents not nearly so great a breach
with convention as has hitherto been supposed.

   Both poems, it is true, are conspicuously organized around
a triple temptation and capitalize upon the identity crisis harbored within that formula. Thus as F. Michael Krouse contends, Jesus must "parry Satan's thrusts without revealing His
identity . . . [and] conceal the very source of His power. The
parallel with Samson lies in Samson's revealing his Nazarite-
ship." As Krouse also reports, the parallelism between Jesus
and Samson is also secured through the *agonistes* epithet here
given to Samson but more usually attributed to Christ.[21] And

[19] *Three Heavenly Treatises, Concerning Christ* (London: Printed for John Budge,
1612), p. 129; cf. *De Doctrina Christiana*, VI, 338.
[20] Andrew Milner, *John Milton and the English Revolution: A Study in the Sociology
of Literature* (Totowa: Barnes and Noble, 1981), p. 207.
[21] *Milton's Samson and the Christian Tradition* (Princeton: Princeton Univ. Press
for the Univ. of Cincinnati, 1949), pp. 101, 115. Following Rupert of St. Heribert,
Krouse also proposes that "The lion which rushed upon Samson in the road to Timnath
was equivalent to Satan tempting Christ in the wilderness" (p. 52); and later, with

there is a still more striking, and disturbing, parallel: Samson's story, like Jesus', was frequently cast as a saint's life; yet by the time *Samson Agonistes* was published, the Samson story was being used in such contexts to mark the degeneration, not regeneration, of the hero-saint. A positive is converted into a negative example, a warning; a life not to be imitated jars with the example set by Jesus, every aspect of whose life, especially the phase of it spent in the wilderness, was subject to imitation. There is no small irony in Milton's choice, as an epigraph for his poem, of the Aristotelian proposition, "Tragoedia est imitation actionis seriae, etc." (twice repeated), and of his then presenting as the subject of his tragedy Samson, whose life was universally acclaimed as inappropriate for imitation and who, in comparison with Jesus, is a "false resemblance . . . , / An empty cloud" (IV.320-21).

---

reference to the placement of *Paradise Regained* and *Samson Agonistes* in the same volume, Krouse argues that for anyone coming to Milton's tragedy immediately after reading this "vivid portrayal of Satan's temptations of Christ . . . , Samson was not simply Samson here, nor Dalila simply Dalila" (p. 123). Furthermore, Krouse pushes an analogy between the pinnacle temptation and Harapha's temptation of Samson (pp. 128-30). Finally, Krouse would interrelate both *Paradise Regained and Samson Agonistes* with *Paradise Lost:* "Samson stands for more than the victorious Nazarite, the faithful Champion of God. He brings to full circle the immense story which Milton took up in *Paradise Lost* and continued in *Paradise Regained.* . . . But *Paradise Regained* did not complete the cycle. . . . It was left to demonstrate the victory on the human level. Samson's story, paralleling as it does the story of *Christus Victor*, reveals him as *Homo Victor*, a palpable exemplification of the meaning to Man of his Redemption" (pp. 132-33). Without denying the interconnection of all these poems, my own argument presents an alternative to Krouse's conclusion. The first of the parallels observed by Krouse was formulated in the seventeenth century by Benjamin Keach: "*Sampson* in respect of his great Strength, as some conceive, was a Type of Christ. . . . He conquered a stout Lion in the Desert, hand to hand, as it were: So Christ overcame the roaring Lion, the Devil, in the Wilderness and made him flie" (*Troposchematologia: Types and Figures; or, a Treatise of the Metaphors, Allegories, and Express Similitudes, & c. Contained in the Bible* [London: Printed for John Hancock, 1682], p. 418). In addition to the parallelisms tabulated by Krouse, Robert Burton implies another—that Samson, like Jesus, has few wants in the wilderness: Samson requires only water, and Jesus does not even need bread (*The Anatomy of Melancholy*, ed. A. R. Shilleto [3 vols.; London: George Bell and Sons, 1893], II, 181).

It was once thought that "the connexion between *Paradise Regained* and *Samson Agonistes*, originally accidental, is not kept up"; that the lack of connection between these poems is nonetheless compensated for by the planned continuities between Milton's epics, with *Paradise Regained* relating to *Paradise Lost* as "its sequel."[22] This peculiarity, even perversity, of poetic placement is accompanied by an unobserved and no less curious paradox of interpretation: typological tradition, almost always frustrated and even sometimes subverted in these poems, provides the logic of connection between them, affirming their status as companion pieces—the twin halves, legitimate if not identical, of a single poetic statement.

Typological tradition yields important supporting props for the argument that the connection between these poems, their placement together in the same volume, the tragedy subordinated to the brief epic, is neither accidental nor capricious but a deliberate, deft calculation on Milton's part. This is not to say that typological connections sanction typological readings of either poem, only that such connections are a bond between these poems in which the ironies of those connections are dissuasive of such readings, at least of the sort that stress similitudes rather than discrepancies, simple equivalents over multivalencies. Nor is this to say that *Paradise Regained* does not exhibit obvious, and obviously important, links with *Paradise Lost* (see, e.g., I. 1-7; II. 133-34, 349; IV. 150, 606-08), only that those with *Samson* are of equal interest and interpretively, perhaps, of more importance. Typological tradition itself accounts for the fact, as Rajan notices, that interconnections between these poems "both play against and play upon each other."[23] Samson may not be mentioned in *Paradise Re-*

[22] *The Poetical Works of John Milton*, ed. David Masson (3 vols.; London: Macmillan, 1882), III, 2, 4.

[23] "To Which Is Added *Samson Agonistes*," in *The Prison and the Pinnacle*, ed. Rajan, pp. 90-91.

gained nor Jesus in *Samson Agonistes*, but the two figures are nevertheless made to face one another in the 1671 volume and in such a way as to pit an emergent against a failed prophet and the bright light of vision against the darkness of the subjected plain.

As the once secure link between Samson ending the lives of the Philistines and Christ coming to end life on earth is broken, the Samson story, losing its analogy with the Second Coming, is correlated all the more insistently with the First Coming; and then as the analogy between Samson's final days, and Christ's, loses its potency, another correlation, this time between Samson's trials as a judge and those of Jesus in the wilderness, achieves prominence. A new set of analogies secures this linkage, behind which stands the typologist's tendency to correlate temptations in the Old Testament with those of Jesus in the New, comparing a whole complex of previous temptations, one with the other, and thereupon contrasting them all with those experienced by Jesus in the wilderness. Thus Lancelot Andrewes observes, "that which was in the olde Testament the Temptation of *Meribah*, is here in the new Testament the Temptation of Wildernes: that which was there the Temptation of *Massah*, is heere the temptation of the Pinacle." Later, Andrewes conjoins the pinnacle temptation and Samson's hurling down the pillars, Samson in this regard representing the foolish in the world, those who "have begun in the spirite" but who "will ende in the flesh," in contrast with Jesus who, overcoming the flesh, triumphs in the spirit.[24] From this analogy others eventually are spun.

The episodes at the pillars and on the pinnacle had been explained in terms of divine impulsion but could also be used to differentiate true from false inspiration, as well as to illustrate the propositions that God never leads men to a stage or

---

[24] *The Wonderfull Combate (for Gods Glorie and Mans Salvation) betweene Christ and Satan* (London: Printed by John Charlwood, 1592), ff. 43ᵛ, 74.

theater but only to the Word, that nothing is ever lost by waiting upon divine providence. The episode at the pillars and the kingdoms temptation had also become linked within a perspective from which each was regarded as illusory: "I finde, although a man have the strength of *Sampson* . . . all are nothing, all are but fantasticall . . . to the eye: as those Kingdomes which the *Divell* offered to Christ."[25] In Samson's rending of the lion is seen Jesus in the wilderness subduing the devil, Samson here emerging as "a notable type of Christ vanquishing and triumphing over Satan that roaring Lion . . . by the sole vertue of his own power."[26] Samson and Jesus are equally prisoners in this life, and each is shown—Samson with the lion, Jesus in the desert with Satan—being exercised during "initiatory encounters," although for all their similarity, this type-casting eventually yields to the perception that Jesus, a spiritual Samson, is "the better *Nazarite*,"[27] a stronger, more perfect, hence more glorious Samson—a victorious not a defeated hero, a spiritual warrior rather than one to blood inured.

These sorts of analogies are cited with growing frequency to emphasize, through Samson, the humanity of Jesus; and each of these figures, in his tearing down the bar and opening the gates into paradise, is regarded as a deliverer, Samson

[25] Edward Vaughan, *A Plaine and Perfect Method for the Easie Understanding of the Whole Bible* (London: Printed by T. S., 1617), p. 3; and Daniel Dyke, *Michael and the Dragon, or Christ Tempted and Satan Foyled* (London: Printed by John Beale, 1635), pp. 216, 355.

[26] I quote from John Downame et al., *Annotations upon All the Books of the Old and New Testaments* (2 vols.; London: Printed by Evan Tyler, 1657), I, no pagination: note to Judges 14:6. See also John Trapp, *Annotations upon the Old and New Testament* (5 vols.; London: Printed by Robert White, 1662), I, 84.

[27] See Joseph Hall, *Contemplations on the Historical Passages of the Old and New Testaments* (3 vols.; Edinburgh: Willison and Darling, 1770), I, 331, 340, 351 (see also p. 361); Joseph Salmon, *A Rout, A Rout, or Some Part of the Armies Quarters Beaten Up* (London: Printed for G. C., 1649), p. 30. See as well Thomas Taylor, *Christ Revealed: or the Old Testament Explained* (London: Printed by M. F., 1635), p. 56, and Trapp, *Annotations upon the Old and New Testament*, I, 89.

commencing what is left for Jesus to complete.[28] The situations of Samson and Jesus reinforce such analogies, with Jesus in the wilderness and Samson at Gaza both being isolated and alone in their suffering and from that posture inviting reflection upon their private and public persons, the natural and the spiritual man, the nature and proof of divine authority, the prospects for apocalyptic deliverance, and the efficacy of millennial expectations. Often the product of such reflections is a Samson motivated by private desire, a natural man whose claims to divine impulsion are unwarranted, an agent in a broken apocalypse who himself provides a profound critique of millenarianism. Such a Samson, in turn, emerges as a foil for the heroism of Jesus, the false and fallen prophet standing against Jesus who is the agent of divine vision and the spirit of true prophecy. "The noblest duell that ever was fought, was between Christ and the Divell," according to Daniel Featley, "and the pitched field was the *wildernesse*."[29] All duels fought in the wilderness advance for comparison, although not all of them match this one in nobility.

The wilderness episodes—Samson's temptations and Jesus'—become linked, it seems, only for the purpose of differentiating them and, in the process, of neutralizing the Samson story by subordinating it to Christ's. In *Eikon Basilike*, for example, the experiences of Charles I are correlated with those of Job, Jonah, David, and Solomon and, more interestingly and importantly, with those of Samson and Christ. "The solitude they have confined Me unto, adds the Wilder-

---

[28] See, e.g., Pordage, *Mundorum Explicatio*, pp. 233-34, and Thomas Taylor, *Christs Victorie over the Dragon: or Satans Downfall* (London: Printed for R. Dawlman, 1633), p. 470.

[29] *Clavis Mystica: A Key Opening Divers Difficult and Mysterious Texts of Holy Scripture* (London: Printed for Nicolas Bourne, 1636), p. 56. But see, too, Nathaniel Fiennes, who slides easily between allusions to the Samson story and to the episode of Jesus standing on the pinnacle (*Private Papers of State* [1640], ed. John Rushworth [8 vols.; London: Printed for D. Brown et al., 1721-22], IV, 180).

nesse to my temptations," writes Charles (or his spokesman), who has already analogized his own experiences with those of Christ on the mountain and pinnacle and drawn from those analogies the lesson that the kingdoms are not worth gaining— nothing is worth gaining—by wrong and violent means. The Samson story is thereupon alluded to in order to instance that one just does not, should not, readily submit to others:

> This were as if *Sampson* should have consented, not
> only to binde his own hands, and cut off his haire,
> but to put out his own eyes, that the *Philistins* might
> with the more safety mock, and abuse him; which
> they chose rather to doe, then quite to destroy him.[30]

The Samson story is at once a positive and a negative example: follow Samson in not submitting to the enemy, but follow the enemy rather in mocking without destroying; now be like Samson and now like his Philistine oppressors.

Not just here but commonly in the seventeenth century, whenever the Samson legend disagrees with that of Jesus, it is subordinated to, then corrected by, the New Testament story. That Milton has this sort of contrastive relationship in mind is suggested by the intertextual connections involving *Paradise Regained* and *Samson Agonistes* and the ironies attending them. Milton's brief epic casts a beam of light through the gloom of history as it is figured in *Samson Agonistes*. From one point of view, *Samson* contains the sad reality, the elemental despair that issues forth from the failed idealisms of *Paradise Regained*; from another, it is as if *Samson* contains the illusion and *Paradise Regained* the true reality. *Samson*, that is, transforms the historical reality into an illusion, whereas *Paradise Regained* would wrest from history its potentiality and thereby transform idealisms into the reality of history. Neither poem

[30] *Eikon Basilike* (London: n. p., 1648), pp. 206, 77; see also pp. 31, 72, 208, 211.

reduces to an ideology, but both strike a relationship with an ideology of which each is more than a mere reflection. Both poems, that is, foster a perception of their opposing ideologies, each looking at a distance upon the other, and, as Terry Eagleton claims of analogous forms of ideological confrontation, "contribut[ing] to our deliverance from the ideological illusion."[31]

Typology is a habit of mind—sometimes a vital part, other times not, of the consciousness of a culture. In the seventeenth century, typology was very much a part of that consciousness, so much so that an audience of readers would have discerned in *Paradise Regained* implicit reference to the Samson story and, conversely, in *Samson Agonistes* reference to the wilderness temptation of Jesus. There is, however, explicit connection between these poems, for in Milton's brief epic Jesus refers to the people of Dan taking up with idols in the aftermath of Samson's tragedy; in the Preface to *Samson Agonistes*, Milton himself sets the view of tragedy expressed here within the perspective afforded on the same genre both by the Jesus and Satan of *Paradise Regained*. The two poems are interconnected in these instances by allusion but more often by an elaborate system of echoing. Such allusions are the equivalent of scholia transferred from the margins into the text itself. These allusions, but even more emphatically the "rebounds of intertextual echo," as John Hollander theorizes, "distort the original voice," in the instance of these poems, the voice of Jesus, "in order to interpret it." Each poem is an echo chamber for the other with "language answering language" and in a "kind of phonetic mimicry," which, again to quote from Hollander, produces "analytic irony" out of this dramatic and typological play.[32]

[31] *Marxism and Literary Criticism* (Berkeley and Los Angeles: Univ. of California Press, 1976), p. 19.

[32] *The Figure of Echo: A Mode of Allusion in Milton and After* (Berkeley and Los Angeles: Univ. of California Press, 1981), pp. 111, 21, 24.

It has been said that "Milton's return to the Old Testament allows him to incorporate both the Jesus and the Satan of *Paradise Regained* within his new, and for him more inclusive, hero."[33] And it is true that these two poems are interconnected but in subtler, more confounding ways: not by quotation and paraphrase but by allusion and echo that, creating dissonances and discontinuities, call for differentiations between heroes, with Samson emerging from such contrasts not as a more encompassing but as a diminished version of the Jesus of *Paradise Regained*. In fine, Samson is less like Jesus than like Satan and perhaps still more like the Adam of *Paradise Lost* who to whatever glories born, in the words of Milton's brief epic, falls "Degraded by himself" (IV.312). In turning from *Paradise Regained* to *Samson Agonistes*, Milton, as he had previously done, must change his notes to tragedy and present an action deemed by Luther and others unworthy of imitation.

Samson the judge and Jesus the king, both rising to their heroic stature when they reach "youth's full flower" (*PR* I. 67; cf. *SA* 938) are also both represented as images of a decidedly different deity, the one whose law is vengeance, the other whose only law is love. Others in Milton's century had been preoccupied with ruling in the style of God, but here Milton's concern is with an anterior question: what is, or should be, God's style? The sinister, squabbling gods of *Samson Agonistes*—"thou shalt see, or rather to thy sorrow / Soon feel, whose God is strongest, thine or mine" (1154-55)—are so personated as to make not only Dagon but Samson's "God" seem ridiculous (cf. *PR* IV.342). In the face of Jesus are to be found "glimpses of his Fathers glory" (I.93), is to be seen the "True Image of the Father" (IV.596). In the figure of Samson, the Chorus discovers only "The Image of [God's] strength" (706), the image of a snarling, combative deity.

---

[33] G. Wilson Knight, *The Golden Labyrinth: A Study of British Drama* (New York: W. W. Norton, 1962), p. 127.

That is, Jesus reveals the totality, is in every respect the similitude of deity, whereas Samson is but an aspect, a manifestation of the dark side of a deity; and it is a deity who
produces through Samson the claims for justice which express
themselves in vengeance and violence, the very qualities that
the God of Milton's epics cannot brook. Nor apparently can
Milton himself; for in *De Doctrina Christiana*, he insists that
God takes no pleasure in destruction or death, not even in the
destruction and death of the wicked (VI, 173). If Jesus is an
image, Samson is a mere shadow of God.

It is of some moment that, in *Paradise Regained*, Satan
tempts Jesus to fashion himself in what will be the image of
Milton's Samson so "that all the world / Could not sustain thy
Prowess, or subsist / In battel" (III.18-20) and to employ
force (a means Satan had already rejected [I.97] to deliver
his people from servitude [IV.380-84]—a means that Jesus
himself now rejects as "argument / Of human weakness rather
then of strength" (III.401-02). Jesus, "unarm'd," chases his
enemies "with the terror of his voice" (IV.626-27). "For
Milton there is no strength except spiritual strength, and no
conflict except mental conflict," says Northrop Frye; "hence
the prophecy that the Messiah will defeat the serpent can only
be fulfilled by a dramatic dialogue."[34] Representations of temptation and strife can be only inward, with both poems belonging to a species of prophecy and sharing with prophecy a
profound interiority.

The trials of Jesus and Samson alike are centered in a mental
theater. Before Jesus goes to the temple he is afflicted with a
swarming multitude of thoughts (I.196-97), and then enters
the wilderness, journeys into himself "with holiest Meditations
fed" (II.110), achieving finally an "untroubl'd mind"
(IV.401). Not the Jesus but the Satan of *Paradise Regained*

[34] *Spiritus Mundi: Essays on Literature, Myth, and Society* (1976; rpt. Bloomington:
Indiana Univ. Press, 1983), p. 202.

anticipates the mental and emotional state of Samson. Like Satan who is "inly rackt" (III.203), "Perplex'd and troubl'd" (IV.1), and eventually "swoln with rage" (IV.499), Samson's mind is a turmoil of "restless thoughts, . . . like a deadly swarm / Of Hornets arm'd" (19-20), with the patience he seems later to have won exploding into the rage that produces the temple holocaust. Samson's is "a troubl'd mind," tumored and festering with wounds (185-86). Jesus may cause the "fiery Serpent" to flee his path as he enters the wilderness (I.312); but as we learn from Genesis and its commentators, and as Milton remembers in *Samson Agonistes* in the image of the "ev'ning Dragon" (1692), "Dan [or Samson] shall judge his people. . . . Dan shall be a serpent in the way, a horned snake in the path" (Genesis 49:16-17).[35]

If the fiery serpent is one that kills by burning and scorching, it is a fit emblem of Samson, or at least of that dimension of his history remembered by Milton in his projected title, *Samson pursophorus*. The evening dragon, the fiery serpent, may also remind us of the fiery Lucifer and the prophecy of

[35] See *The Complete Poetry of John Milton*, rev. ed., ed. John T. Shawcross (Garden City: Doubleday, 1971), p. 618, n. 30. From Luther onward, Samson was customarily identified as the serpent in the way, the viper in the path; see *Luther's Works*, ed. Jaroslav Pelikan et al. (55 vols.; St. Louis: Concordia Press; Philadelphia: Fortress Press, 1955-76), IX, 281-82. For an elaboration of this tradition, see Rollenson, *Twelve Propheticall Legacies: or Twelve Sermons vpon Iacobs Last Will and Testament* (London: Printed for Arthur Johnson, 1612), esp. pp. 143-53. As Rollenson shows, Dan was often taken to be a generic name for Samson. The fiery dragon is associated with the devil, temples, and idolatry, and also emblematizes treacherous destruction in Edward Topsel's *The History of Four-footed Beasts and Serpents*, 2nd ed. (1607; London: Published for G. Sawbridge, 1658), p. 703. For another Old Testament passage sometimes thought to refer to Samson, see the following one from the Book of Amos: "And I raised up your sons for prophets, and of your young men for Nazarites. *Is it* not even thus, O ye children of Israel? saith the Lord. But ye gave the Nazarites wine to drink; and commanded the prophets, saying, Prophesy not" (2:11-12). But of those raised up as a Nazarite, Samson is just as commonly regarded as singular in being the one who is also allowed to fall justly into the hands of his enemies.

disaster in Book XV of Ovid's *Metamorphoses*, of the threats of murder and of death which come at a time when history should be undergoing a metamorphosis and entering a new phase; when like a phoenix, having grown old, history should rise up again in another form. The eagle, though not an Ovidian image here, makes much the same point. In *Areopagitica*, Milton had already elided Samson and this secular bird which, in the parlance of Revelation's commentators, emblematizes the human condition: mankind occupying a middle zone between angels and beasts, traveling above the earth but below the sun, in a region of shadow and error. For all the intimations of an apocalypse, none seems to occur, however. Instead of holy are unholy transformations, the earth continues to be drenched in blood; thoughts which should have been turned to peace are still on war, killing, death. The apocalypse of history is not going to occur without a metamorphosis of mind, an alteration of consciousness, which in its contracted form is represented by Milton's Samson and in its expanded form, by the Jesus of *Paradise Regained*.

Jesus and Samson both make signally important appearances at a temple, the one as a youth and later as an adult, the other only as an adult. The experience at the temple is the initiation of Jesus' career, contributes to the formation of his public posture fully achieved atop another temple. In the case of Samson, however, the same experience terminates a public career and involves a juxtaposition of the public good with private motives. Jesus commits himself to the former, whereas Samson subordinates the former to the latter. The liberation of their people, the deliverance of their respective nations, is an issue foregrounded in both poems, but in such a way as to discriminate Jesus' finer moral tones from Samson's cruder sensibility. Commencing his public life by going to the temple ostensibly to learn but actually to teach, Jesus eventually goes atop the temple to learn; he finds himself where Samson loses himself, defines and discovers himself where Samson, even if inadvertently, destroys himself.

In *Paradise Regained*, Jesus avers:

> I went into the Temple, there to hear
> The Teachers of our Law, and to propose
> What might improve my knowledge or their own;
> And was admir'd by all, yet this not all
> To which my Spirit aspir'd, victorious deeds
> Flam'd in my heart, heroic acts, one while
> To rescue *Israel* from the *Roman* yoke,
> Then to subdue and quell o're all the earth
> Brute violence and proud Tyrannick pow'r,
> Till truth were freed, and equity restor'd:
> Yet held it more humane, more heavenly first
> By winning words to conquer willing hearts,
> And make perswasion do the work of fear;
> At least to try, and teach the erring Soul
> Not wilfully mis-doing, but unware
> Misled; the stubborn only to subdue. (I.211-26)

If Jesus goes from the temple to the desert and, later, from the temple-top returns to civilization as a deliverer of the oppressed, Samson goes from the temple to his death, at the temple surrendering his own role as a deliverer of his people. *Samson Agonistes* begins with a recollection that "Promise was that I / Should *Israel* from *Philistian* yoke deliver" (38-39) and proceeds into the irony that "this great Deliverer" Samson now finds himself "Eyeless in *Gaza* at the Mill with slaves, / Himself in bonds under *Philistian* yoke" (40-42). Unlike Jesus, who commits himself to mental fight, Samson, even at the end, is defying others "to the trial of mortal fight" (1175). His "fist is free" (1235), ready to engage in "the force of Conquest" (1206) in order to effect "The desolation of a Hostile City" (1561). "*Mortal fight*" is just "another phrase in chivalry"[36] in this poem, another component of the romance tradition of which the Satan of *Paradise Regained* is so enamored and Jesus so scornful.

At the temple, Samson declares:

> Now *of my own accord* such other tryal
> I mean to shew you of my strength, yet greater;
> As with amaze shall strike all who behold . . .
>
>   . . . those two massie Pillars
> With horrible convulsion to and fro,
> He tugg'd, he shook, till down they came and drew
> The whole roof after them, with burst of thunder
> Upon the heads of all who sate beneath,
> Lords, Ladies, Captains, Councellors, or Priests,
> Thir choice nobility and flower. . . .
> *Samson* with these immixt, inevitably
> Pulld down the same destruction on himself;
> The vulgar only scap'd who stood without.
>   (1643-59; my italics)

What Samson does, by his own admission, is done of *his own accord*; he kills, and killing, we are told, is an act never coming from God but "meerely from Satan."[37] The Semichorus, not Samson, attributes his action to divine impulsion: "With inward eyes illuminated / His fierie vertue rouz'd" (1689-90). The action is performed impulsively, without reflection on liberation and deliverance and without regard for the authority of inspiration such as is displayed by Gideon in another of the inset narratives in the Book of Judges. And if Samson's final act is performed subsequent to "winning words," they are not of the sort meant "to conquer willing hearts, / And make perswasion do the work of fear" (*PR* I.222-23). That anyone

[36] *The Poetical Works of John Milton*, 5th ed., ed. Henry John Todd (4 vols.; London: Rivingtons, 1852), III, 287.
[37] Dyke, *Michael and the Dragon*, p. 219.

escapes the catastrophe, mindlessly wrought upon the multi-tudes, is Milton's, not Samson's, devising. *Paradise Regained* ends with Satan bringing Jesus to his "Fathers house" (IV. 552) and with Jesus, here becoming one with his Father, "Home to his Mothers house private return[ing]" (IV.639), ready now to enter upon his ministry and "begin to save mankind" (IV.635). *Samson Agonistes*, on the other hand, con-cludes with a Samson who, having failed in his divine mission, is returned publicly, by "funeral train / Home to his Fathers house" (1732-33) where he is crowned not with immortal but with earthly fame, not with amaranthus but with laurel, and thereupon built an earthly monument. Samson's people, we learn in the aftermath of this tragedy, are now without a deliverer.

The fame won by Samson is the same fame extolled by Satan in *Paradise Regained* but rejected by Jesus:

> For what is glory but the blaze of fame,
> The peoples praise . . .
> This is true glory and renown, when God
> Looking on the Earth, with approbation marks
> The just man, and divulges him through Heaven
> To all his Angels, who with true applause
> Recount his praises. . . . (III.47-48, 60-64)

On earth, says Jesus, "glory is false glory, attributed / To things not glorious, men not worthy of fame" (III.69-70). The hero of Milton's tragedy is a "secular bird" (1707), his fame and glory recounted on earth as the people's praise and won by means just the opposite of those recommended by Jesus: "Without . . . violence; / By deeds of peace, by wisdom em-inent, / By patience, temperance" (III.90-92). While his body dies, Samson's fame survives—in time, in history; it is a secular fame generated by a people who now legendize the dead Samson, making of him an earthly idol.

Manoa, having through most of the play forgotten about Samson's mission, may at its end proclaim that Samson has brought freedom to his people (1714-15), but we know from the Book of Judges that Samson has brought no freedom at all, and we learn this too from *Paradise Regained*:

> Should I of these the liberty regard,
> Who freed. . . .
> Unhumbl'd, unrepentant, unreform'd,
> Headlong would follow; and to thir Gods perhaps
> Of *Bethel* and of *Dan*? no, let them serve
> Thir enemies . . . (III.427-32)[38]

Samson was, of course, the first hero of the tribe of Dan and as a hero summed up in himself the failings of his own people. Moreover, by the criterion formulated by Jesus in *Paradise Regained*, Samson seems to be no hero at all. Here Jesus explains why all Samson's efforts, including his exertions at the temple, must be judged untimely:

> What wise and valiant man would seek to free
> These thus degenerate, by themselves enslav'd,
> Or could of inward slaves make outward free?
>
> (IV.143-45)

Timely delays amount to an avoidance of brute violence and are a way of keeping faith in time of trouble. The cause was

---

[38] "The sense seems to be this," says Todd, quoting Charles Dunster: " 'Who, if they were freed from that captivity, which was inflicted on them as a punishment for their disobedience, idolatry, and other vices, would return to take possession of their country, as something to which . . . they had long been unjustly deprived; without shewing the least sense . . . of God's goodness in pardoning and restoring them. This change in their situation would produce none whatever in their conduct, but they would retain the same hardened hearts, and the same wicked dispositions as before, and most probably would betake themselves to their old idolatries and other abominations'," which, as Jesus knows, is precisely what the Israelites do in the aftermath of Samson's tragedy; see *The Poetical Works of John Milton*, ed. Todd (1801), IV, 216.

too good to have been fought for. Moses Wall says as much to Milton in 1659:

> . . . let us pity humane Frailty when those who had made deep Protestations of their Zeal for our Liberty both spiritual and civill, and made the fairest offers to be asserters thereof, and whom we thereupon trusted; when those being instated in power, shall betray this good Thing committed to them, and lead us back to egypt, and by that Force which we gave them, to win us Liberty, hold us fast in Chains. . . . (VII, 511)

Through Jesus Milton says as much here and, in *A Treatise of Civil Power*, addressing the same issue, expresses similar sentiments: God's glory is fulfilled not by strength but by weakness, "by force, inward and spiritual, not outward and corporeal"; for "force neither instructs in religion nor begets repentance or amendment of life, but, on the contrarie, hardness of heart, formalitie, hypocrisie, and . . . everie way increase[s] sin" (VII, 266, 269).

Central to both poems are their respective heroes' claims to divine authority and their commissions to the cause of liberation. The narrator of *Paradise Regained* speaks of the "Spirit who ledst this glorious Eremite / Into the Desert" (I.8-9), and Jesus recalls the same moment:

> . . . I knew the time
> Now full, that I no more should live obscure,
> But openly begin, as best becomes
> The Authority which I deriv'd from Heaven.
> And now by some strong motion I am led
> Into this Wilderness. . . . (I.286-91)

Jesus continually invokes that "Authority" who brought him hither and will bring him hence (I.335-36). The aforementioned speech by Jesus finds a counterpart in Milton's tragedy:

> . . . I begin to feel
> Some rouzing motions in me which dispose
> To something extraordinary my thoughts. (1381-83)

What those extraordinary thoughts are we are never told but can surmise that, nurtured by Samson's desire for revenge, they involve some program for its execution. When Jesus "on was led," he was also disposed to "thoughts / Accompanied of things past and to come / . . . as well might recommend / Such Solitude before choicest Society" (I.299-302): "How to begin, how to accomplish best / His end of being on Earth, and mission high" (II.113-14) of deliverance, a matter about which Samson thinks less than, and differently from, Jesus— a matter which becomes a preoccupation for him not from the moment he enters upon his judgeship but in the moment when, blinded, he is placed in prison and, for all practical purposes, relieved of his judgeship. Then he thinks of times past and the present, "what once I was, and what am now" (22), tardily remembering the "Promise . . . that I / Should *Israel* from *Philistian* yoke deliver" (38-39). He does not initially recall that his charge is to *begin* the work of deliverance but assumes that in his own lifetime he is to accomplish a full deliverance.

If in *Paradise Regained* the prophetic narrator confirms that Jesus goes into the desert, "the Spirit leading" (I.189), the prophetic poet responsible for composing "The Argument" to *Samson Agonistes* allows no more than that Samson was "perswaded inwardly" that the call to the temple "was from God"; the Chorus urges Samson on, *hoping* "the Holy One / Of *Israel*" will be his guide, that the same spirit which "first rusht" on Samson will be "in thee now at need" (1427-28, 1435-37). Manoa declares unequivocally, but only in the aftermath of the tragedy, that "all this" was accomplished "With God not parted from him, as was feard" (1718-19). What casts doubt on such claims at the end of the play are Samson's own seemingly mindless claims early on in the play: "what I motion'd was of God . . . / . . . I thought it lawful from my former act" (222, 231). Such doubts are compounded by the contexts in which such claims are made, of Samson's patently unlawful marriages, of his indiscriminate slaughtering not once but many times. The dubious character of Samson's early assertions is accentuated by Manoa himself: "thou didst plead / Divine impulsion . . . / . . . I state not that" (421-22, 24). *Samson Agonistes* is yet another reminder, says John Knott, of what in prose works and epics alike is always Milton's target for criticism: "The real thrust of Milton's attack . . . is directed against those who appropriate to themselves 'the Spirit of God' "—a gesture that curtailed their liberty no less than the liberty of others.[39]

It may be folly to be ruled by the individual conscience when supposedly divine commands are at odds with God's law. In such circumstances, Milton implies in *De Doctrina Christiana*, to abrogate the law is to go down into Egypt and into the house of bondage. For Samson the judge to abrogate the law is curious indeed, for "the Judges were a sort of Magistrate inferior to kings, and could neither make new laws, nor impose any tributes, but were the supreme Executors of Gods Laws and Commands."[40] The "high exploits" Samson credits himself with having performed, while "Full of divine instinct" (525-26), are without exception unlawful under the Old Dispensation and are of the sort ridiculed by Jesus in *Paradise Regained*. Although he comes to displace the law, Jesus never breaks the law; subject to the law, Samson repeatedly transgresses it, confusing a physical with a spiritual stimulus and mistaking an internal impulse for a divine prompting. Helen

---

[39] *The Sword of the Spirit: Puritan Responses to the Bible* (Chicago: Univ. of Chicago Press, 1980), p. 124.

[40] Matthew Poole, *Annotations upon the Holy Bible* (5 vols.; London: Printed by Robert Roberts, 1688), "Argument" to Judges. See also Henry Robinson, *A Moderate Answer to Mr. Prins Full Reply* (London: Printed for Benjamin Allen, 1645), pp. 19-24.

Damico understands the situation exactly: "in both origin and consequence . . . , the heroes' 'motions' in *Paradise Regained* and *Samson Agonistes* differ markedly and may be seen as representative of the generative and destructive aspects of inspiration."[41]

I was led—the very language is crucial by virtue of its presence in the one poem and virtual absence from the other (see *PR* I.192, 252, 299). The Spirit leads, it never drives, and never does it compel a man to violence. There is the suggestion here that Jesus, not Samson, is being led on, a little further onward by each temptation, into a world of vision, the very word "led" being "expressive of a prophetic afflatus and illumination" and serving, like a code word, to authenticate the inspiration, making clear it is of God and not Satan.[42] In the words of Lancelot Andrewes, "Christ was not hastie, but stayed Gods good time" and was thus able to realize and complete his mission.[43] The dialectic within *Paradise Regained* that pits the false against the true prophet operates intertextually as well. It is Samson, like Satan, who abuses prophecy and follows it "to his fatal snare" (*PR* I.441). Jesus, in contrast, stands as "an inward Oracle" (I.463) and, led himself, leads others into the truth of the divine vision, away from which Samson was often thought to have fallen.[44] Samson, from the

---

[41] "Duality in Dramatic Vision: A Structural Analysis of *Samson Agonistes*," *Milton Studies*, 12 (1979), 105.

[42] I quote from Hugh Farmer, *An Inquiry into the Nature and Design of Christ's Temptation in the Wilderness* (London: Printed for A. Millar, 1761), p. 42 (see also pp. vi, 36, 40-41); see, too, Joseph Hall, *Contemplations upon the Remarkable Passages in the Life of the Holy Jesus* (London: Printed by E. Flesher, 1679), p. 64.

[43] *The Wonderfull Combate*, p. 98.

[44] In *The Sealed Book Opened* (London: Printed for Anthony Williamson, 1656), William Guild identifies Samson with the third angel of the Apocalypse, the star called wormwood, who, falling away from the divine vision, Samson-like, burns up the teachings of God (p. 65). On the other hand, in *Gods Love-Tokens, and the Afflicted Mans Lessons* (London: Printed by Richard Badger, 1637), John Trapp identifies Samson with the Beast's party and hence with those rebuked in Revelation 3:19 (p. 114).

vantage point afforded by *Paradise Regained* and the evidence provided by Milton's tragedy, never "reigns within himself, and rules / Passions, Desires, and Fears" (II.466-67); in fact, by such standards he must be numbered among those unfit to rule because they are "head-strong . . . / Subject . . . to Anarchy within, / Or lawless passions" (II.470-72).

Paradise Regained and especially *Samson Agonistes* dwell upon the annunciation of their respective heroes' births by way of focusing upon their respective commissions for deliverance. That is, in analogy with Old Testament narrative art, Milton builds into his poems type-scenes like the annunciation and allows them, through differences in similar patterns, to operate interpretively, indeed as guides to interpretation. Immediately, Samson asks, "wherefore was my birth from Heaven foretold / Twice by an Angel" (23-24)? And upon seeing the forsaken Samson, Manoa asks, "For this did the Angel twice descend" (361)? Samson remembers again that his "birth from Heav'n [was] foretold" by a "Heavenly message twice descending" (635); and when Samson has gone forth to the temple, the Chorus recollects "the Angel of thy Birth . . . / . . . his message . . . / Of thy conception" (1431, 1433-34; cf. *PR* I.238-54; IV.502-06). The birth narrative in the Book of Judges, no less than these recollections of it in Milton's poem, prepare us, as C. F. Burney has noticed, "for a Gideon or a Samuel, keenly alive to the fact that he holds a divine commission, and upheld in his performance of it by consciousness of the divine support. Samson, however, proves to have no commission at all, and recognizes no higher guide than his own wayward passions."[45] Through the Chorus's remembrance of the great theophany of Samson's birth at the crucial moment that he goes forth to the temple, Milton juxtaposes the beginning and end of Samson's story, his life and

[45] *The Book of Judges with Introduction and Notes* (London: Rivingtons, 1918), p. 337.

death, his onetime divine commission and his own impetuous act of hurling down the pillars of his "own accord" (1643). A life that began in marvel is thus shown by Milton to have ended in tragedy.

In contrast with Samson, who affects public life to perform a private act, Jesus, while "Affecting private life" (III.22), fixes his attention upon the "public good" (867), "Musing and much revolving in his brest, / How best the mighty work he might begin / Of Saviour to mankind" (I.185-87). The prophetic narrator announces that "the time is come" and pleads with the God of Israel to arise and vindicate his glory: "free thy people from thir yoke" (II.43, 48; cf. II.35-36). Neither Jesus nor Satan ever forgets the commission of deliverance; they simply disagree on when the time for deliverance will be, on the conditions under which it can be pursued, and on the methods by which it can be won. It remains an irony that Satan's own insistence that Jesus proceed without delay, despite the fact that the people are not ready and with physical force as the means, anticipates the attitudes of Samson which Jesus himself feels obliged to resist. The only way of finally crediting Samson as a deliverer is to adopt the casuistry of T.S.K. Scott-Craig and then argue for "the equivalence of ransom and redemption," for ransoming as a symbolic form of deliverance.[46]

Early in *Samson Agonistes*, Milton's protagonist remembers, apparently after having for some time forgotten, his commission to liberate his people from their oppressors (38-40, 225-26, 368-72). Yet the very idea of Samson as a deliverer gets swallowed up in a double irony: that in subduing Samson Dalila has delivered the Philistines from this deliverer (982-86), and that in presenting Samson to his enemies the Israelites have delivered themselves of their own deliverer. The issue

---

[46] "Concerning Milton's Samson," *Renaissance News*, 5 (1952), 47; see also p. 48.

throughout most of the play becomes, again ironically, "To prosecute the means of [Samson's] deliverance" (603; cf. 1453-54) with Manoa first, then Dalila, functioning as the principals in a plan necessitating that Samson surrender his role as deliverer, even self-deliverer, and eventuating in Death's becoming Samson's deliverer (1571-73). Only after his death is Samson proclaimed a deliverer (1661-63, 1714-15) by those for whom deliverance is a delusion as their subsequent history shows. *Samson Agonistes* begins with "The breath of Heav'n fresh-blowing, pure and sweet, / With dayspring born" (10-11), which by the end of the poem "proves / Abortive as the first-born bloom of spring / Nipt with the lagging rear of winters frost" (1575-77). Though Samson is wounded in the immortal part at the conclusion of *Samson Agonistes*, his life is here rendered as a tragedy and Samson himself as one of those who, though he may think like a revolutionary, feels as a Philistine. The holocaust at the pillars is a moment of explosion when a certain mind-set, a certain set of values, moves outward into society in the form of laws, moral codes, theological sanctions that in *Samson Agonistes* are being subjected to review. The psychology that produces this explosion, as it reaches outward to and becomes rooted within history, is objectified and legalized in those religions of cruelty such as Joseph Hall enunciated for the age of Milton. Samson's tragedy, then, is a tragedy for human history and especially for the history of Milton's own time.

Samson Agonistes breathes ironies, but none of them so confounding as the irony emerging from the fact that Milton presents his "Tragedy," along with his encomium of tragedy as "the gravest, moralest, and most profitable of all other Poems," against the backdrop of *Paradise Regained*. Milton may designate *Samson Agonistes* "A Dramatic Poem," but he is equally emphatic that *Samson* is "Of that sort of Dramatic Poem which is call'd Tragedy" and in "The Argument" to *Samson*, in its final sentence, again calls his poem a "Tragedy." We must read this play as a poem but without forgetting that as a play *Samson* enters into a conspiracy with its audience; we must be attentive to image and structure, to *all* poetic features, even as we read margins and blank spaces and generally engage the features of dramatic discourse in our interpretations as well. Milton's reminder that this work was not intended for the stage is doubtless a bow to the censor but not finally a reverential one and, rather like similar declarations in Byron's later plays, is a signal that context is important, that spaces are to be filled in. *Paradise Regained* is the important context for *Samson Agonistes*, providing the program notes, as it were, for Milton's pioneering example of mental theater. At the very heart of *Samson Agonistes* is the biblical sense and conception of tragedy, which, as Schneidau remarks, "is tied up with a sense of awe at the way God's destiny continually violates human expectation."[47] If drama always engages author and audience in a conspiracy, Christian drama of the tragic sort often seems to rise up as a statement of, and often against, God's own conspiracy against the human race, His consigning it to a tragic destiny.

In the Preface to *Samson Agonistes*, Milton singles out Aeschylus, Sophocles, and Euripides as "the three Tragic Poets unequall'd yet by any," having just gone out of his way to have the Satan of *Paradise Regained* praise the Greek drama about which Jesus himself is so circumspect. "*Lyric* Odes," along with poems "higher sung" by Homer, precede Satan's offer of "what the lofty grave Tragœdeans taught / In *Chorus* or *Iambic*, teachers best / Of moral prudence, with delight receiv'd / In brief sententious precepts, while they treat / Of

[47] *Sacred Discontent*, p. 259.

fate, and chance, and change in human life; / High actions, and high passions best describing" (IV.257-58, 261-66). Not only is there an inversion of what are usually the second and third items in a generic triad, with Satan seeming to value tragedy over epic—that is, the order of experience which, through his fall, he introduces to the Christian cosmos; hence the literary genre of which he is the originator and still the chief sponsor—but there is a continuing fixation on the very topics that consume the literary interest of the devils and are the object of Milton's ridicule in *Paradise Lost* (II.546-61). Jesus, on the other hand, subordinates the classical ode to the Christian hymn, epic poetry and classical oratory to Christian prophecy, thereby privileging what is "God inspir'd" over what Satan inspires, even as he praises the efficacy of Satanic tragedy "where moral vertue is express't / By light of Nature" and thus all is not quite lost (IV.350-52).

There is, then, no small irony in the generic representations and arrangement of the 1671 poetic volume: an epic-prophecy singing the virtues of the Christian deity sits alongside a tragedy exposing the vices of such deities as are personated by the Philistines no less than by Samson; a poem that is God-inspired huddles with a poem the source of whose revelation is the "light of Nature"; a prophecy anticipatory of apocalypse is teamed with a tragedy functioning as a warning prophecy and teeming with violence and death. Here Samson stands exposed as one of those who understands not God's ways but only the ways of men.

In *A Treatise of Civil Power*, Milton makes clear what the "labor of exposition" involves when the concerns of a text are religious and ethical and when the text itself derives from "light of nature without revelation from above." The highest truths are "above the reach and light of nature" and are inaccessible "without revelation from above." A text that derives from the light of nature, without such revelation, is "liable to be variously understood by humane reason"; such things "as are enjoined or forbidden by divine precept" are likely to be greatly misunderstood without such light as is afforded by the "Spirit within us," which always leads in a direction that accords with the voice of Jesus in the Gospels. We are never molested by the Spirit and made to perform acts out of harmony with the teachings of Jesus (VII, 242). The bearing of this passage on interpretation of *Paradise Regained* and *Samson Agonistes* should be immediately obvious: a tragedy deriving from the light of nature requires the sort of revelation afforded by *Paradise Regained*; without the sense of proportion offered by the brief epic the tragedy is apt to be too variously inter-preted—or simply misinterpreted.

The generic movement in the 1671 volume is from epic and prophecy to tragedy, from composite genres to tragedy now purged of its comic mixture. The movement from *Par-adise Regained* to *Samson Agonistes*—from a New to an Old Testament subject, from a Christian prophecy to a classical tragedy—constitutes a regressive maneuver, and implicit in it is the suggestion that any man, any age, is capable of either comedy or tragedy. These are not different forms but com-peting ideas in, variant aspects of history, which seems forever, and especially in Milton's own time, to be veering away from its potentiality and falling over again into the old reality. Like scriptural history, real history should exhibit the superseding of law, justice, and bond by grace, mercy, and forgiveness—an expected progression that Milton presents as a reversal, the lechery and violence of *Samson Agonistes* following love and peace and thus blocking the emergence of the new world anticipated by *Paradise Regained*. The temptations of Samson and Jesus, especially at the pillars and on the pinnacle, are encounters with a future shut down by Samson but opened by Jesus. As such, *Samson* represents the dominant ideology of Milton's age, one which served as an obstacle to a Revolution's success and which *Paradise Regained* would invalidate. *Samson* is a symbolic inversion, a counter-commentary, on the myth of Milton's brief epic. The actualities of history are here made to face the historical idealism, are taunted by it, but in such a way that both poems are finally a summoning to spiritual adventure. And even if one presents a positive and the other a negative example, the collective force of the volume is to make each reader a partner in a poetic resurrection and a party to the anticipated reconstruction of history.

Only for those (and Milton is not among them) who read the Judges narrative as if it were an Old Testament Book of Revelation verging on a divine comedy, and then read *Samson Agonistes* in like fashion, will it seem that Milton's poem is "unlike other tragedies" because "it is tragedy beyond tragedy" as surely as is *The Tempest*.[48] It is true that, especially in his early prose writings, Milton had locked arms with a clique of rebels who read the Book of Revelation as an invitation to revolution and who used that invitation as a licence for transforming society, at their own will, in anticipation of the imminent end. What Milton came to realize, however, is that Revelation provided him with an alternative: as he had done, let us say in *Areopagitica*, he could make of current history the theater in which the apocalyptic drama was playing itself out; or he could implode that history, as he does in *Paradise Regained*. Through Revelation, he could generalize current history into endtime or, through Judges, could particularize that same history back into the midst of time, making of his own times not a deadend but a road leading to a future postponed. It was easy to lift from the pattern of the Civil War years the apocalyptic paradigm, to collapse history into the final days. Milton's contemporaries did just this; Milton himself did this for a while but was also moved by the catastrophe of the present times to do something else: "to know the apoc-

[48] Knight, *The Golden Labyrinth*, p. 128.

alypse, express it, mourn it, and transcend it," for if catastrophe (although the author from whom I quote is writing about another catastrophe) "is the presumption of man acting as a destroyer, then the fashioning of catastrophe into a new set of tablets is the primal act of creation carried out in the image of God."[49] Images of destruction can be transmuted into acts of creation; a world in ruins can rise up again so that the whole dead world dances under a sky full of stars.

The world of *Samson Agonistes* may not yet be beyond tragedy, but the tragic vision of this poem *is* unlike other tragedies because it is so encompassing, so much more inclusive than that of most such poems: *Samson* is a human tragedy recounting the tragedy of civilization and of its supposedly civilizing religions. In the fullest sense, *Samson Agonistes* is a *Christian* tragedy. In one way, G. Wilson Knight is right to credit Milton with surpassing his dramatic rivals "since his religious assumptions enable him to create a semi-superman of appalling realism," although even this observation is askew insofar as Milton himself would perceive *that* Samson as the creation of others' (and of what ought to be outmoded) religious assumptions. Still further askew is Knight's extension of this observation:

> That said, we must admit that many subtleties are by-passed; there is naturally no facing of Christian love, nor any involvement in the more complex problems of statesmanship; and the final emphasis is on wrath and destruction.

In this, Knight concludes, Milton is unlike Racine who perceives a deeper connection, a fairer balance, between religion and statecraft, an achievement won by Racine through the placement of *Athalie* within the framework of New Testament

---

[49] David Roskies, *Against the Apocalypse: Responses to Catastrophe in Modern Jewish Culture* (Cambridge, Mass.: Harvard Univ. Press, 1984), p. 258.

prophecy.[50] There is no love in *Samson*, just odious hypocrisy on both sides, and "despotic power" (1054). There *is* love in the 1671 poetic volume, however. Here love confronts hatred as Jesus and Samson are made to front one another.

In *Samson Agonistes*, the final emphasis is on destruction, *human* destruction; but the poem is also set within a perspective that takes account of the complex interplay between religion and politics and that assimilates such concerns to New Testament prophecy, especially the drama of the Apocalypse. Whereas the prophetic promise of a new paradise may be dashed in the tragedy of history, there is still an interrogation of that tragedy, an emergent understanding of failed history, out of which is born an improved, an enlarged consciousness that eventuates in the restoration of hopes for regaining paradise if not beyond history, then on earth, *precisely on earth*, and if not now, then in the future. The driving energies toward apocalypse, which are released in *Paradise Regained*, may be frustrated and forestalled by the retreat of *Samson*, and of Milton's own age, into the world of tragedy. Yet *Samson Agonistes* remains a drama of regeneration, but only in the special sense that it would effect regeneration through the representation of degeneration. In the idiom of *De Doctrina Christiana* (VI, 453), Samson may exhibit renovation that would take place naturally, "that . . . affects only the natural man"; it is only the Jesus of *Paradise Regained* who figures forth "Renovation . . . supernaturally" and thus the spiritual renovation and redemption for which *Samson Agonistes* has been wrongly celebrated.

The generic regression represented by the placement of *Samson Agonistes* after *Paradise Regained*, by the withdrawal from narrative art into voiced discourse, from epic into tragedy, from prophetic promises into historical actualities, finds its scriptural counterpart in Old Testament narratives like the Book of Judges, which, though sometimes regarded as epic,

---

[50] *The Golden Labyrinth*, pp. 128-29.

are rather "a deliberate avoidance of epic." As Robert Alter
explains, "the vigorous movement of biblical writing away
from the stable closure of the mythological world" and of epic
is also a movement toward "indeterminacy," wherein "the
shifting causal concatenations, the ambiguities of a fiction [are]
made to resemble the uncertainties of life in history."[51] Milton's own final avoidance of epic and withdrawal from apocalypse are simply that—avoidances of both but rejections of
neither. The future that once seemed a certainty is now a
"perhaps," with tragedy paradoxically opening a way beyond
itself as if to say there can be no new future by evading reality;
only by encountering it and, more, by understanding it will
there be a metamorphosis of mind enabling a metamorphosis
of history. Milton had delineated the oppressive patterns of
history in the closing books of *Paradise Lost*, but a prophet
must do more: he must search history for its failings, for the
reasons that such patterns still pertain (as he does in *Samson
Agonistes*); he must also show the way out of them (as he does
in *Paradise Regained*).

Milton must have understood, as Northrop Frye has now
alerted us, that the historical books of the Bible are no more
history than the Gospels are biography; history just does not
possess the neat patterns that a book like Judges would impose
upon it. Not history *per se*, Judges is more exactly an envisioning of history or a fictive history, investing repetition with
significance and structure with meaning. In this kind of history, man is presented "as under a trial and subject to judgement": a program of action is offered that, "while it cannot
ignore history, may often set itself in opposition to history.
"This," says Frye, "is most obvious with myths of deliverance"[52]—separate, discrete, contending myths of deliverance—that Milton poses against one another in his volume of

[51] *The Art of Biblical Narrative* (New York: Basic Books, 1981), p. 27.

[52] *The Great Code: The Bible and Literature* (New York: Harcourt Brace Jovanovich,
1982), p. 49. See also Frye's *The Myth of Deliverance: Reflection on Shakespeare's
Problem Comedies* (Toronto: Univ. of Toronto Press, 1983).

1671. There is drama within each poem and a drama of perspectives generated by their juxtaposition. The one poem speaks of peace, the other urges defiance and wreaks devastation. Within these contending perspectives, moreover, alternative courses of action are set forth, one that binds men down to the cycles of history, another that would liberate them from those cycles; one that conceives of history as a divine comedy, another that perceives in history a rehearsal for all the events of human tragedy.

Paradise Regained and *Samson Agonistes* are both reflections on history, projecting different scenarios for it and representing, through their separate protagonists, different phases of it. According to the tripartite conception of history, popularized by commentators on the Book of Revelation, history under the rule of nature is displaced by history under the rule of the law and, eventually, of grace. Commonly, the birth of Samson was used to mark the beginning of the second phase, while Christ's nativity inaugurated the final phase of history.[53] Samson and Jesus are juxtaposed in history, then, just as in parallel fashion they will be juxtaposed in the 1671 poetic volume. They are also juxtaposed, as it were, through the biblical subtext of Judges informing the one poem and that of the Book of Revelation informing both. These subtexts contain *the* mythologies of wartime and its aftermath when, as Frye astutely observes, "two essential human concerns invariably loom up in the foreground: survival and deliverance."[54]

George Frederick Handel understood something of this in his adaptation of Milton's tragedy, where Manoa is made to say, "To sorrow now I tune my Song, / And set my Harp to Notes of Woe," whereupon the tragedy itself becomes rife

---

[53] Wayne Dynes elaborated this point in his splendid lecture delivered as part of the Ohio State Univ. Conference on Medieval and Renaissance Apocalyptics (Columbus, Ohio, February, 1981).

[54] *The Myth of Deliverance*, p. 12.

with intimations of apocalypse: the awful voice of the thunder sounding, lofty trumpets blasting, tempests of wrath and avenging whirlwinds, celestial concerts and blazing light.[55] What Handel did not comprehend is that, very pointedly, Milton excises any irenic vision from *Samson Agonistes* where all is dark and deadly, cheerless, comfortless. Only the dark side of the Apocalypse obtrudes upon this play, with the result that it seems as if "Nothing could be less like the Book of Revelation than *Samson Agonistes,* and yet *Samson Agonistes* . . . has for its subject a prototype of the underside, so to speak, of the vision of the Book of Revelation."[56] In their respective structures, however, both *Paradise Regained* and *Samson* mirror the Book of Revelation and derive important aesthetic features from it. *Samson Agonistes* is itself "a 'prophetic tragedy' patterned after Revelation" which, as Lynn Veach Sadler remarks, whatever its final issue, contains within its visionary theater the tragedy of the dragon, of Antichrist, and the tragedy of history.[57] But of more importance perhaps is the analogy that might be drawn between the historical setting of Milton's poems and of the Book of Revelation, which, as Barclay Newman reminds us, *"must be sought in the conflict of ideologies"*:[58] pristine Christianity being locked in combat with later per-

---

[55] *Samson: An Oratorio as Performed at the Theatre in Oxford* (1749), p. 5; see also pp. 1, 6, 24.

[56] Frye, *Spiritus Mundi,* p. 215.

[57] *Consolation in "Samson Agonistes": Regeneration and Typology,* Salzburg Studies in English Literature (Salzburg: Univ. of Salzburg, 1979), p. 204. Cf. Frye, *Spiritus Mundi,* p. 215, and Wittreich, *Visionary Poetics,* esp. pp. 191-212.

[58] *Rediscovering the Book of Revelation* (Valley Forge: Judson Press, 1968), p. 110. It is just this ideological choice that an earlier criticism of these poems blotted out in an aesthetics of balance: "When . . . Milton issued his last two poems together, he laid before the vanquished adherents of the Commonwealth a great alternative. On the one side was the victory of patience and self-repression—the Divine overcoming of evil with good; on the other hand was the triumph of revenge—swift, merciless, irresistible; and . . . the poet leaves the scales balanced between the two" (see J. Howard B. Masterman, *The Age of Milton* [1897; rpt. London: George Bell and Sons, 1909], p. 72).

versions of the faith. Once hidden from, God is now revealed
in history through the similitude of the Son but also through
distorted, antithetical images that are revelations of what he
is sometimes thought to be, but is not. And there is one
singularly important artistic strategy that Milton's poems share
with the Apocalypse: contending visionary panels are set alongside one another in such a way that the first item in a series,
once deciphered, provides a perspective from which the next
item can be interpreted. There is progression within the apparent redaction; for in the Book of Revelation the reformation
of the Church is a prologue to the renovation of history. With
Milton, who believed that every man is a sect of one, the
inaugural event is the regeneration of the individual who, in
turn, becomes a renovator of history.

Milton identifies St. John's high and stately tragedy as his
prototype in the Preface to *Samson Agonistes*, and does so in
the understanding that here is the tragedy of Antichrist and
of all those who resemble him in history. Yet if here we have
the underside of the Apocalypse and its nightmare world of
human history, sitting alongside and as a headpiece to it is the
apocalyptic promise of a paradise to be regained both in future
history and at the end of time. The presence of *Paradise Regained* in the volume and the corrective, interpretive functions
it assumes in relation to *Samson Agonistes* remind us of the
essential difference between early, primitive apocalypses where
the world, despite its horrors, is to be affirmed and the Christian apocalypses which insist that the world is to be improved
upon. The juxtaposition of these poems also reminds us, as
Jacques Ellul might say, that "the last word is not left to
destruction and death. The *truth* is not that of nothingness; it
is life, it is the world related to God, it is the transcendence
of death."[59] As Milton was wont to say: the Scriptures know

[59] *Apocalypse: The Book of Revelation*, trans. George M. Schreiner (New York:
Seabury Press, 1977), p. 50.

no word for *annihilation*. The truth begins in an apocalypse of mind that becomes the prologue to an apocalypse in history. *Samson* records the tragedy of hope: "Nor am I in the list of them that hope," says Samson; "Hopeless are all my evils, all remediless" (647-48). The aftermath of his tragedy is the loss of hope by and for the Israelites, for as he had done with Samson God now departs from them.

In this, *Samson Agonistes* opposes itself to the apocalyptic myth with which *Paradise Regained* is aligned, a myth that survives only because within history there remain hope and liberty for mankind. The time of temptation is the time in the wilderness both for Jesus and Samson; it is their, our, time of testing. As Ellul intones: "The issue here is knowing if man is going to follow Jesus, is going to enter the plan of God, is going to accept this unity with God."[60] Or alternatively, in the instance of *Samson Agonistes*, the issue is whether man will once again follow in the way of Samson, act of his own accord, isolate himself from God, and thereby subvert God's plan for history. Milton recognizes himself and his own age in the character of Samson and so casts Samson off.

To speak of apocalypse with regard to Milton's last poems entails remembering with Dennis Costa that apocalyptic literature "raise[s] questions of belief, moral judgment, death and afterlife within other kinds of fictions. Such a presence confuses, deliberately."[61] *Samson Agonistes*, along with the poem with which it is published, mirrors both the violent revolutionary content of the apocalyptic myth and the cooling off of such religious and political activism into apolitical quietism. Yet instead of veering from one pole to another in this particular dialectic, Milton steers a middle course and, by posing alternatives, offers a way out of an either-or situation.

[60] *Ibid.*, p. 90.
[61] *Irenic Apocalypse: Some Uses of Apocalyptic in Dante, Petrarch and Rabelais*, Stanford French and Italian Studies, 21 (Saratoga: Amna Libri, 1981), p. 2.

The 1671 volume has, for some time, been embroiled in the politics of interpretation—either through *Paradise Regained* it is an appeal for quietism, a plea for the surrender of hopes for a new Jerusalem in history, or through *Samson Agonistes* it is a summons to a final, decisive revolutionary battle. In the case of *Paradise Regained*, the critical effort has been to disengage Milton from utopian thinking; in the case of *Samson*, the effort has been to disengage Milton from thinking altogether.

Paradoxically, it is from just this sort of interpretive politics and critical quagmire that, through contiguous placement, Milton probably sought to remove these poems. If it is not, finally, an invitation to militancy, *Samson Agonistes* emits political signals nonetheless. Neither this poem nor *Paradise Regained* is simply a repudiation of millenarianism; rather both poems, from very different points of view, revive apocalyptic yearnings by revising apocalyptic expectations, revealing what mankind can, and cannot, do as it seeks to establish the millennial kingdom in history. Milton codifies his views on this matter in *De Doctrina Christiana*: "My reply is that there will be no need to his kingdom *for all ages*. . . . Thus his kingdom will not *pass away*, like something ineffectual, nor will it be *destroyed*. Its end will not be one of dissolution but of perfection and consummation" (VI, 627; see also VII, 518-19). Milton, who led the life of the tragic man, would redeem himself and stands ready to redeem others. If *Samson Agonistes* images the ravaged and fragmented world of tragedy, *Paradise Regained*, by offering the possibility for renewal, casts a beam of light upon that world.

Once the Fall has occurred in *Paradise Lost*, God promptly proclaims, and the angels thereupon celebrate, the apocalyptic promise: "Heav'n and Earth renew'd shall be made pure" (X.638) through the agency of the Son, as the angels explain, "by whom / New Heav'n and Earth shall to the ages rise, /

Or down from Heav'n descend" (X.646-48). Milton's fortifying vision, *Paradise Regained* alludes to the apocalyptic horror which *Samson Agonistes* images: "From many a horrid rift abortive pour'd / Fierce rain with lightning mixt, water with fire / In ruin reconciled" (IV.411-13); but the brief epic, acknowledging that proclamations of "Heaven's Kingdom nigh at hand" (I.20) are subject to misconstruction, also urges man to prolong his expectations: ". . . let us wait . . . / Soon we shall see our hope, our joy return" (II.49, 57). Their return depends, though, on the success of Milton's iconoclastic enterprise in *Samson Agonistes*—on that poem's capacity for effectively silencing the archaic world, the life and values of the very world it represents.

It has been understood since the nineteenth century that "Milton passed through a revolution, which, in its last stages and issue, was peculiarly fitted to damp enthusiasm, to scatter the visions of hope, and to infuse doubts of the reality of virtuous principle"; and usually it has been conjectured that *Paradise Regained* and *Samson Agonistes*, Milton's swan songs, are poems of sorrow, effusions of resentment, instead of, what seems more likely, a chief evidence that "the ardor, and moral feeling, and enthusiasm of his youth came forth unhurt, and even exalted, from the trial."[62] Milton's last poems are like

---

[62] W. E. Channing, *Remarks on the Character and Writings of John Milton*, 2nd ed. (London: Printed for Edward Rainford, 1828), p. 27. Hill provides the finest, most moving account of Milton's last years. If the saints were defeated and silenced, still Milton, "almost alone in continuing to exercise his talent as poet and prophet," was "led . . . to take this role not less but more seriously," and in that role he was busy declaring that history "is open: it is what we make of it" (*The Experience of Defeat*, pp. 313, 328). On the matter of Milton's identifying with, and finding hope in, "the educative force of regenerate individuals *like Samson*" (p. 324; my italics), we must simply agree to disagree. On the other hand, we can both agree, I presume, to the proposition set forth by Nicholas Jose: "In *Samson Agonistes* Milton understands why men edge toward easy solutions, or closed pessimism, even as he places those impulses within a larger vision of the high potentiality inherent in history, revealed only as it is inevitably betrayed in a fallen world. . . . No other writer found a way

the Book of Revelation in the profoundest sense: they are poems in which what had once *seemed* the promise of the present time retires into its true proportion. Like Milton's poems, the Apocalypse was written during a dark hour of history, it broke in upon history with its glimmer of hope, it imaged the very darkness that it would disperse. The Book of Revelation represents the despair it would steel mankind against, urging that people keep faith in time of trouble. Like Milton's last poems, the Apocalypse is an enabling book: bringing light out of darkness, joy out of sorrow, its affirmations restore hope to the defeated, raise expectations that have been dashed, and repair a broken world by pointing not beyond history but to a history radically transformed. The battered present is redeemed in the process, for it *is* the present that makes the future possible.

It is one thing to argue, as Mary Ann Radzinowicz does, that Milton "discerned a pattern in history and contemporary affairs of which the life of Samson was paradigmatic" and quite another matter to argue, again with Radzinowicz, that "Milton saw Samson as the historical example of how men should conspire with God to bring about the New Jerusalem." What is compelling about Radzinowicz's argument is that its premises are acute and nearly always right: (1) that in *Samson Agonistes* Milton prophesies "a potential . . . movement through the educative power of the tragedy"; (2) that Milton read Scripture as we should read his poem, "attentive to progressive relevancies" and "unfolding revelation"; and (3) that *Paradise Regained* and *Samson Agonistes* should be read together and interpreted by repeated reference to one another by virtue of the repeated, although muted, references that these poems make to each other.[63] This last principle is but an extension

of transmuting his engagement with political and historical anxieties into Milton's mastering detachment from historical confusion" (*Ideas of the Restoration in English Literature 1660-71* [Cambridge, Mass.: Harvard Univ. Press, 1984], p. 165).

[63] *Toward "Samson Agonistes": The Growth of Milton's Mind* (Princeton: Princeton Univ. Press, 1978), pp. 88, 91, 167, 245.

into the realm of poetry of one of Milton's own principles for interpreting Scripture: if Scripture is to be interpreted by Scripture, as Milton says it should be in *The Readie and Easie Way* (VII, 456; cf. VII, 242), Milton's poems should be interpreted by reference to surrounding poems, *by the poems themselves*; and if the words of Jesus in Scripture dispose of obscurities—in the words of *The Doctrine and Discipline of Divorce*, dissolve the "tedious and *Gordion* difficulties" (II, 340)—then the words of Jesus in *Paradise Regained* may be said to have the same effect on *Samson Agonistes*, making a coffin, as it were, for the apostate Samson (see *Tetrachordon*, II, 664).

From this point of view, what is curious is that Radzinowicz should put forth a conclusion, that Samson is a positive example, which is at odds with such premises and ultimately eroded by them. In *The Doctrine and Discipline of Divorce*, Milton admonishes us to "hold that for truth, which accords most with charity" (II, 340), a principle that holds equally for the truth, or lack of it, in the discrepant interpretations that over the centuries have accrued to both Milton's brief epic and tragedy. As interpretive fictions, Milton's last poems are how-to-live and how-*not*-to-live poems.[64] They demystify their biblical stories, interrogate the ideologies that had accrued to them, and reverse what had become their accepted messages in Milton's age. *Paradise Regained* urges no permanent withdrawal from the active life, only a retreat into contemplation as a prologue to action; *Samson* is no sabre-rattling poem but rather an inquiry into why sabre-rattling should cease. The greatness of both poems resides not in the fact that they transcend their age but in the fact that they bear its imprint so deeply; and a paradox of the poems, certainly, resides in the

[64] See Irene Samuel's elaboration of this idea, at least with reference to *Paradise Regained*, in "The Regaining of Paradise," in *The Prison and the Pinnacle*, ed. Rajan, p. 126. For another attempt to establish linkage between, but also to discriminate, these poems, see Richard Douglas Jordan, "*Paradise Regained*: A Dramatic Analogue," *Milton Quarterly*, 12 (1978), 68.

fact that the scriptural texts from which they derive have such decidedly different claims to truth and thus call for very different orders of interpretation.

The Old Testament texts, Milton explains in *De Doctrina Christiana*, were "handed down . . . in an uncorrupted state" and scrupulously preserved through the ages by "pledged protectors," whereas the New Testament was repeatedly tampered with and corrupted in the course of transmission, a fact which leads Milton to remark:

> I do not know why God's providence should have committed the contents of the New Testament to such wayward and uncertain guardians, unless it was so that this very fact might convince us that the Spirit which is given to us is a more certain guide than scripture, and that we ought to follow it. (VI, 588-89)

The Samson story is preserved in a pristine, the story of Jesus in a corrupted, text. As interpretive fictions, then, Milton's brief epic and tragedy will relate very differently to their biblical originals. In the first instance, a broken narrative line in the historical books, such as one finds in Judges, allows for a certain amount of adjustment in matters of chronology but never in matters of doctrine. If the text of the Old Testament is tainted, it is tainted by later interpreters—"defiled with [their] impurities" (VI, 117); but in the second instance the text itself is tainted and so must be interpreted by a creative, prophetic spirit. Milton's privileging of biblical over pagan stories, together with the different truth claims he attributes to the texts of the two testaments, are a dissuasive to those who argue of the Samson story what might more reasonably be argued of Milton's revisions to classical mythology, that he "transforms and ennobles the material of antiquity," and further, that he contributes "to an evolutionary ennoblement of the [Samson] story," that his version of that story "reveals considerable emancipation from the fetters of the old tale."[65]

For Milton, the issue is not the rendering of the old tale in the Book of Judges but new, and disfiguring, interpretation from which he would release the Samson story by a new representation of the Judges narrative. The representation is simply a restoration of original meaning. In *Paradise Regained*, on the other hand, Milton must re-present the Gospel narrative in such a way as to wrest from a set of corrupted texts a story misunderstood through the ages: "unrecorded left . . . , / Worthy t'have not remain'd so long unsung" (I.16-17). The re-presentation is a decipherment of the original story whose meaning is only now being fully comprehended. *Samson Agonistes* recovers an old revelation. *Paradise Regained* bursts forth with a new revelation that opens the Gospel narrative and authenticates it. Neither poem is really "another book of scripture"; but as Maureen Quilligan says of *Paradise Lost*, each poem "may function, by virtue of its divine inspiration, in ways analogous to Scripture."[66] As we read the Bible, so we should read these poems; and if the Bible, as Blake maintained, is the great code of art, then it may very well provide both these poems with a code for their decipherment.

[65] See, e.g., Kenneth Fell, "From Myth to Martyrdom: Towards a View of Milton's *Samson Agonistes*," *English Studies*, 34 (1953), 145, 148, and see also p. 147.

[66] *Milton's Spenser: The Politics of Reading* (Ithaca: Cornell Univ. Press, 1983), p. 152. And Mary Nyquist offers this exacting formulation: in *Paradise Regained* and *Samson Agonistes* "we are made aware of Milton's effort to put his imagination in the service not so much of Scripture as of Scripture represented in what might be its historical objectivity" ("The Father's Word / Satan's Wrath," *Publications of the Modern Language Association*, 100 [1985], 196). For a different, interesting hypothesis, but one weakened by its taking no notice of what Milton himself says about the textual status of the two testaments, see Herman Rapaport, who argues that Milton chooses Old Testament texts because they are "mutilated, decapitated. . . . Milton is quite willing to valorize . . . the fallen, blind discourse of Hebrews as he does in *Samson Agonistes*" (*Milton and the Postmodern* [Lincoln: Univ. of Nebraska Press, 1983], pp. 215-16).

It is of some interest to, and perhaps even a piece of corroborating evidence for, the foregoing argument that, whereas *Paradise Lost* is an informing context for the major long poems of the Romantic period, *Paradise Regained* and *Samson Agonistes* enjoy the status of subtexts sometimes within the same work, as in Wordsworth's *The Prelude* and Mary Shelley's *Frankenstein*, but more often in related, even interrelated, works such as Blake's *Milton* and *Jerusalem*, Byron's *The Prophecy of Dante* and *Marino Faliero*, Shelley's *Prometheus Unbound* and *The Cenci*, or even Blake's early sketches, or prose-poems, "Samson" and "Then She bore Pale desire." This is no place to stretch out such a thesis, or to follow out its implications; but it is an occasion for reflecting upon the logic of conjoining works by employing *these* Miltonic poems as subtexts. Through their own intense interrelatedness, *Paradise Regained* and *Samson Agonistes* can assert and sanction not only the interrelatedness of other works, but a special kind of interrelatedness: dialectical in nature, with contending perspectives that, instead of sitting side-by-side, are subdued the one to the other.

Hans Robert Jauss has tutored us into a new perception of literary history and of what matters in such histories. From him we have learned to ask, "which historical moments are really the ones that first make new that which is new in a literary phenomenon," and to what degree is "this new element . . . already perceptible in the historical instant of its emergence"?[67] Efforts at resistance and evasion are evidence that there is something to resist and evade. From the very beginning, interpreters of Milton's last poems attempted to nudge them into the boundaries of orthodoxy: *Paradise Lost* and *Paradise Regained* only *seemed* to erode the theology that these poems actually meant to promote; *Samson Agonistes* only *seemed*

[67] *Toward an Aesthetics of Reception*, trans. Timothy Bahti (Minneapolis: Univ. of Minnesota Press, 1982), p. 35.

to challenge current views of male supremacy which Milton must have intended to foster. For some in his own time and for some time later, "Milton the poet and Milton the politician were two different men." If Milton's *poems* were thought to be "orthodox in every part," lest they come to seem otherwise, it was deemed best to keep Milton out of "present political squabbles" by putting to rest John Toland's argument for a political aspect to the epics and by diverting attention from *Samson Agonistes*, whose political aspect seemed so pronounced that it could not easily be averted. There were dissenting voices, of course, urging that "Milton may be proved to have deviated considerably from the scripture-account of things, both in the historical and doctrinal passages of [*Paradise Lost*]" and then insisting that his poems be "read and studied . . . as an *oracle*":

> Milton combated superstition and tyranny of every form and of every degree. Against them he employed his mighty strengths, and like a battering ram, beat down all before him.[68]

But such voices did not become a chorus until the onset of Romanticism when *Samson Agonistes*, now construed not just as a personal allegory, is read as a layering of allegories with Samson now figuring Milton, now the failed revolutionaries, and now the entire English nation and with Milton, in the process, achieving differentiation from Samson. With Romanticism, the poetics of self-allegorization moved into another realm.

Within the history of criticism, Milton's Romantic interpreters enjoy special status, for under their aegis we pass from simplistic reception of Milton's poetry into a deep critical understanding of it. In the history of Milton criticism, it is

[68] *Memoirs of Thomas Hollis*, comp. Francis Blackburne (2 vols.; London: Printed by J. Nichols, 1780), II, 509; I, 93, 141, 145, 146.

the Romantics who mediate "between passive reception and active understanding"[69] and who thus disclose meanings that previous generations resisted, even shielded. With the Romantics, early but scattered approval of Milton's last poems, sometimes even the early shock registered at their implications, moderates into an understanding achieved through the recognition that these poems, interconnected in design and purpose, possess a competitive rather than reflective relationship with institutionalized morality and canonized theology. Byron's imitative poems provide an impressive instance of such criticism.

Yet, if the most exacting analogues to Milton's poems are provided by *Prometheus Unbound* and *The Cenci*, it is because they comprehend most completely, and thus focus most strikingly, the logic of interrelatedness in Milton's 1671 volume. The model for presentment afforded by these poems is different from the one offered by the 1645 *Poems of Mr. John Milton*, which has its own rationale and rhetoric and which, in any event, stands behind other Romantic volumes, most notably *Songs of Innocence and of Experience* and *Lyrical Ballads*. What *Paradise Regained* and *Samson Agonistes* together offer is a model for dialectical opposition figured in generic strife and figuring forth different modes and extents of consciousness: that of Samson and Beatrice Cenci on the one hand, and that of Jesus and Prometheus on the other. There are distinct modes of prophecy, both Milton and Shelley seem to be saying, distinct stances for the prophet to assume, and decidedly different modes of consciousness exhibited by him. There are Samson and Beatrice, Jesus and Prometheus; but there is also the poet, imbued with the consciousness of the former and aspiring to that of the latter. This double consciousness—its discrepant awareness and binocular vision—is the crucial feature of Milton's 1671 poetic volume and its chief contribution

[69] *Towards an Aesthetics of Reception*, trans. Bahti, p. 19.

to a visionary poetic. These poems in conjunction bring us to the awareness that, like the poets themselves, their protagonists are sometimes prophets and sometimes fakes. The Danites, Northrop Frye has said, see only as far as the Old Dispensation and their dim awareness allow them to see.[70] Jesus, Milton, and Milton's fit audience (both contemporary with the poet and now) see further—*and beyond*. That is finally where such a poetic leads: each poem has its own integrity but also looks beyond itself, while the poems collectively, and simultaneously, impress themselves upon human consciousness, which they stretch, and then press upon human history, which they would salvage.

[70] *Spiritus Mundi*, p. 226.

INDEX